MIKE'S WORLD

Edited by
Asa McKercher and Galen Roger Perras

MIKE'S WORLD

Lester B. Pearson and Canadian External Affairs

UBCPress · Vancouver · Toronto

26 25 24 23 22 21 20 19 18 17   5 4 3 2 1

Printed in Canada on FSC-certified ancient-forest-free paper (100% post-consumer recycled) that is processed chlorine- and acid-free.

Library and Archives Canada Cataloguing in Publication

Mike's world: Lester B. Pearson and Canadian external affairs / edited by Asa McKercher and Galen Roger Perras.

Includes bibliographical references and index.
Issued in print and electronic formats.
ISBN 978-0-7748-3528-2 (hardcover). – ISBN 978-0-7748-3529-9 (pbk.).
ISBN 978-0-7748-3530-5 (PDF). – ISBN 978-0-7748-3531-2 (EPUB).
ISBN 978-0-7748-3532-9 (Kindle)

1. Pearson, Lester B., 1897-1972. 2. Canada – Foreign relations – 1945-. I. McKercher, Asa, editor. II. Perras, Galen R. (Galen Roger), editor

FC620.M55 2017   971.064'3   C2017-905429-5
C2017-905430-9

Canada

UBC Press gratefully acknowledges the financial support for our publishing program of the Government of Canada (through the Canada Book Fund), the Canada Council for the Arts, and the British Columbia Arts Council.

This book has been published with the help of a grant from the Canadian Federation for the Humanities and Social Sciences, through the Awards to Scholarly Publications Program, using funds provided by the Social Sciences and Humanities Research Council of Canada.

Printed and bound in Canada by Friesens
Set in Zurich and New Century Schoolbook
by Artegraphica Design Co. Ltd.
Copy editor: Joanne Richardson
Proofreader: Judith Earnshaw
Indexer: Cheryl Lemmens

UBC Press
The University of British Columbia
2029 West Mall
Vancouver, BC V6T 1Z2
www.ubcpress.ca

To Kaiti Perras (1991–2014)

Contents

Part 2: Pearson the Pragmatist

Part 3: Pearson the Idealist

John English

Foreword

There is something maddening about Mike Pearson. His ambiguities irritated Walter Gordon, whose personal wealth and network smoothed Pearson's path to the Prime Minister's Office. He infuriated his close wartime companion Dean Acheson, who found Pearson's ambiguities during the Cold War sanctimonious and dishonest. For his principal Progressive Conservative antagonist, John Diefenbaker, Pearson represented a pretentious, isolated central Canadian elite that, in the eminent and angry historian Donald Creighton's opinion, had deceitfully taken Canada down the perilous American road in the postwar years. Many on the Canadian left simultaneously attacked the sole Canadian Nobel Peace Prize recipient. As a federal civil servant at the Cold War's height, Pierre Trudeau wrote angry denunciations of External Affairs Minister Pearson to diplomats in Pearson's department. As the Cold War was beginning to thaw in 1963, Trudeau publicly denounced the "defrocked prince of peace,"[1] who cravenly collapsed under American pressure and accepted nuclear weapons for Canada.

Later critics on the left, including Yves Engler, Ian McKay, and Jamie Swift, are determined to undermine the image of Pearson as, in the words of McKay and Swift, "a master diplomat, a father of the United Nations, a self-deprecating man of peace, and the prime minister who helped usher in medicare, bilingualism and Expo 67."[2] For these critics, Pearson was too much an apologist for the British Empire for which he fought in his youth and for the American Empire that he served in his later life. Critics on the right were equally vehement and politically more influential. Foreign Affairs Minister John Baird insisted that the "Lester Pearson Building" be removed from his business card, ordered a tribute to Pearson's Nobel Prize be taken off the departmental website, and, with much offence intended, named the structure beside the Pearson Building the John G. Diefenbaker Building. More seriously, Harper Conservatives publicly lamented the welfare state that Pearson's government put in place and attacked the multilateralism and peacekeeping emphasis associated with Pearsonian internationalism.

The fury of fierce extremes that the mostly amiable, often clumsy, and physically ordinary Pearson endured during his prime ministerial years left a mark on historical assessments of him. His success – indeed, his celebrity – prior to 1957 occurred, as Denis Stairs wrote, because the government's policies made Canadians "feel good – proud of our motives and our accomplishments alike in a dangerous and shrinking world."[3] In the 1960s, as colonies became nations, Quebec trembled with nationalism, Americans stumbled into Vietnam, and the young shucked off old ways, Pearson suddenly seemed a relic of the past, not at all the right leader for different times. As the editors and authors of this volume explain, Pearson found the end of the "good times" difficult. A child of the Methodist manse who avidly read Rudyard Kipling and G.A. Henty, Pearson refused to see only dark shadows lurking over the legacy of the British Empire. Similarly, the creation of the state of Israel after the horrors of the Holocaust captured his imagination, and he ignored those shoved aside by the birth of the new state. A supporter of conscription in both world wars, the unilingual Pearson was ill-prepared for Quebec's and France's challenges in the 1960s to his notions of federalism and Canadian external relations. An admirer of the United States' role in the postwar construction of the United Nations system, he refused to join those who excoriated its actions and depreciated the need for American leadership in a bipolar world. Moreover, he seemed to have a deaf ear when protesters cried out for new conceptions of human rights. And he was not "Pearsonian" when it came to the Canadian Arctic. This excellent collection clearly points out these weaknesses and ambiguities in Pearson and his policies.

While this volume also captures the contradictions and weaknesses of Pearson, it also underlines his importance. Even for his detractors, it is hard to imagine Canada without him. A recent survey of scholars ranked Pearson fifth among Canadian prime ministers even though he served only five turbulent years in minority governments. Among the young who were surveyed, he displaced Macdonald and ranked behind only King and Laurier, who served twenty-two and fifteen years, respectively. In Quebec he ranked third, while his successor Trudeau, who tied him among the younger scholars, ranked seventh in his native province.[4]

It is often said of Winston Churchill that he contained multitudes, but through his long life those many ingredients remained remarkably consistent and unchanging. An imperialist he was born, an imperialist he died. He retained his faith in the military, the British aristocracy and its traditions, and the essential superiority of Englishness. Lester Pearson was born a devout Christian in a British Canadian family in which the values of small town Ontario were honoured and cherished. Later, he was the sole Canadian prime minister to serve in uniform at a war front. Yet the multitudes within the deceptively complex Pearson were increasingly an inconsistent blend, one that responded to and reflected the tragic and brilliant century in which he lived. Had Pearson left politics after his disastrous defeat in 1958, would Canada have had national medicare, the maple leaf flag, official bilingualism, the Canada Pension Plan, racially unrestricted immigration, the unification of the armed forces, and, not least, Pierre Trudeau? *Mike's World* traces how deeply his imprint remains. For critics and admirers, for better and for worse, Mike Pearson remade Canada.

Notes

1 Trudeau quoted in Denis Smith, *Gentle Patriot: A Political Biography of Walter Gordon* (Edmonton: Hurtig, 1973), 119.

2 Ian McKay and Jamie Swift, *Warrior Nation: Rebranding Canada in an Age of Anxiety* (Toronto: Between the Lines, 2012), 107.

3 Denis Stairs, "Canada in the 1990s: Speak Loudly and Carry a Bent Twig," *Policy Options* (January/February 2001): 44.

4 Stephen Azzi and Norman Hillmer, "Ranking Canada's Best and Worst Prime Ministers," *Maclean's* (7 October 2016), http://www.macleans.ca/politics/ottawa/ranking-canadas-best-and-worst-prime-ministers/.

Acknowledgments

This project began out of our shared belief that there is too little written about Canadian international history and our sense – dare we, as Canadians, admit such a thing – that American foreign relations historians do things so much better than those of us above the forty-ninth parallel. While each US president seems to have, at minimum, a volume of essays devoted to probing his foreign policy choices and legacies, such a thing has not been done in Canada. Given the marginalization of Canadian international history – what one scholar recently likened to a "tragedy" – such a development is not surprising. But it is lamentable. Hence this book, which gathers together emerging and established scholars to analyze the foreign policy legacy of Canada's most influential diplomat and to do so from a range of vantage points, some laudatory, others condemnatory, but all bringing important insights to our understanding of the complications surrounding this man and his times.

Obviously, this collection is the result of the efforts of more than just us two. First and foremost, thanks go to our contributors, each of whom took the time to prepare incisive papers, to respond to suggestions made both by the reviewers and us, and to do both more or less on time. We would be remiss also if we did not thank our editors at UBC Press: Emily Andrew, who first spearheaded this project before heading off to greener pastures at Cornell and then Randy Schmidt, who saw it through to completion. And our thanks to UBC Press's production team: Holly Keller, Joanne Richardson, and Cheryl Lemmens. Thanks, too, to John English for authoring a foreword and to the reviewers for their comments and criticisms (most of which were fair!).

While we are both thankful for the support of our partners, families, friends, and colleagues, we dedicate this book to the memory of Kaiti Perras.

Acronyms

ACND	Advisory Committee on Northern Development
AECL	Atomic Energy Canada Limited
ASTEF	Association pour l'organization des stages en France
BANQ	Bibliothèque et Archives nationale du Québec
CFPF	Central Foreign Policy Files
CIIA	Canadian Institute of International Affairs
CIPO	Canadian Institute of Public Opinion
CIR	Canada India Reactor
CRTC	Canadian Radio-Television Commission
CYC	Company of Young Canadians
DCER	*Documents on Canadian External Relations*
DEA	Department of External Affairs
DHH	Directorate of History and Heritage Archive
DND	Department of National Defence
DOMREP	Mission of the Representative of the Secretary-General in the Dominican Republic
ECLA	(UN) Economic Commission for Latin America
EEC	European Economic Community
ENA	École nationale d'administration
FAO	Food and Agriculture Organization
FLQ	Front de libération du Québec
GATT	General Agreement on Tariffs and Trade
GLWQA	Great Lakes Water Quality Agreement

IADB	Inter-American Development Bank
ICC	International Control Commission
ICSC	International Commission for Supervision and Control in Indochina
IDRC	International Development Research Centre
IAEA	International Atomic Energy Agency
IJC	International Joint Commission
ILO	International Labour Organization
LAC	Library and Archives Canada
LBJL	Lyndon B. Johnson Library
MAE	Ministère des Affaires Étrangères
MFN	most favoured nation
MLF	multilateral (nuclear) force
NAI	National Archives of India
NARA	National Archives and Records Administration (US)
NATO	North Atlantic Treaty Organization
NAUK	National Archives of the United Kingdom
NAWAPA	North American Water and Power Alliance
NGO	non-governmental organization
NORAD	North American Air Defense Command
NPT	Non-Proliferation Treaty
OAS	Organization of American States
ONUC	Opération des Nations Unies au Congo
PCO	Privy Council Office
PTBT	Partial Nuclear Test Ban Treaty
QUA	Queen's University Archives
RAPP	Rajasthan Atomic Power Project
SACEUR	supreme allied commander Europe
SEATO	Southeast Asia Treaty Organization
SSEA	secretary of state for external affairs
UAR	United Arab Republic
UDHR	Universal Declaration of Human Rights
UN	United Nations
UNEF	United Nations Emergency Force
UNFICYP	United Nations Peacekeeping Force in Cyprus
UNIPOM	United Nations India-Pakistan Observation Mission
UNMOGIP	United Nations Military Observer Group in India and Pakistan

UNRRA	UN Relief and Rehabilitation Association
UNSC	United Nations Security Council
UNSCEAR	United Nations Scientific Committee on the Effects of Atomic Radiation
UNTSO	United Nations Truce Supervision Organization
UNYOM	United Nations Yemen Observation Mission
USSR	Union of Soviet Socialist Republics
VOW	Voice of Women

MIKE'S WORLD

Asa McKercher and Galen Roger Perras

Introduction
Lester Pearson and Canadian External Affairs

No figure has had a greater impact upon Canada's recent foreign policy than Lester Pearson. As Liberal prime minister from 1963 to 1968, but especially as secretary of state for external affairs (SSEA) from 1948 to 1957, "Mike," to his friends, has been credited with having charted a course in which Canada took on an active global role as a helpful fixer seeking to mediate disputes and promote international cooperation. For those Canadians who recall this era fondly, Canada's reputation as a peaceable "middle power" was cemented when Pearson won the 1957 Nobel Peace Prize for his peacekeeping efforts during the Suez Crisis of 1956. Acclaiming this achievement as a stunning success, journalists covering events at the United Nations crowed that "Canada is almost a magic word here" and that there had been a "break-through to new levels of responsibility for Canada in the world."[1] Suez appeared to be the capstone to a "Golden Decade" of achievement in Canadian foreign policy, with Pearson, backed by a cohort of internationalist-minded diplomats, looming large. Their achievements, and this era, have inspired much myth-making about Canada and its international role. In a 1961 debate on Canada's place in the world, poet Douglas LePan, a former diplomatic colleague of Pearson, remarked: "The world is suffering from many kinds of frustrations and will continue to do so. In such a world there is a particular role for Canada. What that role is depends on what sort of an image you have of a heroic Canadian. For myself, I think of Mike Pearson at the United Nations at the time of Suez, producing a resolution that set up the United

Nations Emergency Force and that got the world by a very awkward corner." Four decades later, another controversial and influential Liberal foreign minister, Lloyd Axworthy, reflected: "Mike Pearson was *the* role model. I became an admirer and a Liberal ... Pearson represented to me the quintessential qualities of a Canadian." For journalist Charles Lynch, Pearson "walked funny and he talked funny, but he acted very seriously indeed, and his diplomatic achievements, speaking for Canada at the height of its world prestige and influence ... made him the Canadian of the century."[2] In such characterizations, Pearson personified a notion of Canada as an altruistic, outwardly focused honest broker.

Pearson was part of a generation of policy makers who shepherded Canada into the United Nations and the North Atlantic Treaty Organization (NATO), moves reflective of a new internationalist spirit and a commitment to collective security in contrast to the view that Canada, protected by three oceans, was a "fire proof house, far from inflammable materials."[3] Having been in the thick of two catastrophic wars in their lifetimes, Pearson and his fellow Canadian diplomats seized upon multilateralism and global governance as means to avoid a third conflagration, one that now threatened nuclear destruction. Beyond involvement in the UN and NATO, under their watch Canada made its first commitments to foreign aid and development under the Colombo Plan and participated in a liberal economic order centred on the World Bank and the General Agreement on Tariffs and Trade. Pearson also insisted that Article 2 of the North Atlantic Treaty – the Canadian Article – should promote economic and social cooperation with the aim of making NATO more than a military alliance. Then, of course, there was Pearson's storied action during the Suez Crisis when he spearheaded the creation of a UN peacekeeping force that helped to end the fighting. Though motivated by a keen sense of Canada's national interest, an idealist spirit also guided Pearson and others. It is this appeal to Canadians' "better angels" that has proved so captivating.

Although only one of many officials charting Canada's more active course in the world, Pearson became synonymous with this global approach – and as the lengthy list of his publications at the end of this volume attests, he thought deeply about international relations and Canada's place in the world. His admirers have contended that he was a "brilliant exponent of Canadian foreign policy," that he "epitomized the middle power practice," and knowing internationalism "gave Canada an influence beyond its size or stature, allowing it to punch above its weight," he oversaw "a chapter of our history of which Canadians are rightly proud."[4] Liberals, naturally, have made much of this history and of Pearson. In a 2005 call for an active global role Paul Martin Jr., then prime minister, looked to Pearson's development of peacekeeping as the genesis of an approach in which Canada had "had a major hand in devising the innovative arrangements our world requires." Ten years later, in the midst of a bitterly contested federal election campaign, another former Liberal prime minister, Jean Chrétien, asked Canadian voters to "choose a government in line with our great tradition of peace-building, initiated by Mr. Pearson and promoted by all of his successors until the arrival of the Harper administration." Given these invocations of Pearson and his legacy, is there little wonder why Liberal leaders have been diagnosed with "Nobel Fever"?[5]

Yet Pearsonianism, and its progenitor, had an influence outside of Liberal Party circles. One critic of Pearson, or at least of the mythologizing around the Suez Crisis, had decried the 1957 Nobel Prize win for its "harmful effect on the Canadian military because it began the process whereby Canadians view their soldiers as the world's natural peacekeepers." For similar reasons, former Conservative senator Hugh Segal has derided the "largely mythical 'Pearson in Suez' peacekeeping heroic innovation narrative."[6] On a more positive note, as two political scientists noted recently, their students still "embrace a nostalgic image of Canada – the helpful fixer, the peacekeeper, the altruistic good international citizen" that contrasts with the more assertive Canadian foreign policy practised at present.[7] Perhaps this yearning for Canada "the peaceable kingdom" reflects youthful idealism, a shallow misreading of the past by political science undergraduates, or simply the power of the myths surrounding Pearson, Canada as a middle power, and the Golden Decade of Canadian foreign policy.

Myths "idealize" in that "they select particular events and institutions which seem to embody important cultural values and elevate them to the status of legend." Moreover, they are "agents that generate and condition historical action" and "gain their potency from their ability to persuade."[8] Has what has become known as Pearsonianism had such a lasting influence because of its idealism and its persuasiveness? Certainly, Pearson himself was persuasive – a necessity for a diplomat – for Canada's policy during the Golden Decade often was less than idealistic. But it was his "vision of Canada and the new world order that was largely accepted, and then remembered, by the Canadian people."[9] Among historians, the middle power ideal and, by extension, the Pearsonian age, have lost some of their lustre, with nuanced studies showing that, instead of being magnanimous internationalists, Pearson and his generation of diplomats were conscious of their limited capabilities, mindful of their place in the Western camp, and cognizant of the need to assist their allies.[10] Not that Canada did not support international organizations; far from it. Rather, these scholars emphasize that, during this Pearsonian era, Canadian diplomatists were frequently cautious and pragmatic even as the public latched onto the middle power rhetoric. The Canadian people, one of Pearson's diplomatic colleagues once lamented, forgot "Pearson the pragmatist."[11]

In part, this discovery – not that Pearson hid it – of Pearsonian pragmatism has been why recent years have been tough on Pearson and his legacy. In growing numbers, critics on the left have emphasized that Pearsonianism in action was a far cry from the "progressive internationalism" that Pearson, his colleagues, and subsequent Liberal politicians proclaimed.[12] In this telling, Pearson's foreign policy during his time both as SSEA and as prime minister was blindly anti-communist and pro-Israeli, suspicious if not hostile towards "Third World" nationalism, promoting Western economic interests and export-driven and growth-based development, and slavishly supportive of the United States. Further, Pearson saw the world through "paternalistic" lenses, a racially driven outlook whitewashed by rhetoric about Canada as a selfless international actor.[13] Thus, much of Pearson's record of international achievement reads as a list of shameful conduct. As Ian McKay and Jamie Swift note, a paradox surrounds Pearson: "[his image] as 'Canada's peacemaker general,' the epitome of Canadian civility in a disordered world, stands in contrast to his activities as a fierce cold warrior."[14] Such criticism is not new. Pearson's left-wing critics have long decried the "bankruptcy" of his approach to world affairs. Pointing to how Pearson backed Washington "to the hilt" on Vietnam, these detractors also emphasize his 1963 decision to reverse the Liberal Party's opposition to nuclear weapons, a move that paved the way for Ottawa's acceptance of this weaponry and that led a future Liberal prime minister, Pierre Trudeau, to denounce Pearson as the "defrocked priest of peace."[15] In these interpretations, Pearson is not the nebbish of conservative disdain, but someone who took firm, reactionary positions and is even a "major criminal, really extreme."[16] It might seem odd to associate the word "extreme" with Pearson, a political moderate and diplomat par excellence. But for many on the left, Pearsonianism has far different, and far more sinister, implications for Canada's global role than as a reflection of dewy-eyed internationalism. "If Pearson's foreign policy was to be summarized," noted his most vociferous contemporary critic, "the best words to describe it would be violent or unjust not peaceful or internationalist."[17] Some of these criticisms sit far outside the realm of reasoned historical debate. But the questioning of Pearson's record, and how Canadians remember him, is important.

Criticism has come from the right as well. In Ottawa, until quite recently, Pearson's stock was low, a result of former Conservative prime minister Stephen Harper's efforts to placc a conservative stamp on Canada, thereby erasing much of the liberal – and Liberal – heritage in place after he assumed power in 2006. Hence, the reinstatement of the designations "Royal" to the air force and the navy – a reversal of a Pearson policy; the downplaying of the fiftieth anniversary of Pearson's introduction of Canada's maple leaf flag; an emphasis on members of the military as warriors rather than as peacekeepers; the defunding of the Pearson Peacekeeping Centre, leading to its closure in 2013; and what John Baird, Canadian foreign minister from 2011 to 2015, called the move "from brokerage" to "a values-based foreign policy." Pearson, as noted, was the honest broker personified. "As you know," Harper remarked in 2014, "we have brought in a different approach to foreign affairs from previous governments, previous Liberal governments," whose stance was to "'go along to get along.' Whatever the consensus is, just sign on to it. We have taken stronger stands when we view that important issues, important interests and important values, are at stake."[18] Such comments by Harper and Baird echo those of Howard Green, SSEA in John Diefenbaker's Progressive Conservative government from 1959 to 1963. Green also took umbrage with Pearsonianism, stating in 1960: "The time has come to drop the idea that Canada's role in world affairs is to be an 'honest broker' between the nations. We must decide instead that our role is to determine the right stand to take on problems, keeping in mind the Canadian background and, above all, using Canadian common sense."[19] No wonder that the Harper Tories looked to Diefenbaker, Pearson's political nemesis, to frame the recent political past. They had planned to christen a new heavy icebreaker with Diefenbaker's name; in 2010, they created the annual John Diefenbaker Defender of Human Rights and Freedom Award; and, in 2014, they renamed Ottawa's former City Hall after Diefenbaker. The John G. Diefenbaker Building, now housing Canadian diplomats, lies but a stone's throw from the Global Affairs Canada headquarters, a building named for Pearson. The Harper government's values-based foreign policy was characterized by some as "bullhorn diplomacy" and by others as a betrayal of Canada's supposed impartial, multilateral role on the world stage. "The Conservative government," one detractor asserted, "has taken Canada so far from its foreign policy roots and exposed this country as such a high-profile outlier, it defies explanation."[20] Pearson is credited with laying these roots; thus, tough times, indeed, for Mike and for the myths that surround him.

That Pearson could be the target of such criticism from the right *and* the left is not surprising. Since Pearson was a diplomat and a political centrist, not an ideologue, it is only natural that he could represent different things to different people. After all, here was a man who was anti-communist but was also accused by McCarthyites of being a communist himself – conservative newspaper baron and renowned isolationist Colonel Robert McCormick, editor of the *Chicago Tribune,* once dubbed Pearson "the most dangerous man in the English-speaking world."[21] A paradox arises from Pearsonian foreign policy's blend of realism with idealism, a mixture no doubt appealing to political centrists but appalling to those on the ends of the political spectrum. What Liberal hagiography and the continued sniping at him from the right and the left both underline is that Pearson looms over debates about Canada's global role. "Such was Pearson's impact" on foreign policy, writes journalist Andrew Cohen, "that no prime minister since has failed to evoke his legacy or tried to escape his shadow."[22] Indeed, although Pierre Trudeau eventually trumpeted peacekeeping and embarked, at the end of his time in office, on a quixotic quest for world peace, immediately after succeeding Pearson as prime minister in 1968 he had sought to repudiate the honest broker role. Meanwhile, in the judgment of the US State Department in 1960, Diefenbaker's Tories were "haunted by the international prestige which Canadians think was achieved" by Pearson.[23] American sneering aside, Pearson possessed considerable stature, another reason for his position both as a source of inspiration and as a lightning rod for criticism.

The son of a Methodist pastor, Pearson lived a comfortable if itinerant early life across southern Ontario. His early world was very British, nourished by Canada's imperial heritage, and it left its mark on him. "We are British as well as Canadian," he told his undergraduate students in 1927, adding: "One need not be accused of boastful flag-waving, in saying that, on the whole, the good from the Empire has far exceeded its evils."[24] His own undergraduate history degree at the University of Toronto was interrupted by the onset of the First World War, prompting Pearson and thousands of his contemporaries to rush to defend the imperial metropole. Enlisting in 1915, he served in Greece in a hospital unit and then trained as a pilot in Britain, his military career terminating when he was struck by a London bus and by the onset of what now would be termed post-traumatic stress disorder. Back in Toronto, he finished his BA and then worked at a Chicago abattoir before winning a fellowship to Oxford, excelling in sports if not in academics. Next, Pearson spent five years as a history professor at the University of Toronto. Though he did not publish, rather than perish, in 1928 he joined Canada's small Department of External Affairs (DEA), a ministry dominated by Prime Minister William Lyon Mackenzie King.[25]

While his initial diplomatic work was tedious, Pearson pleased his superiors, advancing in the ranks to serve as first secretary at the High Commission in London from 1935 to 1941 and then as the deputy chief of mission to Canada's Legation in Washington in 1942. These were Canada's two most important overseas posts – Britain and the United States being Canada's principal allies, part of the so-called North Atlantic Triangle – and Pearson's international outlook was no doubt shaped by his exposure to life among Britons and Americans, the "English-speaking peoples" who dominated much of the globe prior to the postwar implosion of formal imperialism. The years in which he served in London and Washington were difficult. Watching the events of the later 1930s as the world again descended into war, he complained that King's "do-nothing" foreign policy had left him "thoroughly disheartened and disillusioned." By 1938, he had rejected the isolationism and appeasement of his superiors, asking: "Would our complete isolation from European events (if such a thing were possible) save us from the effects of a British defeat; and, even if it did, could we stand by and watch the triumph of Nazidom, with all that it stands for, over a Great Britain which, with all her defects, is about the last abode of decency, reason and liberty on this side of the water?"[26] The war turned Pearson – and his generation of Canadian diplomats – into internationalists, backers of collective security, and opponents of totalitarian aggression.

Yet Pearson had to move carefully as King remained cautious about engaging with the world. In late 1947, the prime minister was irate over Pearson's shepherding of a United Nations plan to partition Palestine: "The truth is that Pearson with his youth and inexperience and influenced by the persuasion of others around him, had been anxious to have Canada's [external affairs] figure prominently in world affairs."[27] Still, King had handpicked Pearson, promoting him to ambassador in Washington in 1944, and then, in 1946, to under-secretary of state for external affairs – deputy minister – making Pearson the third most influential person in the foreign policymaking apparatus after the SSEA and prime minister. Pearson made the jump to the second most important position in 1948, abandoning his civil service sinecure for a seat in the House of Commons, representing the northern Ontario constituency of Algoma East and almost a decade of continuous travel. Asked in 1955 where he made his home, he quipped: "On a C-5, I think."[28] It was on board this plane, in the East Block of the Parliament Buildings, and in conference halls and meeting rooms across the globe, that, with Prime Minister Louis St-Laurent and a host of able and like-minded diplomats, he set Canada – for good or ill – upon its Pearsonian course.

Like Pearson, St-Laurent believed that Canada must be more involved in the world than it had been under King, though this idealism, and that of many within Canada's postwar diplomatic corps, was matched by a realistic belief in what Canada could accomplish. In his memoirs, Pearson recalled that, in these years, he and his colleagues "always asked ourselves not only 'What kind of Canada do we want?' but 'What kind of world do we want?'" But he admitted, too, that he, at least, "was not so naïve as to think that we could decisively, or even importantly, influence the policies of the Great Powers, but I hoped we could influence the environment in which they were pursued."[29] Here was the peculiar blend of idealism and realism so characteristic of postwar Canadian foreign policy. Pearson was the poster boy for this policy, becoming perhaps the most famous Canadian in the world. Beyond his activities as SSEA, he was one of NATO's "three wise men," was the president of the UN General Assembly in 1952, and twice contended for the position of UN secretary-general, in 1945 and 1952, with his candidacy opposed by the Soviets and by the Americans, a telling reflection of the paradoxical nature of Pearsonianism. The Korean War from 1950 to 1953 exposed this paradox, for Pearson supported Canadian involvement not only to defend the notion of collective security that upheld the postwar order, but to resist communist aggression; in effect, it seemed to be a war for peace, and he helped to broker an eventual end to the fighting.[30] His involvement in similar crises and negotiations marked a departure from the wariness of the King years. The result, was that, as one British military analyst wrote of Pearson in 1955, "in the post war world, in which Canada is still something of a novelty, he has become a world figure in his own right." Four years later, the young US senator John F. Kennedy paid homage to Pearson as "the guardian of good sense," a statesman who "enjoyed the confidence of very many nations," and "the chief architect of the Canadian foreign service, probably the best in the world."[31] Pearson was, reflected one of India's foremost diplomats, among those "rare personalities who have combined wisdom with power," while Tanzanian president Julius Nyerere called him "the Great Liberal."[32] These views are testament to Pearson's international renown, or at least to the postwar prestige of Canada and its diplomats, and serve as a reminder that the Golden Age myth had a basis in fact.

While foreigners were beguiled by the bow-tied Canadian, it is worth recalling that Pearson served as SSEA when Canada's relative international prominence was high thanks to the weakness of war-ravaged Europe and East Asia and the domination of much of the globe by imperial powers. In effect, then, there were few competitors for the international limelight and Pearson had the great luck to head a remarkable foreign service at a time when Canada, by default, was important globally. Moreover, he and his team had St-Laurent's support. After all, it was St-Laurent who, in 1947, had given voice in his famous Gray Lecture at the University of Toronto to a more active though still pragmatic Canadian role in the world.[33] Regrettably, the world of the late 1940s was entering into a Cold War, and Pearson and St-Laurent placed Canada firmly in the Western camp for they saw the Soviet Union as an aggressive force threatening collective security. As early as March 1946 Pearson had counselled: "The United States and the United Kingdom should convert the United Nations into a really effective agent to preserve the peace and prevent aggression.

This means revising it radically. If the Russians veto such a revision, agreed on by others, a new organization must be created which, as the guardian of the peace for all nations, and not merely the English-speaking ones, can function without the Russians and, as a last resort, against them."[34] Under Pearson and St-Laurent, Canada was an active Cold War combatant, both at home and abroad. Canadians generally supported this stance. As late as 1963, the year Pearson assumed the prime ministership, most Canadians in a national sample saw "communism as a danger to the West." While 47 percent of the same sample disagreed that nuclear war was an acceptable means to defeat communism, 42 percent backed such an apocalyptic solution.[35] Thus, postwar idealism was matched by the reality of great power politics and by a fear of ideological threats to Canada's liberal order. Pearson, however, was wary of the bomb and aware of the grim realities of nuclear warfare. In 1960, on national television, he declared, sensibly enough, that it would be "better to be Red than dead," thereby inciting the ire of Canadian and American conservatives.[36]

Beyond the Cold War, though often linked closely to it, Canadians also wrestled with the fallout of decolonization. As Pearson once reflected: "It may be that in the verdict of history a hundred years or so from now, it will be agreed that of the communist revolution in Russia in 1917 and the emergence of independent Asian countries after World War II – the latter revolution will be considered in its long-range impact as more important than the former."[37] He was right, of course, as the end of empire and the emergence of dozens of new states had a profound impact on international affairs while also inspiring oppressed minorities in Canada itself. Canadian responses to decolonization were decidedly mixed. While Canada often backed its Western allies in retaining their imperial holdings, there were instances, Suez most notably, in which Ottawa sided with anti-colonial nationalism. Just eight months before the Suez Crisis, Pearson had asked reporters: "If we hold colonial territories against the wishes of their inhabitants are we going to be stronger or weaker in the long run?"[38] During the Pearsonian era, decolonization and the Cold War were two of the factors that shaped the world and, with it, Canadian foreign policy.

In 1957, the Pearson–St-Laurent compact came crashing down. An election that year saw Diefenbaker's Progressive Conservatives end the Liberals' twenty-two-year-long run in power. During the Diefenbaker interregnum, foreign policy sounded different. There was more positive bluster about the British Commonwealth and disarmament; more negative bluster about the Soviets and the United States. Still, the contours remained Pearsonian: adherence to the UN, to the Atlantic alliance, and to the US alliance, and the seemingly inexorable realignment of Canadian trade southwards. After all, Diefenbaker and Pearson were similar men, and "the Chief" shared Mike's idealism, if not his pragmatism.[39] In the interim, Pearson had become both Liberal leader and a politician. The Opposition years were tough, with the New Democratic Party, formed in 1961, squeezing the Liberals on the left. Pearson rebuilt his party and whittled away at the Tories. "I doubt," one of his star MPs later recalled, "whether there was any other period of his life when Mike Pearson's diplomacy was more consistently needed or employed to better effect." But, as one journalist put it: "The crackle of intellectual electricity that brought him the Nobel Peace Prize seemed only to hamper Pearson in the cut and thrust over domestic issues."[40] If Diefenbaker was more of a politician than a statesman, Pearson was the reverse.

Despite his initial fumbling, after six years in Opposition, Pearson and the Liberals claimed victory, although astute campaigning by a defiant Diefenbaker limited Pearson to a minority government. There would be a second minority win for the Liberals in 1965, and Pearson resigned and retired in 1968, spending his twilight years first as an adviser to the World Bank and then as chancellor of Carleton University where he led seminars in Canadian foreign policy until his death in 1972.[41] As for his five-year prime ministership, the consensus then and since, as J.L. Granatstein put it, was that "Pearson was a great success as a diplomat. He was not, however, a great success as a prime minister."[42] His time in office seemed plagued by perennial scandal and incompetence, the latter tendency exemplified by the failure to win a majority. That he did not do better as Canada's leader is, on its face, surprising given his skill as a negotiator. As for Prime Minister Pearson's handling of global affairs, there "was no room in the 1960s for the great initiatives of the 1940s." Rather, as Robert Bothwell observes: "Optimism and commitment were transformed into worry and indecision, as much on the public's part as on the government's. The sixties as far as Canadian foreign policy was concerned ended with a whimper."[43]

Though Canadians welcomed the fact that the 1960s ended without an atomic "bang," in this volume, our contributors examine Pearson's foreign policy record and the paradoxical clash between idealism and pragmatism that undergirds Pearsonianism. While the tendency in international history of late has been to move away from elite-focused works towards a welcome emphasis on the social contexts, grassroots, and communities among which elite policy makers moved, Pearson's legacy deserves attention given his continued importance to the framing of debates about Canada's role in the world. Indeed, one is tempted to draw connections to the influence of President Woodrow Wilson in the US context. For nearly a century Wilsonianism has served as a model and a foil for discussion about US foreign policy, with adherents of Wilson – like those of Pearson – advocating internationalism and global engagement. Pearson, though, mixed his idealism with pragmatism. The latter meant that Canadian diplomats were not simply "going along to get along," but it did not mean that Pearson and company were a pack of McCarthyite warmongers. Rather, Pearson's conduct in foreign affairs sprang from mixed motives. Though Pearson was a partisan for the West in the Cold War, he was deeply concerned by the confrontational and interventionist nature of US foreign policy. He was hopeful yet sceptical that internationalism and multilateralism could prevent a major war; realizing that colonialism was on the wane and opposed to being drawn into decolonial conflicts, he was supportive of Canada's Western European allies, many of whom were imperial powers. Concerned about both global poverty and the inequality between the First World and the Third World, Pearson championed Canadian economic interests. In short, Pearsonianism was contradictory. Perhaps contradiction has served as fodder for myth-making; but, in any event, Canadians should neither look back too wistfully on this bygone era nor engage too readily in iconoclasm. After all, Pearson won a Nobel Peace Prize for a reason.

Gathering together scholars of Canadian international history, the present volume wrestles with the contradictions of Pearson and Pearsonianism and, ultimately, with the resulting myths surrounding Canada's role in the world. Some of our contributors take deeply critical positions; others offer considerable praise for Pearson. Together, they provide a sustained analysis of the record of a man who, for better or worse, still influences Canada's international identity and much of Canadian thinking about its global posture.

While much has been written about Pearsonian foreign policy during the Golden Age, especially about both Suez and the creation of Israel, comparatively little has been written about Canada's role in the world from 1963 to 1968.[44] Within the limited work on this era, much of the focus is on Pearson and the Vietnam War, an understandable preoccupation as this conflict was one of the period's signal issues, engaging passions and exposing deep societal divides. Pearson's response to the war has recently been characterized as "balancing war and peace," a fitting description that carries with it that sense of Pearsonian paradox.[45] Beyond Vietnam, other studies have intently explored Prime Minster Pearson's relations with the United States.[46] But, despite historians' and the public's deep interest in the 1960s, there has been little focus beyond these areas. Indeed, the recent spate of historical interest in Canada's 1960s has dealt mainly with domestic rather than international history.[47] So, the chapters in this volume analyze Pearsonian foreign policy during an important period in Canadian and global history, pushing past – though not ignoring – the Golden Era into the 1960s.

Pearson was prime minister in trying times. Leading two minority governments, at home he faced English and French Canadian nationalisms, management of an increasingly interventionist state, rapid technological change, intergenerational strife, and a youthful identification with the Third World that called into question Canada's postwar foreign policy status quo with its Pearsonian identity tied firmly to the Western cause in the Cold War and to Anglo-Saxon notions of liberty and progress.[48] Abroad, the 1960s saw important changes that affected Canada's global position. The recovery of Western Europe and Japan created fresh economic pressures even as declining British influence meant that, for Canadians, Britain was a diminishing counterweight to American influences; the dissolution of formal European empires, the emergence of a plethora of new states, and the rise of Third World nationalism created new opportunities as well as new dangers; and an aggressive Soviet foreign policy that aimed, in the words of Soviet premier Nikita Khrushchev, to "bury" the West raised old fears even as a growing sense of détente created new hopes. At the pinnacle of its power, though the United States sought to "pay any price, bear any burden" in its Cold War crusade, by decade's end Washington was mired in an intractable war, its moral and material superiority in doubt. There were new challenges, too, often thanks to pressures exerted by the growing ranks of non-governmental organizations, many of which were concerned about international human rights and about the environment. Indeed, the 1960s saw a growing global consciousness and inter-connectedness leading to a great sense that it was a "crucial decade."[49] The world was very different than when Pearson had been SSEA, and, as prime minister, he also had to focus on domestic issues. Thus, he left much of the handling of foreign policy to his own SSEA, Paul Martin Sr., an openly ambitious Liberal warhorse who had his own priorities, which created tension between the two men.[50] Still, Pearson acted in foreign affairs. That he did not do a better job of charting Canada through these troubled seas seemed self-evident to observers at the time. "Instead of leading the people through this maze of change," wrote journalist Peter Newman, "the Pearson-Diefenbaker generation of politicians droned on, caught up in the vain hopes of a long-gone epoch, viewing their own peculiar Kiplingesque world through the rear windows of the flag-fluttering limousines in the age of moonflights, mass marches and mod."[51]

When it came to his handling of foreign policy, was Prime Minister Pearson out of his depth? Did he achieve successes? Or was his record a mixed one, reflective of the paradoxes that surrounded him? Moreover, what does his foreign policy record at the time tell us about how Canadians in the 1960s viewed Canada's place in the world? The contributors to this collection explore how Pearson and, by turns, Canadians wrestled with this era of rapid change at home and abroad. Yet the authors' focus is wider for, while examining Pearsonian policy in the 1960s, it traces Pearson's thinking on issues over his career, a lens that allows us to consider policy over several decades and to probe differences between the Golden Decade and the Sixties. What were the changes in his views, for instance, on East-West relations, on Canadian connections to Britain, on the United Nations, and on the emerging Third World? Furthermore, the authors connect Pearson's foreign policy decisions with domestic issues and link external events with developments at home. In connecting Pearson with the world in which he lived, they draw attention to the thinking that inspired his worldviews, including the ways in which he reflected wider trends within Sixties Canada and how Canadians shaped, responded to, and engaged with international affairs in this period. Last, contributors address the myth-making surrounding Pearson and Pearsonianism with an eye towards assessing his record and reputation and doing so not uncritically.[52]

The book has three sections. In the first, the authors assess various aspects of Pearsonianism and its legacy. Indeed, in his contribution Robert Bothwell deals with this concept head-on in a probing exegesis of a term frequently invoked but all too frequently misunderstood. In a similar vein, Michael Carroll and Adam Chapnick explore areas synonymous with Pearsonianism – peacekeeping and the United Nations, respectively – highlighting the idealism that informed Pearson's thinking and the realism that guided his policies. As for policy making, Greg Donaghy looks at the professional relationship between Pearson and Paul Martin. Having had his own goals in foreign affairs, Martin's imprint is felt throughout the book. Switching gears somewhat, Stephen Azzi places Pearson's foreign policy in its domestic setting both in terms of Liberal political activities and with regard to the decade's emblematic upheavals.

The chapters in our second section examine the more pragmatic side to Pearsonian foreign policy. First, Jennifer Tunnicliffe focuses on rights promotion, an issue just beginning to captivate Canadian and global attention in the 1960s. As she stresses, Pearson's handling of and belief in the promotion of human rights internationally was neither inspired nor inspiring. A similar portrait emerges from Peter Kikkert, Adam Lajeunesse, and P. Whitney Lackenbauer's analysis of Pearson's dealings over Arctic sovereignty, a long-standing issue in Canadian foreign policy and one on which, they note, Pearson was distinctly "un-Pearsonian." In analyzing Canadian actions in the Middle East – from which sprang Pearson's greatest triumph, the United Nations Emergency Force – Maurice Jr. M. Labelle offers a highly critical analysis of what constituted Pearsonianism. While Pearson took a hardnosed stance toward issues in the Middle East, he showed considerable caution in addressing developments in Latin America and the Caribbean, long an area that most Canadians had ignored. John Dirks indicates why Pearson's caution may have been shrewd even as Paul Martin hoped to see Canada play a larger hemispheric role. Finally, as Lara Silver shows in her chapter, although Pearson was a product of British Canada and of Oxford, he had a complicated relationship with Britain, thanks to fraying imperial ties and a declining global empire.

Our third section contains chapters stressing the more idealistic side of Pearsonianism. While the early 1960s witnessed tense Cold War crises over Berlin and Cuba, the rest of the decade saw an emerging East-West détente. Pearson, notes Timothy Andrews Sayle, had long been convinced of the need to build bridges to the Soviet bloc, and so his views aligned well with the prevailing post-Cuban Missile Crisis spirit that sought to defuse Cold War tensions. Like many Canadians in the postwar era, Pearson saw a role for Canada in building bridges not just between East and West but also between the West and newly independent states. As Ryan Touhey demonstrates, nowhere was this ethos more in evidence than in South Asia. Meanwhile, growing détente also had an impact upon trans-Atlantic relations, as did changing US nuclear policies. In her chapter, Isabel Campbell charts Pearson's efforts to understand the shifting strategic landscape in Europe and its effect on NATO, an alliance that he had helped to create and to which he was deeply attached. In Europe, and elsewhere, Pearsonianism clashed with Gaullism. Offering fresh insights into the hostile Franco-Canadian relationship, Brendan Kelly shows how Pearson's difficulties in dealing with French president Charles de Gaulle touched on the most pressing domestic question at the time – namely, Canada's future as a united country. Also emphasizing the interplay between the global and the local, in our final chapter, Norman Hillmer, Daniel Macfarlane, and Michael Manulak examine Pearson's record in environmental diplomacy. Like human rights, environmentalism was emerging as a serious issue in the 1960s and it was a matter in which Pearson displayed considerable interest, particularly for the time period.

The image of Pearson that emerges from this volume is that of a paradoxical policy maker who shrewdly pursued what he perceived to be Canadian interests while also seeking to foster cooperation along liberal internationalist lines. If there was a conflict here, as many of our authors note, it occurred because, as Barbara Ward once observed, his "principles made him an idealist, his sensibility a realist."[53] Mixing pragmatism and idealism, he directed Canada through a troubled time both at home and abroad. That he continues to inspire debates about Canada and its role in the world speaks not simply to the power of myth and of self-aggrandizing notions of Canada as a middle power, a peacekeeper, and an honest broker, but to the legacy of a man who for two decades, and for better or for worse, was Canada's face to the world.

Notes

1 Grant Dexter, "Mr. Pearson's Objective Achieved," *Winnipeg Free Press*, 26 November 1956; Maxwell Cohen, "A New Responsibility in Foreign Policy," *Saturday Night*, 19 January 1957.

2 Douglas LePan, *The Price of Being Canadian*, ed. D.L.B. Hamlin (Toronto: University of Toronto Press, 1961), 46; Lloyd Axworthy, *Navigating a New World: Canada's Global Future* (Toronto: Vintage, 2004), 32; Charles Lynch, *You Can't Print That! Memoirs of a Political Voyeur* (Edmonton: Hurtig, 1983), 158–59.

3 Senator Raoul Dandurand, quoted in John Hilliker, *Canada's Department of External Affairs: The Early Years, 1909–1946* (Montreal and Kingston: McGill-Queen's University Press, 1990), 97.

4 Donald Masters, *Canada in World Affairs, 1953 to 1955* (Toronto: Oxford University Press, 1959), 4; Jennifer Welsh, *At Home in the World: Canada's Global Vision for the 21st Century* (Toronto: HarperCollins, 2004), 134; Andrew Cohen, "Pearsonianism," in *Pearson: The Unlikely Gladiator*, ed. Norman Hillmer (Montreal and Kingston: McGill-Queen's University Press, 1999), 153; Paul Heinbecker, *Getting Back in the Game: A Foreign Policy Playbook for Canada* (Toronto: Dundurn, 2011), 60. See also Erika Simpson, "The Principles of Liberal Internationalism According to Lester Pearson," *Journal of Canadian Studies* 34 (1999): 75–92; and John Holmes, *The Shaping of the Peace: Canada and the Search for World Order, 1943–1957* (Toronto: University of Toronto Press, 1979).

5 Government of Canada, *A Role of Pride and Influence in the World: Overview* (Ottawa: Foreign Affairs Canada, 2005); Jean Chrétien, "Canada Must Reclaim Its Role as a World Leader," *Globe and Mail*, 12 September 2015; David Pugilese, "Nobel Fever," *Saturday Night*, May 1997.

6 J.L. Granatstein, *Who Killed the Canadian Military?* (Toronto: HarperCollins, 2004), 14; Hugh Segal, "Foreign Policy and the Senate: Microscope and Telescope in Turbulent Times," in *The Harper Era in Canadian Foreign Policy: Parliament, Politics, Canada's Global Posture*, ed. Adam Chapnick and Christopher J. Kukucha (Vancouver: UBC Press, 2016), 245.

7 Heather Smith and Claire Turenne Sjolander, "Conversations without Consensus: Internationalism under the Harper Government," in *Canada in the World: Internationalism in Canadian Foreign Policy*, ed. Heather A. Smith and Claire Turenne Sjolander (Toronto: Oxford University Press, 2013), i.

8 Daniel Francis, *National Dreams: Myth, Memory, and Canadian History* (Vancouver: Arsenal Pulp, 1997), 11; Paul Cohen, *History in Three Keys: The Boxers as Event, Experience, and Myth* (New York: Columbia University Press, 1997), 212.

9 Adam Chapnick, *The Middle Power Project: Canada and the Founding of the United Nations* (Vancouver: UBC Press, 2005), 148.

10 Greg Donaghy, ed., *Canada and the Early Cold War, 1943–1957* (Ottawa: Department of Foreign Affairs and International Trade, 1998); Hector MacKenzie, "Golden Decade(s)? Reappraising Canada's International Relations in the 1940s and 1950s," *British Journal of Canadian Studies* 23 (2010):

179–206; Adam Chapnick, "The Canadian Middle Power Myth," *International Journal* 55 (2000): 188–206.

11 Ross Campbell, "Pragmatism," in Hillmer, *Unlikely Gladiator*, 161.

12 Mark Neufeld, "'Happy Is the Land That Needs No Hero': The Pearsonian Tradition and the Canadian Intervention in Afghanistan," in *Canadian Foreign Policy in Critical Perspective*, ed. J. Marshall Beier and Lana Wylie (Toronto: Oxford University Press, 2010), 135. For a critique of liberal internationalism in the Pearsonian era, see David Meren, "The Tragedies of Canadian International History," *Canadian Historical Review* 96 (2015), 544–48 and 557.

13 John Price. *Orienting Canada: Race, Empire, and the Transpacific* (Vancouver: UBC Press, 2011), 236.

14 Ian McKay and Jamie Swift, *Warrior Nation: Rebranding Canada in an Age of Anxiety* (Toronto: Between the Lines, 2012), 134. See also Linda McQuaig, *Holding the Bully's Coat: Canada and the US Empire* (Toronto: Doubleday, 2007), 159, 148. On the paradoxes around Pearson, see Norman Hillmer, "Pearson and the Sense of Paradox," in Hillmer, *Unlikely Gladiator*.

15 J.W. Warnock, "Canadian Policy in Vietnam: 'Ready Aye Ready,'" *Canadian Dimension*, May-June 1965; Trudeau, quoted in Denis Smith, *Gentle Patriot: A Political Biography of Walter Gordon* (Edmonton: Hurtig, 1973), 119.

16 Noam Chomsky, "Foreword," in Yves Engler, *Lester Pearson's Peacekeeping: The Truth May Hurt* (Vancouver: Fernwood, 2012), 9.

17 Engler, *Pearson's Peacekeeping*, 146.

18 L. Ian MacDonald, "A Conversation with John Baird," *Policy Options*, April 2012; Steven Chase, "Transcript: Harper Explains Why He Still Wants to Be Prime Minister," 17 December 2014, http://www.theglobeandmail.com/news/politics/transcript-harper-explains-why-he-still-wants-to-be-prime-minister/article22129003/.

19 Canada, House of Commons, *Debates*, 10 February 1960, 930–31.

20 John Ibbitson, "Harper's Handling of Ukraine the Latest Outrage for Old-School Observers," *Globe and Mail*, 20 March 2014; Tim Harper, "Stephen Harper's Lightning Quick Foreign Policy Overhaul," *Toronto Star*, 4 December 2012; Roland Paris, "Canada's Decade of Diplomatic Darkness," *Globe and Mail*, 24 September 2014.

21 Quoted in John English, *The Worldly Years: The Life of Lester Pearson, 1949–1972* (Toronto: Knopf, 1992), 88.

22 Andrew Cohen, *While Canada Slept: How We Lost Our Place in the World* (Toronto: McClelland and Stewart, 2003), 3.

23 J.L. Granatstein and Robert Bothwell, *Pirouette: Pierre Trudeau and Canadian Foreign Policy* (Toronto: University of Toronto Press, 1990), xiii; James Lay, "Memorandum for the National Security Council," 24 May 1960, and attached Department of State report "Certain Aspects of United States Politico-Military Relationships with Canada," Dwight Eisenhower Presidential Library White House, Office of the NSA, NSC Series, Policy Papers, box 26, fol. NSC 5822.

24 Lecture notes, 1927, Library and Archives Canada (LAC), Lester Pearson Papers, vol. 15. See also Phillip Buckner and R. Douglas Francis, ed., *Canada and the British World* (Vancouver: UBC Press, 2006).

25 Early life drawn from John English, *Shadow of Heaven: The Life of Lester Pearson* (Toronto: Lester and Orpen Dennys, 1989).

26 Dexter to Ferguson, 12 November 1937, Queen's University Archives, Grant Dexter Papers, series S01, subseries SS03, file 007; Pearson to Skelton, 4 November 1938, LAC, RG 25, vol. 54, file 319-2.

27 Diary entry, 18 December 1947, LAC, William Lyon Mackenzie King Papers.

28 Press Conference, 29 September 1955, LAC, James Minifie Papers, vol. 27, file Press Conference – Canadian 1955.

29 Lester Pearson, *Mike: The Memoirs of the Right Honourable Lester B. Pearson*, vol. 2 (Toronto: University of Toronto Press, 1973), 32, 35.

30 George Egerton, "Lester B. Pearson and the Korean War: Dilemmas of Collective Security and International Enforcement in Canadian Foreign Policy, 1950–1953," *International Peacekeeping* 4 (1997): 51–74; and Greg Donaghy, "Blessed Are the Peacemakers: Canada, the United Nations, and the Search for a Korean Armistice, 1952–53," *War & Society* 30 (2011): 134–46.

31 Adrian Liddell Hart, "The Voice of Canada," *Saturday Night*, 15 October 1955, 16; John Kennedy, "The Terrain of Today's Statecraft," *Saturday Review*, 1 August 1959.

32 Rajeshwar Dayal, "The Power of Wisdom," *International Journal* 29 (1973–74): 110; MacDonald to Pearson, 10 August 1964, LAC, Pearson Papers, vol. 267, file 810.3 1964.

33 Louis St-Laurent, *The Foundations of Canadian Policy in World Affairs* (Toronto: University of Toronto Press, 1947).

34 Pearson to King, 11 March 1946, *Documents on Canadian External Relations, 1946* (Ottawa: Supply and Services Canada, 1977), 2046.

35 On the polling numbers, see Robert Bothwell, *Alliance and Illusion: Canada and the World, 1945–1984* (Vancouver: UBC Press, 2007), 214. See also Robert Teigrob, *Warming Up to the Cold War: Canada and the United States' Coalition of the Willing, from Hiroshima to Korea* (Toronto: University of Toronto Press, 2009); Reg Whitaker and Gary Marcuse, *Cold War Canada: The Making of a National Insecurity State, 1945–1957* (Toronto: University of Toronto Press, 1995).

36 See Pearson to Heeney, 30 May 1960, LAC, Arnold Heeney Papers, vol. 1, file 15.

37 Quoted in I. Norman Smith, "Pearson, People, and Press," *International Journal* 29 (1973–74): 18.

38 Department of External Affairs, *Statements and Speeches*, 21 March 1956.

39 J.L. Granatstein, "Pearson and Diefenbaker: Similar Men?" and Christina McCall, "The Unlikely Gladiators: Pearson and Diefenbaker Remembered," in Hillmer, *Unlikely Gladiator*. For recent, nuanced views of Diefenbaker's foreign policy, see D.C. Story and R.B. Shepard, eds., *The Diefenbaker Legacy: Politics, Law and Society since 1957* (Regina: Canadian Plains Research Centre, 1998); Kevin Spooner, *Canada, the Congo Crisis, and UN Peacekeeping, 1960–1964* (Vancouver: UBC Press, 2009); Patricia McMahon, *Essence of Indecision: Diefenbaker's Nuclear Policy, 1957–1963* (Montreal and Kingston: McGill-Queen's University Press, 2009); and Asa McKercher, *Camelot and Canada:*

Canadian-American Relations in the Kennedy Era (New York: Oxford University Press, 2016).

40 Lionel Chevrier, "The Practical Diplomacy of Lester Pearson," *International Journal* 29 (1973–74): 129; Peter Newman, "The Man behind the Party's New Mike Pearson – He's Still a Diplomat in Politics," *Maclean's*, 22 October 1960, 12. For an assessment of the impact of Pearson's minority governments on his foreign policy, see John English, "Foreign Policy and Minority Government: The Cases of Lester Pearson and Pierre Trudeau," in Chapnick and Kukucha, *Harper Era*, 41–47. On domestic policy, see Penny Bryden, *Planners and Politics: Liberal Politics and Social Policy 1957–1968* (Montreal and Kingston: McGill-Queen's University Press, 1997).

41 Kevin Brushett, "Partners in Development? Robert McNamara, Lester Pearson, and the Commission on International Development, 1967–1973," *Diplomacy and Statecraft* 26 (2015): 84–102.

42 J.L. Granatstein, *Canada 1957–1967: Years of Uncertainty and Innovation* (Toronto: McClelland and Stewart, 1986), 199.

43 Robert Bothwell, *Pearson: His Life and World* (Toronto: McGraw-Hill, 1978), 181.

44 On Suez, see Antony Anderson, *The Diplomat: Lester Pearson and the Suez Crisis* (Fredericton: Goose Lane Editions, 2015); Michael K. Carroll, *Pearson's Peacekeepers: Canada and the United Nations Emergency Force, 1956–67* (Vancouver: UBC Press, 2009); Michael B. Oren, "Faith and Fair-Mindedness: Lester B. Pearson and the Suez Crisis," *Diplomacy and Statecraft* 3 (1992): 48–73; Michael G. Fry, "Canada, the North Atlantic and the UN," in *Suez 1956: The Crisis and Its Consequences*, ed. Wm. Roger Louis and Roger Owen, 285–316 (Oxford: Clarendon Press, 1989). On Israel, see David Bercuson, *Canada and the Birth of Israel* (Toronto: University of Toronto Press, 1985); Eliezer Tauber, *Personal Policy Making: Canada's Role in the Adoption of the Palestinian Partition Resolution* (Westport, CT: Greenwood Press, 2002); Anne Hillmer, "Here I Am in the Middle: Lester Pearson and the Origins of Canada's Diplomatic Involvement in the Middle East," in *Domestic Battleground: Canada and the Arab-Israeli Conflict*, ed. David Taras and David Goldberg, 125–43 (Montreal and Kingston: McGill-Queen's University Press, 1989).

45 Andrew Preston, "Balancing War and Peace: Canadian Foreign Policy and the Vietnam War, 1961–1965," *Diplomatic History* (2003): 73–111; and Andrew Preston, "Missions Impossible: Canadian Secret Diplomacy and the Quest for Peace in Vietnam," in *The Search for Peace in Vietnam, 1964–1968*, ed. Lloyd Gardner and Tedd Gittinger, 117–43 (College Station: Texas A&M University Press, 2004). For recent attention on the societal divides caused by the war, see Tarah Brookfield, *Cold War Comforts: Canadian Women, Child Safety, and Global Insecurity* (Waterloo: Wilfrid Laurier Press, 2012), 161–88; David S. Churchill, "Draft Resisters, Left Nationalism, and the Politics of Anti-Imperialism," *Canadian Historical Review* 93 (2012): 227–60; Jessica Squires, *Building Sanctuary: The Movement to Support Vietnam War Resisters in Canada, 1965–73* (Vancouver: UBC Press, 2014).

46 Greg Donaghy, *Tolerant Allies: Canada and the United States, 1963–1968* (Montreal and Kingston: McGill-Queen's University Press, 2002); Dimitry

Anastakis, *Auto Pact: Creating a Borderless North American Auto Industry, 1960–1971* (Toronto: University of Toronto Press, 2005); Stephen Azzi, *Walter Gordon and the Rise of Canadian Nationalism* (Montreal and Kingston: McGill-Queen's University Press, 1999); and Bruce Muirhead, *Dancing Around the Elephant: Creating a Prosperous Canada in an Era of American Dominance, 1957–1973* (Toronto: University of Toronto Press, 2007).

47 Lara Campbell, Dominique Clément, and Greg Kealey, eds., *Debating Dissent: Canada and the 1960s* (Toronto: University of Toronto Press, 2012); Bryan Palmer, *Canada's 1960s: The Ironies of Identity in a Rebellious Era* (Toronto: University of Toronto Press, 2009); Dimitry Anastakis, ed., *The Sixties: Passion, Politics, and Style* (Montreal and Kingston: McGill-Queen's University Press, 2008); and M. Athena Palaeologu, ed., *The Sixties in Canada: A Turbulent and Creative Decade* (Montreal: Black Rose Books, 2009).

48 Jeremi Suri, *Power and Protest: Global Revolution and the Rise of Detente* (Cambridge, MA: Harvard University Press, 2003).

49 Diane Kunz, *The Diplomacy of the Crucial Decade: American Foreign Relations during the 1960s* (New York: Columbia University Press, 1994). See also Frank Gavin and Mark Atwood Lawrence, *Beyond the Cold War: Lyndon Johnson and the New Global Challenges of the 1960s* (New York: Oxford University Press, 2014).

50 See, for instance, Greg Donaghy, "Red China Blues: Paul Martin, Lester B. Pearson, and the Chinese Conundrum, 1963–1967," *Journal of American-East Asian Relations* 20 (2013): 190–202.

51 Peter Newman, *The Distemper of Our Times: Canadian Politics in Transition 1963–1968* (Toronto: McClelland and Stewart, 1968), xiii.

52 Regrettably, contributors dealing with Africa, with development, and with immigration backed out of the project.

53 Barbara Ward, "What Shrewd yet Visionary Voice," in *"Freedom and Change": Essays in Honour of Lester B. Pearson*, ed. Michael G. Fry (Toronto: McClelland and Stewart, 1975), 244.

Part 1:

The Pearsonian World

Robert Bothwell

1 Pearson and Pearsonianism

Pearson and Pearsonianism have not had a good press lately. For many years, "Pearson" and the policies and practices he is believed to have originated, which have been lumped under the vague title "Pearsonianism," defined the Canadian way of diplomacy. Before we turn to Pearson the man, let us look at Pearson the idea or, as his critics would prefer, Pearson the myth. Idea and myth are called Pearsonianism, a uniquely Canadian meaning – because there are lots of Pearsons in the world and therefore a wonderful variety of "Pearsonian" ideas.[1] In this chapter I propose first to look at Pearson's relations with Pearsonianism and then to examine a case in which he put his beliefs into practice. The practice, I argue, is inseparable from the belief system, a mixture of ideology and professionalism that characterized the Canadian approach to foreign affairs from the early years of the twentieth century to the beginning of the twenty-first. It has also led to confusion and sometimes error on both the right and the left – as Pearson might have said, not unfamiliar territory for either extreme.

Pearsonianism was not one idea, but a jumble. Historian Stephen Azzi considers that it was "composed of several elements." There was "traditional liberal internationalism, the belief that it is possible to have a truer peace than armed truce" among sovereign states. Working from the fact of state sovereignty, "international institutions should promote peace through collective security or conciliation." Pearson's approach melded the liberalism of William Ewart Gladstone, the liberal icon of the nineteenth century, with the ideas of Franklin Roosevelt, the liberal champion of the twentieth. Thus, Pearson desired "to promote security, prosperity, and human rights abroad."[2] As Norman Hillmer points out, Pearson did not confuse his influence or Canada's with Gladstone's or Roosevelt's. Canada was a secondary power and must combine its power with that of other countries, which, in the mid-twentieth century, meant the United States.[3] Accepting American leadership was not difficult. The United States, too, was a liberal democratic country as well as a neighbour, its merits and its faults well known to Canadians and, especially, to Pearson, who had lived in the United States and had close relatives there. Meanwhile, the British connection continued, and a feeling of solidarity with the democracies of Western Europe, and a desire, based on wartime experience, to be internationally engaged, as Pearson's superior, External Affairs Minister Louis St-Laurent, put it in the Gray Lecture of 1947.

To liberal internationalism should be added professionalism, for diplomacy was Pearson's profession and one to which he was well suited. Diplomacy was not new, to be sure, and it had always been recognized that some were better at it than others. Embassies, legations, consulates, and foreign offices were all embodied by the beginning of the nineteenth century. Diplomats while abroad had a well understood set of privileges essential to their function, being immune from arrest or overt mistreatment by their sovereign host. Representing their own sovereign, they were expected to live up to certain standards of behaviour, including a lifestyle appropriate to the dignity of the sovereign they represented. They were also, to some degree, free "from outside social pressures." Diplomats dealt with other diplomats, sometimes lived with other diplomats, and were judged by their peers rather than by laypeople.[4] A diplomat's effectiveness depended on reputation, and reputation was earned by "good faith, discipline and loyalty," as a later academic analyst puts it.[5]

Where the reputation counted was not so much within one's own foreign service (though of course it bore on such considerations as promotion) as inside those of other countries. According to the American political scientist Robert Rossow, the crucial objective is to minimize "distortion and friction in cross-cultural communications and operations."[6] As Alan Gyngell and Michael Wesley argue, diplomats "need to understand the interests of others in order to pursue better the interests of the government for which they work";[7] in other words, they must possess the quality of empathy, to which Pearson's biographer Antony Anderson adds patience and congeniality.[8] Gyngell and Wesley add, perceptively, that this quality is often at the root of a distrust that diplomats' political masters feel for the profession – the idea that their diplomats have "gone native" or in some other way have forgotten or ignored the basic interests or character of the country that employs them. This is particularly the case when politicians find it difficult to identify intellectually or socially with their diplomats.

As long as the inhabitants of the political system were more or less in sync, socially and intellectually, with their diplomats, the most serious clashes could be avoided. In the early nineteenth century, diplomatic posts were grace-and-favour appointments of a distinctly privileged background, sometimes drawn from the aristocracy, sometimes from a foreign secretary's cabinet of relatives, and sometimes from politics. Cross-cultural differences existed but were mitigated by a common social background among the various privileged envoys. By 1900, aspiring diplomats in many countries, including Britain,[9] were chosen by competitive examination, and, by the 1920s, the practice was nearly universal among Western countries. It was accompanied by decompression in the strictly aristocratic traditions of the various foreign services, although for some purposes the rich were highly valued for the maintenance of standards of entertainment that democratic governments believed they could not afford.[10] It was natural for the fledgling Canadian Foreign Service to adopt this model,[11] and for Lester Pearson, MA (Oxon.) to sit a competitive examination to become a member of the Department of External Affairs.[12] It was not a profession he had initially chosen – indeed, he had tried several before lighting on the foreign service. As it turned out, the man was made for the moment, and the moment for the man.

Pearson rose rapidly in the civil service. The DEA was the prime minister's own department and was headed by Canada's most influential civil servant, O.D. Skelton, the under-secretary for external affairs. Talented foreign service officers were bound to come to their superiors' notice, and if the person doing the noticing was the prime minister, it was possible to move rapidly up the scale. In Skelton's eyes, Pearson embodied "good faith, discipline and loyalty," and while serving on the Canadian delegation at the League of Nations he came to understand "cross-cultural communications and operations." Pearson was deputy minister or under-secretary before he was fifty, and minister or secretary of state for external affairs by the time he was fifty-one – Mackenzie King's last appointment to the cabinet.

Canada, abroad, was Pearson, and, consciously or unconsciously, successive Canadian governments followed in his footsteps. That is, until recently. "The Harper government," as it liked to be called, made it plain that Pearson's legacy was at best obsolete, at worst flawed if not downright immoral. Ironically, the historical left has reached the same conclusion as Harper and his historical handmaidens – but for the opposite reasons and employing "liberal/Liberal" as a term of scorn.[13]

Pearson might not have been surprised. He was, after all, a son of the Methodist manse and familiar with the gospel verse, "A prophet is not without honour, but in his own country, and among his own kin, and in his own house."[14] A historian by training, he knew that reputations rose and fell, and that one century's hero was a villain in the next. A member of the generation that achieved Canadian sovereignty from the British Empire, he worried that his country's sovereignty might be frittered away: in other words, that Canada would move from one form of colonial dependence to another, preserving the forms of a sovereign state while losing its essence, the power of self-determination. Complete autonomy, he also came to see, was a delusion. No state was completely autonomous, and smaller states like Canada were bound to be influenced, often decisively, by larger ones. Behind Pearson's every policy there lurked the concern that sometimes, on some issues, Canada would not be able to say "No."

The ability to say "No," however, was cradled within a larger affirmative mandate. Pearson was not only of the generation that witnessed the coming of Canadian independence in the 1920s and 1930s, he was also part of the generation that experienced the Great Depression and the Second World War. Even the most obtuse recognized that the Depression was an international phenomenon and that national boundaries were not proof against economic disaster. On the political side, the failures of 1930s' diplomacy made it clear that "peace was indivisible."[15] Many observers at the time believed that Canada could not survive either depression or war: among them was Pearson's professional superior, Skelton. His was a counsel of despair for a war he could not prevent, though once war was declared Skelton did his best to mobilize Canada for what he thought was a very uncertain conflict.

The war, however, was won. Better still, the Great Depression was overcome, a collateral benefit from the conflict. Even more, the Canadian government devised policies for economic and social reconstruction, including generous veterans' benefits that gave returning soldiers a chance that they would never have received in the unequal society of the 1920s or in the misery and despair of the Depression. Pearson had little to do with devising these policies, but he and the country gained immeasurably from them. Canadians in the 1940s presumed that there was such a thing as Canadian society – they would have found the notion that there was not very strange – and that what helped one sector, one group, or one region in society helped all. To adapt a phrase that became familiar – all too familiar – in the 1980s and 1990s, a rising tide raised all boats. A happy country and a united country were also very strange, but with prosperity and unity underpinning government, it became possible to envision a positive foreign policy.

It should not be forgotten that Pearson was also a professional diplomat. That was not necessarily a good thing. A sovereign Canada needed representation abroad, but, as one of Pearson's friends, Hume Wrong, cynically wrote, all that was needed for that was a suit, a briefcase, and calling cards. The expense of actually sending a person to fill the suit and distribute the cards was unnecessary. There were moments in the 1930s when Canadian diplomats must have wished they could be somewhere, anywhere, other than the League of Nations or the International Labour Organization, fleeing from conferences on the insoluble refugee problem as Jews and other proscribed people sought to escape Adolf Hitler's expanding empire. Canada, its government paralyzed by the fear of offending anybody, did very little to help.

Diplomats meet, speak, and seek common ground. Obviously, when they do they exchange information and seek positive outcomes. When that is not possible, they try to postpone the many evil days that human folly and the human imagination can devise. In the 1930s it seemed they could do little else. American diplomats met Canadian diplomats, and the Canadians met the British, and during the war they met many others in the hothouse of governments-in-exile that was wartime London. During the war the action was elsewhere, in military headquarters and in strategy meetings among the Big Three or Four or Five – the great powers and their leaders, Roosevelt, Churchill, and Stalin.

To the surprise of some of Canada's leaders the Second World War had not produced domestic catastrophe. During the war, high taxes and rationing were twinned with a soaring gross domestic product and the virtual disappearance of unemployment. Both were sustained by a high civilian morale and a national commitment to the war and ultimate victory over Hitlerism. The government could therefore take an expansive and even generous approach to foreign affairs. Circumstances gave prosperity a very long run. Though a low level of unemployment did re-emerge and the economy suffered occasional setbacks, Canadians' standard of living rose steadily for over thirty years from the early 1940s until the mid-1970s. This was the span and more of Pearson's career as an ambassador, deputy minister, minister, and prime minister, the period in which he defined as well as implemented policy. He could do this with the confidence that his country could back him up, with money and with the things that money could buy, such as a large professional military, or an aid budget, or contributions to United Nations peacekeeping.

There was also a generational change at work. The cautious Mackenzie King, definitely a leader from another era (born 1874), gave way to a slightly younger man, Louis St-Laurent (born 1882). A politician only since 1941, St-Laurent was not encumbered with King's attitudes towards the outside world, and thus he was a transition to a new generation. King's world was the one he had known as a young man, leavened by his experience of the First World War and the disasters it had almost brought upon Canada. King realistically chose to leave before his number was up – a happy contrast with his contemporary Winston Churchill, who remained active in politics as prime minister long past his prime. There was a happy contrast, too, between King and St-Laurent as far as Canadian foreign policy was concerned. St-Laurent handed it over to younger men: finance to Douglas Abbott, defence to Brooke Claxton, and external affairs to Pearson. With St-Laurent's trust and support they ran Canada's external policies into the mid-1950s.

An active Canadian foreign policy was, under the circumstances, a safe bet. The victory of 1945 was the triumph of collective security. That lesson had been driven home to all the allied powers, but, most important, it had taken root in the United States, reversing decades of political isolationism. Pearson and other allied diplomats, not to mention their American colleagues, treated the change in American opinion as a fragile flower to be fertilized and encouraged by every means imaginable. Without American support they believed that

Europe would lapse into chaos and that the beneficiary would be the Soviet Union. One totalitarian power would succeed another, unifying the continent under Joseph Stalin. Stalin already dominated Europe east of the Elbe, behind which the Soviet military and secret police were hard at work imposing friendly governments by intimidating and eliminating non-communist politicians. All this was consistent with Stalin's record in the 1930s, spiced as it was with purges and assassinations, and the record was no secret.

Pearson had no need to put on reactionary spectacles when he looked at European events or Stalin's accomplishments. True, he and his senior colleagues sometimes used British bifocals out of habit and affection, and the British had no hesitation in telling the Canadians what they saw just the other side of the English Channel. The lenses for the Canadians, as for the British and Americans, were firmly liberal and, more precisely, liberal-democratic. Dictatorships and tyrannies were beyond the pale, that is, outside the ambit of Canadians' cultural vision. In 1946–47, that meant eyes focused above all on Europe. As Canadian ambassador in Washington, Pearson got an advance glimpse of Winston Churchill's "Iron Curtain" speech of 1946, and, as under-secretary and then minister of external affairs, he saw the emergence of communist one-party states in Eastern Europe, backed up by secret police terror, purge trials, and the Soviet military. It should not therefore occasion surprise that Pearson was firmly anti-communist and, by extension, an enthusiast for an American-led Western alliance.[16]

There were, however, other circumstances that Pearson had to consider. The first was the atomic bomb. The bomb raised the stakes in international relations exponentially. As a senior government official, he was well aware that Soviet agents were scrambling to uncover atomic secrets in Canadian laboratories; but, as a realist, he knew that, in the long run, atomic weaponry was no secret. What the Americans and their junior partners, the British and Canadians, had made and exploded in 1945 could be and would be built by somebody else – namely, the Russians.

The question, therefore, became: "How could atomic warfare be prevented?" The United Nations furnished a partial solution, allowing states of all kinds to be represented and their arguments and propaganda given a protected public forum. The UN itself might serve as some kind of supervisory authority for the control of atomic energy, perhaps a far-fetched idea but, with no other idea on offer, worth pursuing. The pursuit was the thing, and the longer the better: to quote T.S. Eliot, "the journey not the arrival matter[ed]." Anything that postponed nuclear conflict was desirable. A nuclear war was the final, the ultimate evil, so much so that Pearson indicated that he would rather accept communist victory than see the world incinerated. "Better red than dead," he told a television audience. As we now know, had there been a nuclear war, "dead" was the likely outcome, a point on which various other statespersons agreed.[17]

If the prevention of war was the object, more than ever before, it was necessary to deal with the ideological adversary. This could be trying. Propaganda bubbled on all sides, though what was particularly noticeable were the fumes of Soviet sloganeering. Reliable information was scarce and contacts restricted. Canadian diplomats, cocooned in the Western community in Moscow, consistently reported from 1945 on that Stalin was not interested in and was not aiming for war.[18] He would try everything short of war, but, if firmly resisted, he would hesitate to take the final step. That remained true even after the explosion of the Soviet atomic bomb in the summer of 1949, though it was placed under great strain by the outbreak of the Korean War in June 1950.

The Canadian government was surprised but pleased by the Truman administration's decision to resist the communist invasion of South Korea and to seek UN sanction for its actions. Fortuitously, because the Soviet Union was boycotting the Security Council at the time, UN approval was available, and so the Korean War was fought, officially, between the United Nations on one side and North Korea and Communist China on the other. The St-Laurent government welcomed the UN sponsorship, and when Canadian troops sailed for Korea they travelled under UN auspices.

Before Canadian troops could get to Korea, the UN (American) army suffered a heavy defeat. In the wake of this defeat there was panic. In December 1950, Pearson and Defence Minister Claxton reported to the cabinet that a real danger of war existed and that Canada should be prepared one more time to send an expeditionary army to Europe, this time to fight off Stalin's legions.[19] That would be quite a task because the Soviets could easily overrun Europe as far as the English Channel before effective help from North America could arrive. The newly fledged North Atlantic Treaty Organization, which Pearson had helped to create as both diplomat and minister, was swiftly militarized, and a Canadian army brigade and air division was sent to garrison Europe, along with the Americans and the British. Pearson, ever the optimist, hoped they would not be there too long; as it happened, the Canadian force was not finally withdrawn until 1992.

Canada's participation in the Korean War did not mean that relations with the Truman administration and Secretary of State Dean Acheson were entirely harmonious. Acheson was an old friend of Pearson, and remained so, but, facing tremendous domestic political pressure, he took out some of his frustrations on Pearson, whom he believed to be entirely too compromising in seeking an end to the war. Acheson even took his case against Pearson to the Canadian cabinet, which heard him out and then continued to give the external affairs minister its collective confidence.[20] Differences with Acheson were largely a matter of atmospherics.

The most fortunate event in the early Cold War was the death of Stalin in March 1953. Stalin's departure improved the tone of international relations, and, most important, put into power a collection of politicians who favoured negotiation over confrontation. Negotiations soon occurred between the Western powers and North Korea and China, and then between the West and North Vietnam, China, the Soviet Union, and various neutral states, of which the most significant was India.

Pearson, as Ryan Touhey emphasizes in Chapter 12 (this volume), regarded India as especially important, even crucial. As a senior participant in the British Commonwealth, the Canadian government was aware of the progress of decolonization and saw in it the most important eventual change in the international balance of power. India, as the Commonwealth's biggest member in terms of population, and as a functioning democracy with a congenial government headed by Jawaharlal Nehru, held pride of place in Canadian eyes. India, hoped St-Laurent and Pearson, would be Canada's and the West's link to the developing postcolonial world. Such links would furnish an alternative to communism. With Stalin gone, the Soviet Union could more credibly launch a peace offensive, drawing on the positive qualities of Nikita Khrushchev, the power behind the Soviet establishment after 1953. It became important to draw closer to India. A visit from St-Laurent; the appointment of a senior Canadian diplomat, Escott Reid, to New Delhi;

and frequent contacts between Pearson and Indian defence minister Krishna Menon at the UN established a habit of consultation and collaboration.

India was both neutral and neutralist in the Cold War. Prime Minister Nehru was a leader of the Non-Aligned Movement, and, at the United Nations, India seemed to take the lead among its Afro-Asian members. These were still a minority at the UN, but it did not take deep thinking to see that the numbers would soon increase and form a majority in the General Assembly. The Indian government paid close attention to the colonial wars of the 1950s and, especially, to the war between the communist Viet Minh and the French in Indochina. When St-Laurent, during his visit to New Delhi in January 1954, let it be known that he was no supporter of the French in Indochina, Nehru was favourably impressed.[21]

That war moved into a crisis in the spring of 1954. The French, already war-weary, faced defeat at a remote fortress named Dien Bien Phu, where a significant part of the colonial army was surrounded and outnumbered. If Dien Bien Phu fell, the war was over, both strategically and politically. Military opinion in the United States and Canada held that, unless something happened to change the nature of the war, the remaining French forces would also be defeated and the French empire in Indochina would come to an end.[22] Politically, there was no more appetite in France for a war that had lasted eight years for no particular objective that made any sense to the French electorate and, increasingly, to the French political class. A project for American intervention with the possible use of nuclear weapons got Pearson's attention; as far as he could he discouraged the American government from any such idea. Fortunately, President Dwight Eisenhower also believed that, in this case, nuclear weapons were an unthinkable option. Dien Bien Phu surrendered, the French sued for peace, and France's allies scrambled at a conference in Geneva in the summer of 1954 to save what they could from the debacle.

Canada attended the Geneva Conference, but only because it had been involved in the Korean War, which was also being wound up. There was a ceasefire for the duration of the conference, and this turned into a longer truce when the conference agreed that the French would surrender northern Vietnam to the Viet Minh, evacuate their forces, exchange prisoners, and move populations for those who wished to go north, to the communist zone, or south, to the area the French and their allies still occupied. Once these essential housekeeping tasks were completed, there would be elections in Vietnam to determine the future of the country. Most of the conference signed the final document, including, most crucially, the Viet Minh and France. The government of what would become South Vietnam, however, did not sign, nor did the United States. The Americans contented themselves with a statement that they would not obstruct the agreements, one for each country, collectively called the Geneva Accords.

In order to stabilize the Indochinese states, the Geneva Conference resorted to a device used in Korea – an international truce commission. The experience in Korea was not particularly happy, in part because the commission was divided equally – half communist and half Western. There could never be a decision because there could never be a majority. Indochina would be different. There would be three truce commissions, one each for Vietnam, Laos, and Cambodia, and each commission would have three members, including a neutral chair, India. The communist member would be Poland, and that left only a member representing Western interests. India and China let it be known that they would prefer Canada. The French, the Americans, and the British had no objections, though Canada was not at the top of the American list of preferences.

It remained to tell the Canadians. The British foreign secretary, Anthony Eden, took on that task. To make a long story short, St-Laurent and Pearson accepted. The under-secretary, Jules Léger, scurried to find the money to pay for this unexpected mission and worried about the impression it would make on economically inclined MPs and an unprepared public, but, by August, preparations for a diplomatic expedition to Indochina were well under way.[23] In any case, given the prosperity of the mid-1950s and the high tax rates the economy could sustain, there was really no problem in finding the cash for the International Control Commissions.

Telling the Canadian contingent on the commission what to do was another matter. Once Pearson had found a suitably respectable chair for the Canadian delegation in Sherwood Lett, a wartime brigadier and a corporate lawyer from Vancouver, he had to issue him instructions. This he did in a letter dated 24 August 1954.[24]

Any important document, particularly one that would be parsed by a distant and somewhat autonomous Canadian mission, had to be very carefully drafted. Line diplomats did the drafting. Though Pearson was a good and fluent writer, he seldom had time to compose his own statements and speeches, and this case was no different. But, unusually, Pearson spent considerable time on the instructions, and the draft document is littered with clarifications and insertions in the minister's hand. There can be little doubt that the instructions were genuinely Pearson's and not the product of osmosis and consensus within his department.

First Pearson rehearsed the Canadian government's reasons for taking on the task of supervising the Indochinese ceasefire. It would help secure peace in Southeast Asia, and peace was in everybody's interest – in effect, peace was indivisible and any effort to secure it was justified. Identifying Canada firmly as a member of the Western camp, he noted that the Geneva Accords offered at least the possibility of keeping Laos and Cambodia from "Communist domination in the immediate future," while allowing for the building up of a capacity for military and political resistance to communism south of the demarcation line between North and South Vietnam. These important strategic objectives dictated Pearson's next instruction, which was, broadly, that the control commissions had to be made to work.

The commissions' job was the "supervision, observation, inspection and investigation" of any truce violations. Their most important mandates were to implement the relocation of military forces, release of prisoners, observation of the various demarcation lines between the opposing sides, and the prevention of the introduction of any new military forces and munitions. The commissions had no executive power, but they embodied the consensus of the Geneva Conference – meaning East, West, and neutrals – that the peace was overwhelmingly desirable and must be maintained. Undoing the work of the conference so soon after its completion would not be tolerated.

Finally, there were elections, which the Geneva Accord governing Vietnam prescribed for 1956. The Viet Minh had agreed to forgo the immediate fruits of their military triumph (i.e., driving out the French completely and occupying the whole country) for victory on the installment plan – elections in 1956 covering the whole country – a process that they reasonably believed they would win.

It followed that Canada's approach should be guided by two considerations. First, it was indeed true that Canada represented the Western bloc. For the commissions to function, however, the commissioners must get along, assess evidence in common, and reach a collective conclusion. That meant that they had to deal objectively with the questions before them. The phrase Pearson used was "judicial impartiality." This was not a new concept in Canadian external relations. Canadians many times served on international commissions, mainly with Americans, on bilateral issues that were often of crucial importance to Canada, though usually of marginal interest to the United States. Instead of arguing as adversaries, the Canadians usually sought agreement as to the facts, building common ground. This kind of approach was not unique to Canada or to Canadian-American relations. The Canadian approach can be considered to be a form of mediation, something the Americans were known to favour – as between Russia and Japan in 1905, or between the parties in the Mexican civil war in 1914, or between various French factions in Algiers in 1942.

Great negotiations such as the Paris Peace Conference of 1919 attempted, sometimes fruitfully, to discover the facts of any given case and to base their conclusions on them.[25] In 1946, the Canadian delegate to the UN commission on atomic energy struggled to find common ground between the Soviet Union and the United States. He was not successful. At the Paris Peace Conference and at the UN the parties concerned were deeply divided, and, in the 1946 negotiation, the Soviets and the Americans not only deeply distrusted each other but the Americans, at least, considered the Soviets to be morally repellent. Nevertheless, the negotiation occurred.

The Indochinese commissions were of the same ilk. The alternatives for the time being were too dreadful to contemplate so the commissions, somehow, had to work. In Pearson's judgment, the Canadians should not waste their time binding up the wounds of France's remaining colonial interests. The French empire in Indochina was finished, and any attempt to give it renewed life would not only fail but also alienate the local population, making the advance of communism all the more likely. Nor should the Canadians seek to create a Western ally or allies. Non-communist governments were good enough and, in fact, the best that could be expected. Implicitly, Pearson was suggesting that they would be neutral, a proposition that the Americans found distasteful though not completely unpalatable.

Here, plainly, was the Indian influence, conveyed through Nehru and Krishna Menon directly to St-Laurent and Pearson, and filtered through the Canadian high commissioner to India, Escott Reid. "Canada enjoys extremely good relations with India," Pearson wrote, "based on our common membership in the Commonwealth, our common heritage of British institutions and a deep feeling of mutual respect." It was true that India's policy of non-alignment was not Canada's, but it was to be respected even when Canadian observers might think the Indians to be in error in their estimate or interpretation of a given international phenomenon. Pearson did not mean that the Canadians should forget their own government's pro-Western orientation, or the fact that, despite the occasional political eruptions (McCarthyism, for example) in the United States, Canadians generally and correctly esteemed their principal ally. The best way to deal with the Indians was through "an attitude of scrupulous fairness and impartiality."

The third member of the commission, Poland, was of course communist, and bad things could be expected from that side: "obstruction, deceit and bad faith." "Nevertheless," Pearson instructed Lett, "you will do your best to establish good working relations with your Polish colleague." "Courtesy and good humour" were the best guides to dealing with the Poles, even if, as good communists, they might be abusive in return.

The Canadians were to show impartiality not only inside the commissions but also in their daily contacts with the interested parties in Indochina. They were to treat the French with caution, bearing in mind that the Indians distrusted them and disapproved of their role in Indochina. The Americans were more difficult. Canada had "very close and friendly relations" with the United States, but the Canadian representatives on the commissions were public beings, whose every action might be scrutinized. The commission had to be made to work, and, though Pearson did not put it this way, that meant that it had to develop a kind of internal organizational culture all its own. Accordingly, Lett and his staff were to keep "the demands of judicial objectivity and discretion" always in mind. As with contacts with the French, the impression the Canadians would make on the Indians was very much on Pearson's mind.

The commissions set to work. As predicted, the Poles were often obstructive, and the Indians voted with them more often than the Canadians would have liked. Some of the issues put before the commissions were painful – especially Catholic refugees from the north trying to move south – and the results were often very unsatisfactory. Yet Pearson's rules of conduct had a strange and unexpected echo.

Many years later, one of the Polish commissioners, Mieczyslaw Maneli, wrote a memoir in which he fondly remembered his Canadian colleagues and praised precisely the qualities that Pearson had laid down in 1954 – fairness, objectivity, and good humour.[26] In Robert Rossow's terms, the Canadians showed "good faith, discipline and loyalty," the hallmarks of diplomatic professionalism.

The initial stage of the commissions' work was, relatively speaking, successful. The French and their allies evacuated northern Vietnam, which became the Democratic Republic of Vietnam (North Vietnam) under the communist leader Ho Chi Minh. The rest of the country became, in short order, the Republic of Vietnam (South Vietnam) under Ngo Dinh Diem, a nationalist who seems to have loathed the French and the communists equally. Though Diem could be reasonably described as authoritarian, arbitrary and frequently brutal, his southern republic certainly did not equal the north on what we might call the dictatorship scale. In establishing his rule, Diem drew in the Americans. Their arrival coincided with the departure of the French, who finally left in 1956, turning over their headquarters in Saigon, the southern capital, to the Canadians.

Diem's view of the International Control Commission (ICC) matched his (correct) understanding that it would push for elections in 1956. Opposed to the elections for obvious reasons, he also despised the ICC, particularly its Indian members, who had a very uncomfortable time of it in Saigon. American pressure presumably kept Diem in line and preserved the ICC, but on the issue of elections Washington agreed with Diem: the notion of free and fair elections under a communist government was an absurdity. Elections on the East European or Soviet model always turned in implausible majorities of 99 percent for the communists. The record of communist dissimulation and obstruction during the movement of refugees was a harbinger of what would happen during the election – and after, to those Vietnamese who identified with the French or with the Ngo Dinh Diem government. Even if the elections were genuinely free and fair the Americans conceded that the communists would win. As a consequence, the Eisenhower administration supported Diem's refusal to go along with them.

It was a momentous decision, and, as we now know, a rash one. It was true that it was a Hobson's choice. From India, High Commissioner Escott Reid did his best to promote an Indian idea that the elections in Vietnam should go forward, with their inevitable result, in return for which the two remaining Indochinese states, Laos and Cambodia, would remain non-communist, with an international guarantee of their security that would include India.[27] Or the Americans could proceed with what would now be called "nation building," training the South Vietnamese army to the point at which it could successfully resist attacks from the North Vietnamese. In 1954–55, there were American voices that argued that the United States should cut its losses and retreat from the mainland of Southeast Asia, concentrating its attention on its offshore clients, Taiwan and the Philippines. But to do so was to run counter to a principal tenet of Republican Party dogma, one that dominated American thinking for the next twenty years: that there was nothing the United States could not accomplish, once it put its mind to the task. This being the case, to abandon territory and millions of people to the communists was to run counter to the laws of electoral physics. Any administration rash enough to accommodate the communists would be a sure loser in the next elections, and American elections were always only two years away. John Foster Dulles, the Republican secretary of state, understood this point very well. Dulles thought one of the choices before the United States was accepting defeat. He did not see the issue clearly, for the basic question was really whether to accept defeat now or face defeat later.

Pearson, the documents show, took the elections seriously. To prepare, he hired a political scientist, ostensibly an expert on elections, to go to Vietnam and see what could be done. Dulles and Pearson were reported to have shouted at one another behind closed doors, and we shall never be sure what the shouting was about. The timing of the incident, which took place in Pearson's office in Ottawa, fits with the issue of Vietnamese elections in March 1955.[28] The outcome, however, is not in doubt. The political scientist was told to pack his bags and return to Toronto.[29] There would be no elections.

Though it was unknowable at the time, the derailing of the elections issue marked the beginning of a new and querulous phase in Canadian-Indian relations. Nehru was disappointed, and he also had his misgivings about the United States confirmed. The Canadians wondered whether the ICC should be terminated but eventually decided that something was better than nothing. The Indians wanted to stay and so did the Poles. Perhaps something would turn up. What did turn up over the next fifteen years was a Pandora's Box of troublesome minutiae, bitter squabbling over trivia, and steadily worsening relations between the Canadians and Indians. Instead of reinforcing Canadian-Indian relations, the ICC undermined them. All this in a climate in which daily highs ranged in the mid-30s, Celsius, and air conditioning was reserved for only the highest ranks. Worse, in the view of the Canadians in Saigon, this could go on indefinitely. The Canadian mission in Vietnam lasted nineteen years, plus two more years of ordinary diplomatic relations. In the end it was unsuccessful. It was unsuccessful not only internally, creating bad feelings between the Canadians and the Indians and helping to alienate the two countries from each other,[30] but also in its larger mission of preventing, or at least mitigating, war. The Americans intervened massively, something that Canadian diplomacy had hoped to prevent, and then lost, more or less as Pearson predicted. The North Vietnamese solved the problem by driving out the Americans and then by conquering what was left of South Vietnam.

Canada's role (and Pearson's) in Vietnam has been criticized, sometimes justly, from positions on the left, right, and centre. The main charges, however, are unjust. To the right, Pearson demonstrated lamentable "equivalence" between East and West. That charge is easily disproved. Pearson conceived Canada's role to be to represent the best interests of the West, both through the ICC's immediate mission in Vietnam and through conciliating India and improving its conception of the West and, in particular, of the United States. Moreover, the Canadians' behaviour in Saigon, sharing information and opinions with the Americans, can hardly be described as contrary to Western interests, more narrowly defined. Yet, to those on the right, Pearson and Pearsonianism are curiously insufficient. Pearson was not the shining moral exemplar that they wanted, and Pearsonianism was a doctrine that was too prone to compromise, leaving principle and purpose in the ditch.

It is true that delay and obfuscation are tools of diplomacy. It is also true that expediency and time-serving can substitute for strategy and patience, and sometimes be mistaken for those qualities. It does not follow that diplomats actually enjoy using them, or that they prefer to live for the moment, with no hope or expectation of a better world to come. Diplomats like to feel some purpose and some accomplishment, and the Canadians who served on the ICC in the 1950s and 1960s were for the most part no exception.

Stephen Harper was careful not to mention Pearson when he praised Canada's stand against communism during the Cold War as an example of principle in practice. As prime minister he preached against what he and his speechwriters saw as elements of Pearsonianism. "There have been times when we've fallen short, heeded the calls of those who preferred to see Canada sidelined, to see Canada serve as a neutral bystander instead of a principled actor," he intoned in a speech in Toronto on 30 May 2014. He went on to condemn "those who preached moral-equivalency and who said that Canada should learn to accept totalitarian communism as just another option."[31] There are echoes – disapproving echoes – of "better red than dead."

To the left, there is a lively tradition of condemnation of Canada's Liberal governments for standing aside when great moral considerations were at stake, or for behaving in a manner that betrayed what they claimed to be their own principles.[32] Generally speaking, Liberals like Pearson are denounced for going along with (American) policies that they knew were wrong or misguided, or for remaining silent when principle should have dictated otherwise. For the left, too, Pearson's conception of the world is a point of irritation – a world of great powers, all of them greater than Canada. The importance of these powers shaped Canadian policy: the Soviets were seen as antagonists, the British as close kin, and the Americans as the world's richest and most powerful nation. Then there were the Indians, who, to Pearson's mind, represented the future as well as a window on the present. It was a realist perspective, less moralistic and prescriptive, as I have noted, than Dean Acheson and his "Stern Daughter of the Voice of God." It was, above all, what a professional diplomat had to do.

Some diplomats, and some politicians, too, yearn for a simpler life with more vivid solutions. A younger contemporary of Pearson's, Keith Laumer, an American diplomat, conceived an alternate world in which junior diplomats ruled the roost, while their elders, who were always portrayed as deficient in brains and character, did their best to ignore whatever hostile elephant happened to be trampling around the conference room. Fortunately, in this world the enemy was obvious – reptilian, with five eyes, easily spotted in a crowd except by the bureaucratically obtuse. Harper would have approved and would have applauded the hero of Laumer's tales. This was a young diplomat, Jame Retief, who was as quick with his fists as with his wit, and who reliably advanced the good and frustrated the evil. Retief and his author must have enjoyed living in a universe painted in bright primary colours, and they tell us a cracking good yarn – for in the end Retief's adventures are all the same.[33] In Retief's house are many mansions, and one does not have to exercise much imagination to predict a line-up of statespersons waiting to get into a more straightforward world in which virtue is always its own reward. Pearson's world, unfortunately, was more like *Fifty Shades of Grey* – with complications and usually without the sex.[34] In that indistinct world, problems were seldom easily solved, if they could ever be solved by human intelligence or action. The danger usually lay in applying simple formulas to get an easy solution. Dulles specialized in that. Pearson did not.

Notes

1 The usage of "Pearsonian" as applied to foreign affairs usually identifies the user as a Canadian writer. In the larger world, "Pearsonian" refers to ideas related to the scientist and statistician Karl Pearson. This suggests that Canadian foreign affairs commentators might consider finding a new word.

2 Stephen Azzi to author, 6 December 2014.

3 Norman Hillmer and Jack Granatstein, *Empire to Umpire*, 2nd ed. (Toronto: Nelson, 2007), 206.

4 See Robert Rossow, "The Professionalization of the New Diplomacy," *World Politics* 14 (1962): 561–75, from which this and following quotes are drawn. Having trumpeted "the new diplomacy" in his title Rossow nevertheless traces some of its elements back to the Napoleonic period and the diplomacy of the nineteenth century.

5 Rossow, "Professionalization," 563.

6 Ibid.

7 Alan Gyngell and Michael Wesley, *The Making of Australian Foreign Policy* (Cambridge: Cambridge University Press, 2003), 129.

8 Antony Anderson, *The Diplomat: Lester Pearson and the Suez Crisis* (Fredericton: Goose Lane Editions, 2015), 82.

9 See the reference in Gilbert and Sullivan's *Iolanthe* to making the House of Lords subject to "competitive examination," or to the "modern major general" (a professionalized officer) in *Pirates of Penzance*. This notion still has some possibilities for institutions such as the Canadian Senate.

10 Peter Larkin and Vincent Massey, high commissioners for Canada in London in the 1920s and 1930s, fitted the "useful rich" category. On the decline of aristocratic credentials, see John English, *The Life of Lester Pearson: The Shadow of Heaven* (Toronto: Lester and Orpen Dennys, 1989), 190–91.

11 John Hilliker, *Canada's Department of External Affairs: The Early Years, 1909–1946* (Montreal and Kingston: McGill-Queen's University Press, 1990), 118–21.

12 It would seem that the competition attracted Pearson more than the job, though he did think that diplomacy "would be a very interesting profession." Pearson, quoted in Anderson, *Diplomat*, 59. See also Norman Hillmer, *O.D. Skelton: A Portrait of Canadian Ambition* (Toronto: University of Toronto Press, 2015), 162–64.

13 Leftish disapproval encompasses "liberal-nationalist" historiography as well as the history of "liberal nationalists" in Canadian international relations. See David Meren, "The Tragedies of Canadian International History," *Canadian Historical Review* 96 (2015): 534–66. See also the response by the international relations historian and Pearson biographer, John English, in English, *Life of Lester Pearson*, 567–75. For both left and right, "liberal" is more a term of abuse than admiration.

14 See Mark 6:4, King James Bible.

15 The phrase is attributed to Soviet foreign minister Maxim Litvinov.

16 This has been a matter of some discussion among left-leaning Canadian historians, fascinated by the wickedness they perceive in the United States. While they occasionally admit that Stalin and the Soviet Union were not especially admirable, most of their fire is reserved for the United States.

17 See Tom Nichols, *No Use: Nuclear Weapons and US National Security* (Philadelphia: University of Pennsylvania Press, 2014), 17ff.

18 On this point Canadian, American, and British diplomats agreed. See John Lewis Gaddis, *George F. Kennan* (New York: Penguin, 2011); and Robert Bothwell, *Alliance and Illusion* (Vancouver: UBC Press, 2007), 197.

19 Cabinet Conclusions, 28–29 December 1950, LAC, RG 2.

20 Cabinet Conclusions, 22 November 1952, LAC, RG 2. Acheson later encapsulated his irritation with Pearson and Canada in an essay entitled "Stern Daughter of the Voice of God." He was criticizing Canadian moralizing, but the title is more appropriately applied to his own fulminations. Himself a child of the British Empire and Edwardian Canada, Acheson lived up to the best imperial standards in his "du-haut-en-bas" view of Pearson.

21 The war was more than a simple colonial conflict: it was also a war between different groups of Vietnamese, Laotians, and Cambodians so that the "Forces de l'Union française" fighting the Viet Minh included thousands of anti-communist Vietnamese and other nationalities.

22 Pearson to Lett, 24 August 1954, LAC, RG 25, vol. 4629, file 50052-A-40-pt.1.

23 John Hilliker and Donald Barry, *Canada's Department of External Affairs: Coming of Age, 1946–1968* (Montreal and Kingston: McGill-Queen's University Press, 1995), xxx; Bothwell, *Alliance and Illusion;* John English, *The Worldly Years: The Life of Lester Pearson, 1949–1972* (Toronto: Knopf, 1992), 94–95.

24 See above, note 19.

25 The best-known example of an enduring and mostly successful international organization is the bilateral International Joint Commission between Canada and the United States. It operates as an investigatory body and reaches its decisions by consensus. At Paris, Sir Robert Borden struggled with the question of the Greco-Albanian border, while Arthur Sifton, his minister of customs and a Canadian delegate, worked on the regulation of European ports and waterways and aerial navigation – quite successfully, even if his fellow citizens had difficulty following just what it was he had done.

26 Mieczyslaw Maneli, *War of the Vanquished: A Polish Diplomat in Vietnam* (New York: Harper and Row, 1971), 34–35, 43.

27 Escott Reid, *Radical Mandarin: The Memoirs of Escott Reid* (Toronto: University of Toronto Press, 1989), 274–77.

28 Conversation with Arthur Menzies, Ottawa, 2005. Menzies headed the Far Eastern Division in the Department of External Affairs. Unfortunately, Menzies, who knew what the shouting was about, chose to be coy and did not divulge it. See *Foreign Relations of the United States, 1955–1957*, vol. 27 (Washington, DC: Government Printing Office, 1992), document 342. Most of the day's events took place in public, but before they started Pearson and Dulles met for twenty minutes in private. The announced subject under discussion was the publication of diplomatic papers relating to the Yalta Conference in 1945.

29 The political scientist Donald Smiley became an ornament of the political science department at the University of Toronto.

30 Canada and India also quarrelled over the Indian development of an atomic bomb, to which Canadian technical and scientific aid had unwittingly contributed. In diplomacy it takes at least two to tango, and Indian diplomacy should share the blame for poor Canadian-Indian relations.

31 Speech by Stephen Harper to the Tribute to Liberty organization, 30 May 2014 (formerly on the Government of Canada website). The main target was obviously Trudeau and his government, though the descriptions of his actions and policies might have seemed strange to those who participated in them. Pearson, who had not engaged in the Vietnam War, and considered it ill-advised, was collateral damage.

32 Perhaps the best and most considered of these is Reg Whitaker and Gary Marcuse, *Cold War Canada: The Making of a National Insecurity State* (Toronto: University of Toronto Press, 1996). Robert Teigrob focuses more on the construction of opinion in his *Warming Up to the Cold War* (Toronto: University of Toronto Press, 2009). He spends considerably more time on the follies of US policy and the Canadian reaction thereto than on the links that people at the time, often rightly, considered important. The book with the greatest recent impact is Ian McKay and Jamie Swift, *Warrior Nation: Rebranding Canada in an Age of Anxiety* (Toronto: Between the Lines, 2012). Not all their material is unfamiliar to other historians: indeed, at times it seems that they have just discovered fire or reinvented the wheel.

33 On Retief, see Keith Laumer, *Retief in the Ruins* (New York: Baen Books, 1986), which is number thirteen in the Retief saga. Readers are encouraged to send their surplus copies to any member of the former Harper cabinet, or to Donald Trump and his counsellor, Steve Bannon, who might find this alternate world comforting. To judge from the evidence, they have already implemented an agenda that would have gladdened Retief although, unlike our hero, they have not been very successful.

34 There was, however, Charles Ritchie. See Victoria Glendenning and Judith Robertson, *Love's Civil War: Elizabeth Bowen and Charles Ritchie* (New York: Simon and Schuster, 2009).

Michael K. Carroll

2 Pragmatic Peacekeeping
The Pearson Years

The fact that Lester Pearson's name is often associated with peacekeeping should not surprise Canadians. In 1957 he was awarded the Nobel Peace Prize for his role in bringing about a resolution to the Suez Crisis, and the chair of the Nobel committee commended his "powerful initiative, strength, and perseverance to restore peace in situations where quick, tactful, and wise action ha[d] been necessary to prevent unrest from spreading and developing into a worldwide conflagration."[1] This was high praise indeed for Canada's secretary of state for external affairs, and it was well deserved.

Yet peacekeeping has not always been popular in Canada. The defeat of the Liberal government in 1957, in part, can be traced back to peacekeeping and the implied abandonment of Britain and the support for the United States that went along with it. The Canadian military also initially saw peacekeeping as a distinctly "unmilitary" endeavour that took it away from its main duty of fighting against the Soviet menace. Yet a myth has nonetheless evolved that Canada is, by its very nature, an altruistic peacekeeping nation. This myth is neither helpful nor accurate. As Ross Campbell, one of Pearson's former colleagues at the Department of External Affairs, once lamented: "Pearson the pragmatist has been forgotten by the public and, to some extent, by successor Canadian governments in their zeal to promote exclusively the image of Pearson the UN protagonist."[2] It should be noted, as Adam Chapnick does in Chapter 3 (this volume), that, while Pearson firmly backed the United Nations and believed it to be an important aspect of Canada's foreign policy, his pursuit of foreign policy, whether during his tenure as secretary of state for external affairs or as prime minister in the 1960s, was always conducted with an eye towards what was perceived to be Canada's national interest.

Peace has always been in Canada's interest, and looking towards the postwar era, Pearson and the rest of the world saw the United Nations as a possible arbiter of peace. As the Canadian ambassador to the United States, Pearson gave an address to the United Nations Forum in Washington, DC, in April 1945, in which he stated:

> What we must do is not abolish force, but put enough force at the disposal of a world authority to prevent aggression by convincing the aggressor that he will be quickly and effectively chastised if he misbehaves. Swift and sure punishment meted out by an international authority, if it could be achieved would be as effective in preserving international peace as our policing system is in preserving domestic peace.[3]

Pearson clearly had the lessons of the 1930s and appeasement in mind and looked to prevention as the key. But he understood that, if necessary, any supranational organization must be prepared to back up its rhetoric with the use of force. He was also realistic enough to realize that a police force under international control was clearly not possible in the immediate future. But, during this same speech, he commented:

> There does not seem to me to be any valid reason, however, why we should not start with a *small* international force for limited purposes ... a beginning of an international force ... It is the ultimate and to me the only hope of peace among the nations.[4]

Pearson returned to this common theme in early 1948. In a speech entitled "Peace through the United Nations," he made the case that

> the UN must, if it is to be effective, have adequate force under its sole control to implement its decisions. This force must be capable of being brought into action quickly as a result of an international decision which cannot be blocked by any one power.
>
> You will of course complain that this is impractical and impossible. My reply is that at the moment it certainly is, but that it is

an objective which must be reached, a purpose that must be realized. The alternative is international anarchy.[5]

The UN made some tentative steps to deal with regional conflicts in the late 1940s, but while Pearson, as a diplomat, was in a position to influence Canadian foreign policy, he could not direct it. And under the leadership of Prime Minister William Lyon Mackenzie King, international involvement was not always seen to be in Canada's interest.

When the first UN peace mission to oversee the situation in Palestine was created in 1948, Canadians were nowhere to be found. Considering that role to be a drain on resources and a thankless task, King doubted that the Canadian public would support military operations in distant lands. He also feared that, judging from the divisive nature of Canada's participation in both world wars, peacekeeping would exacerbate problems related to national unity.

The following year, when the UN approached Canada about participating in an observer mission in Kashmir (known as the United Nations Military Observer Group in India and Pakistan [UNMOGIP]), to help keep the peace between India and Pakistan, King had since retired but, according to Minister of National Defence Brooke Claxton, cabinet was "allergic" to the idea. However, in 1949, the issue was not decided by cabinet, instead being deferred to the new prime minister, Louis St-Laurent, and his SSEA, Lester Pearson.[6]

Pearson and St-Laurent constituted a new breed of politician compared to King – they were internationalists – and were more than willing to expand Canada's role in the world. However, neither Pearson nor St-Laurent were internationalists for idealism's sake alone. International credibility was gained by joining UNMOGIP, and the cost of seconding four military officers for UN duty was negligible. In 1954, while five additional soldiers were deployed to the United Nations Truce Supervision Organization (UNTSO) serving in the Middle East, it was not until 1956 that peacekeeping really became a household term in Canada.

When Egypt nationalized the Suez Canal in July 1956, it did not immediately appear to have much immediate relevance to Canada. As Ralph Campney, the minister of national defence, put it: "It is primarily a European matter ... not a matter which particularly concerns Canada. We have no oil there. We don't use the Canal for shipping."[7] But Pearson knew from his time as a diplomat that what affected the great powers, particularly Britain, sooner or later would have an effect on Canada.

The Suez Canal's nationalization struck an economic blow to the United Kingdom to be sure, but perhaps more important was its psychological impact. Seeking to gauge British sentiment first-hand, Pearson made a visit to London in August 1956, a trip that caused him great concern. As he reported upon his return: "The British and the French haven't cooled down in the least. The way they talk about Suez is enough to make your hair stand on end."[8] The Canadian military attaché in London also reported that "it [was] not a question of whether military action [would] be taken but rather a matter of how and when."[9]

The threat of military action was of concern to Pearson not only for international peace and security in the Middle East – it had the potential to escalate into a full-blown nuclear affair between the superpowers – but also because it threatened unity within the British Commonwealth, NATO, and the Anglo-American alliance. As Pearson wrote to Norman Robertson, Canada's high commissioner in London: "We are not very happy here about developments and where they are leading. But we have no desire to be critical unless and until we can come up with some constructive ideas of our own."[10] While Pearson had sympathy for British aims, he disagreed with the way in which Britain was pursuing its policy in the Middle East. Thus, he reported to St-Laurent in September that "we should be very careful in this interim period in saying or doing anything which would give the impression that Canadian association or support is something that can be taken for granted."[11] Remaining above the fray and not being too closely aligned with British policy – or American policy, for that matter – would make it easier for Canada to act as an arbitrator if and when the opportunity arose.

Pearson and the Canadian diplomatic corps carefully monitored events and negotiations as they continued throughout the early autumn. Towards the end of October it appeared as if things were quietening down in the Middle East. The Israeli invasion of Egypt on the morning of 29 October 1956, however, changed everything. Within a week of the attack, Britain and France had joined the military fray, the Soviet Union was threatening nuclear strikes against London and Paris, and relations between the UK and the US sank to an all-time low. From the Canadian perspective the Suez Crisis had opened Pandora's Box, unleashing competing interests among Canada's most important allies and threatening dramatic repercussions for NATO, the Commonwealth, and the United Nations – the cornerstones of Canadian foreign policy.

While the Security Council was dealing with the issue of Suez, Canada quietly bided its time. However, once discussions were transferred to the General Assembly Pearson sped to New York on 1 November 1956. As an old UN hand, Pearson knew most of the representatives by name. He had contended for the position of secretary-general in 1945 and again in 1952 – his candidacy was vetoed by the Soviets – and his hard work over the years, including his tenure as the president of the General Assembly in 1952, had earned the respect of most delegations. Canada, throughout the early 1950s, had also gained a reputation at the UN for objectivity and consensus building.

In the early morning of 2 November, the General Assembly passed a resolution calling for an immediate ceasefire and the withdrawal of all troops in the Suez region. Canada was one of the six notable abstentions in this vote, with Pearson reasoning that the resolution was inadequate in dealing with the essence of the crisis. As he explained Ottawa's position to the General Assembly:

> The resolution does provide for a cease-fire and I admit that that is of first importance and urgency. But it does not provide for any steps to be taken for a peace settlement ... I therefore would have liked to see a provision in this resolution authorizing the Secretary-General to make arrangements with Member States for a United Nations force large enough to keep these borders at peace while a political settlement is being worked out.[12]

This provided the basis for what became known as the Canadian resolution. And while the Americans immediately signalled support for the initiative, it was not an easy sell. Opinions in the General Assembly were diverse and debates were often heated. Even Dag Hammarskjöld, the UN secretary-general, was by all accounts initially critical of the Canadian proposal and doubted it had any chance of success.

Pearson brought Hammarskjöld onside, and with the experienced Canadian diplomats in New York – Bert MacKay, Geoff Murray, and John Holmes – he took the lead in explaining the resolution to all and sundry. The resolution shrewdly avoided going into specifics, simply leaving the details of the force up to the secretary-general. It passed the General Assembly by a vote of fifty-seven to zero, with nineteen abstentions. According to one observer, the resolution succeeded because "the result was a set of general principles which pleased nobody 100% but which everyone could, without too much reluctance, accept."[13]

This resolution ultimately brought about the creation of the United Nations Emergency Force (UNEF), though the composition of the force was not what Pearson had originally envisioned. Canadian military and political officials had recommended a sizable fighting force – the size of a division – with tanks, infantry, fighter aircraft, and paratroop elements. The realities of state sovereignty, however, dictated a much less robust force. UNEF became a six thousand strong, lightly armed force, comprised of ten different nations – with Canada's contribution of one thousand support troops forming the backbone of the operation. In the words of the secretary-general, UNEF was designed to be "paramilitary in nature [though] not a force with military objectives."[14] Pearson also lamented that peacemaking did not follow hand-in-hand with peacekeeping. As UNEF was not designed to become an indefinite military fixture in the Middle East, he asserted that "the intervention of the United Nations was incomplete and only partially successful."[15] In Pearson's opinion, the UN failed to take advantage of the atmosphere of crisis and anxiety to tackle the underlying problems of the Arab-Israeli crisis – evidence that he saw peacekeeping as a means and not an end.

While UNEF was left to languish in the desert, Pearson and his colleagues found themselves in the Opposition benches until they returned to form the government after the 1963 federal election. Foreign policy, as a matter of course, was generally the domain of now prime minister Lester Pearson and the SSEA, Paul Martin.[16] As Greg Donaghy has stressed, the relationship between Pearson and Martin was complex, and while Pearson respected his minister's abilities, there was tension between them. A watchful eye was cast over foreign affairs but, as prime minister, Pearson's attention was increasingly preoccupied by domestic affairs and, according to Donaghy, "a reluctance to undermine his minister's authority obliged Pearson to tread carefully when he entered Martin's domain."[17] Yet, as Donaghy shows in Chapter 4 (this volume), Pearson's and Martin's foreign policy experience allowed the Liberal government to hit the ground running when they returned to office in April 1963.

In terms of peacekeeping, not much had changed in the previous five years. UNMOGIP, UNTSO, and UNEF remained ongoing, and a modestly successful mission had been deployed for less than a year in 1962–63 in West New Guinea/West Irian. The only major peacekeeping initiative during the Diefenbaker interregnum was the UN mission to the Congo (ONUC [Opération des Nations Unies au Congo]), which, due to the impending withdrawal of the Indian infantry contingent and the substantial costs that the operation posed for the United Nations' continued solvency, was in the process of being scaled back before being disbanded completely in 1964.

Within two months of taking up the reins of power, however, Pearson's government had to contemplate a new peacekeeping operation when a request came from the United Nations to supply an air unit for a mission to be deployed to Yemen (United Nations Yemen Observation Mission [UNYOM]). Caught in the throes of a civil war, Yemen's strategic location on the southern tip of the Arabian Peninsula at the mouth of the Red Sea made it an important geographical pawn in the Cold War. With American, British, and Soviet interests in the region, Yemen's civil unrest was further exacerbated by the intervention of both Egypt and Saudi Arabia. Believing that "the crisis threatened to split the Arab world," UN Secretary-General U Thant sent Ralph Bunche, UN under-secretary-general for special political affairs, to the region on a fact-finding mission.[18] Bunche's assessment that "Yemen could become a Cuba in the Near East" only highlighted the extreme importance and unpredictability of the issue.[19]

The Department of National Defence (DND) and the Department of External Affairs held differing opinions on the value of Canadian participation. In cabinet, Martin pushed for Canada's involvement, while the minister of national defence, Paul Hellyer, argued that UNYOM could prove to be yet another expensive, dangerous, and indeterminate mission whose success "seemed very uncertain."[20] Yet UNYOM had a mandate supported by all of the major protagonists – the Soviets had abstained on the vote – and Pearson ultimately decided that, while Yemen itself had very little direct importance to Canada, the issue of peace in the Middle East demanded Canada's attention. In cabinet discussions Martin referenced Canada's "enviable reputation in UN peace-keeping activities" as a rationale, while Pearson pronounced that "Canada was almost bound to participate in the observation group."[21]

In fact, Canadian forces personnel seconded from UNEF and UNTSO were already in Yemen on an interim basis as part of a UN advance party. Despite the uncertain prospects for success, the Yemen operation had many important factors in its favour. Having escaped the seemingly omnipresent Russian veto in the Security Council, UNYOM had, at the very least, tacit superpower support. The major parties involved – Yemen, Egypt, and Saudi Arabia – agreed to a supervised disengagement plan. And perhaps most important, Cairo and Riyadh agreed to finance the mission, albeit only two months at a time. Optimistically, U Thant thought UNYOM might only be needed for two months but that it "would not be required for more than 4 months."[22] The DND's continued reticence notwithstanding, cabinet approved Canada's contribution to UNYOM on 13 June 1963. About fifty Royal Canadian Air Force pilots and technicians served for just over a year.

UNYOM was a small observer force of approximately two hundred personnel tasked with "observing, certifying, and reporting" on the disengagement of Egyptian and Saudi Arabian forces, a task that one analyst deemed to be "hopeless from the start."[23] Canada's ambassador in Cairo, Robert Ford, shrewdly noted: "UNYOM cannot and was not intended to stop hostilities between Republicans and Royalists inside Yemen"; rather, the mission was "a face-saving cover for this Saudi-UAR disengagement which would prevent a direct confrontation possibly engulfing [the] whole Mideast in war."[24] With a limited albeit worthy mandate, the Canadian forces personnel assigned to UNYOM made the best of a difficult situation. However, much as Hellyer had originally warned, the mission did not go as planned. The disengagement by the United Arab Republic (UAR) and Saudi forces was a fiction, reconnaissance planes often came under ground fire, and the "two- to four-month mission" lasted for fourteen months. Less than two months into the mission, UNYOM's commanding officer, Major-General Carl von Horn, resigned in protest over lack of support for the mission. And, while the Canadian commander preferred to remain optimistic, the living and working conditions in Yemen were best described as "atrocious."[25] Pearson's cabinet reassessed Canada's contribution to UNYOM in January 1964, after the mission had been scaled back by almost half, and again in July 1964, but never proposed to withdraw.[26]

When the UN finally pulled the plug on UNYOM in September 1964, few in the Canadian military were disappointed.[27] With a limited mandate and no peace to keep, the UN faced a difficult task in Yemen, with the civil war raging on for four years after UNYOM's departure. It was not until after the third Arab-Israeli War in 1967 that regional actors actively pursued a meaningful peace, allowing the Republicans to claim victory and establish the Yemen Arab Republic in 1968. While the peacekeeping mission in Yemen was far from a success, it was not an abject failure. Conflict was contained and the Middle East did not erupt into a global conflagration. In this, diplomats in Ottawa, and at the UN in New York, found some solace.

While the mission in Yemen was ongoing, the Liberal government was following through on an election promise to undertake a comprehensive review of defence policy. The result, the 1964 *White Paper on Defence* is a document that historian Sean Maloney contends "was a departure from previous defence statements: it was explicit, clear, and public."[28] While the defence of Canada and support for NATO were still mainstays of Canadian policy, for the first time peacekeeping was explicitly identified as a priority in determining foreign and defence policy.[29]

Wanting to make a strong impression and take charge of his department, Paul Hellyer enthusiastically embraced the defence review process. Hellyer's initial draft, however, was preoccupied by the Soviet threat and NATO's importance, and it was coloured by his low opinion of the UN's ability to serve the interests of peace. Consequently, Pearson was "appalled" by the report.[30] After receiving cabinet input, Hellyer's revised draft embraced a wider perspective of Canadian defence priorities and more accurately represented the views of Pearson and the DEA. The final version of the White Paper was strikingly different from the first iteration. Recognizing the inextricable link between foreign and defence policy, it states: "It is essential that a nation's diplomacy be backed up by adequate and flexible military forces to permit participation in collective security and peacekeeping, and to be ready for crises should they arise."[31]

The formal inclusion of peacekeeping in defence prioritization was important, but it was not intended to be interpreted – as some were wont to do – as a fundamental reorientation of Canadian policy. NATO and defending Canada were still the main priorities for, as Hellyer quipped: "If that [i.e., peacekeeping] were the objective, why on earth would we have launched a 1.5 billion dollar, 5 year re-equipment program? ... For a UN role alone, an order of blue berets and billy sticks might suffice."[32] Peacekeeping did not make up a large proportion of Canada's military budget at the time, but Pearson's pragmatism was slowly spreading to Canadian forces brass, who were coming to understand that peacekeeping's popularity with Canadians could be leveraged for increased appropriations. With the crisis in Cyprus worsening, the White Paper's release in March 1964 provided an opportunity for the government to align actions with its published rhetoric.

Located in the eastern Mediterranean Sea, Cyprus was a former British colony populated by a Greek majority and a Turkish minority. Though relations between the two groups had always been strained, the international community took particular notice after riots erupted in December 1963 over proposed constitutional amendments put forward by the ethnically Greek president of Cyprus, Archbishop Makarios. Pearson was sceptical that Greek and Turkish Cypriots would ever find common ground. But Cyprus was a fellow member of the Commonwealth and, more important to policy makers in Ottawa, Greece and Turkey were both NATO members. Talk quickly turned to the possibility of a peacekeeping force to stave off a full-blown war.

London and Washington originally envisioned a peacekeeping force under NATO's auspices, but the idea was rejected out of hand by Makarios. Host nation consent, while at times troubling, was considered by officials in Ottawa as imperative for the success of any mission. Should the government of Cyprus accept a peacekeeping force, Paul Martin informed his NATO allies that Canada would give the request "sympathetic consideration."[33] Though Makarios had made it very clear that only a UN force would be acceptable, the British were hesitant to raise the issue of Cyprus at the UN for fear of Soviet meddling. Instead, they floated the idea of a Commonwealth peacekeeping force that would include Canada. This proposal incited fears in Quebec about being associated with what could be perceived as resurgent colonial aims on the part of the British – a domestic concern that was heightened by the fact that the battalion on standby duty was the Quebec-based Royal 22nd Regiment.[34] To Ottawa's relief, Britain finally placed the issue of Cyprus before the UN Security Council on 18 February 1964.

Pearson was not oblivious to the difficulties that lay ahead. He was troubled by the fact that the secretary-general "appeared to be taking it for granted that Canada would be willing to participate," yet they both knew that it would be difficult for Canada to turn down a request for peacekeepers.[35] Arthur Andrew, the Canadian high commissioner to Cyprus, also warned the DEA, "should it be decided to send troops ... in my judgement it will not[,] repeat not[,] be a short or easy job."[36] The British and Americans were anxious to solve the problem and avoid any Cold War fallout, and there was increasing domestic interest in Canada's peacekeeping response.

When questioned in the House of Commons about possibly deploying Canadian troops to Cyprus on 19 February, Pearson stated that it was "premature to speculate" as the issue was still under discussion by the UN Security Council. However, he outlined the conditions that would have to be met for the government to make a commitment. A paramount stipulation was for the force to have a composition and mandate "to contribute to peace and stability in the area" and for the mission not to be of an "indefinite duration."[37] Not mentioned, but also a concern, was the issue of peacekeeping finance, which was preoccupying much of the United Nations' time and sapping Canadian enthusiasm for the UN. Clearly, UNEF's lessons and inadequacies were front and centre in the prime minister's thinking.

The UN Security Council finally passed the resolution authorizing the mission to Cyprus (United Nations Peacekeeping Force in Cyprus [UNFICYP]) on 4 March 1964, at which point U Thant called on Brazil, Canada, Finland, Ireland, and Sweden to join Britain and form the nucleus of the operation. Unlike previous missions, "which everyone [fought] to get into,"[38] governments hesitated to commit to UNFICYP. Ottawa, for its part, was still apprehensive about aspects of the mission's mandate, consultative mechanisms, duration, and financing. In an aide-memoire to U Thant, the Canadian government outlined its concerns and sought clarification on twenty-one issues.[39] The unspoken issue was that all wanted this to be a multinational force, and no nation wanted to be tarnished by colonialism should it end up keeping the peace with only Britain.

As the finer points of diplomacy were discussed in Ottawa and New York, and sabres were rattled in Ankara and Athens, violence escalated on Cyprus as Greeks and Turks sought to entrench their positions in advance of a UN-imposed settlement. Britain also raised the stakes by threatening to withdraw its support for UNFICYP if a force was not in place by 12 March. Geopolitical imperatives ultimately helped sway the Pearson government's reaction. As Pearson recognized:

> The stakes are high ... Failure of the United Nations and the international community on this crisis will put in jeopardy the whole peacekeeping function of the UN, the function on which the whole concept and organization of the UN is based. The League of Nations received its death blow in Ethiopia. We must prevent the UN suffering the same fate through failure in Cyprus. Furthermore, armed conflict between two NATO members, Turkey and Greece, will end NATO in its present form.[40]

NATO's importance was also recognized by Washington, and on 12 March President Lyndon Johnson intervened personally and called Pearson to see if Canada could take the lead in paving the way for a UN peacekeeping force. Johnson felt constrained by the Russians and Cold War realities, but Canada, he believed, was in a position to get the ball rolling.[41]

Martin had flown to New York the previous day to discuss the situation with U Thant and was dismayed by the "passivity" of the secretary-general.[42] Believing that U Thant did not comprehend the gravity of the situation, Martin took it upon himself to confer with his counterparts in Stockholm, Helsinki, and Dublin. With a conditional pledge from Ireland, Sweden also committed to the force, thus meeting the Canadian threshold for a multinational operation. With the arrival of the twelve-hundred strong Canadian contingent in Cyprus on 13 March, U Thant proudly reported that UNFICYP was ready to keep the peace.

The secretary-general's pronouncement was a bit premature for, upon their arrival and without the support of the other contingents, the Canadians essentially were left "twiddling their thumbs."[43] It was close to a month before UNFICYP was fully functional, but the international community's declared intention towards Cyprus provided enough heft for the Americans to send a strongly worded telegram to Ankara informing the Turks to "keep their shirts on."[44] With peace seemingly ensured, Lyndon Johnson called Pearson to express his gratitude for the Canadian action, asking: "Now, what can I do for you?" Pearson replied that he did not have anything in mind at the moment but later admitted that it was nice to know that he "had some credit in the bank."[45]

All was not smooth sailing for the new peacekeeping operation, but whatever growing pains were to be had were certainly preferable to the alternative of war. For the Liberal government in Ottawa, the military contribution to UNFICYP was also preferable to awkward questions about why Canada had not done more to facilitate peace or support the UN.[46] Yet, in the rush to keep the peace, few of Canada's "twenty-one demands" had been met with any satisfactory responses. The force was indeed multinational, but confusion lingered over the mandate and ability of the peacekeepers to use force. When cabinet re-examined the mission in September 1964, while there was little chance of withdrawing the Canadian contingent, ministers recognized that Canada was the "largest and the only really professional one in the Force and [that] its withdrawal in present circumstances would almost certainly make the United Nations peacekeeping force in Cyprus impossible."[47] Peace among NATO allies in Cyprus seemingly required a continued Canadian presence. But to help maintain the status quo of the Cold War and to facilitate improved Canadian-American relations, Canada's contribution to UNIFCYP seemed a small, if ongoing, price to pay. As the mission was again reviewed in December 1964 with no end in sight, Canada once again twisted the ongoing financial thorn in the side of the UN and suggested revisiting the voluntary nature of contributions to finance ongoing peacekeeping operations.[48]

Following up on the perceived success of the UNFICYP's deployment as well as the equally troubling dissolution of the UN mission in the Congo, Pearson returned to the familiar theme of "Keeping the Peace" when he was invited to deliver the Dag Hammarskjöld Memorial Lecture at Carleton University in May 1964.[49] The topic was a natural one for Pearson and was most fitting given Hammarskjöld's legacy. And it also allowed Pearson to push forward the agenda of a standby force for the United Nations. Pearson had been a long-time advocate of a UN military force, but he was realistic enough to know that it was untenable in the Cold War political climate. This being the case, he set his sights a bit more modestly.

In his address to the General Assembly in September 1963, Pearson proposed: "There should be an examination by interested governments of the problems and techniques of peace-keeping operations. This could lead to a pooling of available resources and the development in a co-ordinated way of trained and equipped collative forces for UN service to meet possible future demands for action under the blue flag of the United Nations."[50] An initial attempt to coordinate a meeting with Denmark, Finland, the Netherlands, Norway, and Sweden had to be rethought when the meeting was criticized by Moscow for its overly NATO orientation. Finland, given its geographical location, and Sweden, being a neutral nation, were also nervous that the discussions about peacekeeping might become embroiled in Cold War concerns. The second time around, in his May 1964 address, Pearson simply proposed "discussions with certain other governments, primarily of military problems arising out of past and current peace-keeping operations."[51]

Attempting to leave politics to the side, the Ottawa Peacekeeping Conference held in November 1964 brought together military officers and bureaucrats with direct peacekeeping experience. As Paul Martin explained to the Standing Committee on External Affairs prior to the conference:

> The aim of what we have in mind would be to review the past experience of United Nations peacekeeping operations and to discuss special military problems which have been encountered in the course of those operations ... The proposal is a modest one, and is the first step in showing what might be done in a practical way to improve the present stand-by arrangements. The conference will largely be exploratory and at the working level.[52]

Invitations went out to the twenty-seven nations that had contributed one hundred or more personnel to a UN mission, with representatives from twenty-three countries ultimately attending.[53]

Recognizing that peacekeeping "has now become a practical necessity in the conduct of international affairs," Pearson and Canadian policy makers sought to provide a forum for practitioners from various nations to "exchange views on the practical and technical problems encountered in UN operations and pool ideas based on their actual experience."[54] Some suspected the motives behind the conference, but even Paul Hellyer, who was not "overly optimistic that any startling progress would be made," still agreed that "it would be a step forward."[55]

The meeting made no "startling progress," but then again it was never expected to.[56] Important lessons were shared, limitations were identified, and it became very clear that the issue of sovereignty was a difficult hurdle to overcome. The conference, however, opened lines of dialogue between states on an important topic, with the hope of improving peacekeeping down the road. One unexpected outcome of the Ottawa talks was the creation of the UN Special Committee on Peacekeeping Operations in February 1965. Commonly known as the Committee of 33 and formally introducing "peacekeeping" to the UN vernacular, this new body was authorized by the General Assembly to specifically deal with issues relating to peacekeeping. Initially taken as a sign of hope by some, the Committee of 33 quickly became bogged down in the financial crisis that threatened to tear the world body apart.

Peacekeeping is an expensive undertaking. When Pearson's government came to power in 1963, the UN was $110 million in debt, and $100 million of that debt was directly attributable to unpaid assessments for UNEF and ONUC. Some nations, such as the Communist bloc and France, refused to pay peacekeeping assessments as a matter of principle; others simply pled an inability to pay. As Adam Chapnick (Chapter 3, this volume) stresses, this issue annoyed the fiscally responsible Canadians.

As of 1 January 1964, the Soviet Union and twenty-one other nations were officially in arrears for more than two years of their UN assessments, which left them subject to having their ability to vote revoked under Article 19 of the Charter. Ottawa assumed that most of the non-communist nations would pay enough of their arrears to evade sanction, but this still left the Soviet Union, four of its satellites, and the United Arab Republic refusing to pay. Canada and its allies had long adhered to the belief that peacekeeping costs were a collective responsibility. Yet, as a showdown loomed over Article 19, it became increasingly obvious that, potentially, "the United Nations would become exactly the kind of debating society which the USSR had always favoured and [that] its capacity for collective action would be seriously damaged."[57] Some adroit political manoeuvring made it possible to navigate through the 19th General Assembly, but the concessions required ultimately left collective financing as a non-starter. As future peacekeeping missions now were to be funded on a voluntary basis, the UN's ability to sustain peace and security operations had no secure footing and was left to the whims of its membership.[58]

Much like the voluntary financial arrangements for the Cyprus mission, Western nations were fully aware that they would have to foot the bill for any new peacekeeping operation authorized outside of the Security Council. Large missions certainly were out of the question, but sometimes the costs of peacekeeping were considered worthwhile compared to the less pleasant alternatives. When a civil war broke out in the Dominican Republic in spring 1965, the Security Council authorized the Mission of the Representative of the Secretary-General in the Dominican Republic (DOMREP) to observe and report on the negotiated ceasefire. Lasting for almost a year and a half, DOMREP was not financially onerous given that, at its height, the entire mission sported just two military observers at a cost of less than $300,000. Canada contributed one officer to DOMREP,[59] and the involvement was not deemed important enough even to make its way on to Pearson's agenda for cabinet. Canada did not have particularly close relations with the Dominican Republic, nor was it a member of the Organization of American States (OAS), nor, as John Dirks makes clear in Chapter 9 (this volume), was Pearson much interested in Latin America. The United States, however, landed twelve thousand marines on the Dominican Republic's shores to protect Americans threatened by the fighting; they were joined by an OAS peacekeeping force of almost seventeen hundred soldiers.[60]

More directly connected to Canada was the flare up of hostilities along the Indo-Pakistani border in September 1965. Connected to both nations through the Commonwealth and mindful of the geopolitical importance of the subcontinent, Pearson quickly offered himself as a potential mediator. Though his services were politely declined, Ottawa supported efforts to achieve peace through the United Nations.[61] While UNMOGIP already had a presence on the ground in Kashmir, its resources were spread thin and additional peacekeepers were quickly dispatched to the region.[62] To facilitate peace along the rest of the border, the UN Security Council authorized the creation of the United Nations India-Pakistan Observation Mission (UNIPOM), which, at its height, had fewer than one hundred military observers. In existence for only eight months, UNIPOM effectively observed the withdrawal of both Indian and Pakistani military forces from the border region. While success was the result of both states' willingness to disengage, UNIPOM has the distinction of being one of the few peacekeeping missions that had both a measure of success and a limited duration.

By the mid- to late 1960s, Canada was the largest contributor to UN peacekeeping efforts. Peacekeeping had become one of a number of ways in which Canada was able to project itself onto the international stage, support its allies, and contribute to a peaceful international environment. All of these elements were pluses for Canada. Peacekeeping also provided a measure of international credibility and goodwill, and, perhaps more important, it was domestically popular. Real world exposure with a dash of idealism was very appealing to Canadians and how they viewed themselves, particularly against the backdrop of growing American military involvement in Vietnam. The request by the Egyptian government on 16 May 1967 for UNEF's withdrawal, however, sounded a wake-up call.

Officials in Ottawa were concerned that UNEF's removal was a prelude to war on the part of the Egyptians. With eight hundred Canadian soldiers and air force personnel on the ground in the Middle East, a war was the last thing anyone wanted. For Pearson, there was also a personal element involved. Having been so closely associated with UNEF's creation it was difficult to witness the peacekeeping force's dismemberment. While not attempting to directly contest the issue of sovereignty and host-nation consent, the Canadian position was that the issue should be brought before the Security Council or, at the very least, the General Assembly. Yet U Thant thought the UN had no legal grounds on which to stand. Legally speaking, the secretary-general's interpretation was correct, although Pearson thought that U Thant should have used his office's prestige to exercise more moral authority over the question.

Plans for evacuation estimated that it would take about six weeks for UNEF troops to be withdrawn, though the UN Secretariat hoped that arrangements could be expedited.[63] The bulk of the force's logistical support and air transport services was provided by the Canadian contingent, and officials in New York acknowledged that they would be among the last to leave. Yet, as the crisis escalated, some in Ottawa began to question the speed at which the UN withdrawal was proceeding. With Canadian troops slated to be the last to come home, there was a concern that their safety could be compromised should events in the Middle East get out of hand.[64] After a lengthy discussion, cabinet decided to seek a hastened withdrawal of the Canadian contingent from UNEF. However, before U Thant could even be informed of the Canadian decision, he received a letter from the Egyptian government ordering the Canadian contingent's withdrawal within forty-eight hours.

Citing unfriendly statements and actions by Canada as the cause – views that, as Maurice Jr. M. Labelle suggests in Chapter 8 (this volume), were not unfounded – the UAR declared that it was "desirous to prevent any probable reaction from the people of the United Arab Republic against the Canadian forces in UNEF, which may have undesirable reflection on the United Nations."[65] While it is doubtful that the Egyptian government had the interests of the Canadian Forces at heart, the expedited withdrawal of the Canadian contingent likely saved lives. When the Six Day War broke out between Israel and its Arab neighbours less than a week later, the costs for UNEF were dear: fifteen peacekeepers killed and seventeen injured.

As UNEF was ordered to withdraw from Egyptian territory and the Canadian contingent was singled out for immediate departure, self-doubt crept into the Canadian psyche. Pearson, however, sought to ensure that any public uncertainty was short-lived by reiterating Canada's steadfast support for the United Nations and promising Canadian participation in any future efforts to advance the interest of peace in the Middle East.[66] Unfortunately for Pearson, he did not live to see the return of Canadian peacekeepers to Egypt with UNEF II's deployment in 1974.

Peacekeeping, as it developed on the global stage, was a far cry from what Pearson had originally envisaged. Peacekeeping was meant to be a means to an end. Operations were not intended to be indefinite fixtures on the landscape but were to provide a temporary respite allowing for the negotiation of the larger issues. Pearson regretted not insisting on a stronger mandate to deal with the underlying issues of the Arab-Israeli crisis in 1956, though at the time it would have delayed, if not derailed, the peacekeeping effort. In each crisis that came before the UN, time was of the essence lest a regional conflict escalate to include the superpowers. In this, peacekeeping had some value. International stability was preserved, alliances were held together, and Canadians believed that peacekeepers were making a difference. This was all in Canada's national interest, with a dash of altruism to help the medicine go down.

Peacekeeping, in many respects, was the perfect fit for a middle power such as Canada. It was a technique that, in the time and space provided by the UN Security Council, allowed for a mechanism that reduced tensions between the superpowers and mitigated the possibility of brushfire conflicts escalating to a nuclear level. That Canada could act in the cause of peace at the United Nations – and on the world stage – in a way the United States could not, appealed to Pearson's idealism. While not without its costs and dangers, peacekeeping was considered by Pearson, and most Canadians, to be a worthwhile endeavour to help keep the world safe from itself. Canada did not engage in peacekeeping for the Americans or because it was a disinterested party. It engaged in peacekeeping because it was a strong member of the Western alliance and because of the innate belief that peace has always been in Canada's national interest. For Lester Pearson, the lamentable factor was that, in most cases, peacekeeping did not lead to lasting peace.

Notes

1 Gunnar Jahn, "The Nobel Peace Prize 1957, Presentation Speech," http://www.nobelprize.org/nobel_prizes/peace/laureates/1957/press.html.
2 Ross Campbell, "Pragmatism," in *Pearson: The Unlikely Gladiator*, ed. Norman Hillmer (Montreal and Kingston: McGill-Queen's University Press, 1999), 161.
3 "The International Use and Control of Force," address to the United Nations forum, Washington, DC, 2 April 1945, LAC, Lester Pearson Papers, vol. 1, file 15.
4 Ibid. Emphasis in original.
5 Lester Pearson, "Peace through the United Nations," address to the Annual Dinner of the Toronto Board of Trade, 26 January 1948, Directorate of History and Heritage (DHH), file 653.003 (D29).
6 "Canada and Peacekeeping Operations," report no. 4, Canadian Forces Headquarters, 22 October 1965, DHH; Cabinet Conclusions, 13 January 1949, LAC, RG 2, vol. 2643.
7 Quoted in James Eayrs, "Canadian Policy and Opinion during the Suez Crisis," *International Journal* 12 (1957): 99.
8 Blair Fraser, *The Search for Identity: Canada, 1945–1967* (Toronto: Doubleday, 1967), 155.
9 Foulkes, quoted in J.L. Granatstein, *A Man of Influence: Norman A. Robertson and Canadian Statecraft, 1929–1968* (Ottawa: Deneau, 1981), 299.
10 SSEA to High Commissioner in United Kingdom, 7 August 1956, in *Documents on Canadian External Relations* [*DCER*], *1956–1957*, vol. 22, pt. 1 (Ottawa: Department of Foreign Affairs and International Trade, 2001), 140–42.
11 Delegation to North Atlantic Council to SSEA, 17 September 1956, in *DCER, 1956–1957*, vol. 22, pt. 1, 163–64.
12 Official Records of the General Assembly, 562nd Plenary Meeting, ES-I, 1 November 1956.
13 Quoted in Peter Calvocoressi, *Suez: Ten Years After*, ed. Anthony Moncrieff (New York: Pantheon Books, 1967), 133.
14 UN doc. A/3302, 6 November 1956.
15 Comments by Pearson to questions put to him by Yousuf Karsh, September 1958, LAC, Pearson Papers, vol. 89.
16 Walter Gordon, *A Political Memoir* (Toronto: McClelland and Stewart, 1977), 279–80.

17 Greg Donaghy, "Minding the Minister: Pearson, Martin and American Policy in Asia, 1963–1967," in Hillmer, *Unlikely Gladiator*, 131; John Hilliker and Donald Barry, *Canada's Department of External Affairs: Coming of Age, 1946–1968* (Montreal and Kingston: McGill-Queen's University Press, 1995), 250, 252–54; interview with Geoffrey Pearson, 13 August 2002, Ottawa.
18 U Thant, *View from the UN: The Memoirs of U Thant* (Toronto: Doubleday, 1978), 49; see also PERMISNY to DEA, 30 April 1963, LAC, RG 25, vol. 5438, file 11282-B-40-pt.1.
19 Brian Urquhart, *Ralph Bunche: An American Odyssey* (New York: Norton, 1993), 365.
20 Cabinet Conclusions, 13 June 1963, LAC, RG 2, vol. 6253.
21 Ibid.
22 UN doc. S/5321, 2nd Report of the Secretary-General to the Security Council on developments relating to Yemen; "Report No. 13, Canada and Peacekeeping Operations Yemen – UNYOM," 19 December 1966, DHH; PERMISNY to DEA, 30 April 1963, and PERMISNY to DEA, 28 May 1963, LAC, RG 25, vol. 5438, file 11282-B-40-pt.1. In an 8 May memo, Robert Ford, the Canadian ambassador to Egypt, said: "We would be deluding ourselves in assuming that UN operation in Yemen will be of short duration."
23 Rosalyn Higgins, *United Nations Peacekeeping 1946–1967: Documents and Commentary*, vol. 1: *The Middle East* (Oxford: Oxford University Press, 1969), 653.
24 Cairo to DEA, 21 June 1963, LAC, RG 25, vol. 5438, file 11282-B-40-pt.1.
25 "Report No. 13, Canada and Peacekeeping Operations Yemen – UNYOM," 19 December 1966, DHH; Major-General Carl C. von Horn, *Soldiering for Peace* (London: Cassell, 1966). For a very pointed description of why "morale disintegrated" in UNYOM, see Leonard V. Johnson, *A General for Peace* (Toronto: Lorimer, 1987), 53–54.
26 Cabinet Conclusions, 3 January 1964, LAC, RG 2, vol. 6264; Cabinet Conclusions, 25 June 1964, LAC, RG 2, vol. 6265.
27 According to the official DND report, "a more ill-conceived or disorganized mission than that in Yemen cannot be visualized." See "Report No. 13, Canada and Peacekeeping Operations Yemen – UNYOM," 19 December 1966, DHH.
28 Sean Maloney, *Canada and UN Peacekeeping: Cold War by Other Means, 1945–1970* (St. Catharines, ON: Vanwell, 2002), 181.
29 Canada, Department of National Defence, *White Paper on Defence* (Ottawa: Queen's Printer, 1964), 24.
30 Tom Kent, *A Public Purpose: An Experience of Liberal Opposition and Canadian Government* (Montreal and Kingston: McGill-Queen's University Press, 1988), 312; Hilliker and Barry, *Canada's Department of External Affairs*, 279. See also Paul Hellyer, *Damn the Torpedoes: My Fight to Unify Canada's Armed Forces* (Toronto: McClelland and Stewart, 1990), 44–47; Gordon, *Political Memoir*, 278–79; Greg Donaghy, *Grit: The Life and Politics of Paul Martin Sr.* (Vancouver: UBC Press, 2015), 207–8.
31 Canada, *White Paper on Defence*, 11.
32 Hellyer, quoted in Robert Bothwell, *Alliance and Illusion: Canada and the World, 1945–1984* (Vancouver: UBC Press, 2007), 262.

33 Quoted in Donaghy, *Grit*, 209.
34 Cabinet Conclusions, 14 February 1964, LAC, RG 2, vol. 6264. See also Alastair Taylor, David Cox, and J.L. Granatstein, *Peacekeeping: International Challenge and Canadian Response* (Toronto: CIIA, 1968), 171–72.
35 Cabinet Conclusions, 4 February 1964 and 5 March 1964, LAC, RG 2, vol. 6264.
36 Quoted in Andrew Burtch, "'Tact, Diplomacy and an Infinite Store of Patience': Cyprus and Canadian Peacekeeping," *Canadian Military History* 19 (2010): 2.
37 House of Commons, *Debates*, 19 February 1964, 6.
38 Ralph Bunche, quoted in Urquhart, *Ralph Bunche*, 270.
39 See Alan James, *Keeping the Peace in the Cyprus Crisis of 1963–64* (Houndsmills: Palgrave, 2002), 103; Donaghy, *Grit*, 211.
40 Maloney, *Canada and UN Peacekeeping*, 216.
41 Lester Pearson, *Mike: The Memoirs of the Right Honourable Lester B. Pearson*, vol. 3 (Toronto: University of Toronto Press, 1975), 134–35.
42 Paul Martin, *A Very Public Life*, vol. 2 (Toronto: Deneau, 1985), 547.
43 James, *Keeping the Peace*, 111.
44 Ibid., 109.
45 Pearson, *Mike*, 3:135.
46 Cabinet Conclusions, 10 March 1964, LAC, RG 2, vol. 6264.
47 Ibid., 25 September 1964, LAC, RG 2, vol. 6265.
48 Ibid., 17 December 1964, LAC, RG 2, vol. 6265.
49 Lester Pearson, "Keeping the Peace," *Survival* 6 (1964): 150–58.
50 Ibid., "Before the Eighteenth Session of the United Nations," in *Words and Occasions* (Toronto: University of Toronto Press, 1970), 216.
51 Pearson, "Keeping the Peace," 156.
52 Quoted in Taylor, Cox, and Granatstein, *Peacekeeping*, 179–80. See also "Peacekeeping Meeting," draft of Statement by the Minister to the House of Commons on Monday, 26 October 1964, LAC, RG 24, vol. 10131, file 21-14-1-2-pt.4.2.
53 Aide-Memoire, "Meeting to Exchange Experiences on United Nations Peace Keeping Operations," 17 October 1964, LAC, RG 24, vol. 10131, file 21-14-1-2-pt.4.1.
54 Ibid.
55 Quoted in John Macfarlane, "Sovereignty and Standby: The 1964 Conference on UN Peacekeeping Forces," *International Peacekeeping* 14 (2007): 601.
56 Ibid.
57 Article 19 and the Financing of Peacekeeping Operations, n.d. (late February or early March 1965), LAC, RG 25, vol. 10132, file 21-14-1-4.
58 For an analysis of the UN's financial crisis as it pertained to Canada and peacekeeping, see Michael K. Carroll, *Pearson's Peacekeepers: Canada and the United Nations Emergency Force, 1956–1967* (Vancouver: UBC Press, 2009), 57–97.
59 See Lieutenant-Colonel Paul Mayer, *I've Had a Good Innings* (Renfrew, ON: General Store Publishing House, 2006).
60 United Nations, *Blue Helmets: A Review of United Nations Peace-Keeping,* 3rd ed. (New York: UN Department of Public Information, 1996), 654.

61 Cabinet Conclusions, 8 September 1965, LAC, RG 2, vol. 6271.

62 UN, *Blue Helmets*, 138.

63 PERMISNY to DEA, 19 May 1967, LAC, RG 24, vol. 21596, file 2-5081.2.

64 Memorandum for the Minister, 22 May 1967, DHH, 112.3H1.001 (D18).

65 "Evacuation of Canadian Contingent, May-June 1967, Mahomoud Riad to U Thant," United Nations Archives, S-316, box 9, file 1. See also Rikhye – Gaza to the Secretary-General, 27 May 1967, DHH, 112.3H1.001 (D18).

66 Bruce Hutchison, "Canada Repledges Peace Aid," *Christian Science Monitor*, 2 June 1967.

Adam Chapnick

3 Pearson and the United Nations
Tracking the Stoicism of a Frustrated Idealist

No Canadian has ever been as regularly associated with the United Nations as has Lester Pearson. In one analyst's apt words, "as a civil servant, as secretary of state for external affairs, and as prime minister, Pearson conveyed and indeed personified the marriage of Canadian national interest to world order under the United Nations."[1] As many contributors to this volume attest, Pearson's attachment was personal: two world wars and the Great Depression convinced him that the international community would not survive the twentieth century without an effective universal organization dedicated to "the establishment of peace and orderly progress."[2] Such thinking complemented his view of Canada as a necessary, albeit limited, actor in the Cold War international system.

UN Secretary-General Kurt Waldheim once referred to Pearson's approach to the United Nations as "practical idealism." The Canadian was "one of the most loyal and energetic supporters of the enterprises of the world organization and had a remarkable understanding of its possibilities and its limitations."[3] John English's description of Pearson's initial response to the UN's creation – "as much as could be expected but certainly less than what was needed"[4] – conveys a similar sense of a man who did not permit his dreams to prevent rational thinking about the possibilities and limitations of international organization during the Cold War. Add Pearson's outspoken disdain for "the polemical warfare" that too often characterized General Assembly debates,[5] and one obtains a clear picture of his UN mindset. Some challenges, including peacekeeping and promoting economic development, called for United Nations engagement. Others, like resolving great power conflict, exceeded the organization's reach. Perhaps most important, there was a way of doing UN business, a quiet, orderly, conservative diplomatic method that served the organization well.

This chapter argues that, from his experience as a diplomat at the UN's inception through his five years as Canada's prime minister, Lester Pearson viewed the UN through a lens of perennially frustrated idealism. While his evident frustration led some analysts to label Pearson a realist,[6] the emotion he invested in the organization suggests otherwise.[7] Pearson was realistic enough to comprehend the limits of what the UN could and could not achieve, but the resignation he expressed when the organization repeatedly disappointed him was that of an idealist whose heart had been broken.

For the purposes of this volume, focused as it is primarily on the foreign policy of Lester Pearson as prime minister, it is critical to briefly acknowledge the context that prompted much of Pearson's frustration in these later years. Not only was Canada changing in the 1960s (see Stephen Azzi, Chapter 5, this volume), the UN was also in a state of "transition."[8] An organization initially dedicated to the maintenance of world peace that had quickly morphed into an outlet for Cold War diplomatic confrontation transformed once more during the 1960s. As the UN grew from 76 members in 1955 to 113 in 1963, the power of the so-called non-aligned states to shape the international agenda increased significantly.[9] The shift in the balance of influence contributed to the election of the Burmese diplomat, U Thant, as secretary-general (1961–71). U Thant was committed, wrote one biographer, "to a new world order in which colonialism and its vestiges would be eradicated and economic resources more equitably apportioned."[10] His efforts coincided with the 1964 UN Conference on Trade and Development, a symbol of the new-found importance of international development to the UN community. With that emphasis, however, came a crisis in the organization's fiscal health. The non-aligned states called on the UN to do more – more peacekeeping, more development assistance, more involvement in other issues that had formerly been the exclusive domain of the great powers – but it lacked the resources to pay for such engagement. Pressures therefore emerged on wealthier

Western nations, Canada included, to contribute beyond their "fair" share. While such calls were heeded, they also led to increasing levels of national disappointment with the UN.[11]

Historically, noted one foreign report, Canadians had approached the UN with an unrepentant idealism. For them, the UN Charter was "the highest expression of the global community's wishes."[12] By 1968, however, Canada's capacity for influence was limited. As the Afro-Asian group challenged the US and the Union of Soviet Socialist Republics (USSR) without intermediaries, the General Assembly could no longer be swayed by Canadian diplomatic exhortations. In spite of its increased contributions to the UN's regular and supplementary budgets, Ottawa's capacity to effect change had diminished.[13] Nonetheless, Pearson himself remained stoic to the end.

At the practical level, Pearson understood Canada's role in the UN in functionalist terms.[14] He drew from two basic premises. First, a non-great power's influence in world affairs ought to be determined on a case-by-case basis, dependent on the capacity of the state to contribute to a given international issue – Canada's functional principle. Second, promoting a stable and prosperous international order was a primary Canadian national interest. Pearson therefore advocated significant involvement in issue areas in which Canada could provide added value, while he demonstrated less interest in areas dominated by the great powers. Finally, his approach to policy development at the UN combined a confidence in his personal diplomatic abilities with a recognition of both the skills of the ministry beneath him and the responsibility of his government to keep the public informed.

Pearson's understanding of the role of the UN in international society was inspired by his experience during the organization's founding conference. His priorities then had been twofold: (1) create a structure strong enough to prevent war among the great powers without sacrificing the flexibility required to keep them engaged; and (2) build robust social and economic agencies able to promote and foster prosperity among rich and poor nations alike.[15] Later, as secretary of state for external affairs, his speeches emphasized the UN's role as "a symbol of the community of nations and peoples," bounded by "a set of principles or code of ethics which member governments have promised to observe."[16] This normative conception was meant to encourage the great powers to persevere when their interests as members of the organization appeared to be stifled.

The UN also had a "parliamentary" role. It brought, Pearson argued, "the democratic process – and the pressure of public opinion – to bear in the handling of international issues; even on those totalitarian states which have been successful in isolating their peoples from contacts with others and from the direct impact of United Nations discussions."[17] It was, therefore, part of the Western arsenal in the Cold War and of particular interest to non-great power states such as Canada. Finally, the UN must meet "the problems of poverty, disease, ignorance, and backwardness, or what is in UN circles called 'underdevelopment.'"[18] Pearson returned to these themes as leader of the Liberal Opposition.[19]

In 1963, Prime Minister Pearson was pleased to note that the community of nations that he had advocated had established "the machinery for fighting brush fire wars, for persuading powers to seek peaceful solutions, for coordinating activities of the specialized agencies and other bodies, [and] for channeling and administering international assistance."[20] He could support the UN's important, if limited, intervention in the Congo as "a practical necessity in the conduct of international affairs," as he did when he spoke before the eighteenth session of the General Assembly soon after taking office.[21] His memoirs echo similar themes.[22] The UN "was at least a foundation for a new world on which we could build,"[23] he wrote in Volume 1. "I was not so naïve to think that we could decisively, or even importantly, influence the policies of the Great Powers," he added in Volume 2, "but I hoped we could influence the environment in which they were pursued."[24]

Pearson's lack of naiveté is clear. From the organization's founding through his time as prime minister, he recognized the limits of the UN's capacity to effect change. To function, the world organization had to include an active and engaged United States, but even then it could never be expected to resolve great power conflicts. Such thinking led Pearson to accept Washington's and Moscow's demands for a veto over Security Council affairs in 1945.[25] He did so reluctantly, expressing his frustration candidly to Secretary-General Trygve Lie in 1948 and publicly upon accepting the Nobel Peace Prize in 1957: "Certainly, the idea of an international peace force effective against a big disturber of the peace seems today unrealizable to the point of absurdity," he said.[26] Indeed, as leader of the Opposition, Pearson was adamant that the best way to preserve the UN's integrity was to limit what was asked of it. The UN could only do what member states, and particularly the great powers, allowed it to do. During the Cold War, the UN's room to manoeuvre was limited.[27]

As prime minister, Pearson promoted the North Atlantic Treaty Organization – an alliance that he had helped found – as an important corollary to the UN. In his 1963 address to the General Assembly, he averred that the world organization was "no substitute for national foreign policy or bilateral diplomacy," adding that the UN Charter itself acknowledged "that there are other peaceful means of solution, regional and limited collective arrangements, outside of the United Nations but consistent with its principles which member states can employ."[28] Under his leadership, the Department of External Affairs twice published reports explicitly warning Canadians that the UN could not function effectively without a legitimate budget nor could it manage conflict between or among the great powers.[29]

To Pearson, what limited success could be achieved at the United Nations depended largely on the quality of international diplomacy.[30] As he made clear in 1948, global change was best effected "not by aggressive nationalism but by earning the respect of the nations with whom we co-operate."[31] Four years later, having just been elected president of the General Assembly, he told members of the UN Correspondents' Association that the only way the world organization could meet its goals would be through "patient negotiation and compromise, in private meetings and in public debate."[32] When he addressed the General Assembly in 1952, he re-emphasized the importance of accepting the possible.[33] He also cited the need to balance public communication and outreach with the need for private space for quiet diplomacy. "I know that without the active participation of world agencies of communication and information, this experiment in world organization could not succeed," he said in his first address to the General Assembly after his term as president expired, "because it would not be able to secure popular support. But the United Nations has, or should have," he added, "a private as well as a public face ... [I]t is not essential, as I see it, indeed it is often harmful, for the negotiation of policy always to be conducted in glass houses which are often too tempting a target for brickbats."[34] Pearson maintained this thinking as Opposition leader, speaking out regularly in favour of "the normal processes of diplomacy," "small diplomatic successes," and "piece-meal, and at times uneasy, bargaining."[35]

Pearson's unshakable belief in quiet diplomacy was even more apparent when he was prime minister. When questioned in the House of Commons about the conflict between Greece and Turkey in Cyprus in 1964, he stressed that the problem could "only be solved in a climate of moderation and compromise."[36] In a DEA discussion of decolonization in 1966, Ottawa emphasized the need for "orderly evolution."[37] Faced also in 1966 with questions in the House of Commons about possible Canadian recognition of Communist China at the UN, but mindful of American pressure to preserve the status quo, Pearson noted the "fundamental obstacles" preventing "further and equitable progress," and he warned members of Parliament not to expect significant change in the immediate future.[38] In the Pearson government's 1966 report on Canada's UN experience, Ottawa explained that, when SSEA Paul Martin's efforts to reach a compromise within the General Assembly looked unlikely to succeed, the Canadian delegation elected not to press the matter.[39] The prime minister's caution was evident again the following year in cabinet debates over imposing sanctions on Rhodesia's white minority regime. On 14 February 1967, when Martin urged immediate approval of the necessary regulations to meet the Security Council's 15 February deadline, Pearson refused. More time, he claimed, was needed to ensure the support of the minister of trade and commerce, who could not attend the meeting, and for Pearson to verify that this Security Council initiative would not commit the UN to actions that it lacked the capacity to undertake effectively.[40]

In sum, for Lester Pearson, the UN was an unfinished project, necessary to promote peace and prosperity but limited in its effectiveness by the need to maintain great power support in the midst of a cold war. Diplomacy was therefore critical, as was a willingness to accept, if not encourage, incremental progress.

Canada, Prime Minister Pearson believed, was aptly positioned to support and promote such progress. Indeed, preserving an international system having the United Nations as its focal point was "a basic foundation" of Canadian foreign policy.[41] As a 1966 DEA publication made clear, "Canada was ready and willing, when the Charter system of security was found to be wanting, to put into practice the theory of functional contributions to the United Nations which she had advocated from the beginning."[42] Functionalism specified not only where Canada could contribute but also where it would be less helpful. At the UN under Pearson, Ottawa made its greatest impact on (ultimately unsuccessful) efforts to establish an international police force, on the debate over the funding of UN peacekeeping operations, and on the expansion of the UN's development assistance mandate. Canada was significantly less engaged on questions involving the Security Council, be they related to expansion of the membership or to Canadian candidacy for a non-permanent seat.

As prime minister, Pearson told the House of Commons: "We in Canada have always regarded participation in United Nations peacekeeping operations as a fundamental obligation of United Nations membership."[43] His statement was as much a long-held personal view as it was a national one. As SSEA during the Korean War, Pearson initiated a Canadian tradition of keeping an infantry battalion on perpetual stand-by for UN service.[44] Almost immediately after helping to form the UN Emergency Force in Suez, he wrote an extended article for the American periodical *Foreign Affairs* advocating the establishment of a permanent UN peacekeeping authority, or at least "a permanent mechanism by which units of the armed forces of member countries could be endowed with the authority of the United Nations and made available on short notice for supervisory police duties."[45] Suez, he repeatedly made clear, was a compromise. In the future, the international community had to do better.[46]

When he became prime minister, Pearson faced a Canadian public enamoured with peacekeeping and with the positive accolades and reputation that it had brought them as a people.[47] As Michael Carroll notes in Chapter 2 (this volume), when he represented Canada at the UN General Assembly that September, Pearson called on the organization to operationalize Secretary-General U Thant's recent call for states to set aside personnel who could be made available to the UN on short notice. As befitted an advocate of functionalism, Pearson also noted that his country had already done so. He then went further, calling on states with a history of peacekeeping leadership to meet to formally discuss best practices.[48]

Upon his return to Ottawa, Prime Minister Pearson worked with his SSEA and his minister of national defence to turn such words into action.[49] The onset of the crisis in Cyprus, also discussed in greater detail in Carroll's chapter, made his call for a permanent force that much more urgent. The Cyprus mission, he wrote in a widely read article in *Maclean's*, demonstrated "the folly of not organizing in advance so that that UN [could] operate effectively."[50] The article advocated that "a number of middle powers, whose credentials and whose motives are above reproach ... work out a stand-by arrangement among themselves consistent with the United Nations charter."[51] As he had done previously, Pearson pledged that Canada would show leadership to make this happen. His words were almost immediately heralded by the *Economist* and then again by U Thant when the latter spoke to a joint meeting of both houses of Canada's Parliament a few weeks later.[52] Ottawa hosted a meeting of military experts to consider the technical aspects of UN peace-keeping operations that November.[53] Regrettably, controversy over how UN peacekeepers were and would be funded quickly derailed any potential progress.[54]

Pearson had been mindful of how the UN was to pay for peacekeeping from the moment he helped establish the United Nations Emergency Force in late 1956. Indeed, in the autumn of 1957, Canada's delegation argued before the General Assembly that funds for peacekeeping had to come from everyone "as a symbol of collective sharing in the collective effort for peace."[55] Although a 1962 advisory opinion from the International Court of Justice legitimized Ottawa's position, neither the Soviet Union nor France would cooperate. Thus, when Pearson spoke to the General Assembly in 1963, UN debt had reached $120 million. As prime minister, Pearson's position had not changed: "If the United Nations decides in accordance with recognized and legal procedures to engage in peacekeeping operations," he said, "the expenses should be borne collectively by the whole membership, in accordance with Assembly decisions on apportionment ... If we do not give the organization the financial support that it needs for discharging its responsibilities, its very existence will be endangered."[56]

Given Soviet and French intransigence on the funding issue, when it came time to finance the mission to Cyprus in 1964, U Thant solicited volunteers. As the functional principle dictated, Canada contributed both militarily and financially and then used those contributions to justify its persistent and outspoken advocacy to deal harshly with delinquent states. Since Article 19 of the UN Charter dictated that donors in sufficient arrears could lose their right to vote in the General Assembly, and since by late 1964 thirteen states, most notably France and the USSR, were in that very position, Ottawa's policy became more challenging. As he had throughout his public service and parliamentary career, Pearson compromised. Canada continued to pay more than its fair share, and no states were ever denied voting rights. As that result did not sit right with Canadians, public support for peacekeeping softened.[57]

The public was more supportive of the prime minister's efforts to promote international development. Pearson had been focused on "economic and social matters" at the global level since the UN's founding conference in 1945. "The primary task of the new world organization," he told a Los Angeles Town Hall Club then, "must be to remove the social and economic as well as the political causes of international friction and international dispute."[58] Pearson's memoirs of his experience as foreign minister reaffirmed that commitment.[59] Two weeks before the 1958 election that gave the Progressive Conservative John Diefenbaker his unprecedented majority, Pearson spoke about development assistance through the UN in functionalist terms on the CBC: "Canada has a good record in this field," he said, "but we can and should do more unless a deterioration of our whole domestic economy made that quite impossible."[60]

As prime minister, Pearson continued to argue that "security and welfare are interrelated, parts of the same problem."[61] Canada's performance, however, at least according to an internal DEA study in 1965, was less impressive. Appended to Under-Secretary of State for External Affairs Marcel Cadieux's report to Paul Martin on Canada and the UN was a critical summary of the national approach to development assistance. "It is submitted," read the memo,

> that in spite of the developments of the past twenty years, including the growth of the United Nations' economic and social programme (and Canada's substantial contributions to it), the influx of new members, and the vital relationship of economic development to their political stability, Canada still has not readily accepted the concept of balance between the importance of political and security matters on the one hand, and economic, social and humanitarian affairs on the other. This is reflected in our approach to this latter group of issues at the United Nations, which is essentially passive and negative ... If we want other nations to share our aspirations for an organization with an effective capacity to maintain the peace, we shall have to respond positively to their ambition that the United Nations should achieve capacity to combat the situation in which

the gap between the "have" and "have not" countries is increasing rather than diminishing.[62]

While the evidence is circumstantial, there is reason to believe that Canada's performance on the development assistance file disappointed the prime minister. Upon his retirement, he wrote and spoke out forcefully in favour of greater regard for economic and social insecurity.[63]

If Pearson's commitment to peacekeeping and economic development was consistent with functionalism, his relative *lack of interest* in certain elements of Security Council affairs was equally so. Whereas Canada's military could contribute meaningfully to global conflict management efforts, and the Canadian economy could support investments in international development, Canada lacked the great power authority – and veto power – to substantively influence Security Council discussions. As a result, the DEA was hardly interested in standing for a seat on the United Nations Security Council (UNSC) in the late 1940s.[64] And while Ottawa certainly took its role seriously in 1948 and 1949,[65] there is little reason to believe that Pearson saw non-permanent membership as critical. Indeed, in 1953, as SSEA, he advised against pursuing an unexpected opportunity to reacquire a seat in 1954, four years before Ottawa had expected to stand for its second UNSC term.[66]

Pearson does not seem to have discussed the Security Council in detail as Opposition leader, and he appears to have played no role in the 1963–65 dialogue both within Canada and among its Western allies that contemplated the potential loss of a Commonwealth UN seat on an expanded Security Council.[67] One can be more certain that he "never seriously considered becoming a candidate" for non-permanent membership on the Security Council for the 1967–68 period until it was suggested to Ottawa by London and others.[68] When Canada's great power allies made it clear in 1966 that they hoped Ottawa would assume the Security Council seat the following year, Paul Martin responded positively. Pearson, however, was less enthused: "The important thing is to show no particular desire to take on this responsibility,"[69] he wrote. Canadian diplomats did not confirm Ottawa's willingness to stand for election until 23 August 1966, just a few months before the General Assembly met for the election. In its report on the decision to stand, the DEA described itself as having been "willing to take on the *burden* to prevent difficulties over the possible nominations of Greece and Spain."[70] For Prime Minister Pearson, a Security Council seat was a necessary contribution to the stability and credibility of the organization as a whole. It was not, however, a position that would allow Canada, or its representatives, to shine.

As shining at the UN mattered to Pearson, his attitude towards how Canada's foreign policy process was managed at meetings in New York was shaped extensively by his own personal history. The desire to be noticed was based on two complementary ideas. The first, consistent with the historian Michael Bliss's argument that Pearson's ambition has been unduly exaggerated, was that the functional principle dictated that Ottawa make an effort to lead.[71] The second was personal. As Norman Hillmer argues: "For all his success at representational diplomacy, Pearson had some disdain for it. He wanted to be at the centre, to be a *working* diplomat."[72] Indeed, two academics who knew him when he taught at Carleton University after leaving politics suggest that Pearson would have preferred the UN secretary-generalship – a position for which he was considered, and denied by a Soviet veto, twice[73] – over Canada's prime ministership.[74] His election as president of the General Assembly in 1952 was also hardly accidental.[75]

Although Canada's international standing in the postwar period certainly helped, Pearson was a frequent candidate for UN leadership positions in part because of his superior communications skills. Those skills, combined with his unshakable belief that the public had a right to be informed of its government's actions on the world stage, left him comfortable briefing Canadians on the organization all the way through his time as prime minister.[76] When he assumed office in 1963, Pearson outlined the national approach to world affairs in the speech from the throne. "The principles of Canadian external policy are those of the United Nations charter," remarked the governor general: "to maintain peace with justice and respect for human rights with fundamental freedoms; and to promote the welfare of all peoples by international co-operation." Pearson's government would "seek solutions to international problems by diplomacy and negotiation."[77]

In the House of Commons, Pearson sometimes handled questions on UN affairs personally. On Cyprus in 1964, for example, he argued that the situation demonstrated that "the United Nations, with all its weaknesses and imperfection, [was] indispensable in keeping the peace at times of crisis."[78] He similarly defended the organization in spite of its flaws when U Thant called on UNEF to withdraw from Egypt in

1967.[79] And while he only spoke to the General Assembly as prime minister once, he asked specifically to see the texts of his SSEA's subsequent speeches to the group in advance.[80]

Taking personal responsibility for Canada's UN experience did not prevent Prime Minister Pearson from allowing DEA members diplomatic latitude during their work in New York.[81] In 1967, for example, during a debate over the Middle Eastern crisis, Pearson explained the actions of Canada's permanent representative to the UN at meetings of the Security Council as follows: "Yes, Mr. Speaker, he is acting on instructions from the government of Canada. But as I am sure my hon. friend will appreciate, in present circumstances the Canadian representative, subject to decisions in principle that have been taken, must be given a certain leeway in carrying them out."[82] In general, as Greg Donaghy makes clear (Chapter 4, this volume), even though he was never fully confident in his SSEA's personal abilities, Pearson concentrated his own involvement at the head-of-government level, leaving his diplomatic officials a degree of flexibility to translate the government's vision into action, similar to the flexibility he had received in the 1940s and 1950s.[83]

As Michael Carroll points out (Chapter 2, this volume), when Canada's UN peacekeepers were expelled from the Middle East in 1967 self-doubt entered the Canadian psyche. Robert Bothwell argues that Canadians' disappointment led many, including Pierre Trudeau's successor government, to believe "that an inward-looking policy, concentrating more narrowly on Canada, was the proper response to a world where Canada's role was no longer appreciated."[84] Moreover, around the world, by 1968, the UN appeared to be in trouble. As one analyst has noted, thanks largely to decolonization, "the UN could now claim more persuasively than ever before to speak for the peoples of the world, but in some ways, it could do less than ever for them."[85] Pearson, however, never gave up.[86] Cynics called his foreign policy "feckless," comparing Canada under his government to "the flower child ... hoping not to become involved in international disputes and seeking only to do good among the deserving poor and give wise counsel of the wicked super-states."[87] Such criticism is too harsh. Pearson persevered because his long international career had taught him that the UN, however flawed, promoted the Canadian national interest. It was, and had to be, a critical element of a Cold War world order conducive to Canadian security and prosperity.

Notes

The author thanks David Banoub for research assistance.

1 Peter Gellman, "Lester B. Pearson, Collective Security, and the World Order Tradition of Canadian Foreign Policy," *International Journal* 44 (1988–89): 70.

2 Statement by the Secretary of State for External Affairs and President of the United Nations General Assembly, 22 December 1952, LAC, Lester Pearson Papers, vol. 63, file UN General, 1947–57. See also Norman Hillmer, "Pearson and the Sense of Paradox," in *Pearson: The Unlikely Gladiator*, ed. Norman Hillmer, 3–18 (Montreal and Kingston: McGill-Queen's University Press, 1999).

3 Kurt Waldheim, "Lester Pearson and the United Nations," in *"Freedom and Change": Essays in Honour of Lester B. Pearson*, ed. Michael G. Fry (Toronto: McClelland and Stewart, 1975), 13 and 12.

4 John English, *Shadow of Heaven: The Life of Lester Pearson* (Toronto: Lester and Orpen Dennys, 1989), 262.

5 Lester Pearson, *Words and Occasions* (Toronto: University of Toronto Press, 1970), 213.

6 See, for example, Hillmer, "Pearson and the Sense of Paradox," in Hillmer, *Unlikely Gladiator*, 3.

7 English, *Shadow of Heaven*, 314.

8 Bernard Firestone, *The United Nations under U Thant, 1961–1971* (London: Scarecrow Press, 2001), xxiv.

9 For a list of UN members, see "Growth in United Nations Membership, 1945 to Present," http://www.un.org/en/sections/member-states/growth-united-nations-membership-1945-present/index.html.

10 Firestone, *United Nations*, xx.

11 Reid to Ignatieff, 29 March 1966, LAC, Escott Reid Papers, vol. 34, file 11; Policy Review: Canada and the United Nations, appended to Cadieux to Martin, 26 March 1965, LAC, Paul Martin Papers, vol. 226, file 22; Charlotte S.M. Girard, *Canada in World Affairs, 1963–1965* (Toronto: CIIA, 1980), 8–10; Firestone, *United Nations*, 61, 102–3. For Pearson's view of the changes, see his "Before the Eighteenth Session of the United Nations," 19 September 1963, in Pearson, *Words and Occasions*, 214; and Lester Pearson, "What Future for the United Nations?" *New York Times*, 27 September 1959.

12 Internal memo, 23 July 1968, Ministère des Affaires Étrangères, Archives Diplomatiques, Paris, Ministère des Affaires Étrangères Records, 83QO/oc 105.

13 Policy Review: Canada and the United Nations, appended to Cadieux to Martin, 26 March 1965, LAC, Martin Papers, vol. 226, file 22; Hadwen to Under-Secretary of State for External Affairs (USSEA), 7 December 1964, LAC, Martin Papers, vol. 226, file 21; Lester Pearson, *Mike: The Memoirs of the Right Honourable Lester B. Pearson*, vol. 2 (Toronto: University of Toronto Press, 1973), 134; Alastair Buchan, "Concepts of Peacekeeping," in Fry, "Freedom and Change," 18.

14 On functionalism in the UN context, see Adam Chapnick, "'A Great Small Country on the International Scene': Looking Back at Canada and the United Nations," *International Journal* 67 (2012): 1063–72.

15 English, *Shadow of Heaven*, 262, 288. See also Geoffrey Pearson, *Seize the Day: Lester B. Pearson and Crisis Diplomacy* (Ottawa: Carleton University Press, 1993), 162.

16 Lester Pearson, *Democracy in World Politics* (Princeton: Princeton University Press, 1955), 66. See also "The United Nations – Review and Preview – 1945, 1955, 1965," 22 June 1955, San Francisco, LAC, Pearson Papers, vol. 63, file UN General, 1947–57; and Pearson, "Town Meeting of the World," [24 June 1955], in Lester Pearson, *The Four Faces of Peace and the International Outlook* (Toronto: McClelland and Stewart, 1964).

17 Pearson, "The United Nations – Review and Preview," LAC, Pearson Papers, vol. 63, file UN General, 1947–57.

18 Pearson, *Democracy in World Politics*, 72.

19 See, for example, Pearson "The New Face of Diplomacy," in Pearson, *Four Faces of Peace*, 43; Pearson, "The United Nations and Peace," in Lester Pearson, Ernest A. Gross, and Sir Patrick Dean, *A Critical Evaluation of the United Nations* (Vancouver: UBC Press, 1961), 11, 18; and Pearson, "What Future for the United Nations?"

20 Pearson, "Room for Hope," 24 October 1963, in Pearson, *Four Faces of Peace*, 129.

21 Pearson cited in "The Prime Minister Addresses the UN," *External Affairs* 15 (1963): 339.

22 Pearson's post-retirement lectures are consistent with his memoirs, suggesting that his thoughts in the 1940s and 1950s resonated during his time as prime minister. See Pearson, "A Poor Thing, but Our Own," in Lester Pearson, *Peace in the Family of Man* (Toronto: Oxford University Press, 1968), 82.

23 Lester Pearson, *Mike: The Memoirs of the Right Honourable Lester B. Pearson*, vol. 1 (Toronto: University of Toronto Press, 1972), 283.

24 Pearson, *Mike*, 2:35.

25 English, *Shadow of Heaven*, 262, 300.

26 Pearson to Lie, 27 May 1948, LAC, Pearson Papers, vol. 63, file UN General, 1947–57; Pearson, "The Four Faces of Peace," 11 December 1957, in Pearson, *Four Faces of Peace*, 12.

27 Pearson, "The United Nations and Peace," 2 February 1961, in Pearson, *Four Faces of Peace*, 114, 119.

28 Pearson, "Before the Eighteenth Session of the United Nations," 219.

29 Department of External Affairs (DEA), *Canada and the United Nations 1963* (Ottawa: DEA, 1964), 8; and DEA, *We the Peoples ... Canadians and the United Nations, 1946–1965* (Ottawa: Queen's Printer, 1966), 57.

30 John Holmes, "The Unquiet Diplomat – Lester B. Pearson," *International Journal* 62 (2007): 291–309.

31 Pearson, "Some Principles of Canadian Foreign Policy," January 1948, in Pearson, *Words and Occasions*, 69.

32 Pearson, "To the United Nations Correspondents' Association," 11 November 1952, in Pearson, *Words and Occasions*, 118.

33 Statement by the Secretary of State for External Affairs and President of the United Nations General Assembly, L.B. Pearson, 22 December 1952, LAC, Pearson Papers, vol. 63, file UN General, 1947–57.

34 Statement by the Chairman of the Canadian Delegation to the Eighth Session of the United Nations General Assembly, L.B. Pearson, 23 September 1953, LAC, Pearson Papers, vol. 63, file UN General, 1947–57. See also, Pearson, *Democracy in World Politics*, 64–65.
35 Pearson, "The New Face of Diplomacy," in Pearson, *Four Faces of Peace*, 43; Pearson, "The United Nations and Peace," 2 February 1961, in Pearson, Gross, and Dean, *A Critical Evaluation of the United Nations*, 12.
36 House of Commons, *Debates*, 13 March 1964, 913.
37 DEA, *We the Peoples*, 72.
38 House of Commons, *Debates*, 15 November 1966, 9898. On US pressure, see Greg Donaghy, "Red China Blues: Paul Martin, Lester B. Pearson, and the China Conundrum, 1963–1967," *Journal of American-East Asian Relations* 20 (2013): 190–212.
39 DEA, *Canada and the United Nations 1966* (Ottawa: DEA, 1968), 4.
40 The story can be followed through the cabinet conclusions of 26 January, 14 February, and 21 February 1967, LAC, RG 2, vol. 6323. See also Thomas Hockin, "External Affairs and Defence," in *Canadian Annual Review for 1967*, ed. John Saywell (Toronto: University of Toronto Press, 1968), 248.
41 Pearson, quoted in "A Face of the World," *External Affairs* 17 (1965): 84.
42 DEA, *We the Peoples*, 56. See also "Growth of the Canadian Foreign Service," *External Affairs* 18 (1966): 240–42.
43 House of Commons, *Debates*, 13 March 1964, 913.
44 Michael K. Carroll, *Pearson's Peacekeepers: Canada and the United Nations Emergency Force, 1956–67* (Vancouver: UBC Press, 2009), 40. See also Pearson, *Mike*, 2:122.
45 Lester Pearson, "Force for U.N.," *Foreign Affairs* 35 (1957): 401–2, 404.
46 Pearson, *Four Faces of Peace*, 12–13; Pearson, "United Nations and Peace," 115–16.
47 Girard, *Canada in World Affairs*, 278; Peyton Lyon, "External Affairs and Defence," in *Canadian Annual Review for 1964*, ed. John Saywell (Toronto: University of Toronto Press, 1965), 219.
48 Pearson, "Before the Eighteenth Session of the United Nations," 19 September 1963, in Pearson, *Words and Occasions*, 215–16.
49 Martin to Pearson, 29 October 1963, and Hellyer to Pearson, 15 November 1963, LAC, Pearson Papers, vol. 271, file 820.22.
50 Lester Pearson, "A New Kind of Peace," *Maclean's*, 2 May 1964, 9.
51 Ibid., 11. See also Lester Pearson, "Keeping the Peace," *External Affairs* 16 (1964): 240–53.
52 "Minute Men for Peace," *Economist*, 16 May 1964; Text of Address by Secretary-General U Thant to Joint Meeting of Both Houses of Canadian Parliament, 26 May 1964, LAC, Pearson Papers, vol. 271, file 822.21.
53 For conference planning details, see Ross Campbell to USSEA, 3 June 1964, LAC, Pearson Papers, vol. 271, file 820.22. For details on the conference itself, see Carroll, Chapter 2, this volume.
54 Girard, *Canada in World Affairs*, 329.
55 William Barton, "Who Will Pay for Peace? The UN Crisis," *Behind the Headlines* 24 (1965): 5. See also DEA, *Canada and the United Nations 1964*, 21.

56 Pearson, quoted in "The Prime Minister Addresses the UN," *External Affairs* 15 (1963): 343. See also Carroll, *Pearson's Peacekeepers*, 70; and Pearson, "Keeping the Peace," *External Affairs* 16 (1964): 252.

57 For more detail, see Barton, "Who Will Pay for Peace?"; Carroll, *Pearson's Peacekeepers*, 89–97; DEA, *Canada and the United Nations 1964*, 12; DEA, *Canada and the United Nations 1966*, 2; and J.L. Granatstein, "Canada: Peacekeeper – A Survey of Canada's Participation in Peacekeeping Operations," in *Peacekeeping: International Challenge and Canadian Response*, ed. Alistair Taylor (Toronto: CIIA, 1968), 181.

58 Pearson, "Canada at the San Francisco Conference," 4 June 1945, in Pearson, *Words and Occasions*, 65.

59 Pearson, *Mike*, 2:123. See also Pearson, "The Need Is Great," 3 June 1956, in Pearson, *Four Faces of Peace*, 175.

60 Pearson, "We Can't Buy Friends," 18 March 1958, in Pearson, *Four Faces of Peace*, 232.

61 "The Prime Minister Addresses the UN," *External Affairs* 15 (1963): 339.

62 Policy Review: Canada and the United Nations, appended to Cadieux to Martin, 26 March 1965, LAC, Martin Papers, vol. 226, file 22.

63 Lester Pearson, "The UN at 25," *Saturday Review*, June 1970. See also his lecture, "Co-operation through Economics," in Pearson, *Peace in the Family of Man*.

64 John Hilliker and Donald Barry, *Canada's Department of External Affairs: Coming of Age, 1946–1968* (Montreal and Kingston: McGill-Queen's University Press, 1995), 78.

65 Hector Mackenzie, "Knight Errant, Cold Warrior or Cautious Ally? Canada and the United Nations Security Council, 1948–1949," *Journal of Transatlantic Studies* 7 (2009): 453–75.

66 Pearson to USSEA, 9 March 1953, LAC, Pearson Papers, vol. 63, file UN General, 1947–57.

67 Canadian discussions of council expansion can be found in LAC, RG 25, vol. 12145, file 24-13-4-2-pt.15. It took two years for Ottawa to forsake the idea of a Commonwealth seat and join the Western European and Others Group. See David Bosco, *Five to Rule Them All: The UN Security Council and the Making of the Modern World* (Oxford: Oxford University Press, 2009), 101–3.

68 Youde to UK Mission in New York, 20 April 1966, National Archives of the United Kingdom (NAUK), DO 181/17. On the initial Canadian thinking at the departmental level, see Cadieux, Memorandum for the Minister, 13 May 1966, LAC, RG 25, vol. 12145, file 24-13-4-2-pt.15.

69 Pearson, Minute on Gordon Robertson to Pearson, 19 May 1966, LAC, Pearson Papers, vol. 280, file 823 Secret. See also Martin to Mission in New York, [May 1966,] LAC, RG 25, vol. 12145, file 24-13-4-2-pt.15; Gordon Robertson to Cadieux, 25 May 1966, LAC, Basil Robinson Papers, vol. 14, file 1; and the June through August 1966 correspondence in NAUK, DO 181/177.

70 DEA, "Final Reports: Twenty-first Session: United Nations General Assembly, New York, 1966," LAC, RG 25, vol. 3470, file 6-1966/4, emphasis added. See also Thomas Hockin, "External Affairs and Defence," in *Canadian Annual Review for 1966*, ed. John Saywell (Toronto: University of Toronto Press, 1967), 216.

71 Michael Bliss, *Right Honourable Men: The Descent of Canadian Politics from Macdonald to Mulroney* (Toronto: HarperCollins, 1994), 220.
72 Hillmer, "Pearson," in Hillmer, *Unlikely Gladiator*, 10. Emphasis in original.
73 Documents on his first candidacy can be found in LAC, Pearson Papers, vol. 63, file UN Secretary-General 1946. Pearson underplayed his disappointment in his memoirs. See Pearson, *Mike*, 1:280. John English's interpretation that Pearson "wanted to face the challenge of being a 'great man'" is significantly more convincing. See English, *Shadow of Heaven*, 297. On his second opportunity, see Pearson, *Mike*, 2:125–29; LAC, Pearson Papers, vol. 64, file UN Secretary-General 1952–53.
74 Peyton Lyon and Bruce Thordarson, "Professor Pearson: A Sketch," in Fry, *Freedom and Change*, 3.
75 For the records of this campaign, see LAC, Pearson Papers, vol. 64, file UN – President, 1951.
76 Hilliker and Barry, *Canada's Department of External Affairs*, 47. See also Pearson, *Mike*, 2:33; and Pearson, "Which Way Will It Go?" in Pearson, *Peace in the Family of Man*, 103.
77 House of Commons, *Debates*, 16 May 1963, 6.
78 Ibid., 10 August 1964, 6627.
79 Ibid., 24 May 1967, 534. See also UK Mission in Canada to Foreign Office, 30 May 1967, NAUK, FO 61/19; and House of Commons, *Debates*, 8 June 1967, 1290–91.
80 Canadian Delegation UN to Ottawa, 23 September 1965, LAC, Pearson Papers, vol. 271, file 822. On the limitations of the attention that Pearson could give to foreign affairs as the leader of two minority governments in a time of large-scale domestic change, see Girard, *Canada in World Affairs*, 345; and Carroll, *Pearson's Peacekeepers*, 72.
81 On his historical experience, see Pearson, *Seize the Day*, xiv; Hilliker and Barry, *Canada's Department of External Affairs*, 8, 9, 45, 47, 87; and English, *Worldly Years*, 49. On Pearson's experience as prime minister, see Hilliker and Barry, *Canada's Department of External Affairs*, 253–54; and English, *Worldly Years*, 314. See also Greg Donaghy, Chapter 4, this volume.
82 House of Commons, *Debates*, 14 June 1967, 1513.
83 On Cyprus, see Pearson, House of Commons, *Debates*, 16 February 1964, 6; Girard, *Canada in World Affairs*, 294–304; Peyton Lyon, "External Affairs and Defence," in Saywell, *Canadian Annual Review for 1964*, 229–31; and Thomas Hockin, "External Affairs and Defence," in Saywell, *Canadian Annual Review for 1967* (Toronto: University of Toronto Press, 1968), 255.
84 Robert Bothwell, "Canada's Moment: Lester Pearson, Canada, and the World," in Hillmer, *Unlikely Gladiator*, 28.
85 Mark Mazower, *No Enchanted Palace: The End of Empire and the Ideological Origins of the United Nations* (Princeton: Princeton University Press, 2009), 199.
86 J.L. Granatstein, "External Affairs and Defence," in *Canadian Annual Review for 1968*, ed. John Saywell (Toronto: University of Toronto Press, 1969), 254;

Granatstein, "Canada: Peacekeeper – A Survey of Canada's Participation in Peacekeeping Operations," in Taylor, *Peacekeeping*, 185.

87 Butterworth to Department of State, 4 September 1968, Lyndon B. Johnson Presidential Library, National Security File, Country File, box 166.

Greg Donaghy

4 C'est la Guerre
The Diplomacy of Mike Pearson and Paul Martin

Paul Martin's appointment as secretary of state for external affairs in Lester Pearson's government was widely anticipated but not universally welcomed. He was often perceived as too ambitious and overly serious, prompting journalists Peter and Christina Newman to mock the "special patina of old-world statesmanship [he] laid on thick" for cabinet's swearing-in on 22 April 1963.[1] Though some assessments were generous – reporter Peter Stursberg, an old friend, described the new foreign minister as "larger than life and twice as eye-popping" – most were careful and judicious.[2] In a "cabinet of experts," Martin was judged an "admirable choice," which made "suitable use of the talents of a veteran." Doubts about the Windsor MP were offset by the confident expectation that the prime minister would "exercise his unique talents in this field."[3] That was certainly the view in the Department of External Affairs, whose occupants welcomed the Liberal victory as a return to a "sort of normalcy." "So far as I am concerned," Ambassador Charles Ritchie sighed happily in his diary, "I am dealing with someone familiar. Mike Pearson has already telephoned me 3 or 4 times."[4]

Martin and Pearson, who shared a similar liberal-internationalist worldview, were clearly the two most important Canadian foreign policy makers from 1963 to 1968. Staunch cold warriors in the postwar decades, they sensed the emerging reformist ethos of the 1960s. They acknowledged the changes in global order required by the waves of postcolonial nationalism sweeping Africa and Asia, by Europe's strong postwar recovery, and by the youthful demands of civil society for a voice in policy. But their focus was often elsewhere, and theirs was not the harmonious or productive relationship that Canadians had once anticipated. A career politician, Martin was a strong and independent-minded minister with foreign policy credentials that rivalled Pearson's. Entering his sixties, he knew that this was his last chance to score the kind of policy success that would guarantee his lifelong ambition to be prime minister. A man in a hurry, he was anxious for action, by himself if necessary. In contrast, Pearson was weakened by successive minority governments and scandal and burdened with a heavy domestic agenda. Almost equally powerful within the minority Liberal governments of the mid-1960s, neither man was willing or able to displace the other.

Balance initially encouraged collaboration. Pearson handled summits while Martin toiled in the diplomatic trenches, each ignoring minor irritants and small slights to achieve early Canadian triumphs in North American resource diplomacy and in post-imperial Cyprus. But manageable differences over tactics, timing, and priorities flared uncomfortably amid the wreckage of the Vietnam War, which escalated sharply in 1965. Driven hard by ambition and his unbridled faith in negotiation – he once argued that "it is hard to single out why a meeting is useful. The very fact that it is held means that it is good" – Martin inserted himself (and Canada) into the global search for peace in Indochina.[5] Unable to rein in his minister, Pearson sniped from a distance as the war upset their partnership, fuelled resentments, and complicated policy making in Ottawa.

By the spring of 1963, Martin was at the height of his power. First elected as a Liberal MP in the Windsor riding of Essex East in 1935, he had risen steadily through government ranks for thirty years, carving out a place for himself as the Liberal Party's leading progressive spokesman. An early disciple of radical economist John Maynard Keynes, Martin favoured state intervention in the economy long before it was fashionable. During the Great Depression, he campaigned for social and economic reform, demanding unemployment insurance, old age pensions, and labour rights. "That's not socialism," he insisted, "it is social justice."[6]

As Martin's striving ambition, his "lugubrious" personality, and his outspoken progressivism tested relations with Prime Minister William Lyon Mackenzie King, he remained on the backbenches as Canada plunged into the Second World War. But when King and the Liberal Party, under pressure from the left, embraced a postwar reform agenda in 1943, Martin's forward-looking reputation proved useful, and he was appointed parliamentary secretary for the minister of labour.

Articulate and sincere, Martin had an immediate impact selling Liberal reform to Canadian labour. "The workers trust him," wrote *Montreal Labour* in 1945, "they know he will leave nothing undone."[7] King, valuing Martin's role as labour's spokesman in caucus, elevated him to the junior cabinet portfolio of secretary of state in April 1945. The job reinforced Martin's liberal standing. He played a key part in winning Canadian workers the right to unionize during a strike at the Ford Motor Company in 1945. The next year, he steered the first Canadian Citizenship Act through the House of Commons as the country shed the vestiges of its imperial heritage. Impressed by his parliamentary skill, King promoted Martin to minister of national health and welfare in December 1946.[8]

Martin remained at the health and welfare ministry for the next decade, a pivotal figure in the Liberal government's campaign to build a more equitable postwar welfare state. He recruited a team of reform-minded doctors and administrators, and pushed them hard. His deputy minister, George Davidson, described him as "the most difficult and demanding Minister I ever worked for and at the same time the most worthwhile, the most rewarding."[9] In the spring of 1948, Martin sponsored a program of federal health grants that injected $30 million annually into public health and hospital construction, creating the infrastructure required for public health care.[10] He tackled Ottawa's miserly and despised means-tested old age pension in 1950, replacing it with a universal benefit that eventually added $300 million annually to the federal budget. Other significant victories followed, including a national hospital insurance program in 1956–57.

Constant outreach cemented Martin's stature as a leading Liberal. He nurtured his contacts with the press, exchanging gossip and secrets for headlines. As health minister, he bolstered publication budgets and PR staff. Martin's name arrived monthly in millions of Canadian homes alongside pension and baby bonus cheques. "He is the government's Santa Claus," wrote one journalist, "its good fellow who helps the sick and the aged and the needy. He is the housewives' 'sugar daddy.'"[11] Martin crossed Canada endlessly, addressing health care workers, ethnic groups, and labour unions, doing small favours and pocketing political debts. He enjoyed talking to students of all kinds and was in constant demand as an "A-List" speaker at Liberal rallies.

The most prolific speaker in cabinet, he delivered more than 150 speeches every year. The *Montreal Gazette* estimated that he gave more speeches during the 1954 summer recess "than any three other cabinet ministers combined."[12]

Nor was Martin intimidated by Pearson's diplomatic reputation and his Nobel Peace Prize. By 1963, he had his own impressive record to defend. As a teenager when the First World War ended and the League of Nations was created, Martin readily absorbed the era's heady internationalism. After law school and graduate studies at the University of Toronto, he pursued international law at Harvard and Cambridge in the late 1920s, attending the quixotic summer courses offered by Sir Alfred Zimmern's Geneva School of International Studies. He watched the League of Nations Assembly at work in 1930, a rare experience for a young Canadian, before returning to Canada and settling in the "border city" of Windsor. Exposed to cross-border issues and drawn by President Franklin Roosevelt's New Deal politics, Martin became a shrewd and sure-footed judge of his American neighbours and their country.

Martin's interests were broad. He was active locally and nationally in the Canadian Institute of International Affairs (CIIA) and the League of Nations Society. As a young MP, he tracked the rise of fascism in Europe and Asia, proposing measures to strengthen Canada's foreign policy in his maiden speech to the House of Commons in June 1936. It was an ambiguous effort, mixing support for the League with twists of North American isolationism. "Good stuff Paul," teased one MP, "tho' I am not sure any one is clear or can be clear while he holds onto the League with one hand and onto the continent of North America with the other."[13] But King and Windsor voters liked his careful approach, and the speech gave Martin credibility with the country's foreign policy pundits at the CIIA's annual Lake Couchiching conference on public policy.

Martin added practical experience to his résumé. He attended League of Nations assemblies in 1936 and 1938, experiences that reinforced his support for the postwar United Nations. In 1944–45, he joined official delegations to International Labour Organization (ILO) conferences, managing the subcommittee charged with defining relations between the ILO and the UN. Word of his diplomatic "skill, fairness, and good humour" followed him home.[14] He regularly headed missions to meetings of the UN's Economic and Social Council in the mid-1940s, and he served as deputy chairman of Canada's delegation to the UN General Assembly in 1949. Despite Cold War tensions, he revelled in the UN's promise of international cooperation and its willingness "to bite into everything."[15]

Martin's UN responsibilities increased in the 1950s. At the General Assembly in the fall of 1952, he worked with, but independently of, Mike Pearson to close the gap dividing American and Indian diplomats over the fate of prisoners of war in Korea.[16] He impressed rising diplomat Jules Léger and leading Canadian journalists, who profiled him under the headline, "Martin Emerges as Seasoned Negotiator at UN Meetings."[17] He took complete charge of Canada's UN delegation for the first time in 1954. Defying Pearson's advice to retreat, he successfully pursued a joint disarmament resolution with the Soviet Union. Pearson had succumbed to "cold feet," Martin bragged in his memoirs, but he had not, winning praise from UN Secretary-General Dag Hammarskjöld for "an admirable job."[18]

Martin did even better in 1955. With Pearson absent, he brokered a deal to resolve a Cold War deadlock on admitting new members to the UN, revitalizing the world body and setting it on the road to universality. Forty years later, diplomat-scholar John Holmes still regarded it as "one of the most remarkable feats in the history of the General Assembly."[19] Martin treasured the praise, especially from old friends. "You have done something at the United Nations which has made your friends very proud and countless people in Canada and elsewhere very grateful," wrote Governor General Vincent Massey, one of his earliest backers, "so as one of those both proud and grateful I wanted to say so."[20] The widespread approval strengthened his confidence in his diplomatic skills and judgment, and in his capacity to act independently.

Two lengthy trips abroad rounded out Martin's diplomatic education. During a sixty-three-day goodwill tour of Asia in 1956–57, he visited Indochina, Singapore, India, Pakistan, Australia, and New Zealand. The Canadian met the continent's leading postcolonial figures, and wrestled with Asia's enormous scale and its vital importance in the struggle for world peace. Martin visited the Middle East too. He marvelled at Israel's progress but was shaken by Arab instability and evidence of Cold War intrigue. The treks gave Martin the same confidence in his independent judgments about Asia and the Middle East as he had in his views on the UN or the US. Apart from Pearson himself, it is unlikely that Canada ever had a secretary of state for external affairs more prepared for the job.

Martin's independent political standing and his solid foreign policy credentials would have complicated his relations with any prime minister. But his long and fragile personal relationship with Pearson only made their situation more difficult. Though Pearson was six years older, the two men were near contemporaries. They had known each other since the 1920s; their paths had crossed at the University of Toronto, where Pearson taught history and Martin was a student. Though they moved in different circles, their friends and colleagues overlapped, and they kept in touch with short notes marking personal or professional milestones, each acknowledging a talent worth cultivating.

This easy friendship changed in 1948 when Pearson left the Department of External Affairs to become foreign minister. As Martin had wanted that role, he viewed Pearson as an interloper and, increasingly, as a rival for the party's top post. But Prime Minister Louis St-Laurent expected his ministers to get along, and the budding rivalry was easily contained. Indeed, Martin campaigned for Pearson during his first election, and the two became political allies. They shared a strong internationalist bent and a left-liberal perspective on domestic issues in a "high-tory" cabinet that was sceptical of both. Pearson and Martin valued their mutual support, but they were not close.

The Liberal leadership contest in 1958 added distance and antipathy. Martin accepted Pearson's victory, but defeat rankled. He resented his leader's easy rise to prominence when he had had to fight so hard for a seat and a cabinet post. "He was the beneficiary of the establishment," Martin said later. "He took advantage of this, perhaps unconsciously, but he took advantage of it and it helped him considerably."[21] Quite simply, as their colleague Paul Hellyer later put it, "Martin felt that Pearson had his job and [Martin] felt that he could do it better."[22]

In turn, Pearson disliked Martin's raw ambition and often suspected his politician's reflexes. In his memoirs, Pearson mocked Martin's "parliamentary debating skill – never using one simple word when fifty were needed to confuse and frustrate our political foes."[23] But in Opposition and as prime minister of a minority government, Pearson had to rely on Martin. This was especially true since many Canadians questioned Pearson's political judgment and his ability to handle Progressive Conservative leader John Diefenbaker. As a result, Pearson treated his colleague on the Opposition front bench "with kid gloves and showed him lots of consideration."[24] There were warm notes of appreciation, high-profile jobs and foreign travel, and hints that Martin would be named to the external affairs portfolio in due course.

With Pearson's blessing, party insiders reminded Martin of "the value (for the future) of him being 100% behind his Leader in thought as well as in word." As Ralph Maybank wrote to Pearson: "These friends do not think the future actually belongs to Paul, but I guess they will talk to him that way."[25] Martin rallied and remained "totally loyal" to Pearson.[26] It suited both politicians to establish a basis for mutual cooperation, though neither let go of the resentments and suspicions that lay at the heart of their uneasy partnership. Journalist and Pearson supporter Grant Dexter, no lover of Martin, came away from a talk with Pearson in April 1962 spitefully cheered by the thought that Pearson "really ha[d] no illusions about Paul."[27]

Despite their freighted history, Martin and Pearson cooperated easily during the Liberal government's first eighteen months in office. While Pearson captured early headlines with high-profile visits to British prime minister Harold Macmillan and US president John Kennedy, Martin spent much of his first six months on the job in committee backrooms, mostly occupied with tackling the deadlocked Columbia River Treaty. North America's fourth largest river, the untapped Columbia flowed from British Columbia to Oregon. After decades of study, International Joint Commission engineers had concluded that joint development would maximize its potential, recommending that the benefits be shared equally between Canada and the US. Diefenbaker had struck a deal with Kennedy in 1961 that traded Canadian upstream benefits for surplus power generated downstream. But that was not enough for BC premier W.A.C. Bennett, whose province owned the resource, and he refused to sign. The treaty also ran into trouble with New Democratic Party and Liberal nationalists who feared that it gave Americans too much control over Canadian resources. The Vancouver Liberal MP Jack Davis called it a "fiasco" and a "sell out."[28] On the eve of his visit to Kennedy's compound at Hyannis Port, with US patience running out, Pearson insisted that Martin fix the stalled treaty.

Under Martin's guidance, senior officials and Liberal politicians quickly hammered out a protocol to the treaty, adding provisions to clarify downstream benefits and Canada's rights over flood control and power generation. Crucially, he convinced Davis to back the plan in time for Pearson to present it to Kennedy as evidence of renewed North American partnership.[29] Tackling Bennett while holding Davis and his nationalist allies on side was tricky business, and Pearson was generous with his praise, assuring cabinet that this was "excellent work under great pressure."[30] Pearson was even happier when Martin cut a final deal with US and BC negotiators in December, saluting him in cabinet for "a big job well done."[31]

Pearson was equally pleased with Martin's triumph the following spring, when Canada led efforts to create a UN peacekeeping force for Cyprus. As Michael Carroll makes clear (Chapter 2, this volume), peacekeeping interested both men, and they worked together in early 1964 to ensure that the government's *White Paper on Defence* embraced it as a mechanism to stabilize the decolonizing states of the global south. Just as they finished their work, the Mediterranean island of Cyprus began unravelling. A former British colony, Cyprus had recently become independent with a cumbersome constitution designed to protect Turkish-Cypriot minority rights. When Greek-Cypriot president Archbishop Makarios tried to amend the Constitution in late 1963, violent civil strife erupted. With Greece and Turkey, NATO allies, itching to intervene, Britain imposed a truce.

As the island tipped towards war in March, anxious Western diplomats looked to the UN for peacekeepers. The most likely contributors were neutral Ireland, Sweden, and Finland, but they, wary of being trapped on Cyprus, hesitated to act. When Britain threatened to leave the island unless relief was in sight, the situation became acute. With the fate of the force hanging in the balance, Martin telephoned his counterparts in Dublin, Stockholm, and Helsinki. This was the kind of personal diplomacy that he loved, drawing on the "political bond between foreign ministers."[32] The Swedes, it turned out, distrusted Finnish intentions and were reluctant to act without another neutral. Coaxing a pledge from Ireland, Martin assured Stockholm of another neutral participant, thus ending the crisis's most dangerous phase.[33]

Martin savoured his triumph, though it was immodest of him to claim in his memoirs that the force came into being solely as a result of his telephone calls or that he was its author.[34] Sweden and Finland were already headed towards a UN force. But with British deadlines looming, Martin forced the pace and gained a day when minutes mattered. For that, he deserved the shower of praise and favourable press coverage that rained on him in the spring of 1964. The Liberal caucus cheered his "matchless job," asking Jim Walker, its chief whip, to pass along its "keen appreciation for [Martin's] efforts and success in the Cyprus dilemma."[35] The *Globe and Mail* gushed about Martin's "quite fantastic diplomacy."[36] Most important, the prime minister was happy. "You are doing a fine job, Paul," Pearson wrote to mark his minister's birthday in June, "and you know how much this means to me. I am more grateful than I can say."[37]

By the end of 1964, however, trouble was brewing. Despite his successes in British Columbia and Cyprus, Martin fretted over his inability to advance his own objectives. His early push to join the OAS, a personal priority since the 1930s, had been blocked by Pearson and the diplomats, who fretted about the dangers of too much American influence. He worried, too, that Pearson had mishandled his recent visit to France, and he wondered about the prime minister's commitment to renewed relations with France. "He just was not at home with French people," Martin later explained.[38] The year ended unhappily for Martin when Pearson and his cabinet colleagues scuttled his plan for a resolution asking the UN to resolve the stand-off over China by seating both the People's Republic of China and break-away Taiwan. Martin squirmed miserably as Pearson nodded wisely and pro-American transport minister Jack Pickersgill fulminated. Canada, "Pick" bluntly advised, should "recognize China the day after the Americans do."[39] It was a humiliating defeat for the foreign minister.

The discomfort was mutual. By early 1965, Pearson was growing increasingly impatient with his foreign minister. Part of the pressure was political. Pearson was doubtless sensitive to the worries of Liberal members who wanted more of Martin, an outstanding House of Commons performer, on the front benches as the party faced fall-out in Parliament from scandals and a bitter debate over Canada's new flag. "Paul has to forget about saving the world," complained beleaguered Liberal MPs in August 1964, "and come give us a hand."[40] The prime minister was angry too about accusations linking Martin to an immigration scandal involving visas for Onofrio Minaudo, a Windsor-based Mafioso.[41] Most important, by early 1965, the war in Vietnam and Canada's close relations with Washington were undermining Pearson's uncertain partnership with Martin. By March, Finance

Minister Walter Gordon was already campaigning for the foreign minister's job.[42]

Vietnam had not been a priority when the Liberals settled into office in 1963, though Pearson and Martin were already familiar with the country and its problems. Since 1954, Canada had served with India and Poland on the International Control Commission that monitored the peace between Ho Chi Minh's communist North Vietnam and its American-backed rival, Ngo Dinh Diem's South Vietnam. Canadian diplomats and politicians, frustrated as Poland and India let communist Viet Cong insurgents undermine the peace with impunity, backed US efforts to shore up Saigon with arms and advisers in search of a stable and non-communist government.

Pearson was more sceptical than his minister about the American role in Asia, but this difference barely registered in 1963. Ottawa's faith in Washington remained rock solid through the spring of 1964, when US secretary of state Dean Rusk asked Canada to send its ICC representative, Blair Seaborn, to Hanoi with a message of unshakeable American resolve. Warning that support for direct intervention would not be forthcoming, Pearson and Martin hesitantly agreed. Seaborn delivered the tough American message, noted Hanoi's equally firm reply, and returned to his Saigon base with the secret Canadian channel open. For Martin, the diplomatic possibilities were tantalizing. Even as the war began to escalate in August 1964, he clung to this secret back channel, sending Seaborn back to Hanoi in August and December, anxiously probing for diplomatic openings.

But Pearson was growing ever more doubtful of American policy, straining relations with Martin. Their varied reactions to their excursion to President Lyndon Johnson's Texas ranch in January 1965 heralded a difficult spring. The informal visit, replete with cowboy hats and bourbon, golf carts and helicopters, beagles and the rustic ranch house, prompted a rattled Pearson to question Johnson's temperament and judgment. "General MacArthur would not have approved," he summed up his trip, "nor, I suspect, John Kennedy."[43] Martin loved Texas. Johnson's casual style and frank talk fascinated him. He was captivated by the president's easy intimacy; both early risers, the two shared a morning coffee in their pyjamas. Martin identified with the self-made president and judged him "an intriguing and powerful personality," commenting: "He had the same kind of drive as me ... LBJ was a strong president."[44] His assessment of the visit could hardly have differed more from Pearson's. "I don't think that you and I," he wrote Rusk warmly, "have ever had more useful or more relaxed meetings."[45]

These different perspectives on Johnson and US leadership mattered as the war in Vietnam intensified in 1965 with stepped-up US air strikes in response to Viet Cong attacks on American bases. Martin remained reluctant to make Ottawa's differences with Washington public, convinced of the traditional virtues of quiet diplomacy. Pearson, however, bowed to the mounting pressure to do something to stop the bombing. U Thant and other global figures had urged him to speak out, confident that he had Washington's ear. American friends, including Vice-President Hubert Humphrey and journalist Marquis Childs, also encouraged him to act. In March, Pearson decided to raise the idea of using a bombing pause to test Hanoi's willingness to talk in a speech that he was soon slated to deliver at Temple University in Philadelphia.[46]

Martin was appalled. "You can't make that speech!" he told Pearson.[47] He urged the prime minister to abandon his plans, suggesting that he raise it privately with Johnson. When Pearson refused, Martin threatened to resign but withdrew his threat when he saw that it had no impact. Predictably, the speech enraged Johnson who berated Pearson over lunch at Camp David. Martin was also beside himself with anger, and when the two Canadians next spoke, they exchanged "some pretty tough words."[48]

Shaken by his rough encounter with Johnson, Pearson was inclined to watchful inactivity in Asia, ready to ease the US burden in Vietnam but only when asked. This was no longer enough for Martin. He worried that youthful protests during the 1965 federal election campaign presaged broad domestic opposition to the war. He was embarrassed by revelations of Washington-Hanoi contacts about which he was ignorant and by charges that Canada was no more than an American stooge on the ICC. Insisting on the need for "extraordinary steps," Martin decided in late January to send retired diplomat Chester Ronning to Beijing and Hanoi, hoping that he might find a way to break the UN deadlock over Chinese representation, convince Beijing to back peace in Vietnam, and determine whether Hanoi's position had shifted under US bombing.

Several factors influenced Martin. While he was clearly driven by his ambitions for the Liberal leadership, his motives were not simply self-serving. He was attracted by the political rewards that the mission would bring to the Liberal Party. "Public opinion in Canada would welcome an initiative," he told Pearson, "which could be presented as a contribution to the search for peace in Vietnam."[49] He was also convinced that Johnson was genuinely interested in talks and that public US statements to this effect were an invitation to act. Ronning would fulfill an American need for a mediator and add to Canada's standing in Washington. Pearson was sceptical but allowed Martin to proceed. To safeguard his own damaged standing in Washington, the prime minister cruelly hung his foreign minister out to dry. The "Ronning mission was Martin's idea," he told US ambassador Walt Butterworth, adding that, "if anything went wrong, his government would disavow any involvement."[50] Rusk dismissed the initiative as inconsequential.

Ronning failed in Beijing, where he was denied entry, and Hanoi. His first mission produced a suggestion from North Vietnamese prime minister Pham Van Dong that Hanoi would begin talks if the US halted its bombing. But Pham added an element of ambiguity by linking this idea to earlier North Vietnamese statements demanding additional US concessions. US diplomats doubted any progress was possible, but an angry Martin convinced US assistant under-secretary of state Bill Bundy to continue the dialogue. There was no give in the next US message, and a chorus of Canadian voices urged Martin to abandon the effort. "It would be a sad ending to our initiative in this matter if we became merely an instrument of USA propaganda or for putting the DRVN [North Vietnam] on the spot," Pearson cabled from Europe.[51]

Martin persisted, however, and Ronning arrived in Hanoi for a second time on 14 June. The results were mixed. North Vietnam, though happy to retain the Canadian conduit, dismissed the US message as nothing "that has not already been published in the western press."[52] As Martin weighed the options, his relations with Washington quickly soured. He was coy about sharing the negative results with the US, insisting that Bundy come to Ottawa to be debriefed. They spent a long afternoon closeted in Martin's East Block office before recessing for dinner at the nearby Chateau Laurier hotel. Martin came with a handful of experts from the Department of External Affairs and allowed them to speak freely. Pleased to note that most of them disagreed with

Martin, Bundy was blunt: "Basically, Hanoi turned Ronning down cold."[53] The evening broke up with boozy tears and hard words on the hotel's front steps.

The Ronning incident and the bickering between Martin and Bundy further eroded Pearson's fading confidence in his foreign minister. He had told Walter Gordon in the fall that Martin was doing "a very poor job at External, where morale is very low," adding in March 1966 that Martin's views on foreign policy no longer mattered.[54] He told friends and colleagues that foreign policy making had been much harder when he was minister.[55] He confided to Minister of National Defence Paul Hellyer that he "wanted to get Paul Martin out of External Affairs: [He] is getting too involved in the Vietnam thing to the exclusion of our overall relations with the US."[56] According to Martin, Pearson asked him to leave his portfolio in the spring of 1966.

But Pearson's views counted for a good deal less in 1966 than they once had. The parliamentary session that spring was among Canada's most disgraceful. Opposition critics brought House business to a standstill over the government's treatment of Victor Spencer, a Vancouver postal clerk dismissed as a spy. Justice Minister Lucien Cardin defended as humane the government's decision to fire Spencer, who was dying of cancer, without charging him. Outraged at the illiberal presumption of guilt, Opposition MPs demanded an inquiry. When Pearson deserted Cardin and caved in to their demands, caucus revolted and challenged his leadership. A handful of angry Quebec ministers threatened to resign, while Cardin fired back with accusations of Progressive Conservative misdeeds. Slowly, the press fleshed out the titillating details of the long-faded dalliance between Gerda Munsinger, a cocktail hostess with ties to East German intelligence, and former Progressive Conservative cabinet minister Pierre Sévigny. The embittered House erupted in scandalous charges and counter-charges. "An absurd nightmare," wrote rookie MP Gérard Pelletier, "a Kafkaesque sort of labyrinth without any exit."[57]

As his memoirs reveal, Martin spied another shot at the chief job as Pearson's leadership teetered during the crisis.[58] But, if tempted, he held his hand, and the chance passed as Pearson righted his government. Martin could afford to wait, for External Affairs had been good for him and he was not about to leave. Peter Newman, who had dismissed Martin's leadership chances as "uncertain" in the previous December, revised his opinion upward.[59] "Once the most outrageously partisan figure in Ottawa," he wrote in February 1966, Martin "has, by sheer force of will, become a dignified foreign minister with a style uniquely his own." He would be "written large" on any list of possible successors.[60]

That was certain. In a March Gallup Poll, 10 percent of respondents named Martin as the next likely Liberal leader; his nearest rivals were Mitchell Sharp at 5 percent and Robert Winters at 2 percent.[61] He did even better in May, when voters were asked to choose between the three potential candidates. Thirty-two percent of them backed him, compared to just 13 percent for Sharp and 10 percent for Winters. With Liberal voters, his support rose to a commanding 38 percent.[62] As the leadership beckoned, Martin's style even became a touch prime ministerial: he abandoned the St. Patrick Street bus, opting instead for a black Chrysler and a chauffeur. As he strode across Parliament Hill – "watching, nodding, smiling benignly" – Ottawa insiders dubbed him "The Presence."[63] Confident and secure, Martin marched on.

After the upsets over Vietnam, Pearson's relations with Martin never recovered their ballast and equilibrium. Indeed, they grew much worse over the next two years. In the fall of 1966, while Martin chased peace in Asia via talks in Moscow and Eastern Europe, Rusk enlisted Pearson to scuttle another China initiative. The drawn out cabinet debate on recognizing Communist China exposed Martin to ridicule as his younger advisers, who wanted reform, laughed at his helplessness. "The discomfited Martin would dodge and weave, as [the advisers] twisted their stilettos," the young diplomat Roy MacLaren recalled, "the whole time punctuated by his loud ahems and various irrelevant flutters."[64] In the new year, Pearson complained again of the lack of reform in Canada's NATO and North American Air Defense (NORAD) policy, lending Walter Gordon his moral support when the outspoken nationalist shattered cabinet solidarity in May to rail against Washington's military alliances and its war in Vietnam. Martin wanted him fired, but Pearson refused.

May and June 1967 were especially difficult. Pearson rejected Martin's advice on handling the Centennial visit of French president Charles de Gaulle, launching instead a cack-handed attempt to recruit Canada's ambassador to France, Jules Léger, as CBC head, a move that seemed to signal his unhappiness with the country's policy towards France. "A mon avis," reflected Under-Secretary Marcel Cadieux, "le Premier Ministre n'est pas disposé à écouter la voix de la raison. Dans ce domaine comme à l'égard du Vietnam, il est obsède pas immédiate et ne semble pas avoir souci des échéances plus lointaines."[65] There was more trouble in June, when war broke out between Israel and its Arab neighbours. Pearson favoured direct dialogue between the major powers, rebuking Martin openly in cabinet for supporting a stronger UN effort and launching his own peace plan without consulting either his minister or his diplomats. "La guerre continue entre M. Martin et le Premier Ministre," Cadieux archly noted.[66]

The conflict persisted through the fall and winter. When Martin blocked Pearson from speculating on UN and NATO reform in a London speech, the prime minister retaliated by prematurely leaking Martin's secret plans for a peacemaking initiative in Cyprus. "En somme," Cadieux sighed desperately, "la guerre entre les deux continue."[67] It was made worse by the tensions stirred by the Liberal leadership convention slated for April 1968. Martin, hurt that Pearson announced his retirement in December 1967 while he was in Europe, was convinced that it was done to harm his chances. He spied Pearson's malevolent hand behind Justice Minister Pierre Trudeau's leadership bid as well. The strain spilled over when Pearson blamed Martin, who was absent campaigning, for letting the Opposition defeat the government's budget bill in February. "It was the first and only time," Martin later recorded, "that we ever really lost our cool with one another."[68] By then, however, it hardly mattered for the two men were barely on speaking terms, their relations marked by an "obvious coldness."[69]

Canada's foreign policy during the 1960s was not fatally compromised by divisions at the top. Despite their differences, Pearson and Martin got along when they had to. This was especially true of their first years in office, which were marked by successes in the Columbia River talks and the Cyprus crisis. Nor did their bitter quarrels over Vietnam ever imperil relations with Washington. Ottawa inched away from the hopeless American crusade so carefully that few observers on either side of the border even noticed.

The impact of Canada's divided leadership was less tangible. The 1960s was a decade of change, heralding a coming era of globalization. The signs were everywhere: in the stirring of economic powerhouses South Korea and Japan, and in the rising political clout of Communist China; in the ferment of West European integration; and in the quickening pace of change across the vast Global South. These were challenges that Ottawa mostly missed. Pearson and Martin, superbly prepared and equipped for their task, ought to have done better. But Vietnam and the bitter personal squabbling between Pearson and Martin diminished their capacity to embrace this larger reality. "Ces conflits ne sont pas," complained Cadieux sadly after observing yet another clash between his two superiors, "de nature à permettre à nos hommes politiques d'aborder les problèmes avec la largeur d'esprit qu'il faudrait."[70] And that was tragic.

Notes

1 Christina Newman and Peter Newman, "Portrait of a New Regime Taking Power," *Maclean's*, 15 June 1963, 16–17, 41–45.
2 Peter Stursberg, "Postmark Ottawa," *Saturday Night*, June-July 1963, 7–8.
3 "The New Pearson Team," *Toronto Star,* 23 April 1963.
4 Charles Ritchie, *Storm Signals: More Undiplomatic Dairies, 1962–1971* (Toronto: McClelland and Stewart, 1983), 52.
5 Story interview with Martin, [1969–70,] LAC, Paul Martin Papers, vol. 353, tape A-7, side 1.
6 "Hecklers Are Busy at Conservative-Liberal Debate," *Windsor Daily Star*, 7 October 1935.
7 "The Royal City of Windsor, Ontario," *Montreal Labour World* [Spring 1944].
8 Jack Pickersgill, *Seeing Canada Whole: A Memoir* (Markham, ON: Fitzhenry and Whiteside, 1994), 286.
9 George Davidson to Martin, 23 June 1965, LAC, Martin Papers, vol. 275, file: Birthday 1965.
10 Paul Martin, Memorandum on Health Insurance, Cabinet Document 659, 20 April 1948, LAC, RG 2, vol. 66, file C-20-5.
11 Richard Needham, "Timber of Two Principal Parties Analyzed for Cabinet Positions," LAC, Martin Papers, vol. 127, clipping file: January to December 1953.
12 "Oratory," *Montreal Gazette,* 18 September 1954.
13 Macphail to Martin, 18 June 1936, LAC, Martin Papers, vol. 121, scrapbooks, 83.
14 Mainwaring, "Memorandum for the Minister of Labour," 23 May 1944, LAC, Martin Papers, vol. 1, file: ILO, Philadelphia, 1944.
15 "Backstage at Ottawa: Johnny Canuck, Diplomat," *Maclean's*, 15 January 1947, 15.
16 Greg Donaghy, "Blessed Are the Peacemakers: Canada, the United Nations, and the Search for a Korean Armistice, 1952–53," *War and Society* 30 (2011): 134–46.
17 "Martin Emerges as Seasoned Negotiator at UN Meetings," *Chatham Daily News*, 7 November 1952. See also I. Norman Smith, "All This UN Talk, Talk, Talk, Is Vitally Important Work," *Ottawa Evening Journal*, 8 November 1952; Mark Harrison, "Canada Rescues UN from 'I-Dotting' Yanks, 'Legal-Minded' British," *Toronto Daily Star,* 28 November 1952; Walter O'Hearn, "Canada's Delegate Is Frank," *Montreal Star*, 28 November 1952.

18 Pearson to Martin, 1 December 1954, LAC, Lester Pearson Papers, vol. 9, file 7.

19 John Holmes, *The Shaping of Peace: Canada and the Search for World Order* (Toronto: University of Toronto Press, 1983), 327.

20 Massey to Martin, 31 December 1955, LAC, Martin Papers, vol. 167.

21 Norah Story interview with Martin, [1969–70,] LAC, Martin Papers, vol. 351, tape 10, side 1.

22 Author interview with Paul Hellyer, 30 July 2006.

23 Lester Pearson, *Mike: The Memoirs of the Right Honourable Lester B. Pearson*, vol. 3 (Toronto: University of Toronto Press, 1975), 39.

24 Author interview with Tom Kent, 23 August 2007.

25 Maybank to Pearson, and enclosure, 8 July 1962, LAC, Pearson Papers, vol. 22, file 313.3, Maybank, Ralph.

26 Author interview with Tom Kent, 23 August 2007.

27 Grant Dexter to File, 5 April 1962, Queen's University Archives (QUA), Grant Dexter Papers, box 1, file: Memos 1957.

28 Quoted in Neil Swainson, *Conflict over the Columbia: The Canadian Background to an Historic Treaty* (Montreal and Kingston: McGill-Queen's University Press, 1979), 246, 248.

29 Martin, Memorandum for the Prime Minister, 7 May 1963, LAC, RG 25, vol. 5181, file 5724-2-40.

30 Martin, Memorandum for Cabinet: Discussions with British Columbia, 5 June 1963, and Martin, Memorandum for Cabinet: Agreement with British Columbia, 26 June 1963, LAC, RG 25, vol. 5181, file 5724-2-40; Cabinet Conclusions, 6 June 1963, LAC, RG 2.

31 Cabinet Conclusions, 11 December 1963, LAC, RG 2.

32 Ibid.

33 Ross Campbell, "Memorandum to Mr. Martin," 13 March 1964, LAC, RG 25, vol. 10130, file 21-14-11-Cyprus. As an anonymous DEA source explained to the Ottawa press, "Ireland triggered Sweden. Actually, the Irish agreement was a bit of a surprise." See "Martin Spurred Cyprus Force Decision," *Toronto Star*, 14 March 1964.

34 Allan James, *Keeping the Peace in the Cyprus Crisis of 1963–64* (London: Palgrave, 2002), 110–11.

35 Walker to Martin, 25 March 1964, LAC, Martin Papers, vol. 251, file EA.

36 Quoted in John Saywell, ed., *Canadian Annual Review for 1964* (Toronto: University of Toronto Press, 1965), 231.

37 Pearson to Martin, 22 June 1964, LAC, Martin Papers, vol. 275, file: Birthday Greetings.

38 Story interview with Martin, [1969–70,] LAC, Martin Papers, vol. 351, tape 2, side 2.

39 Pickersgill, quoted in Donald Page to File, 6 October 1982, Global Affairs Canada, CIH-330, file 7-5-2-7.

40 Peter Jackman, "Parliament: Repatriating Paul for Duty on the Home Front," *Ottawa Journal*, 18 December 1964.

41 For details, see Greg Donaghy, *Grit: The Life and Politics of Paul Martin Sr.* (Vancouver: UBC Press, 2015), 220–21.

42 Escott Reid, Confidential Note, March 1965, LAC, Escott Reid Papers, vol. 33, file 22.
43 Pearson, *Mike*, 3:126–27.
44 Paul Martin, "At the Right Hand: A Record of Canadian Foreign Policy, 1963–1968," manuscript, author's collection, 396.
45 Martin to Rusk, 18 January 1965, LAC, Martin Papers, vol. 226, file 14.
46 Greg Donaghy, *Tolerant Allies: Canada and the United States* (Montreal and Kingston: McGill-Queen's University Press, 2001), 127–30.
47 Quoted in Peter Stursberg, *Lester Pearson and the American Dilemma* (Toronto: Doubleday, 1980), 218.
48 Ibid.
49 Martin, Memorandum for the Prime Minister, 20 January 1966, LAC, RG 25, vol. 9397, file 20-22-Viets-2-1-1.
50 Quoted in George Herring, *The Secret Diplomacy of the Vietnam War: The Negotiating Volumes of the Pentagon Papers* (Austin: University of Texas Press, 1983), 171.
51 Ottawa to Brussels, Tel. Y-405, 6 June 1966, LAC, RG 25, vol. 9404, file 20-22-Viets-2-1-1.
52 Saigon to Ottawa, Tel. 524, 18 June 1966, LAC, RG 25, vol. 9404, file 20-22-Viets-2-1-1.
53 Herring, *Secret Diplomacy*, 197.
54 John English, *The Worldly Years: The Life of Lester Pearson, 1949–1972* (Toronto: Knopf, 1992), 357. See also Walter Gordon, Memorandum: Lunch with LBP, 30 March 1966, LAC, Walter Gordon Papers, vol. 16, file: Memos to L.B. Pearson.
55 Author interview with Richard O'Hagan, 30 June 2012.
56 Paul Hellyer, *Damn the Torpedoes: My Fight to Unify Canada's Armed Forces* (Toronto: McClelland and Stewart, 1990), 209.
57 Quoted in John Saywell, ed., *Canadian Annual Review for 1966* (Toronto: University of Toronto Press, 1967), 15.
58 Paul Martin, *A Very Public Life*, vol. 2 (Toronto: Deneau, 1995), 609.
59 Peter Newman, "Fight for Control of Liberal Party Now Under Way," *Ottawa Journal*, 16 December 1965.
60 Peter Newman, "Strange Case of Paul Martin: A Politician Turns to Statecraft," *Vancouver Sun*, 5 February 1966.
61 Gallup Poll, 31 March 1966, Canadian Institute of Public Opinion (CIPO) Archives.
62 Gallup Poll, 28 May 1966, CIPO.
63 Richard Jackson, "Plot and Counter-Plot and Double Agents," *St. John's Evening Telegram*, 16 November 1966.
64 Roy MacLaren, *The Fundamental Things Apply: A Memoir* (Toronto: University of Toronto Press, 2010), 77.
65 Marcel Cadieux, Diary, 17 May 1967, LAC, Marcel Cadieux Papers, vol. 12, file 12-9.
66 Marcel Cadieux, Diary, 8 June 1967, LAC, Marcel Cadieux Papers, vol. 12, file 12-9.

67 Marcel Cadieux, Diary, 29 November 1967, LAC, Marcel Cadieux Papers, vol. 12, file 12-9.
68 Martin, *So Many Worlds*, 618.
69 "'Impatient' Successor Sparks Pearson Gibe," *Montreal Star*, 22 March 1968.
70 Marcel Cadieux, Diary, 29 November 1967.

Stephen Azzi

5 Lester Pearson and the Substance of the Sixties

Lester Pearson seemed out of place in the Sixties. He was the consummate insider in a time of rebellion, a senior citizen in an age of youth, a weak public speaker in an era of stirring oratory, a man who looked uncertain in a period of passionate conviction. In striking contrast, John F. Kennedy seemed to personify the Sixties. Articulate and attractive, he mastered television, the new medium of political communication. Kennedy's youth and eloquence captured the idealism and hope of an age when people believed that government could solve problems, people could prosper, and the United States could live up to its founding principles. If Kennedy appeared cool and self-assured, Pearson displayed all the awkwardness of a history professor. He was ill-suited for television, unable to simplify issues and dependent on the vague phrases of the professional diplomat. His face was drawn in soft lines, lacking the edges required to stand out on the small screen. His slightly high-pitched voice would have been forgettable if not for the lisp, which seemed more pronounced on television than in person. He swayed as his spoke, his head moving around the television frame as if it were a pendulum, and he smiled at the wrong time, giving him a smug look. Groovy he was not.

Appearances were deceiving. If writer and cartoonist Jules Feiffer could describe Kennedy as "a wonderful stylist and a bad president," it seems right to call Pearson a bad stylist and a superb prime minister.[1] He accomplished more in five years than any other Canadian leader, and his achievements were in tune with the age – except for those that were ahead of their time. For at least half a century after his retirement, the symbols of Canadian identity were those Pearson had given the country: the flag, peacekeeping, bilingualism, public health care, the Canada Pension Plan, and other generous social programs.

In the emerging literature on Canada in the Sixties, Pearson merits only rare mentions. When he does appear, it is as a pro-American prime minister who led a scandal-plagued government. Bryan Palmer's *Canada's 1960s* devotes several pages to political scandals and a few to the fractious flag debate, but ignores health insurance, the Canada Pension Plan, the guaranteed income supplement, and the Pearson government's other considerable achievements.[2] These innovations changed the lives of Canadians but seem not to deserve any attention because they came from elites in Ottawa, not protestors in the street. The grassroots activists were a significant and compelling part of the Sixties story, but important, too, were the politicians and bureaucrats who brought about real and long-term change.

Pearson understood that Canadian society was undergoing a fundamental transformation and that government must change to keep up. The availability of effective birth control altered social mores, fuelling a sexual revolution and transforming the family. Established churches lost much of their influence, as attitudes changed on divorce and countless other issues. In Quebec, the Quiet Revolution of the early 1960s altered views of religion, the state, and society. As the decade wore on, many Quebeckers became dissatisfied with Canada and turned to separatism. A quieter revolution was taking place in English Canada: although remaining in the Commonwealth, Canadians were much less likely to believe that Canada – or even English Canada – was British.

Pearson was an optimist, and he came to power in an optimistic age. Technology was leaping forward, health care was improving, unemployment was low, wages were rising, and the economy was growing. It was a time of abundance, when standards of living rose rapidly and prosperity kindled hope for a better tomorrow. In 1959, pollsters discovered that 52 percent of Canadians thought the world would be a better place in ten years' time, with only 16 percent thinking it would be worse. More than 74 percent of Canadians considered themselves fortunate to live in a time of rapid scientific progress, and 83 percent expected a cure for cancer within twenty years.[3]

Yet the challenges were many. In the midst of plenty, countless individuals remained poor and disadvantaged, as economic and political disparities persisted both within Canada and around the world. In Africa, people demanded self-determination, forging movements that won independence for former colonies. In Western democracies, minorities struggled for recognition of their civil rights. The women's liberation movement in Canada and elsewhere sought equality in the workplace, liberalized divorce laws, legalized abortion, and daycare for children whose mothers worked outside the home. Support for Quebec independence grew rapidly. Successive Quebec premiers demanded greater powers for the provincial government, while a terrorist group, the Front de libération du Québec (FLQ), bombed federal government and corporate targets. *Silent Spring*, the 1962 book by American marine biologist Rachel Carson, exposed the devastating effects of pesticides, fuelling concern for an endangered environment. In Canada – as throughout the Western world – many feared nuclear war and came to distrust the motives of the United States, particularly in light of that country's disastrous intervention in Vietnam.

Slowly, the optimism of the early Sixties turned to disappointment and then to cynicism. The year 1965 was a symbolic turning point, with war breaking out between India and Pakistan over Kashmir, the US occupying the Dominican Republic out of fear that the civil war there would end with a communist victory, and protests against the war in Vietnam becoming common after US president Lyndon Johnson began an extensive aerial bombing campaign and sent large numbers of ground troops to Southeast Asia. The US Congress passed the Voting Rights Act, a triumph for the Civil Rights Movement but one that did nothing to alleviate poverty among blacks. Frustrated by discrimination in housing, education, and employment, blacks in the Los Angeles neighbourhood of Watts rioted for six days. In Selma, Alabama, police attacked peaceful civil rights protesters, clubbing them with truncheons and burning their eyes with tear gas. These events reverberated in Canada. About one thousand Canadians showed their support for the Selma protestors by demonstrating outside the US consulate in Toronto. As many as six thousand gathered at the University of Toronto for a teach-in, a combination seminar and protest, patterned after anti-war rallies on US college campuses. Over the next several years, thousands more protested before the US embassy in Ottawa and US consulates in Toronto and Montreal, demanding that the Americans pull out of Vietnam.

Two songs, both topping music charts in Canada and the US in the pivotal year of 1965, showed the shifting mood of the Sixties. Sonny and Cher's "I Got You Babe" captured the decade's early idealism. It was a goofy love song about two young people who were not at all worried about being broke because they had each other. In stark contrast, "Eve of Destruction" reflected the bitterness and cynicism of the later 1960s. Written by P.F. Sloan and sung – or snarled – by Barry McGuire, the song was an extended rant about violence around the globe, racism at home in the United States, the threat of nuclear war, and the omnipresence of hatred in the world. In the mid-1960s, the cuddliness of "I Got You Babe" gave way to the anger of "Eve of Destruction."

But Pearson was not discouraged, despair being foreign to his nature. He maintained his optimism, always determined to pursue progressive policies. The Great Depression of the 1930s had made social insurance popular; the prosperity of the 1950s and 1960s made it possible. Circumstances had combined to provide an opening for government action, and Pearson knew he had to act quickly to take advantage of it. Because of Pearson's tendency to tell people what they wanted to hear, some commentators have questioned his commitment to reform.[4] Yet he signalled his intent clearly when he chose his closest advisers, radicals promoted over the objections of the Liberal party's old guard. Pearson's top adviser was Toronto businessman Walter Gordon, chair of the policy committee at the party's national rally in 1961 and chair of the Liberal election campaigns in 1962, 1963, and 1965. Gordon dominated the party in the early 1960s, solving financial problems, firing many employees, hiring individuals of his own choosing, functioning throughout as though he were party president.[5] His 1961 book, *Troubled Canada,* called for public health insurance, a contributory pension plan, programs to help areas of low-employment, and measures to ensure that young people could attend university whatever their financial status.[6] When Pearson became prime minister, Gordon became an unusual creature: a finance minister who said "yes" to proposals for new spending. In this, Gordon found an ally in Tom Kent, a former editor of the *Winnipeg Free Press* and Pearson's chief policy adviser. On the far left of the Liberal Party, Kent wrote the party platforms in 1962 and 1963, and worked tirelessly to implement them. Joining him on the party's left wing were Maurice Lamontagne and

Allan J. MacEachen, both of whom worked in the leader's office in the Opposition years and became ministers in the Pearson government. "These were idea men," Pearson later recalled, "with ideas very much in harmony with my own."[7]

The prime minister was not the driving force behind every one of his government's policies. Pearson's role was often to provide strategic direction: he determined the government's priorities and recruited the individuals who designed and implemented programs. He used his talents as a negotiator to keep his diverse party united and to obtain provincial agreement for his programs. Yet he was also the mainspring behind several of the key initiatives and, in some areas, like Canada–US relations and Quebec's place in Canada, played a direct day-to-day role in managing the issue.

No Canadian government did more to help the poor than Pearson's. "There is a moral obligation to assist," he later said. "It is part of the higher nature of man to help those who need help. It is only right for the strong to help the weak, for those who have to share with those who have not."[8] When the Pearson government took office, millions of Canadians lived in poverty.[9] Pearson launched a war on poverty in 1965, overseen by a cabinet committee – with Pearson as chair, MacEachen as vice-chair, and Kent as secretary – and spearheaded by a secretariat inside the Privy Council Office, the prime minister's government department. The initiative's most notable measure was the Canada Assistance Plan, under which the federal government paid half the cost of provincial social assistance programs. Previously, Ottawa had shared the costs of allowances for people with disabilities, the elderly, and the unemployed. Now the federal government would also contribute to nursing-home care, allowances for widows and needy mothers, and a range of other provincial social programs.

One indication of the persistence of poverty was the condition of housing in Canada. In the early 1960s, many Canadians still lived in over-crowded, dilapidated homes. One in ten metropolitan homes lacked adequate plumbing.[10] In response, Ottawa provided low-interest loans to provinces or municipalities, paying up to 90 percent of the cost of constructing low-income housing, and covered half the losses of operating subsidized housing projects. More than 140,000 dwellings were built under the loan program in the next fourteen years.[11]

Poverty was common among the elderly. One problem was that more than half of Canadian workers had no workplace pension, leaving many to live out their final years in destitution. Pearson's government undertook three measures to end poverty among seniors. Old Age Security was raised from sixty-five dollars to seventy-five dollars per month and was made available at age sixty-five instead of seventy. The Canada Pension Plan was launched, covering 92 percent of the workforce and providing about one-quarter of a retired person's income.[12] Finally, the Guaranteed Income Supplement was implemented in 1966, mandating a minimal income for seniors.

The Pearson government recognized that the poor were not evenly distributed across the country but lived disproportionately in rural areas and in the Atlantic provinces. In the early 1960s, more than 40 percent of Canadian farms were not economically viable.[13] In the late 1960s, 40.1 percent of families in Newfoundland and Labrador and 52.5 percent in Prince Edward Island were poor, striking figures when compared to the 12.2 percent of Ontario families and 15.9 percent of British Columbia families that fell into this category.[14] The Pearson government's Area Development Program offered incentives for companies to establish plants in places with high unemployment. The Fund for Rural Economic Development created comprehensive development plans for five chronically poor areas of Canada, promoting industrial development and tourism, and improving infrastructure, services, education, and training. The Manpower Mobility Program offered loans and grants to individuals willing to leave economically depressed areas to take up jobs elsewhere. The Cape Breton Development Corporation phased out the island's dying coal industry, operating the mines for several years while working to diversify the local economy.

The Pearson government also aimed to aid poor communities by harnessing the enthusiasm and energy of youth. The Company of Young Canadians (CYC) fostered community development programs to help disadvantaged Canadians improve their lives. CYC volunteers created drop-in centres for troubled youth, set up food co-ops and credit unions, helped inner-city residents fight plans to tear down homes to make way for new development, and assisted First Nations and Métis to take greater control over their communities. A well-intentioned program, the CYC was highly controversial, in part because of the way the volunteers exploited the organization's autonomy, frequently attacking the government that had created and funded the organization. "It is existing governments, and related power structures, that are by nature pernicious, and ... organizing to fight them is about the most valuable and relevant political action people can perform," one CYC volunteer later wrote, reflecting the view of many of her colleagues.[15] In Quebec, FLQ members infiltrated the CYC. The organization's lax administration reflected the unruly spirit of its volunteers, making it an easy target for critics. These factors led the Pierre Trudeau government to revoke the CYC's independence in 1970 and then to fold it in 1976.

Public health care was the government's most celebrated achievement. Canadians were generally healthy, but not as healthy as people in countries with similar standards of living. Canada's infant mortality rate surpassed that of the US, England and Wales, Denmark, Norway, and Sweden. Life expectancy at birth was higher in Canada than in the US but lower than in other comparable countries.[16] In 1966, the government introduced the Medical Care Act, pledging to cover half the cost of provincial medicare plans so long as they were universal, comprehensive in their coverage, portable from one province to another, and publicly administered on a non-profit basis. After the early 1970s, when the program came fully into effect, no Canadian was denied medical care because of an inability to pay.

The Pearson government also sought to provide access to education for those of limited means. Many young people never finished high school, and only 5 percent, mostly members of the economic elite, attended college or university. Under Pearson, family allowances were extended to cover sixteen and seventeen year olds in school. The government ended the Dominion-Provincial Student Aid Program, an archaic program that had benefitted an average of fewer than three thousand students annually. Instead, Pearson's government created the Canada Student Loans program, which provided assistance to any full-time student in financial need. By 1972–73, 122,000 students were benefitting from the program.[17] Pearson's government also doubled federal spending on universities, allowing them to accommodate baby boomers and growing numbers of working-class students.[18] When Pearson came to office in 1963, only 146,827 full-time undergraduate students were enrolled in Canadian universities. This number almost doubled in five short years, rising to 239,723 by the time he stepped down as prime minister.[19]

The fight against racial discrimination was a defining global struggle of the Sixties. In Canada, the government and courts had slowly recognized the principle of racial equality, but discriminatory laws and regulations remained in force. In 1962, John Diefenbaker's government had moved towards a colour-blind immigration policy but had not travelled the full distance, maintaining quotas on immigrants from South Asia and restrictions on who could enter the country as a sponsored immigrant. Canadian citizens or landed immigrants could sponsor a wide range of relatives from preferred countries (any country in Europe or the Americas, plus Egypt, Israel, and Lebanon), including adult children, siblings, and the siblings' family members. But only a narrow range of immediate relatives from Asia or Africa – spouses, parents, grandparents, and unmarried children under the age of twenty-one – could come as sponsored immigrants. Diefenbaker's government also continued the practice of recruiting immigrants from Britain, Western Europe, and the United States but not from elsewhere. In 1967, Pearson's government eliminated these last vestiges of racial discrimination from Canada's immigration policy, inaugurating a system that assigned points to applicants based on factors such as their education, skills, and age. Canadian citizens and immigrants now could sponsor family members regardless of their country of origin. The Pearson government opened immigration offices in Islamabad, Tokyo, Manila, Port of Spain, and Kingston, Jamaica. Within a few years, Asia became the main source of immigrants to Canada, fundamentally changing the face of Canadian society.

In the 1960s, sexism was still socially acceptable in Canada. Most women were limited to jobs as teachers, nurses, secretaries, and receptionists. Few women worked as school principals, university deans, newspaper editors, or corporate executives. No women, not even female reporters, could attend the annual dinner of the Canadian Parliamentary Press Gallery. No woman was a member of a stock exchange in Canada. Women could not join Ottawa's prestigious Rideau Club or many of the country's other exclusive clubs. In 1963, only six women were elected to Parliament, 2 percent of all MPs. Only one woman – Ellen Fairclough – had ever served in cabinet. No women had served on the Supreme Court of Canada or the highest courts in the provinces.

In 1961, the average income for women was less than half of that for men.[20] This disparity was partly because women were confined to low-paying positions and partly because women were frequently paid less than men for the same job. This was a perfectly legal practice. In a 1968 case, an Ontario Supreme Court judge ruled that it was "common sense" that a policewoman in Sault Ste. Marie should earn less than a policeman in the same city. The woman who had pursued the case was "a menace to the esprit-de-corps" of the force, according to the judge.[21]

Pearson's attitudes towards women are not easy to define. Many writers have simplified his views by recounting the same anecdote. In 1965, Pauline Jewett, an intelligent and capable Liberal MP, asked Pearson if he would appoint her to the cabinet. According to Jewett, Pearson responded that there was already one woman in cabinet and he did not think Judy LaMarsh intended to leave.[22] It is not clear whether Pearson believed there could only be one woman in cabinet or if he was making an inappropriate joke to rescue himself from an awkward conversation. Certainly, there were good reasons for Jewett not to be appointed to cabinet – reasons that had nothing to do with her gender.[23]

Like many men of his era, Pearson was uncomfortable when discussing women's issues. This emerged clearly in a 1972 CBC television program, four years after he left office. When the interviewer asked the former prime minister about "women's lib," Pearson chuckled and seemed to blush: "Well, I think there is an awful lot to be done to bring women into the world [and] ... give them a chance that they've never had. But I find it difficult, myself, to completely ignore the facts of biology." When asked about having Judy LaMarsh in cabinet, he gave an awkward response: "She didn't expect to be treated as a woman – and she wasn't treated as a woman. And that of course is the way it should be." He then followed with a vague explanation of his views on female equality: "I think it's rather silly to ignore the differences completely, and it's equally silly to divide them so that women have one category of occupation and develop it only and men have another."[24]

Yet Pearson had close personal and professional relationships with strong women. As journalist Christina McCall observed, he sought the views of the intelligent women who surrounded him, including his wife and the wives of his friends.[25] He was close to Winnipeg Liberal MP Margaret Konantz, who was a more likely candidate for cabinet than Jewett. He maintained a friendship with Barbara Ward, the British economist who wrote a foreword to the British edition of Pearson's memoirs, describing him as having a "profound sense of everyone else's interest and value."[26] He recognized the ability of his executive assistant, Mary Macdonald, allowing her a great degree of latitude in running his life. In the 1960s, she was the only woman to work as executive assistant to a cabinet minister.[27] Pearson appointed LaMarsh as minister of national health and welfare, a critical portfolio that put her in charge of two of the government's key initiatives: the Canada Pension Plan and health insurance. According to LaMarsh, Pearson was not "anti-female." She never felt that he discriminated against her in a period when discrimination against women was a matter of course.[28]

Pearson believed in the equality of women and in the principle of social justice, though women's issues were not among his highest priorities. In 1964, after confirming that the provinces were committed to a policy of equality of opportunity, his government ratified an international labour convention calling for an end to workplace discrimination based on race, colour, sex, or religion. The convention had been drafted in 1958, but the Diefenbaker government had never ratified it. Pearson then established the Royal Commission on the Status of Women, an achievement that scholars often discount because he only did so after intense lobbying from LaMarsh and the Committee for the Equality of Women in Canada, a coalition of women's organizations that eventually became the National Action Committee on the Status of Women. Much has been made of the account of Laura Sabia, the organization's national chair, who claimed that Pearson refused to appoint the commission but changed his mind three days after she threatened to rally 2 million women in the streets of Ottawa.[29] In fact, Pearson had not rejected the idea of a commission, as Sabia claimed. The same day that the *Globe and Mail* reported on her threat of a mass protest, Pearson circulated a memorandum asking cabinet to consider creating a commission, a document that would have been in the works for at least several days and probably many weeks.[30] Once the commission was appointed, he supported it fully. According to Clerk of the Privy Council Gordon Robertson, Canada's senior public servant, Pearson "took a personal interest in the commission" and asked Robertson to do all he could to help the chair, Florence Bird, in her work.[31] In contrast, Progressive Conservative MP Terence Nugent voiced the views of many men in the 1960s when he dismissed the commission as "utter balderdash":

> Nobody married needs to be educated about the status of women. Anybody with half a brain in his head knows he has to learn two things quickly: to say "Yes, dear" when she is right, and "Yes, dear"

> when she is wrong. That is the situation a man has to cope with, and it needs no royal commission to tell him that.[32]

The commission's impact was significant. It made women's issues the subject of national debate, holding six months of hearings and attracting extensive media coverage. The commission's 1970 report contained a long list of recommendations that aimed for the equal treatment of women under the law and in the workplace: women should receive equal pay for work of equal value and maternity leave benefits; the federal government should appoint more women to the Senate and hire more women in managerial positions; the federal and provincial governments should create a national daycare program to allow mothers to participate in the labour force; and abortion should be legalized for women who were fewer than twelve weeks pregnant and for others if the pregnancy threatened their physical or mental health. In the subsequent decade, most of the recommendations were implemented, in whole or in part, transforming the lives of women in Canada.[33] The commission was, in political scientist Naomi Black's words, "the first success of the second wave of Canadian feminism."[34]

When Pearson became prime minister, Canadian divorce laws were stuck in the nineteenth century. The British North America Act, 1867, had made divorce a federal responsibility, but Ottawa never passed national legislation on the issue. Each province retained the acts that were in effect when it joined Confederation, subject only to amendments by the federal Parliament, resulting in a patchwork of laws across the country. On the request of Ontario's government, Ottawa passed a divorce law for that province in 1930, a replica of England's 1870 legislation. There was no law in Quebec or Newfoundland, meaning that residents of those provinces could only obtain a divorce through an act of Parliament. For residents in nine of ten provinces (all but Nova Scotia), a divorce was granted only if the plaintiff could prove spousal adultery, making it impossible for a woman to end a marriage to a cruel or abusive husband, or to a husband who had deserted her.[35]

Canadian divorce practices lagged behind those of many other Western jurisdictions and domestic opinion. Britain had liberalized its divorce legislation in 1937, recognizing cruelty and desertion as legitimate reasons to dissolve a marriage. In many US states, there were several grounds for divorce, and a plaintiff was not required to offer any proof. In Canada, public opinion was changing rapidly. In 1943, a Gallup Poll showed that 24 percent of respondents thought it too difficult to get a divorce in Canada. By 1960, that number had risen to 39 percent.[36] Just two months after Pearson took office in 1963, Gallup reported that 50 percent now thought it too difficult to get a divorce in Canada, 21 percent thought the requirements were "about right," and 17 percent considered the process "too easy."[37] The Pearson government began to act in 1966, establishing a parliamentary committee to study the issue. In 1968, Parliament passed the Divorce Act, allowing courts to grant a divorce when a marriage had permanently broken down.

Pearson pursued changes to the laws governing reproduction and sexuality. In late 1967, the government introduced extensive revisions to the Criminal Code, proposing to decriminalize abortion and the advertisement or sale of contraceptives. In the 1960s, pharmacists were still fined for distributing contraceptives. Doctors were jailed for providing abortions, and anyone helping a woman to obtain an abortion, including her husband, could also be charged, with the result that the procedure was frequently carried out in unsanitary conditions by people without the necessary training. Thousands of women died from botched abortions. Under Pearson's legislation, it would become legal to advertise and sell contraception, and women could obtain an abortion if a committee of doctors believed her physical and mental health was in danger. Pearson's Criminal Code revisions also decriminalized homosexual acts between consenting adults in private, legislation introduced more than a year before the Stonewall Riots, often seen as the beginning of the gay rights movement in the US. In Canada, public opinion was almost evenly split on the question of whether homosexual sex should be a crime.[38] On this, as on many other issues, Pearson's government was ahead of its times.

The Criminal Code amendments on abortion, contraception, and homosexuality are usually credited not to Pearson but to Pierre Trudeau, who became justice minister in April 1967. Trudeau memorably justified the measures by saying, "the state has no business in the nation's bedrooms" and he was prime minister when the legislation finally passed.[39] Yet others deserve as much or more recognition. Minister of Justice Lucien Cardin drafted and introduced the bill before Trudeau entered cabinet, and the revisions were very much in line with the Pearson government's overall program of reform.

Pearson deserves credit, too, for another justice initiative: ending capital punishment. In the mid-1960s, most Canadians supported the death penalty.[40] Pearson argued that hanging was not a deterrent but the product of "a desire for retaliation and for revenge." Capital punishment "morally diminished" Canadians and could not be justified "in any society that aspires to become truly civilized."[41] When he became prime minister, Pearson effectively abolished the death penalty by insisting that cabinet use its prerogative to commute death sentences. In 1967, Parliament passed a five-year moratorium on capital punishment, except for the murders of on-duty police and corrections officers. The Trudeau government extended the moratorium in 1973 before abolishing capital punishment in 1976. Although LaMarsh often complained of Pearson's lack of backbone, she recognized his "single-minded determination to do away with the death penalty," noting that he "would bring up the death-penalty question again and again."[42]

Pearson showed that same sense of resolve over the place of Quebec in Confederation. Although he spoke French poorly, Pearson understood the situation in Quebec better than virtually any other senior politician in English Canada. He was ahead of many in his own party and far ahead of the Progressive Conservative opposition in recognizing that Canada was experiencing what he called a "serious crisis of national unity."[43] Although Pearson had long favoured a strong central government, he came to believe that some decentralization was necessary to preserve the country. He also understood that the federal government could no longer function almost exclusively in English.

Pearson explained his views in a pivotal speech on 17 December 1962, four months before becoming prime minister. The difficulty was that English and French Canadians understood Confederation differently. For francophones, Canada was a partnership between English and French, "a bilingual and bicultural nation." But for most anglophones, the country was composed of "an English-speaking Canada with a bilingual Quebec." In Pearson's view, Canada needed to become a "true partnership" – and needed to do so soon, before large numbers of Quebeckers turned to separatism. French Canadians should enjoy "equal and full opportunity to participate in all federal government services, in which their own language [would] be fully recognized." The government should work to see that francophones were properly represented in professional and administrative jobs in the public service and that the education system provided the opportunity for young Canadians to become bilingual.[44]

Upon taking office, Pearson quickly ensured a strong francophone presence in Ottawa. Of the twenty-six ministers in his first cabinet, ten were French Canadians, twice as many as there had been at the end of the Diefenbaker era.[45] Pearson encouraged francophone ministers to speak French in cabinet meetings, making him probably the first prime minister to do so. "I was anxious to establish at once that every French-speaking member had the right to use his own language in Cabinet if he so desired," Pearson recalled.[46] In 1965, he decided that his cabinet and caucus needed more robust representation from francophone Quebec, so he recruited labour leader Jean Marchand, journalist Gérard Pelletier, and law professor Pierre Trudeau as Liberal candidates for that year's federal election. Marchand joined the cabinet after the election, and Trudeau became justice minister in 1967. All three men would play key roles in national politics, with Trudeau serving as prime minister for fifteen years.

Three months after taking office, Pearson established the Royal Commission on Bilingualism and Biculturalism. Its mandate was broad: "To recommend what steps should be taken to develop the Canadian Confederation on the basis of an equal partnership between the two founding races, taking into account the contribution made by the other ethnic groups to the cultural enrichment of Canada."[47] Few royal commissions have had as significant an impact on Canada. Not only did the commission's recommendations lead to the recognition of English and French as official languages in Canada, but also its appointment slowed the drift towards separatism in Quebec. "By establishing the commission in Bilingualism and Biculturalism he bought precious time, educated the rest of Canada in the French Fact, and began to change the climate of politics subtly, gropingly, but decisively," wrote journalist Bruce Hutchison.[48] Another journalist, *Montreal Star* editor George Ferguson, agreed: "Another year or two of the Diefenbaker stand-pattism would have ended in rupture. What Pearson gained was time, and time was all important. To say therefore that he saved Confederation is ... no more than the truth."[49]

Pearson has earned similar praise for his solution to the Canada–Quebec conflict over pensions, a skirmish that could have ended disastrously. Before coming to office, the Pearson Liberals had promised to launch a national contributory pension plan. To Pearson's surprise,

Quebec had its own ideas, which were much further developed than those of the federal government. The prime minister showed enormous flexibility, jettisoning his government's proposals and creating a plan on the Quebec model. Pearson could not stop Quebec from operating its own program, but he did ensure that the Canada Pension Plan and the Quebec Pension Plan were identical in all details, including contribution levels and benefits. He also convinced Quebec and the other provinces to accept a constitutional amendment to allow the federal plan to provide survivors' and disability benefits. Pearson's adaptability meant that Canadians ultimately ended up with a better plan, and Quebec did not set off entirely on its own. "I think there was a risk of Confederation coming apart at the seams over that whole social security package, and that was avoided," recalled NDP member of Parliament Stanley Knowles.[50]

Fostering national unity meant ensuring that national symbols had meaning for French Canadians and for the growing number of Canadians whose ancestors came from neither the British Isles nor France. Pearson led the drive to create a distinctive Canadian flag despite indifference in the Liberal caucus and hostility in much of English Canada. He persevered through six months of rancorous debate in the House of Commons, even when advisers urged him to put the flag aside to address more pressing matters. "If he had made up his mind there was something he really wanted to do, he got his own way in the end," cabinet minister Jack Pickersgill later remembered. "This whole flag business showed how tough he really could be."[51] Pearson then proposed that Parliament declare "O Canada" the national anthem. Still reeling from the exhausting flag debate, cabinet ministers recoiled, but Pearson was willing to take on another battle.[52] A parliamentary committee recommended the measure, but a dispute with the song's copyright holders meant that the anthem only became official in 1980, after the English lyrics entered the public domain. Pearson succeeded in creating the Order of Canada, the country's highest honour, despite the opposition of senior cabinet ministers Mitchell Sharp, Jack Pickersgill, and Walter Gordon, who believed it inappropriate for a democratic state to bestow distinctions on individuals. But, as Pickersgill recalled, "Mike wanted it, and when a Canadian prime minister is set on something he gets it, whatever his ministers think."[53]

Pearson's preoccupation with Quebec shaped the choice of his successor. In a word, Pearson made Pierre Trudeau. Pearson recruited the Montreal professor into politics and quickly promoted him to justice minister, a senior portfolio. Pearson cast Trudeau in a leading role at the televised federal-provincial conference of February 1968, where Trudeau captured public attention by confronting Quebec premier Daniel Johnston. Pearson helped persuade a reluctant Trudeau to seek the party leadership. Although Pearson was carefully neutral during the leadership race, his earlier actions had pushed Trudeau within reach of the highest office. Trudeau's confrontational policies towards Quebec have long been disputed, but most agree that he ended FLQ terrorism and won the 1980 referendum on separatism. Trudeau's leadership rivals, Robert Winters, Paul Hellyer, or even the elder Paul Martin, likely could not have accomplished either feat.

With his long experience as a diplomat, Pearson was deeply concerned about international issues, including poverty in the developing world. In 1950, he had attended the Colombo Conference of foreign ministers, which drafted a plan for the economic development of South and Southeast Asia. The next year, Pearson convinced a sceptical cabinet to support the plan, a decision that marked the birth of a formal Canadian foreign aid program. As prime minister, Pearson more than tripled the federal government's international aid budget from $69.5 million in 1963 to $253.2 million in 1968.[54] Pearson also extended Canadian aid for the first time to Latin American countries and francophone Africa. In 1967, he announced plans to establish the International Development Research Centre (IDRC) to study how best to help developing countries. After leaving politics, Pearson chaired both the IDRC and the World Bank's Commission on International Development, which proposed that rich countries give 0.7 percent of their GDP to the developing world, a target adopted by the United Nations General Assembly in 1970.

Pearson understood that the international security situation was changing and that Canadian defence policies had to change with it. Having recovered from the Second World War, Europe was better able to defend itself. At the same time, decolonization had unleashed conflicts in the developing world. In response, Pearson's government shifted the emphasis of Canadian defence policy, the 1964 *White Paper on Defence* reorganizing the Canadian armed forces to transfer resources to peacekeeping and away from NORAD and NATO. As Isabel Campbell notes (Chapter 13, this volume), this reorganization meant that Canadian Forces had to be more adaptable, ready to respond to new circumstances, not least of which was a reduced need for NATO in an era of détente.

One of the government's most contentious measures was to unify Canada's armed forces, a measure that Pearson advocated before Defence Minister Paul Hellyer did.[55] The defence establishment had long been inefficient and wasteful. The 1964 White Paper announced plans to unify the army, navy, and air force into a single service under a new chief of the defence staff. Later governments changed some aspects of these reforms (restoring distinct uniforms and ranks, for instance), but no one reversed the unification of the services, recognizing the value of a more efficient and coordinated military.

Pearson's greatest challenge in foreign affairs was to manage the relationship with the United States. His goal was to maintain a measured distance from Canada's powerful neighbour: close, but not too close. Pearson understood the political, economic, and military benefits of an intimate relationship with the United States, but he had also long worried about the implications of American power. Pearson's first step as prime minister was to undo the damage of the early 1960s, damage caused, in large part, by Diefenbaker's refusal to keep his commitment to arm Bomarc missiles with nuclear warheads. Months before becoming prime minister, Pearson announced that his government would honour the obligation but would negotiate with the US to remove the nuclear weapons from Canada. A few weeks after taking office, Pearson met with John F. Kennedy at the president's summer home in Hyannis Port, Massachusetts. The two men got on exceptionally well in a meeting "tinged with euphoria," to quote Canadian ambassador Charles Ritchie.[56] As historian Greg Donaghy has shown, Pearson's government worked quietly with the United States to solve a range of economic and political problems.[57] Ottawa and Washington negotiated the Auto Pact, a managed trade agreement that stimulated Canadian industry and reduced Canada's chronic trade deficit with the United States.

At the same time, Pearson's government worked to offset the American economic and cultural influence in Canada. Ottawa blocked US banks from expanding their Canadian presence. Parliament created the Canadian Film Development Corporation to help fund Canadian movies and amended the Income Tax Act to encourage Canadian companies to advertise in domestic magazines rather than their foreign competitors. The Canadian Radio-Television Commission (CRTC) began regulating the broadcast industry, replacing the feeble Board of Broadcast Governors, and later imposed Canadian content quotas on radio stations.

Pearson had no doubt that Americans had blundered by intervening in Vietnam, but he believed that public condemnation of the US would do little to solve the problem. He explained his position to cabinet in May 1967:

> The important thing, from the point of view of the government's policy, was to end the war. It was not important at this point to establish blame or responsibility in connection with it ... [T]o concentrate condemnation and criticism on the United States, and to make public pronouncements to that effect, ... made no contribution to the achievement of the objective of ending the fighting.[58]

The prime minister counselled the US to find a face-saving way out, but President Johnson dismissed Pearson's advice. Behind closed doors, Pearson repeatedly advised Johnson to stop the bombing and offer to negotiate with North Vietnam.[59] In April 1965, less than two months after the US launched Operation Rolling Thunder, the sustained bombing of North Vietnam, Pearson called on the US to suspend the operation. In a speech at Temple University in Philadelphia, where he was receiving an award, Pearson suggested that Johnson halt the bombing in the hopes of opening negotiations with North Vietnam. For members of the growing anti-war movement, Pearson's speech was meek. It was not enough that Canada stayed out of the war and urged the US to get out as well: Canada should openly condemn Washington's actions, stop sharing with the US information gained through Canada's membership on the International Control Commission for Vietnam, abrogate the Canada–US defence production sharing agreements, and refuse to sell any materiel to the US. But from an American perspective, Canada had gone too far. Johnson berated Pearson for his speech, and elder statesman Dean Acheson mocked Canadian moralizing, describing Canada as the "stern daughter of the voice of God."[60]

Anti-war protestors play a starring role in the literature on Canada's Sixties, making Pearson appear behind the times; in fact, he was ahead of Canadian public opinion on Vietnam. In 1966, one year after the Temple University speech, a poll showed that 45 percent of respondents thought the Americans should continue or increase their attacks on Vietnam, while only 31 percent wanted the US to withdraw. Only in late 1967 did more Canadians prefer that the US pull out rather than continue the war.[61]

Pearson's decision to stay out of Vietnam had a larger significance. American liberalism died in the Vietnamese countryside in a war that discredited Lyndon Johnson and undermined the US economy. In 1969, Richard Nixon replaced Johnson as president, and the reform movement evaporated. Canadian liberalism survived for a generation, in part because Pearson had the good sense not to send troops to Southeast Asia. After Pearson left office, reform continued under Trudeau, albeit at a slower pace.

Pearson's government did not do everything that needed to be done – no government can. His cabinet paid insufficient attention to several significant issues, such as the desperate state of Indigenous peoples or, as Norman Hillmer, Daniel Macfarlane, and Michael Manulak point out in Chapter 15 (this volume), the environment. Still, the list of the Pearson government's accomplishments is astonishing, particularly since Pearson never had a majority in the Commons and many of his policies fell under provincial jurisdiction, meaning they could only be implemented with the approval of the provinces.

Lester Pearson did not appreciate rock 'n' roll, did not smoke marijuana, did not grow his hair long, and did not wear love beads. But then again, neither did most Canadians in the 1960s. What Pearson did was lead an innovative government, a government that was well in tune with the times and often pushed far ahead of public opinion, the most active government in Canadian history. A new world was dawning, and Pearson helped lead Canada towards it, completing the Canadian welfare state, doing more to help the poor than any other prime minister, beginning the overhaul of the archaic Criminal Code, creating a royal commission to promote women's equality, managing the Canada–US relationship better than could have been expected in those years, updating the symbols of Canada, and practising a flexible federalism that saved the country. He did it all in an awkward – almost bumbling – style, which prevented him from ever winning a majority government and ensured that few Canadians could identify any of his accomplishments at the end of his tenure.[62] At no other time in Canadian politics has there been such a victory of substance over image.

Notes

Thanks to Norman Hillmer and Tim Cook for their valuable comments on the manuscript, to Landon Pearson for sharing her insights on her father-in-law, to Kevin Brushett for help in understanding the Company of Young Canadians, and to Kurt Montgomery and Michael Chiarello for assistance with the research.

1 Jules Feiffer, "007 in the White House," *Newsweek*, 28 November 1983, 83.

2 Bryan Palmer, *Canada's 1960s: The Ironies of Identity in a Rebellious Era* (Toronto: University of Toronto Press, 2009). Similarly, several volumes of essays about the Sixties say little about the Pearson government: Dimitry Anastakis, ed., *The Sixties: Passion, Politics, and Style* (Montreal and Kingston: McGill-Queen's University Press, 2008); Lara Campbell, Dominique Clément, and Gregory Kealey, eds., *Debating Dissent: Canada and the Sixties* (Toronto: University of Toronto Press, 2012); Karen Dubinsky, et al., eds., *New World Coming: The Sixties and the Shaping of Global Consciousness* (Toronto: Between the Lines, 2009); M. Athena Palaeologu, ed., *The Sixties in Canada: A Turbulent and Creative Decade* (Montreal: Black Rose, 2009).

3 Canadian Institute of Public Opinion, poll 279, November 1959, perma.cc/RS2Q-K6GG. "It's Good to Be Alive," *Toronto Star*, 12 December 1959.

4 See, for example, Alvin Finkel, *Social Policy and Practice in Canada: A History* (Waterloo: Wilfrid Laurier University Press, 2006), 157–58.

5 Stephen Azzi, *Walter Gordon and the Rise of Canadian Nationalism* (Montreal and Kingston: McGill-Queen's University Press, 1999), chap. 3; Stephen Azzi, "'It Was Walter's View': Lester Pearson, the Liberal Party and Economic Nationalism," in *Pearson: The Unlikely Gladiator*, ed. Norman Hillmer, 104–16 (Montreal and Kingston: McGill-Queen's University Press, 1999).

6 Walter Gordon, *Troubled Canada: The Need for New Domestic Policies* (Toronto: McClelland and Stewart, 1961).

7 Lester Pearson, *Mike: The Memoirs of the Right Honourable Lester B. Pearson*, vol. 3 (Toronto: University of Toronto Press, 1975), 54.

8 Lester Pearson, "The Case for Cooperation," in *The Crisis of Development* (New York: Praeger, 1970), 32.

9 Economic Council of Canada, *Fifth Annual Review: The Challenge of Growth and Change* (Ottawa: Economic Council of Canada, 1968), chap. 6.

10 Benjamin Schlesinger, *Poverty in Canada and the United States: Overview and Annotated Bibliography* (Toronto: University of Toronto Press, 1966), 29.

11 Lynn Hannley, "Substandard Housing," in *House, Home, and Community: Progress in Housing Canadians, 1945–1986*, ed. John R. Miron (Montreal and Kingston: McGill-Queen's University Press, 1993), 206.

12 Dennis Guest, *The Emergence of Social Security in Canada*, 3rd ed. (Vancouver: UBC Press, 1997), 143.

13 M.W. Menzies, *Poverty in Canada: Its Nature, Significance and Implications for Public Policy* (Winnipeg: Manitoba Pool Elevators, 1965), 32.

14 The Dominion Bureau of Statistics avoided the words "poverty" and "poor," referring instead to "low-income" families. See *Statistics on Low Income in Canada, 1967* (Ottawa: Dominion Bureau of Statistics, 1971), 25.

15 Margaret Daly, *The Revolution Game: The Short, Unhappy Life of the Company of Young Canadians* (Toronto: New Press, 1970), 4–5. On the CYC, see Kevin Brushett's forthcoming *The Uncomfortable Few: The Company of Young Canadians and the Politics of Youth, 1965–1975*.

16 Canada, *Royal Commission on Health Services* [*Report*], vol. 1 (Ottawa: Royal Commission on Health Services, 1964), 150.

17 Organization for Economic Cooperation and Development, *Educational Policy and Planning: Canada, II* (Paris: Organisation for Economic Cooperation and Development, 1975), 9, 40.

18 The federal contribution to university operating expenditures went from $57.1 million in 1963 to $101.3 million in 1968. The federal contribution to capital expenditures rose from $11.2 million to $20.7 million in the same period. See F.H. Leacy, M.C. Urquhart, and K.A.H. Buckley, eds., *Historical Statistics of Canada*, 2nd ed. (Ottawa: Statistics Canada, 1983), series W519 and W526.

19 Ibid., series W455.

20 Jenny Podoluk, *Incomes of Canadians* (Ottawa: Dominion Bureau of Statistics, 1968), 9–10.

21 "Policewoman Chastised for Equal Pay Demand," *Montreal Gazette*, 23 January 1968.

22 Sydney Sharpe, *The Gilded Ghetto: Women and Political Power in Canada* (Toronto: HarperCollins, 1994), 81; Sherrill MacLaren, *Invisible Power: The Women Who Run Canada* (Toronto: Seal, 1991), 235; Patricia Myers, "'A Noble Effort': The National Federation of Liberal Women of Canada, 1928–1973," in *Beyond the Vote: Canadian Women and Politics*, ed. Linda Kealey and Joan Sangster (Toronto: University of Toronto Press, 1989), 45; Gertrude Robinson and Armande Saint-Jean, with Christine Rioux, "Women Politicians and Their Media Coverage: A Generational Analysis," in *Women in Canadian Politics: Toward Equity in Representation*, ed. Kathy Megyery (Toronto: Dundurn, 1991), 138; Linda Trimble and Jane Arscott, *Still Counting: Women in Politics across Canada* (Toronto: University of Toronto Press, 2003), 35; Marilyn Froggatt and Lorraine Hunter, *Pricetag: Canadian Women and the Stress of Success* (Toronto: Nelson, 1980), 145.

23 As Judy LaMarsh explained: "Pauline was quite unpopular in the caucus. I don't think she ever would have made the Cabinet, because she came in and at once showed her disdain for caucus ... she ... practically had nothing to do with members of the caucus, and she was quite sneery to and about them at caucus meetings." Interview with Judy LaMarsh, 28 May 1975, LAC, Peter Stursberg Papers, vol. 15, file 1.

24 The interviewer was Larry Zolf. Weekend, CBC Television, broadcast 31 December 1972, www.cbc.ca/archives/categories/politics/prime-ministers/lester-b-pearson-from-peacemaker-to-prime-minister/pearson-discusses-vietnam-and-womens-lib.html.

25 Christina McCall, "The Unlikely Gladiators: Pearson and Diefenbaker Remembered," in Hillmer, *Unlikely Gladiator*, 66.

26 Barbara Ward, foreword in Pearson, *Through Diplomacy to Politics: Memoirs, 1897–1948* (London: Victor Gollancz, 1973), xiii.

27 LaMarsh, *Memoirs*, 290; Peter Dempson, *Assignment Ottawa: Seventeen Years in the Press Gallery* (Toronto: General Publishing, 1968), 40. The only other woman to work as a senior political aide was Marianne Barrie, special assistant to Revenue Minister Edgar Benson.

28 Interview with Judy LaMarsh, 14 July 1976, LAC, Stursberg Papers, vol. 30, file 3.

29 Sabia's account can be found in Harriet Lyons, "Found Women: More Now and Future Heroines," *Ms.*, March 1973, 16, 18; Sylvia Fraser, "Laura Sabia: Not Exactly Mom and Apple Pie," *Chatelaine*, November 1975, 54–55, 98–99, 102–5; "How Laura Built a Lobby," *Saturday Night*, September 1978, 4. It has been repeated many times in various forms since the 1970s. See, for example: Penney Kome, *Women of Influence: Canadian Women and Politics* (Toronto: Doubleday, 1985), 81–82; MacLaren, *Invisible Power*, 79; Leslie Pal, *Interests of State: The Politics of Language, Multiculturalism, and Feminism in Canada* (Montreal and Kingston: McGill-Queen's University Press, 1993), 113; Peter Li, *The Making of Post-War Canada* (Toronto: Oxford University Press, 1996), 165n3; Susan Merritt, *Her Story III: Women from Canada's Past* (St. Catharines, ON: Vanwell Publishing, 1999), 192.

30 Barry Craig, "Women's March May Back Call for Rights Probe," *Globe and Mail*, 5 January 1967; "Royal Commission on Women," Memorandum to Cabinet, cab. doc. no. 1/67, 5 January 1967, LAC, RG 2-B-2, vol. 6324, file C-20-5.

31 Gordon Robertson, *Memoirs of a Very Civil Servant: Mackenzie King to Pierre Trudeau* (Toronto: University of Toronto Press, 2000), 246.

32 House of Commons, *Debates*, 8 February 1967, 12803.

33 Of 122 recommendations, 43 were implemented by 1979, and another 53 were partially implemented. Canadian Advisory Council on the Status of Women, *10 Years Later: An Assessment of the Federal Government's Implementation of the Recommendations made by the Royal Commission on the Status of Women* (Ottawa: Canadian Advisory Council on the Status of Women, 1979), 8.

34 Naomi Black, "The Canadian Women's Movement: The Second Wave," in *Changing Patterns: Women in Canada*, ed. Sandra Burt, Lorraine Code, and Lindsay Dorney (Toronto: McClelland and Stewart, 1993), 155.

35 In Nova Scotia, cruelty was also grounds for divorce.

36 Both the 1943 and 1960 results are in Canadian Institute of Public Opinion, "Many Unhappy with Divorce Law," *Toronto Star*, 28 April 1960.

37 "Divorce Laws Rated Too Difficult by Canadians," Canadian Institute of Public Opinion, Gallup Poll of Canada, press release, 9 October 1963. The poll was conducted in June.

38 A Gallup Poll showed that 41 percent thought that "homosexual behaviour" conducted in private between consenting adults should be a criminal offence; 42 percent thought it should not be. "Homosexuality: Views Vary," *Ottawa Citizen*, 16 September 1968.

39 "Proposed Law Would Allow Homosexuality," *Toronto Star*, 22 December 1967.

40 "Bare Majority Wants Hanging Kept," *Ottawa Citizen*, 26 February 1966.

41 House of Commons, *Debates*, 16 November 1967, 4370–71.

42 LaMarsh, *Memoirs*, 230.

43 House of Commons, *Debates*, 17 December 1962, 2722.

44 Ibid., 2724–25.

45 Pearson's first cabinet included Lucien Cardin, Lionel Chevrier, Azellus Denis, Jean-Paul Deschatelets, Guy Favreau, Maurice Lamontagne, Paul Martin, Hédard Robichaud, Roger Teillet, and René Tremblay. Paul Martin is the most difficult to categorize. Although English and French were both spoken in Martin's childhood home, his parents, Philippe and Lumina, spoke French as their first language. Martin attended a French high school, Collège St-Alexandre, which "would sharpen Martin's identity as a French Canadian," in the words of his biographer. See Greg Donaghy, *Grit: The Life and Politics of Paul Martin Sr.* (Vancouver: UBC Press, 2015), 7.

46 Pearson, *Mike*, 3:92.

47 Order-in-Council PC 1963–1106, app. 1 in *A Preliminary Report of the Royal Commission on Bilingualism and Biculturalism* (Ottawa: Royal Commission on Bilingualism and Biculturalism, 1965), 151.

48 Bruce Hutchison, *The Far Side of the Street* (Toronto: Macmillan, 1976), 359.

49 George Ferguson, "The Gladiators Withdraw: Ten Years of Pearson and Diefenbaker," *Round Table* 230 (1968): 203.

50 Peter Stursberg, *Lester Pearson and the Dream of Unity* (Toronto: Doubleday, 1978), 197.

51 Ibid., 162.

52 Pearson, *Mike*, 3:281.

53 Douglas Fisher, "The Man Canadians Love to Hate," *Toronto Sun*, 15 July 1998.

54 Robert Carty, "Going for Gain: Foreign Aid and CIDA," in *Ties That Bind: Canada and the Third World*, ed. Richard Swift and Robert Clarke (Toronto: Between the Lines, 1982), 155.

55 Notes of interview with Paul Hellyer, 1 February 1975, LAC, Howard Lentner fonds, R11232, vol. 2, file 11.

56 Charles Ritchie, *Storm Signals: More Undiplomatic Diaries, 1962–1971* (Toronto: Macmillan, 1983), 48.

57 Greg Donaghy, *Tolerant Allies: Canada and the United States, 1963–1968* (Montreal and Kingston: McGill-Queen's University Press, 2002).

58 Cabinet Minutes, 17 May 1967, LAC, RG 2.

59 Pearson, *Mike*, 3:137–48; McGeorge Bundy, "Memorandum for the Record of a Conversation between President Johnson and Prime Minister Pearson, Hilton Hotel, New York, May 28, 1964, 6:15–6:45 p.m.," in *Foreign Relations of the United States, 1964–1968*, vol. 1 (Washington, DC: Department of State, 1992), 394–96; English, *Worldly Years*, 358–79.

60 The line is from Wordsworth's "Ode to Duty." Dean Acheson, "Canada: 'Stern Daughter of the Voice of God,'" in *Neighbors Taken for Granted: Canada and the United States*, ed. Livingston Merchant (New York: Praeger, 1966), 134–47.

61 "Gallup Poll: Canadians Favor Withdrawal of US Troops from Vietnam," *Ottawa Citizen*, 2 November 1967.

62 In early 1968, a Gallup Poll asked which of the government's accomplishments would help the Liberals win votes in the next election. Fully 70 percent could not think of anything. "Most Canadians Can't Think of a Liberal Achievement," *Toronto Star*, 9 March 1968.

Part 2:

Pearson the Pragmatist

Jennifer Tunnicliffe

6 Lester Pearson, Human Rights, and the United Nations

Lester Pearson played a key role in setting Canadian foreign policy from the 1940s to the late 1960s, the period in which the United Nations developed the foundations of its international human rights regime. He was chair of the Canadian delegation to the UN when the General Assembly adopted the Universal Declaration of Human Rights (UDHR) in 1948, and he was Canada's prime minister when the two International Covenants on Human Rights were adopted two decades later. Yet relatively little has been written about Pearson's attitudes towards these developments or human rights more generally.[1] To address this gap, this chapter explores Pearson's relationship to the development and implementation of the International Bill of Rights at the UN from the 1940s until his retirement as prime minister.[2] It considers how Pearson envisioned the promotion of peace and freedom in the postwar period, what he understood to be the role of human rights declarations and covenants within international affairs, how these views changed in response to a growing rights culture in Canada, and how Pearson ultimately shaped Canadian foreign policy towards human rights initiatives at the UN.

In his work with the Department of External Affairs, Pearson promoted freedom, tolerance, and understanding as essential components of peace.[3] He did not, however, view human rights declarations as the most appropriate tool through which to achieve and sustain this peace. Pearson criticized these instruments as too abstract and difficult to enforce, resisting the development of the UDHR and its associated covenants throughout the 1940s and 1950s. In this same period, Pearson opposed the adoption of a domestic bill of rights. While he worked to create greater political, social, and economic equity for Canadians, he believed that Canada's traditional methods for protecting civil liberties were a sufficient guarantee of individual rights and freedoms. Later, as leader of the Opposition and then prime minister, Pearson began to recognize and cautiously respond to the growing public support for human rights laws – an issue emphasized by Stephen Azzi (Chapter 5, this volume) – resulting in a more positive approach to a Canadian bill of rights and, eventually, support for the UN's human rights instruments. Rather than taking a lead role in promoting the inclusion of human rights principles into domestic or foreign policy, Pearson, like many of his contemporaries in Ottawa, reacted to increased pressure from grassroots activists and minority groups in Canada. Therefore, while Lester Pearson may be remembered for his determination to carve out a role for Canada within the postwar international system, it would not be in the area of human rights.

Pearson served in Canada's High Commission in London in the early years of the Second World War. He returned to Ottawa briefly to act as assistant under-secretary of state for the DEA before moving to Washington in 1942 to work in the Canadian Embassy. Through these positions, Pearson became heavily involved in postwar planning. In 1943, he participated in the founding conferences for the Food and Agriculture Organization and the United Nations Relief and Rehabilitation Administration. He was both a Canadian representative at the Dumbarton Oaks Conference, where the great powers debated proposals for an international organization to maintain peace and security after the war, and a delegate to the UN's founding conference in San Francisco in 1945. His participation in these conferences exposed Pearson not only to questions of postwar reconstruction but also to questions of human rights. American non-governmental organizations (NGOs) led the lobbying efforts to include human rights provisions in the Charter of the proposed UN, arguing this formal recognition was essential to any peace settlement. While the United States, Britain, and the Soviet Union all expressed concern over national sovereignty, it was difficult to ignore the pressure from NGOs, particularly when Allied forces had championed rights and freedoms during the war. The introduction of a clause to protect domestic jurisdiction finally convinced the major powers to support the inclusion of a statement on human rights in the Charter.[4] Throughout these debates, Pearson and the Canadian delegation remained non-committal in their comments, speaking only broadly in support of the principles and objectives of human rights.[5]

Pearson did not agree with the NGOs that priority should be given to rights. He did support the concept that freedom was a necessary component of peace, stating, "there can be no enduring and creative peace if people are unfree."[6] In a 1944 article in *Canadian Affairs*, he outlined his view on how best to "get peace and keep it." Pearson drew inspiration from Franklin Roosevelt's "Four Freedoms" speech from three years earlier, highlighting the need for collective security to ensure "freedom from fear" and cooperation in economic development to ensure "freedom from want." He viewed the abstract notions outlined in the UN's human rights provisions as ill-suited to guaranteeing economic, political, and social stability. Pearson criticized the appropriateness of framing the peace settlement in terms of rights, supporting instead a greater focus on the welfare, not the rights, of individuals and states. He argued, "we may get further in this 'welfare' approach to international organization than we ever did along the road of glittering political abstractions."[7] Pearson took a pragmatic approach, emphasizing the need for nations to focus their attention and resources on what he viewed as the practical questions in the process of organizing for peace rather than on the more elusive idea of human rights. For example, in the early 1940s he advocated creating a declaration on the determination of states to deal with the problems of hunger and malnutrition once the war was over.[8] He was pleased that the conferences on food and agriculture, and on relief and rehabilitation, dealt with issues of human welfare. He applauded the "workmanlike approach to practical problems" laid out at these conferences, arguing that "a pint of milk a day for everyone may in the long run prove a greater help to international cooperation and provide a surer basis for international organization than thunderous declarations about the rights of man."[9]

This sense of the limitations of rights declarations shaped Pearson's approach to the early development of human rights laws at the UN. His ideas were in line with those of the majority of DEA policy makers in the 1940s, many of whom continued to worry about the influence of international human rights on Canadian sovereignty.[10] Under William Lyon Mackenzie King's leadership, the Liberal government did not support placing the international protection of human rights within the power and responsibility of the proposed UN.[11] As Robert Bothwell has noted, while human rights principles may have been of concern to the party, they were not the most important issue that Liberals wanted to see governments engage with at the end of the war.[12]

Ultimately, the campaign to include human rights provisions as a part of the UN was successful, and the organization's Charter called upon its member states to promote "universal respect for, and observance of, human rights and fundamental freedoms."[13] To fulfill this obligation, the newly formed UN Commission on Human Rights drafted an international bill of rights, releasing the first component of this bill, the Declaration of Human Rights, in 1947.[14] This declaration would act as a broad statement of principle for member states to follow, and its content generated significant debate in both the Economic and Social Council and at the General Assembly before it was put to a final vote and adopted in December 1948.

When Louis St-Laurent became prime minister in 1948, Pearson replaced him as both secretary of state and chair of the Canadian delegation to the UN. Supported by St-Laurent, and sustained by a "disciplined Liberal majority in Parliament," Pearson and his diplomatic advisers had unusual political latitude in setting Canada's policy towards the UN's human rights initiatives.[15] Pearson advised his government not to support the Declaration. He based this recommendation both on the opinion, within the DEA, that an international bill of rights was unnecessary and out of discomfort with the instrument's content and possible impact on Canadian policy.[16] However, Canada's government was reluctant to outright oppose a declaration on human rights. To give the government time to determine a policy, the DEA advised the Canadian delegation to recommend that the UN delay consideration of the draft until the following year.[17] This was unsuccessful, with the majority of member states, including the United States and Britain, opposing any delay.[18] When cabinet asked Pearson in November 1948 for a recommendation on how to proceed, he warned that the draft Declaration contained "objectionable" articles, including provisions for economic and social rights that could infringe on provincial jurisdiction.[19] Pearson had previously opposed the inclusion of economic rights, arguing that they "alter[ed] the character of the declaration, which was originally intended to be merely a summary of the liberties of the individual."[20] In sum, Pearson recommended that

Canada abstain in any final vote on the Declaration.[21] Cabinet agreed, and Canadian delegates used the argument that several of the draft Declaration's articles fell within provincial jurisdiction as the primary justification for their resistance. The extent to which Ottawa used this constitutional argument to mask deeper concerns over the substance of the document has been a subject of debate among historians.[22] Certainly, Pearson and other members of the DEA were well aware that, as the Declaration was a moral guide with only "quasi-juridical force," it could not bind governments to take any legislative actions that could be challenged by provincial authorities.[23] In a speech to the UN before the final vote, Pearson hinted at some of Canada's substantive problems with the Declaration. He referenced concerns surrounding the document's vague language, the broad scope of its definition of rights, and differences between a codified declaration and Canada's traditional methods of protecting rights and freedoms.[24] Despite these concerns, pressure from the international community persuaded Pearson that an abstention was undesirable as Canada would find itself in a minority alongside the Soviet bloc and South Africa.[25] While the Canadian delegation abstained in the preliminary vote on 6 December to make its point, it changed its position to support the Declaration in the final vote four days later. The Canadian government could therefore claim that it voted for the UDHR, though fear of negative diplomatic implication was its primary reasoning.

Less than a year after the UDHR's adoption, the UN introduced the second component of its International Bill of Rights, a draft covenant. This instrument provided a clearer articulation of the rights outlined in the Declaration and, as a multilateral treaty, would commit signatory states to implement and enforce its provisions. Fierce debate over the appropriateness of including economic and social rights in the same covenant as civil and political rights led to the creation of two separate instruments in 1954.[26] Member states negotiated the content of the resulting International Covenant on Civil and Political Rights and the International Covenant on Economic, Social and Cultural Rights for more than a decade before adopting both instruments in 1966.

Pearson was much less involved in the development of the International Covenants than he had been with the Declaration. As SSEA, he was focused on issues such as the Korean War and the Suez Crisis. In the larger context of Canadian foreign policy in this period, human rights issues were very low on the agenda. There was little pressure from within the House of Commons on the Liberal government relating to international human rights. One exception was Progressive Conservative MP John Diefenbaker, who had criticized the Liberals in 1948 for their lack of effort towards the UDHR.[27] However, Diefenbaker was more personally interested in a national bill of rights than international rights, and he did not follow up on his comments, which allowed the Liberals to avoid having to justify their actions towards the UDHR or the Covenants. When Minister of Justice Stuart Garson wrote to Pearson in 1950, outlining his objections to the first draft covenant, Pearson agreed with Garson's opinion that Canada ought to oppose its adoption.[28] Garson's report eventually became the basis for Canada's policy approach to the Covenants for much of the 1950s. After the Progressive Conservatives won the election in 1957, despite Prime Minister John Diefenbaker's support for a domestic bill of rights, he and his party took little interest in questions of rights internationally. There was much consistency in the policy approach of the Liberals and the Progressive Conservatives towards the UN's human rights covenants.[29] Progressive Conservative opposition to these instruments centred on the same concerns that Pearson had outlined in relation to the UDHR: the language of the document, its definition of rights, the inclusion of economic and social rights in particular, the possible impact of a covenant on Canadian policy, proposed measures of implementation, and questions over jurisdiction, particularly given the legal nature of a covenant.[30]

Pearson's continued resistance to the UN's human rights instruments also reflected his support for the British parliamentary tradition. He referred to the codification of rights reflected in the Covenants as "contrary to the whole spirit of British institutions."[31] His views were in line with the majority of Liberal Party members in the 1940s and 1950s, who took pride in Canada's traditional methods for protecting rights and argued that a bill of rights was unnecessary, both at home and within the framework of the UN. Canada had inherited the British legal and parliamentary system whereby civil liberties and fundamental freedoms were guaranteed by the rule of law and through parliamentary supremacy, not by statute. In fact, Canada had very few laws to explicitly promote rights or protect individuals from discrimination in the immediate postwar period; yet Pearson felt that Canada enjoyed a strong record of respect for human rights. He told the UN in 1948 that Canada was a country where rights and freedoms were "not only a matter of resolutions but also of day-to-day practice from one end of the country to another."[32] Ten years later, in a House of Commons debate over the need for a Canadian bill of rights, Pearson cautioned that

> rights and freedoms are not established or protected merely or primarily or often at all by proclamations of beliefs or written constitutions, but by the slow, sure building of a sound and progressive social, political and economic structure of law, justice and understanding. That has been the British way and it has worked there; and on the whole it has worked with us too.[33]

By the time the Liberals returned to power in 1963, the domestic environment in which Canada was setting its policies towards international human rights instruments had changed. Civil liberties organizations and minority groups spent decades lobbying government to remove discriminatory policies and promote equal citizenship, and they launched public awareness campaigns to reveal the prejudice that existed in Canadian law and society.[34] As a result of the hard work of these grassroots activists, by the end of the 1950s most jurisdictions in Canada had passed fair practices legislation in the areas of employment and accommodation, prohibiting discrimination based on a set list of grounds. Several had also adopted equal pay legislation.[35] Provincial governments enacted legislation dealing with a number of the rights outlined in the draft covenants, including workers' compensation, mothers' allowance, mandatory education, and living accommodations for the aged.[36] Provincial and federal voting acts were amended to drop racial and religious disqualifications, and the federal government changed immigration regulations to take out discrimination based on colour, race, or country of origin.[37] Property laws were rewritten to prohibit discrimination in the sale or leasing of a property, and social welfare programs were created or modified to promote health, old age security, and unemployment insurance. In 1962, Ontario enacted its human rights code and became the first province to establish a commission responsible solely for the administration, promotion, and enforcement of human rights. While many marginalized groups within Canadian society continued to be inadequately protected, these developments demonstrated the impact of Canada's burgeoning human rights movement on domestic policy. Federal and provincial governments had begun to respond to calls for statutory protection of rights and freedoms, and for an enhanced role for the state in maintaining stability and ensuring the equality of its citizens.

Pearson recognized and responded cautiously to these changes. When Diefenbaker's government introduced a bill to formally recognize and declare the existence of certain basic rights and fundamental freedoms for Canadians in 1958, the Liberal Party initiated an internal review of its past policies towards such legislation.[38] The governments of Mackenzie King and St-Laurent had rejected calls to implement a Canadian bill of rights. In fact, one of the arguments against Canada's support for the UDHR had come out of a fear that it would provide ammunition for advocates of a Canadian bill of rights, a document that the Liberals did not endorse.[39] In their 1958 review, however, the Liberals concluded that this past policy had been too inflexible and dismissive of both the importance of a bill of rights to Canadians and its appeal to voters.[40] Realizing that voters now supported rights-related legislation in ways that they had not in the 1940s, Pearson's Liberals changed their position, attacking the shortcomings of Diefenbaker's legislation rather than objecting to its purpose. The Liberals went so far as to argue that Canada needed a constitutionally entrenched bill of rights, with Pearson challenging Diefenbaker to submit his legislation to the provinces for their opinion in order to create a "truly national declaration on human rights and fundamental freedoms."[41] After newly elected Quebec premier Jean Lesage announced in July 1960 that his government supported a bill of rights, Pearson renewed his pressure on Diefenbaker to discuss the bill with the provinces in order to consider the possibility of entrenching it in the Constitution.[42] In a departure from his earlier views on rights declarations, Pearson argued, "there can be no more important questions than those of human rights and fundamental freedoms, and no questions more appropriate for parliamentary consideration."[43]

Notwithstanding this type of rhetoric, Pearson remained tied, at least in part, to the tradition of British constitutionalism. While he acknowledged that "new circumstances, new difficulties and new pressures" may justify "some" departure from Canada's traditional methods of protecting rights, he reminded Parliament that constitutional acts or bills of rights did not always ensure that governments would uphold the rights of individuals. He suggested:

> By the method we have followed over the years we have built up in this country a respect for freedom, a respect for human rights, which is not exceeded in any other free country in the world today. So we have to look at any proposal bearing on this matter in the light of the experience we have had. We have to be very sure before we make a change that it is going to be an effective change, and a change in the right direction.[44]

Ultimately, Diefenbaker's Bill of Rights remained a statute rather than a constitutional amendment. Pearson voted in favour of the bill regardless. As prime minister several years later, he initiated negotiations with the provinces for constitutional change, which included patriation and an entrenched charter of rights and freedoms. Pearson retired before the process of patriation began, however, and the Charter became a project for his successor, Pierre Elliott Trudeau.

By the 1960s, Canada's DEA realized that, due to overwhelming support from other member states, the two International Covenants on Human Rights would eventually be adopted in some form by the General Assembly.[45] Many different factors influenced the government's decision to ultimately support the adoption of these Covenants. First, a growing bloc within the UN openly criticized those states that did not support the instruments. Canadian officials worried about Canada's image among these newly established, and often non-aligned states. Robert Bothwell has argued that these concerns were a matter of self-interest; in order for Canada to exert any influence in the postwar, postcolonial world, it had to maintain the image of the "honest broker," and this required the support, and respect, of non-aligned states.[46] By 1964, DEA analysts emphasized how embarrassing it would be for Canada to be one of the only countries not to support the Covenants' adoption. They argued that the cost of abstention might be that Canada appeared to oppose core values of the international human rights regime: freedom, respect for universal human dignity, equality of peoples, and peace among nations.[47] A second and related factor was the knowledge that Canada's allies, even those that had originally opposed the Covenants, were now more supportive of adoption.[48] Once again, Canada found itself in an undesirable minority. Finally, the legislative and cultural developments at home created an environment in which federal policy makers felt increasingly uncomfortable opposing international rights initiatives. By 1963, when Pearson became prime minister, these pressures had combined to persuade the DEA to recommend that the government take a more positive role not just in the debates over the Covenants but also in human rights programs at the UN more generally.[49] In response, the Canadian delegation began to participate more actively in the article-by-article debates of the Covenants in the General Assembly, preparing itself to vote in favour of the two instruments in 1966. In supporting the adoption of international treaties on human rights that did not include any federal state exemptions, the Canadian government decided that the cultivation, at home and abroad, of an image of Canada as an advocate of human rights, fundamental freedoms, and international justice was more important than any potential constitutional conflicts that could arise as a result of this decision. Federal officials knew, however, that the Covenants would not be binding on Canada unless the government decided to ratify them.

Pearson was prime minister when the UN adopted the International Covenants on Human Rights, but he was not intimately involved in the process. In his memoirs, he recalled that the party was preoccupied with matters it considered to be of greater importance, notably the issue of Quebec and the strength of Canada's federalism.[50] When asked by Opposition leader John Diefenbaker in 1967 if the Liberal government intended to place the newly adopted Covenants before Parliament for approval and ratification, Pearson admitted he was "not as familiar as [he] perhaps should be with these particular international covenants" and promised to look into it.[51] Four days later, he gave a short speech to the House of Commons in which he reversed his earlier opposition to an international covenant on human rights by describing the instruments as a "significant step forward by the international community," reminding the House that the Liberal government had voted in support of the Covenants at the UN the previous year. Pearson applauded Canada's "constructive contributions" to the development of international human rights, downplaying almost two decades of Canadian resistance. He told Diefenbaker that the government would strike an interdepartmental committee to consider the contents of the Covenants and, as a number of the provisions fell within provincial jurisdiction, would consult with the provinces before any steps would be taken towards ratification.[52]

A month later, the DEA forwarded copies of the text of both Covenants to the provincial governments. A letter followed from Pearson asking the premiers to study the instruments and to indicate their willingness to enact the necessary legislation, while also informing the provinces of Ottawa's intention to initiate a federal-provincial dialogue on the topic of the Covenants in the near future.[53] The DEA convened a meeting of the federal Interdepartmental Committee on Human Rights to formulate recommendations for cabinet concerning the question of ratification. This committee recommended that Canada sign on to the instruments at the earliest possible date and work to achieve the required provincial support for ratification.[54] Pearson was content to wait. While the federal Liberals did not oppose ratifying the International Covenants on Human Rights, their foreign policy – as the chapters in this volume attest – was more focused on arms control and peacekeeping initiatives at the UN, Canada's role within NATO and NORAD, increasing international trade, and reducing global economic disparity. As in the immediate postwar period, Pearson and his Liberal government did not view human rights instruments as a component of their foreign policy goals.

The provinces were slow to reply to Pearson's 1967 letter because international covenants on human rights were not a priority for these governments either. Nothing came of the Interdepartmental Committee's suggestion that Canada sign on early to the Covenants, and the Canadian government did not schedule a federal-provincial meeting to discuss international human rights. More than a year after Pearson sent his letter to the premiers, the Canadian delegation told the UN that Canada was "awaiting [an] affirmative reply" from the provinces before pressing forward.[55] Having made initial contact with the premiers, Pearson and his government felt no sense of urgency to sign or ratify the Covenants. Thus, when Pearson stepped down as prime minister in 1968, the situation remained unresolved. It would not be until 1976 that Canada would finally ratify the Covenants.

Lester Pearson was a skilful diplomat who promoted peace, supported the UN, and advocated a strong role for Canada within the international system. The conventional wisdom is that he must have also supported the formation of the UN's human rights regime.[56] After all, he was foreign minister when Canada voted to support the UDHR and then prime minister when the UN adopted the International

Covenants. A close examination of Pearson's attitudes towards human rights declarations in the 1940s and his foreign policy towards an international bill of rights demonstrates that this conventional wisdom is mistaken.

Pearson did not oppose human rights, he simply believed that the rhetoric surrounding these rights was too abstract to have a real effect with regard to promoting justice, peace, and stability in the world. Instead, he supported "the British way" of relying on Parliament to enact progressive and just laws to protect the welfare, not simply the rights, of its citizens. On a practical level, human rights declarations were simply not a priority for Pearson in the context of the post-war world, and he worried about the impact of these instruments on Canadian policy. As a result, he was complicit in the federal government's opposition to the adoption of international human rights instruments from the 1940s to the 1960s. By the time he became prime minister, however, growing support at the UN and at home for human rights principles caused Pearson and his party to rethink their approach – a view in line with Stephen Azzi's emphasis on Pearson as a progressive prime minister. In the 1960s, the Liberals called for a constitutional bill of rights for Canada and voted to adopt the International Covenants. However, these changes were not at the heart of Pearson's foreign or domestic policies. Human rights issues remained peripheral, and no real progress on ratification of the Covenants took place for several years after his retirement. Indeed, as both John Dirks (Chapter 9, this volume) and Tim Sayle (Chapter 11, this volume) make clear, human rights also had little place in Pearson's dealings in Latin America and Eastern Europe, regions in which rights abuses pushed the issue to the forefront of global politics in the 1970s. Instead, Pearson and the federal Liberals separated human rights principles from foreign policy decisions, demonstrating the extent to which human rights concerns remained peripheral. David Webster's study of Canada's bilateral human rights dialogues with China, Cuba, and Indonesia makes clear that this separation was not unique to either Pearson or the Liberal Party. Successive Canadian governments have treated human rights as "an optional extra," avoiding any genuine effort to find effective rights-promotion strategies in foreign affairs.[57]

Since the adoption of the Charter of Rights and Freedoms in 1982, support for human rights has become an increasingly important element of Canadian identity. With this has come a tendency to criticize current governments for their failure to uphold what is perceived to be Canada's tradition of support for human rights at the UN. There is little recognition of the extent to which Canadian policy makers, including respected figures such as Lester Pearson, historically opposed the development of international human rights instruments. This history is important to help better understand Pearson and his policies, and to provide vital context for the Canadian federal government's contemporary approach to human rights initiatives at the UN.

Notes

1 Several studies outline Pearson's role in Canada's opposition to the UDHR and the Covenants: William A. Schabas, "Canada and the Adoption of the Universal Declaration of Human Rights," *McGill Law Journal* 43 (1998): 403–41; Michael Behiels, "Canada and the Implementation of International Instruments of Human Rights: A Federalist Conundrum, 1919–1982," in *Framing Canadian Federalism: Historical Essays in Honour of John T. Saywell*, ed. Dimitry Anastakis and P.E. Bryden, 151–84 (Toronto: University of Toronto Press, 2009); Jennifer Tunnicliffe, "A Limited Vision: Canadian Participation in the Adoption of the International Covenants on Human Rights," in *Taking Liberties: A History of Human Rights in Canada*, ed. David Goutor and Stephen Heathorn, 166–89 (Don Mills, ON: Oxford University Press, 2013).

2 The International Bill of Rights consists of the Universal Declaration of Human Rights (1948); The International Covenant on Civil and Political Rights (1966); The International Covenant on Economic, Social and Cultural Rights (1966); and the Optional Protocol to the International Covenant on Civil and Political Rights (1966).

3 In a 1957 Nobel Lecture, Pearson argued, "if there is to be peace, there must be compromise, tolerance, agreement." He also stated: "There can be no enduring and creative peace if people are unfree." See Lester Pearson, "The Four Faces of Peace," Nobel Lectures, University of Oslo, 11 December 1957.

4 American advocacy groups and smaller states such as Chile, Cuba, and Panama kept human rights on the agenda at San Francisco. See Samuel Moyn, *The Last Utopia: Human Rights in History* (Cambridge, MA: Belknap Press, 2010), 62; Roger Normand and Sarah Zaidi, *Human Rights at the UN: The Political History of Universal Justice* (Bloomington: Indiana University Press, 2008), 127–28.

5 John Holmes, *The Shaping of Peace: Canada and the Search for World Order*, vol. 2 (Toronto: University of Toronto Press, 1979), 44.

6 Pearson, *Four Faces of Peace*; and Lester Pearson, *Diplomacy in the Nuclear Age* (Cambridge, MA: Harvard University Press, 1959), 112.

7 Lester Pearson, "Canada and the Post-War World," *Canadian Affairs* 1 (1944): 2, 7, 12.

8 Lester Pearson, *Mike: The Memoirs of The Right Honourable Lester B. Pearson*, vol. 1 (Toronto: University of Toronto Press, 1972), 248.

9 Pearson, "Canada and the Post-War World," 13.

10 An exception was Escott Reid, who, in 1945, prepared a draft UN charter containing an entire chapter on the importance of human rights. This document was never included in Canada's official documents. See Escott Reid, *On Duty: A Canadian at the Making of the United Nations, 1945–1946* (Toronto: McClelland and Stewart, 1983), 18–23.

11 Kim Richard Nossal, "Cabin'd, Cribb'd, Confin'd? Canada's Interests in Human Rights," in *Human Rights in Canadian Foreign Policy*, ed. Robert O. Matthews and Cranford Pratt (Montreal and Kingston: McGill-Queen's University Press, 1988), 49–50.

12 Robert Bothwell, *Alliance and Illusion: Canada and the World, 1945–1984* (Vancouver: UBC Press, 2007), 21–23.

13 Human rights obligations are set out in the Preamble and in Articles 1 and 55 of the Charter.

14 For an overview of the history of UN human rights formulation and definition, see Louis Sohn, "A Short History of United Nations Documents on Human Rights," *The United Nations and Human Rights*, 18th report (New York: Commission to Study the Organization of Peace, 1968), 39–186.

15 Robert Bothwell, "Foreign Affairs a Hundred Years On," in *Canada among Nations 2008*, ed. Robert Bothwell and Jean Daudelin (Montreal and Kingston: McGill-Queen's University Press, 2009), 29.

16 In Canada, "civil liberties" referred to traditional legal and political rights and did not have the same universal connotation as did human rights at the UN. St-Laurent and Pearson also worried about how a declaration of human rights would limit Canada's ability to pursue informal policies, such as preventing the spread of communism. See Louis St-Laurent to the Canadian Delegation, October 1948, LAC, RG 25, vol. 3701, file 5475-DP-40.

17 John Hackett, Progressive Conservative MP and president of the Canadian Bar Association, advised the draft be referred to the International Law Commission for review. See Hackett to Pearson, October to November 1948, LAC, RG 25, vol. 3701, file 5475-DP-40.

18 Pearson often commented in his reports that the "Western powers" were pressuring Canada to support the quick adoption of a declaration. See, for example, memo (110), Pearson to the Canadian Delegation, 7 October 1948, LAC, RG 25, vol. 3701, file 5475-DP-40.

19 Pearson to Louis St-Laurent and Brooke Claxton, 10 November 1948, LAC, RG 25, vol. 3701, file 5475-DP-40.

20 Pearson to Dana Wilgress, 20 July 1948, LAC, RG 25, vol. 20, file 5475-W-2-4-pt.1.

21 Pearson to St-Laurent and Claxton, 10 November 1948, LAC, RG 25, vol. 3701, file 5475-DP-40.

22 Behiels, "Canada and the Implementation," 151–84; Schabas, "Canada and the Adoption," 403–41; Tunnicliffe, "Limited Vision," 166–89.

23 In fact, the DEA had produced a document for its UN delegates in September 1948 in which it confirmed that a declaration would have only moral sway. See DEA, Instructions for the Canadian Delegation, 21 September 1948, LAC, RG 25, vol. 3701, file 5475-DG-3-40-pt.2.

24 Pearson, "Statement on the Universal Declaration on Human Rights," 10 December 1948, LAC, RG 25, vol. 3701, file 5475-DP-40.
25 Canadian Delegation to SSEA, 23 November 1948, LAC, RG 25, vol. 3701, file 5475-DG-2-40.
26 Normand and Zaidi, *Human Rights at the UN*, 200–12.
27 House of Commons, *Debates*, 9 April 1948, 2857–59.
28 Garson to Pearson, 30 June 1950, LAC, RG 25, vol. 6408, file 5475-W-40-pt.2.2.
29 Several DEA policy advisers remained in their positions throughout the transition from Liberal to Progressive Conservative and back to a Liberal government. As Diefenbaker was not specifically interested in international human rights, he relied on his advisers to guide Canadian policy towards the Covenants.
30 Garson to Pearson, 30 June 1950, LAC, RG 25, vol. 6408, file 5475-W-40-pt.2.2.
31 Pearson to the Canadian Delegation, 25 November 1948, LAC, RG 2, vol. 206, file U-41-H-pt.1.
32 Pearson, Speech to the General Assembly, 10 December 1948, LAC, RG 25, vol. 3701, file 5475-DP-40.
33 House of Commons, *Debates,* 5 September 1958, 4650.
34 On early rights organizations, see Ross Lambertson, *Repression and Resistance: Canadian Human Rights Activists 1930–1960* (Toronto: University of Toronto Press, 2005); Dominique Clément, *Canada's Rights Revolution: Social Movements and Social Change, 1937–1982* (Vancouver: UBC Press, 2008); James W. Walker, "The 'Jewish Phase' in the Movement for Racial Equality in Canada," *Canadian Ethnic Studies* 34 (2002): 1–29.
35 On provincial anti-discrimination laws, see Brian Howe, *Restraining Equality: Human Rights Commissions in Canada* (Toronto: University of Toronto Press, 2000), 8.
36 These developments were all reported to the UN secretary-general. For example, "Report on the UN Yearbook on Human Rights – 1959," LAC, RG 25, vol. 6926, file 5475-W-7-40-pt.3.2.
37 Voting acts were changed in British Columbia, Manitoba, Ontario, Nova Scotia, Newfoundland and Labrador, the Northwest Territories, Saskatchewan, the Yukon, and for the federal government. In 1962, the Progressive Conservative government introduced new immigration regulations granting admission to Canada on the basis of an applicant's "education, training, skills or other qualifications." In 1967, the Liberal government established a "points system" to rate applicants on the basis on qualifications, and it removed "race" from the text of Canadian immigration law.
38 Christopher MacLennan, *Toward the Charter: Canadians and the Demand for a National Bill of Rights, 1929–1960* (Montreal and Kingston: McGill-Queen's University Press, 2003), 145.
39 DEA to Chairman of the Canadian Delegation to ECOSOC, 13 July 1950, LAC, RG 25, vol. 6408, file 5475-W-40-pt.2.2.
40 MacLennan, *Toward the Charter*, 145.
41 House of Commons, *Debates*, 5 September 1958, 4647.
42 Ibid., 1 August 1960, 7376.
43 Ibid., 5 September 1958, 4644.

44 House of Commons, *Debates*, 5 September 1958, 4649.

45 "Final Report on the Thirteenth Session of the Third Committee of the General Assembly," 8 January 1959, LAC, RG 25, vol. 6928, file 5475-W-15-40-pt.7.2.

46 Bothwell, *Alliance and Illusion*, 8.

47 UN Division to Legal Division, "Canadian Position on Draft International Covenants on Human Rights," 25 January 1962, LAC, RG 25, vol. 5118, file 5475-W-15-40-pt.4.

48 Ibid.

49 For example, in 1963, Canada sat for the first time on the UN Commission on Human Rights; DEA to the Minister, "Canada's Candidature for the Human Rights Commission," LAC, RG 25, vol. 6924, file 5475-W-40-pt.16.1.

50 Lester Pearson, *Mike: The Memoirs of the Right Honourable Lester B. Pearson*, vol. 3 (Toronto, University of Toronto Press, 1975), 128.

51 House of Commons, *Debates*, 19 January 1967, 11983.

52 Ibid., 23 January 1967, 12101–2.

53 The steps taken by the federal government to consult the provinces are recorded in Buchan, "Canada in the International Field of Human Rights," 10 May 1974, LAC, RG 25, vol. 13650, file 45-13-2-3-pt.9.

54 Minutes, Interdepartmental Committee on Human Rights Meeting, 9 February 1967, LAC, RG 25, vol. 14947, file 45-CDA-13-1-1.

55 Roquet, Speech to the Third Committee of the General Assembly, 29 November 1968, LAC, RG 25, vol. 14952, file 45-13-1-6-pt.6.

56 Successive governments have promoted the idea that Canada played a key role in the development of the UDHR and its covenants.

57 David Webster, "Canada and Bilateral Human Rights Dialogues," *Canadian Foreign Policy Journal* 16 (2010): 56.

Peter Kikkert, Adam Lajeunesse, and P. Whitney Lackenbauer

7 Lester Pearson and Arctic Sovereignty
A Case of Un-Pearsonian Diplomacy

In a 2011 editorial about Arctic politics, the *Globe and Mail* asserted that Canada must embrace a more "Pearsonian" approach to the region. An international opinion poll had just revealed that the majority of Canadians regarded Arctic sovereignty as the country's most important foreign policy priority and supported deploying more military assets to the region. The survey suggested two things: (1) the North still had the power to inspire Canadian nationalism like little else, and (2) Canadians were much less willing to compromise on Arctic disputes than were their American neighbours. More than 40 percent of Canadians agreed that Ottawa must take a firm stand in defending the region from any foreign challenge. The editorial, suggesting that military force remained an ineffective guard against future sovereignty disputes, concluded: "It's time for a Pearsonian quiet diplomacy on the Northern Front."[1]

With the phrase "Pearsonian diplomacy," the *Globe and Mail* hoped to invoke a model of statecraft based on cooperation, negotiation, give-and-take bargaining, subtlety, and compromise. These principles flowed out of Lester Pearson's long and varied career. Pearson's model insisted that "flexibility in the conduct of foreign policy" was essential to Canada and that it was "unwise, then, to lay down dogmatic priorities and postulates."[2] Rather than working from a fixed and inflexible position, Canada should strive for a middle way formed by moderation, especially when an issue involved the country's close bilateral relationship with the US. In disputes with Washington, Pearson advised that Ottawa should carefully avoid forcing any issue unless "absolutely certain of our case"[3] and confident that there was a "good chance of emerging successful."[4] When Canada faced bilateral disputes, it "usually did better through quiet, rather than through headline, diplomacy."[5]

The *Globe and Mail* made a sober point in suggesting that the Pearsonian model of diplomacy would bolster cooperation and stability in the contemporary circumpolar world. It is ironic, however, that Canada's Arctic sovereignty was one of the few areas of government policy in which Pearson failed to abide by his own guiding principles. Historian Denis Stairs has argued that properly exercising the Pearsonian model of diplomacy requires "a measure of detachment from the issues at hand," something that Pearson lacked when dealing with Arctic sovereignty.[6] Pearson's engagement with Canada's North and, in particular, his thoughts and approach towards the complicated international legal issues involved in terrestrial and maritime claims in the Arctic, is relatively unknown and virtually ignored in his memoirs and biography. He was, however, a committed "northern nationalist" who strove to protect Canada's Arctic interests.[7] Unfortunately, his level of knowledge and acumen on Arctic affairs never matched his interest and enthusiasm.

Throughout his career, Pearson's approach to Arctic sovereignty was clumsy, confused, and frequently threatened to put Canada on an unnecessary collision course with the United States. He failed to consider, or simply ignored, the broader legal interests that informed Washington's position on Arctic sovereignty. His public support of an extreme version of the sector principle, which he believed allowed Canada to claim all the "islands and the frozen sea" even if unoccupied and unexplored, ignored the theory's dubious validity in international law and strong US opposition to its use. As prime minister, Pearson again displayed little awareness of American law of the sea concerns when he attempted to win Washington's recognition of the Arctic Archipelago as internal Canadian waters. This action inspired a sharp American rejection, leading to the withdrawal (or "deferral," as it was labelled at the time) of the Arctic waters from consideration – a decision that highlighted the problems with Pearson's diplomatic approach to Arctic sovereignty more generally.

In the fall of 1929, when Pearson was still a raw recruit at the Department of External Affairs, one of the first files to cross his desk dealt with Canada's Arctic sovereignty. At the request of Under-Secretary of State for External Affairs O.D. Skelton, Pearson explored the controversy surrounding the Sverdrup Islands in the High Arctic, which involved Canada, Norway, and the Norwegian explorer Otto von Sverdrup.[8] Between 1898 and 1902, Sverdrup led his ship, *Fram,* on a scientific expedition to northwest Greenland and into the waters of Canada's Arctic Archipelago, over-wintering for three years on Ellesmere Island. From there, he set out to discover, claim, and partially survey the islands of Axel Heiberg, Amund and Ellef Ringnes, and King Christian.[9] When Sverdrup returned to Norway, he embarked on a lifelong effort to persuade Oslo to pursue his claims. Rather than challenge Canada's claim to the islands, however, Norway permitted Sverdrup to approach Ottawa with an offer to give up any rights he might have in the Arctic Archipelago in return for payment.[10] After reviewing the situation, Pearson concluded that Norway had no rights to the islands and could not challenge Canada's claim, although he suggested paying off Sverdrup to avoid possible controversy or negative publicity.[11] It was during this brief sojourn into the files on Arctic sovereignty that Pearson discovered the sector principle.

The sector principle assumed the use of meridians as national borders, running from a state's eastern and western extremes to the North Pole. All territory bracketed by these lines, discovered or not, supposedly belonged to that country.[12] Canada's Department of the Interior had first employed the principle in a quasi-official manner in 1904 when it published a map that used the 141st and 60th meridians to the North as Canadian boundaries (see map, next page).[13] In 1907, Senator Pascal Poirier proposed a resolution in the Canadian Senate to make a formal declaration of sovereignty based on the sector principle, but no official action followed. On 1 June 1925, however, Charles Stewart, Canada's minister of the interior, told the House of Commons and the world that Canada claimed sovereignty over all land within the Canadian sector up to the North Pole.[14] This proclamation, made in response to a planned American expedition in search of undiscovered land around the Pole, tied Canada to the sector principle – although Ottawa never officially incorporated it into law.[15] By the time Pearson composed his Sverdrup Islands report in 1929, the principle had already attained considerable international influence. In 1926, the Soviet Union made its own massive sector claim, which Soviet

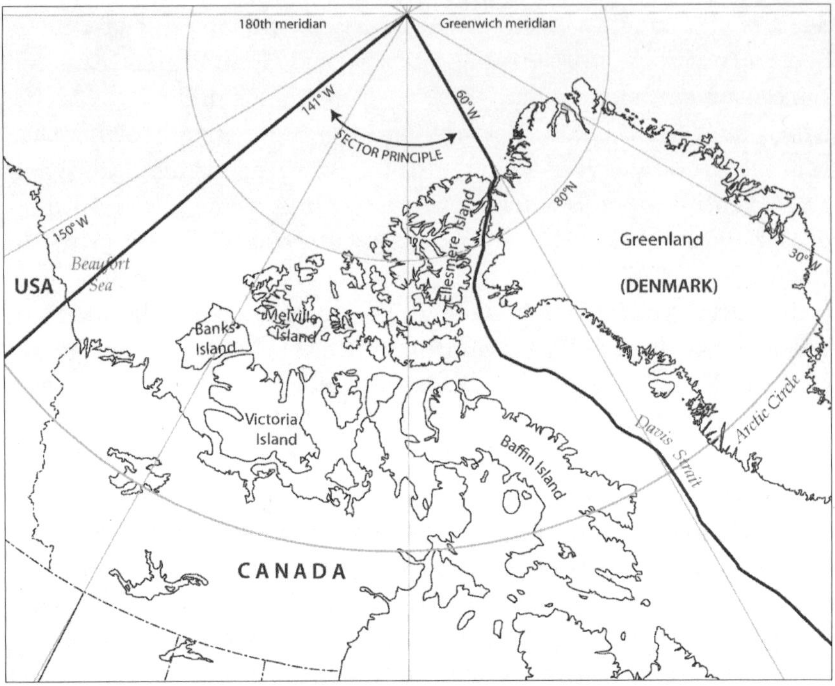

Canada's sector principle. *Cartography by Jennifer Arthur-Lackenbauer*

jurists later insisted included not only land but enclosed Arctic waters as well. Meanwhile, Britain, New Zealand, Australia, and France all claimed vast national sectors in the Antarctic.

To Pearson, dividing sovereignty on the basis of sectors represented a "practical solution of the Arctic question" of how states could acquire sovereignty in the region. Biographer John English points out that, when Pearson wrote his report on the Sverdrup claims, he "made a case for Arctic exceptionalism, the assertion that the Arctic did not fit neatly into existing international law."[16] In more temperate areas, states claimed territory on the basis of effective occupation; however, in the Arctic, similar forms of occupation were more difficult, if not unreasonable, to expect or to sustain.[17] Pearson suggested that the Arctic's unique and harsh conditions, "unlike any visualized by international lawyers in the past," called for new rules and practices – such as the sector principle.[18] While this principle might not be acceptable in other regions, Pearson argued, it offered a tidy solution to potential

Arctic territorial disputes. Through simple, uncomplicated sector lines, Canada could secure its northern possessions.

Even as Pearson wrote his report, however, international opposition to the sector principle mounted. The Norwegians vocally denounced the principle in the Arctic and Antarctic.[19] Although Britain claimed a vast sector of the Antarctic continent, in 1926 it likewise rejected the principle as a means of asserting sovereignty over sea ice.[20] Most important, the US opposed the notion of sectors as it directly violated the Hughes Doctrine. This doctrine, the foundation of American polar policy, rejected the notion that the polar regions were exceptional in any way; instead, the State Department maintained that countries had to settle, colonize, and exploit polar lands before they could successfully claim them.[21] In short, sector claims had no place in the American conception of polar sovereignty. While Pearson was finishing his report, the US Navy declared, in September 1929, that the sector principle represented an illegal attempt by a few of the world's powers to unfairly divide up a large portion of the globe.[22] With such adamant opposition from the United States, the sector principle had little chance of finding international acceptance. Throughout much of his career, however, Pearson clung to the sector principle as the ideal solution to Canada's dilemma of securing sovereignty over a large and inhospitable portion of the circumpolar world.

While minister-counsellor and then ambassador at the Canadian Legation (and later the Canadian Embassy) in Washington during the Second World War, Pearson's central task was, as his biographer phrased it, to "educate the Americans about the sovereignty of Canada."[23] This task kept him heavily occupied, especially after Ottawa's lack of control over the US defence projects in the Canadian northwest began to worry Prime Minister William Lyon Mackenzie King.[24] In combatting an American tendency to act before attaining approval from Ottawa, Pearson argued that Canada "should be particularly careful in forcing the issue with the United States on any matter unless we are willing to pursue the matter through to the end; and unless we have a good chance of emerging successful. In estimating our chances in this regard, we should never lose sight of the relative position of the two countries." Before Ottawa went "to the mat" with Washington, he concluded, it must have an "unanswerable case ... Otherwise, the United States will ignore our arguments, bring up their heavy guns, and we will make a virtue of necessity by giving in. In the end, we will be in a much worse position than if we had not taken the 'firm stand' originally."[25]

Although this philosophy served Pearson well during the war, he seemed to forget it when the Cold War reawakened concerns in Ottawa about potential US threats to Canadian sovereignty in the Arctic Archipelago. As US-Soviet relations deteriorated, North American defence analysts unrolled polar projection maps highlighting the Soviet Union's propinquity.[26] With strategists making nightmarish predictions of hostile bombers penetrating North America's northern approaches to wreak havoc on the continent's industrial heartland, in the spring of 1946 US defence officials bombarded Ottawa with proposals for projects designed to enhance their Arctic capabilities, including several permanent weather stations placed on uninhabited islands in Canada's archipelago.[27] Although American officials repeatedly assured their Canadian counterparts that they had no desire to infringe on Canadian sovereignty, they never offered to recognize Canada's sector claim or title to the islands.[28] The prospect of US-built installations on islands that few Canadians had ever visited worried Ottawa politicians and civil servants,[29] who gave considerable thought to the complex problem throughout 1946 and early 1947.

As Ottawa nervously reflected on its Arctic sovereignty, Pearson felt that Canada had the perfect leverage to force an explicit American recognition of Canada's claims. "I am wondering whether we could not take advantage of the present situation to secure from the United States Government public recognition of our sovereignty of the total area of our northern coasts, based on the sector principle," Pearson wrote to USSEA Hume Wrong in June 1946.[30] If his bid worked, it would secure Canadian control over a large slice of the polar region. In advocating such a move, Pearson was fixated on the Arctic, where he saw a reasonable trade-off that would benefit both countries: granting American bases and defence rights in exchange for recognition of Canadian sovereignty over lands and waters in which the US had little interest beyond its defence requirements. Although Pearson's approach was nationalistic and direct, it was also brash, ill-conceived, and doomed to fail. Not only did Pearson's proposal directly challenge core US legal principles, he seemed uncharacteristically oblivious to Washington's strategic interests.

American decision makers could not consider Arctic sovereignty – and the sector principle in particular – in isolation. As Wrong explained, the State Department would not "fall in line" with Pearson's suggestion "if falling in line means that they are asked to proclaim their adhesion to the sector theory of Arctic sovereignty."[31] Wrong believed that Pearson "underestimate[d] the difficulties" faced by the United States. If the US recognized Canadian sovereignty over its slice of polar territory, it would strengthen the Soviet Union's legal position in the Arctic and that of the claimant states in Antarctica, where Washington still considered making its own territorial claim.[32] Such a scenario would also violate the American position on the freedom of the seas. In July 1946, William Clayton, the first assistant secretary of state for economic affairs, warned Under-Secretary of State Dean Acheson that, if either Canada or the Soviet Union extended the sector to enclose their Arctic waters, "additional and serious problems would arise." The United States would have no option but to vigorously resist any such claims.[33] In short, Washington could not publicly recognize Canada's sovereignty, tied to the sector principle, without prejudicing its broader legal and military interests.

It is striking that Pearson, having so much experience working with the Americans, misunderstood the US position so fundamentally. His forceful approach also contravened his own wartime advice on how Canada should handle its closest ally. Not only did Ottawa not have an "unanswerable case" or even a "good chance" of success, the approach that Pearson advocated would have forced the US to "bring up their heavy guns."[34] Unwilling to push Washington into a position whereby it had to abandon its long held principles on sovereignty to agree with Canada's claims, Wrong advised Pearson to avoid any formal attempt to secure American recognition. Instead, Wrong – and the DEA more generally – opted for a more pragmatic and flexible approach, characterized by careful negotiations and quiet diplomacy. They sought a gradual, implicit US recognition of Canada's sovereignty – a textbook case of Pearsonian diplomacy.

While the DEA refrained from mentioning Canada's sector claim in its discussions with the State Department, Pearson was unwilling to jettison the principle. In a July 1946 article entitled "Canada Looks Down North" published in the influential American journal *Foreign Affairs,* he publicly tied Canada to the sector principle.[35] He explained that Ottawa used the principle to claim Canada's northern mainland as well as the islands and the frozen sea up to the North Pole, the first public indication of a Canadian maritime claim in the Arctic.[36] Although this did not reflect official policy, Pearson's position as ambassador gave the assertion tremendous weight. He used the article to tell the US exactly what he thought belonged to Canada, an example of the loud and public diplomacy he so abhorred. In fact, conveying to the Americans a stronger Canadian connection to the sector principle than the DEA actually embraced would have likely confused matters.

Although the government rejected Pearson's proposals regarding the sector principle, his influence on domestic strategies was more positive. In early 1948, while still USSEA, Pearson took up his appointment on the newly formed Advisory Committee on Northern Development (ACND) and attended its first meetings, in which he fought to improve Canada's Arctic capabilities. After becoming secretary of state for external affairs, Pearson was replaced on the committee by the new acting under-secretary, Escott Reid. Along with Arnold Heeney, Pearson was the chief architect of the "government policy of Canadianization" designed to keep "the Canadian Arctic Canadian." While he doubted that Washington possessed any conspiratorial designs for the region, he insisted that Canada must develop its own capabilities and end its dependence on the Americans for transportation and communications to isolated stations.[37] Pearson avidly supported new icebreakers for service in Arctic waters and endorsed Royal Canadian Air Force efforts to provide air transport for joint Canadian-American defence projects. When it came to practical matters, rather than the more theoretical issue of the legal basis for Canadian sovereignty, Pearson proved adept and pragmatic.[38]

Despite Pearson's important ACND work, his understanding of high-level Arctic issues remained confused and limited. Minister Pearson shocked northern expert R.A.J. Phillips in 1952 when he wondered "how good our claim was to some areas of the Arctic: If it must rest on discovery and continuous occupation, it may well be in future that our claim to some relatively unexplored areas will be shaky indeed."[39] By this point, after years of informal agreements and careful negotiations with the Americans, who had proven respectful of Canada's position even when they disagreed with it, most DEA officials felt that Canada's terrestrial sovereignty in the Arctic was more secure than ever.[40] Pearson's query also flew in the face of decades of Canadian policy, focusing on effective occupation of the region as the principle means of securing sovereignty. In the years that followed, Pearson's insecurities and confusion about Arctic sovereignty, plus his blind faith in the sector principle, raised more questions than they answered.

After the 1955 Canada-US agreement on the Distant Early Warning Line secured an "explicit recognition of Canadian claims to the exercise of sovereignty in the Far North,"[41] Ottawa's primary sovereignty concerns shifted from the Arctic Islands to the waters around them. Should Canada claim all the waters up to the North Pole, only the waters within the Arctic Archipelago, or limit itself to its three-mile belt of territorial waters? In his 1946 *Foreign Affairs* article, Pearson had suggested that the sector principle extended Canadian sovereignty all the way to the North Pole. While there was some international support for this bold proposition, the idea that sea ice and water could be assimilated in such a fashion flew in the face of established international law.[42]

The matter was left unexamined until August 1954, when the presence of Soviet-occupied ice-islands close to the Canadian sector prompted the Defence Research Board to undertake the first focused (albeit cursory) examination of the subject.[43] That same month the DEA, with Pearson as minister, studied the legal validity of the sector principle. Its conclusions were clear: alone, the principle provided an insufficient basis to claim any waters of the polar sector, or even the northern islands themselves. Furthermore, the legal experts concluded it was "most unlikely" that any foreign state would recognize a Canadian claim to the polar sector. Accordingly, they recommended avoiding making any such claim.[44] Whether Pearson approved this memorandum, which was intended to inform the Department of National Defence's response to Soviet activities, is unknown. Nevertheless, the assessment revealed the divergence between Pearson's adherence to the sector principle and his own department's position.

The government's decision to move away from the sector principle in claiming the Arctic waters was confirmed in March 1956 when Prime Minister Louis St-Laurent opted to limit Canada's maritime claim to the waters lying within the Arctic Archipelago. Behind the scenes, cabinet quietly decided that it intended to draw straight baselines around the Arctic Islands to enclose those waters as "inland,"[45] relying on a legal principle established by the International Court of Justice in 1951 when it accepted the validity of a vaguely similar Norwegian claim.[46] Furthermore, Deputy Minister of Mines and Technical Surveys Marc Boyer posited that these lines were meant to represent the maximum, rather than the minimum, of Canada's projected claim.[47] If this was indeed the case, these baselines were not meant to supplement the sector principle but to replace it. Though this course of action was kept secret for the time being, the Privy Council Office (PCO) circulated a letter to all government departments informing them of Canada's principled decision to "lay claim to sovereignty over the waters of these channels." It also instructed government officials to refrain from any action or public statement that might prejudice such a claim.[48] With this, Canada's preferred course of action was apparently set.

Pearson's public statements in the following months, however, demonstrated a lack of understanding about what the Liberal government was trying to accomplish. In April 1956, a *Globe and Mail* story asserted that Canada would soon establish a claim to the Arctic waters.[49] When asked to confirm or deny these assertions, Pearson stated that the article was inaccurate and that Canada had not yet decided "whether we will put this [claim] forward or not at this time."[50] Two weeks later, he was asked about the Norwegian case's effect on Canada's Arctic sovereignty. Pearson explained that baselines were inapplicable in the Canadian case because the distances between the Arctic Islands were too great.[51] That May, the question was revisited during a parliamentary committee hearing. Pearson again raised doubts as to the extent and status of Canada's maritime sovereignty given the ambiguity on the subject in international law. One year later, his statement was passed on to the chair of geography at the University of British Columbia, who had requested clarification of Canada's boundaries for use in American textbooks. Citing Pearson, the DEA admitted that it could provide no clear answer.[52]

Pearson's statements clearly contradicted cabinet's intentions. Straight baselines were the intended basis of Canadian sovereignty, and Pearson should have known that. Further, publicly implying that Canada was unsure of its sovereignty flew in the face of the PCO order to avoid prejudicing that claim. These interviews and public addresses were carefully followed by American diplomats, who dutifully kept Washington informed of events.[53] Statements like Pearson's helped to confirm in their minds that Canada either had no intention of making a claim or was so uncertain as to its potential claim that it could not offer public statements about it.

In subsequent years, Pearson continued to advocate for the sector principle despite the government's clear desire to situate Canadian sovereignty within a more internationally recognized legal framework. In July 1958, as leader of the Liberal Party and Official Opposition, Pearson spoke in the House of Commons about northern development. "We have claimed sovereignty," he asserted, "under what we call the sector theory over the prolongation north, right to their meeting at the north pole, of the east and west extensions of our boundary."[54] George Carty, an executive officer at the Department of Northern Affairs and Natural Resources, was surprised that Pearson would diverge so publicly from the position the Liberals had been trying to establish while in office. "This adds another distinguished name to the list of advocates of the sector theory!" Carty wrote to his deputy minister, R.G. Robertson. "I think we should keep it on file. I have also called it to Mr. [J.S.] Nutt's attention [at Canada's embassy in Washington] who thinks it adds confusion to an already confused situation."[55] One month later, Pearson reiterated his call to extend Canadian control over the Arctic all the way to the Pole, this time specifically mentioning that sovereignty encompassed permanent ice fields covering the Arctic Ocean.[56]

Pearson's choice to continue publicly pushing the sector notion was curious and counterproductive. By the summer of 1958, the DEA recognized that the issue had become totally confused by statements from Pearson and from those of the ruling Progressive Conservatives whose leader, Prime Minister John Diefenbaker, had made northern development a major policy plank.[57] The result was a detailed interdepartmental study on the matter, initiated in August 1958 and concluded the following summer. The conclusions largely mirrored those reached in 1956: Canada should rely on straight baselines to claim the waters of the Arctic Archipelago and should not pursue the sector theory or sovereignty over the waters of the Arctic Ocean.[58] The United States remained the chief stumbling block as it had never recognized Canadian sovereignty beyond a three-mile territorial sea. Nevertheless, DEA lawyer J.L. Delisle intimated that "it is not impossible perhaps that quiet negotiations with the United States ... might achieve reluctant acquiescence from them."[59]

In April 1963, Pearson's Liberals formed the government in Ottawa, and one of the new prime minister's first initiatives was to expand Canada's maritime domain. Having failed to secure a wider territorial sea and broader fisheries jurisdiction at the 1958 and 1960 UN Law of the Sea Conferences, cabinet decided to unilaterally enclose a series of important coastal waters as internal – a designation that subjected them to full Canadian sovereignty.[60] The initiative primarily focused on the east coast, but cabinet decided to include the Arctic waters as well.[61] To move forward with these claims, senior officials recognized that Canada needed American acquiescence. The US, as the world's principal defender of the traditional freedom of the seas and Canada's western neighbour in the Arctic, was the foreign power most directly interested. The Pearson government was confident, therefore, that Canadian sovereignty in these maritime areas would win broader international acceptance if the US could be brought onside.[62] Ottawa, however, grossly underestimated the importance Washington attached to matters of maritime sovereignty, and the assumption that Canada could acquire American support proved a brash overstep.

The Arctic claim that Canada advanced in 1963 was not based on the sector principle. Despite Pearson's long-standing connection to that theory, the DEA and other government departments with a northern interest had decisively rejected its use.[63] Instead, Canada attempted to secure American acceptance of its sovereignty to the waters within the Arctic Archipelago by pointing out the security benefits that would accrue to both nations if it had clear legal authority to bar Soviet vessels from the area. Washington, however, ignored this proposition.[64] During negotiations in late 1963, State Department representatives told their Canadian counterparts that American concerns about the freedom of the seas trumped localized security issues. For a government that recognized Soviet vessels' right to be three miles off the Florida coast, near the vital Cape Kennedy space facilities, Soviet activities in North American Arctic waters were of secondary concern.[65] US officials feared that if Canada was allowed to claim the Arctic (and other) waters, other states would cite this as a precedent to close off waters of strategic significance. For the world's greatest naval power, such an eventuality was unacceptable.

Pearson had again failed to abide by his own maxim: that Canada should only venture to force an issue with the Americans when it was "absolutely certain of [its] case."[66] Simply put, Ottawa lacked confidence in the strength of its case when it came to Arctic waters. The Diefenbaker government had received a "vigorous" rejection from Washington to similar claims that it had tentatively forwarded earlier that year,[67] and the DEA had recently concluded that drawing baselines around the Arctic Archipelago "would be unlikely to stand up to detailed analysis before a judicial tribunal."[68] In this context, as Canadian negotiators should have expected, Washington failed to give way on any of the crucial points.

American opposition compelled Canada to back away from some of its more contentious claims. In February 1964, SSEA Paul Martin informed the Americans that, while Canada was not formally abandoning its sovereignty claims to the Arctic waters, he was officially deferring them. This concession had little impact on the American representatives who threatened to take any of Canada's proposed straight baselines to the International Court.[69] Canada achieved none of its objectives, and State Department documents described the Canadians as pleading for face-saving measures to help "bail them out."[70] Ultimately, Pearson's drive to enclose the Arctic – and the other coastal waters – failed because his government misunderstood the actual and potential global implications of its actions. In 1967, the prime minister conceded that his law of the sea policy had been "singularly unsuccessful."[71]

In April 1968, Pearson's direct role in defining Canadian Arctic policy ended when Pierre Trudeau took over as prime minister. Even in retirement, however, Pearson marched to the beat of his own drum. In 1969, in the immediate aftermath of the American supertanker *Manhattan*'s controversial journey through the Northwest Passage, Pearson ventured to Washington to speak at a NATO conference. On a panel with former Secretary of State Dean Acheson and two former Scandinavian foreign ministers, Pearson reiterated his call for Canada to "assert sovereignty over the Arctic Islands and permanent ice floes." Thus, at a moment of extreme political sensitivity, when the very nature of Canada's Arctic sovereignty was being questioned, and after more than a decade of effort at the DEA to cement Canada's claim to the waters within the Arctic Archipelago by downplaying the sector principle, Pearson clung tenaciously to his long-standing belief that "permanent ice floes should be assimilated with permanent land" and that there was "a good argument" to be made for the sector theory.[72]

As was the case with his 1946 *Foreign Affairs* article, Pearson's statement came at an inopportune moment for Ottawa. Owing to the popular pressure for a more forceful Arctic policy after the *Manhattan,* the DEA was reassessing its position while trying to enforce more discipline in its messaging. Pearson's decision to resurrect the sector principle, while diverging from the official policy line that the DEA sought to implement, further confused the debate about what Canada was trying to claim in the Arctic – a complicated issue that might have benefitted from nuanced, quiet diplomacy had Pearson's personal understandings about sovereignty evolved over time.[73]

From 1929 onwards, Pearson advocated for an extreme version of the sector principle that did not simply see these meridians as lines of demarcation to claim territory (islands) but also as a means of enclosing the waters within and beyond Canada's Arctic Archipelago. In so doing, Pearson went further than most proponents of the principle in the Arctic and Antarctic, who applied it only to land. His ongoing promotion of Canada's sector claim ignored the principle's dubious validity in international law – and its uncertain status in the eyes of many DEA officials, who insisted that effective occupation constituted the real foundation of Canada's claim. Had Ottawa tried to attain formal American recognition of Canadian sovereignty in the Arctic in 1946, based on the sector principle, as Pearson urged on several occasions, Canada's position would have been dramatically weakened by Washington's inevitable rejection owing to US global legal interests. Nonetheless, Pearson continued his dogmatic support of the sector principle well after most senior decision makers in Ottawa recommended and set their sails on a different, more pragmatic, course.

In the mid-1950s, when Ottawa's focus shifted from terrestrial concerns to the status of Arctic waters, the DEA adopted a cautious policy that eschewed any vigorous, explicit assertion of the sector principle. Instead, officials promoted the idea of drawing straight baselines around the Arctic Islands rather than simple longitudinal lines to the North Pole. This policy trajectory was strongly implied in a cabinet decision of March 1956 and clearly laid out in a comprehensive interdepartmental study in 1959, which emphasized the value of avoiding American protests and quietly allowing the passage of time to strengthen Canada's position. Even Pearson's government downplayed the sector theory and highlighted Canada's claims to the waters within the archipelago when devising its sovereignty strategy in the mid-1960s. Pearson, however, either misunderstood or dismissed what the DEA hoped to accomplish and made bold public statements throughout his career that contradicted departmental policy. Thus, despite his well-earned recognition as Canada's foremost diplomat of the twentieth century, Pearson's views on Arctic sovereignty seemed both naive and archaic.

As prime minister, Pearson's failed attempt to secure explicit American recognition of Canada's sovereignty to the waters of the Arctic Archipelago reaffirmed his overly idealistic and immature appreciation of the bilateral relationship when it came to Arctic diplomacy. His ideas and actions were inflexible, immoderate, and loud, indicating a deep misunderstanding of the core political and legal variables involved. Far from giving Canada a "good chance at emerging successful" and with its sovereignty secure, Pearson's unbending views repeatedly placed his country in unwinnable and frequently embarrassing situations. While a fuller understanding of Pearson's Arctic policy will have to await the full release of his papers as well as some still confidential government files, the available record leads us to draw an odd but inescapable conclusion: when it came to the Arctic, Lester Pearson was decidedly un-Pearsonian.

Notes

1 "Consider This: Pearsonian Diplomacy in the Arctic," *Globe and Mail*, 25 January 2011. On the poll, see Jill Mahoney, "Canadians Rank Arctic Sovereignty as Top Foreign-Policy Priority," *Globe and Mail*, 24 January 2011; Jill Mahoney, "In the Arctic, Canada Willing to Fight to Keep the True North Free," *Globe and Mail*, 25 January 2011. EKOS Research conducted the international survey for the Munk School of Global Affairs at the University of Toronto and the Walter and Duncan Gordon Foundation.

2 Lester Pearson, *Mike: The Memoirs of the Right Honourable Lester Pearson*, vol. 2 (Toronto: University of Toronto Press, 1972), 31.

3 Denis Stairs, "Realists at Work: Canadian Policy Makers and the Politics of Transition from Hot War to Cold War," in *Canada and the Early Cold War*, ed. Greg Donaghy (Ottawa: Department of Foreign Affairs and International Trade, 1998), 112–13n9. See "Minister in the United States to the First Secretary, 21 March 1944," *Documents on Canadian External Relations* [*DCER*], *1944* (Ottawa: Queen's Printer for Canada, 1967), 1404–08.

4 Stairs, "Realists at Work," 98–99. See "Memorandum from Minister-Counselor, Legation in United States, to Minster in United States, 18 March 1943," in *DCER, 1943* (Ottawa: Queen's Printer for Canada, 1967), 1138–42.

5 Lester Pearson, *Mike: The Memoirs of the Right Honourable Lester Pearson*, vol. 1 (Toronto: University of Toronto Press, 1972), 68. Pearson believed that

diplomacy with the US should be carried out behind closed doors. The only exceptions were his 1951 public lecture to the Empire Club and the Canadian Club, in which he said that days of smooth and easy relations with the US might be over, and his infamous Temple University speech on American conduct in the war in Vietnam. See Erika Simpson, "The Principles of Liberal Internationalism According to Lester Pearson," *Journal of Canadian Studies* 1 (1999): 83–84, 91n55.

6 Denis Stairs, "Present in Moderation: Lester Pearson and the Craft of Diplomacy," *International Journal* 29 (1973–74): 152.

7 Shelagh Grant identified several Ottawa mandarins as important "northern nationalists," including Hugh Keenleyside and Vincent Massey, but not Pearson. See Shelagh Grant, "Northern Nationalists: Visions of 'A New North,' 1940–1950," in *For Purposes of Dominion: Essays in Honour of Morris Zaslow*, ed. Kenneth Coates and William R. Morrison, 47–70 (North York: Captus, 1989).

8 Gordon Smith, *A Historical and Legal Study of Sovereignty in the Canadian North: Land, 1870–1949*, ed. P. Whitney Lackenbauer (Calgary: University of Calgary Press, 2014), 305–6; Janice Cavell and Jeff Noakes, *Acts of Occupation: Canada and Arctic Sovereignty, 1918–25* (Vancouver: UBC Press, 2010), 245–46.

9 Lyle Dick, *Muskox Land: Ellesmere Island in the Age of Contact* (Calgary: University of Calgary Press, 2002), 218.

10 See Thorlief T. Thorliefsson, "Norway 'Must Really Drop Their Absurd Claims Such as That to the Otto Sverdrup Islands': Bi-Polar International Diplomacy; The Sverdrup Islands Question, 1902–1930" (MA thesis, Simon Fraser University, 2006).

11 Smith, *Historical and Legal Study*, 305–6.

12 For overviews of the sector principle in the polar regions, see Oscar Svarlien, "The Sector Principle in Law and Practice," *Polar Record* 10 (1960): 248–63; Donat Pharand, *Canada's Arctic Waters in International Law* (Cambridge: Cambridge University Press, 1988); and Donald Rothwell, *The Polar Regions and the Development of International Law* (Cambridge: Cambridge University Press, 1996).

13 Curiously, these borders still appear on Canadian maps today. See Pharand, *Canada's Arctic Waters*, 5.

14 An amendment to the Northwest Territories Act insisted that all people entering the sector had to get a permit from Ottawa. Nine days later, Stewart further clarified that Canada claimed "all the territory lying between meridians 60 and 141." See House of Commons, *Debates*, 1 June 1925, 3773; 10 June 1925, 4069, 4084; and Pharand, *Canada's Arctic Waters,* 48–50.

15 Gordon W. Smith, "Sovereignty in the North: The Canadian Aspect of an International Problem," in *The Arctic Frontier*, ed. R. St. J. Macdonald (Toronto: University of Toronto Press, 1966), 215; See Pharand, *Canada's Arctic Waters*. The best introductions to Canada's interwar Arctic sovereignty practice are: Cavell and Noakes, *Acts of Occupation*; and Smith, *Historical and Legal Study*. See also Janice Cavell, "Sector Claims and Counter-Claims: Joseph Elzéar Bernier, the Canadian Government, and Arctic Sovereignty, 1898–1934," *Polar Record* 50 (2014): 293–310.

16 John English, *Ice and Water: Politics, Peoples and the Arctic Council* (Toronto: Allen Lane, 2013), 64.

17 This fact was eventually recognized in international law. See International Court of Justice, *Eastern Greenland Case*, Judgment of 5 September 1933, ICJ Reports, 1933.

18 Lester Pearson, "The Question of Ownership in the Sverdrup Islands," 28 October 1929, quoted in Cavell and Noakes, *Acts of Occupation*, 245–46.

19 See, for instance, Einar-Arne Drivenes and Harald Dag Jølle, *Into the Ice: The History of Norway and the Polar Regions* (Oslo: Gyldendal Norsk Forlag, 2006), 292–94.

20 Amery to Byng, 30 January 1926, LAC, RG 13, vol. 1970, file 542, 1927.

21 S.W. Boggs, Department of State, Office of the Historical Adviser, The Polar Regions: Geographical and Historical Data in a Study of Claims to Sovereignty in the Arctic and Antarctic Regions, 21 September 1933, US National Archives and Records Administration (NARA), RG 59, Central Decimal File 1930–39, box 452, file 800.014, Arctic, 31; and Charles Hughes to Norwegian Minister, 2 April 1924, *Foreign Relations of the United States 1924* (Washington, DC: US Government Printing Office, 1939), 519–20. For more on the development of the Hughes Doctrine and the sector principle, see Whitney Lackenbauer and Peter Kikkert, "The Dog in the Manger – and Letting Sleeping Dogs Lie: The United States, Canada and the Sector Principle, 1924–1955," in *The Arctic Ocean: Essays in Honour of Donat Pharand*, ed. Suzanne Lalonde and Ted McDorman, 216–40 (Leiden: Brill, 2014).

22 Adams to Stimson, 23 September, 1929, quoted in Donat Pharand, *Law of the Sea of the Arctic, with Special Reference to Canada* (Ottawa: University of Ottawa Press, 1973), 142. For more on the American position on the sector principle and the Hughes Doctrine, see Lackenbauer and Kikkert, "Dog in the Manger."

23 John English, *Shadow of Heaven: The Life of Lester Pearson* (Toronto: Lester and Orpen Dennys, 1989), 257.

24 See Vincent Massey, *What's Past Is Prologue* (Toronto: Macmillan, 1963), 371; Clyde Sanger, *Malcolm MacDonald: Bringing an End to Empire* (Montreal and Kingston: McGill-Queen's University Press, 1995), 237–39; Shelagh Grant, *Sovereignty or Security? Government Policy in the Canadian North, 1936–1950* (Vancouver: UBC Press, 1988), 103–15; Stanley Dziuban, *Military Relations Between the United States and Canada, 1939–1945* (Washington, DC: Office of the Chief of Military History, Department of the Army, 1959), 217–28, 331–34; Whitney Lackenbauer, "Right and Honourable: Mackenzie King, Canadian-American Bilateral Relations, and Canadian Sovereignty in the Northwest, 1943–1948," in *Mackenzie King: Citizenship and Community*, ed. John English, Ken McLaughlin, and Whitney Lackenbauer, 151–68 (Toronto: Robin Brass Studio, 2002).

25 Stairs, "Realists at Work," 98–99.

26 Kenneth Eyre, "Custos Borealis: The Military in the Canadian North" (PhD diss., King's College London, 1981).

27 On these US proposals, see Shelagh Grant, *Polar Imperative: A History of Arctic Sovereignty in North America* (Vancouver: Douglas and McIntyre, 2011),

283–300; David Bercuson, "Continental Defense and Arctic Security, 1945–50: Solving the Canadian Dilemma," in *The Cold War and Defense*, ed. K. Neilson and R.G. Haycock, 153–70 (New York: Praeger, 1990); and P. Whitney Lackenbauer and Peter Kikkert, "Sovereignty and Security: The Department of External Affairs, the United States, and Arctic Sovereignty, 1945–68," in *In the National Interest: Canadian Foreign Policy and the Department of Foreign Affairs and International Trade, 1909–2009*, ed. Greg Donaghy and Michael Carroll, 101–20 (Calgary: University of Calgary Press, 2011).

28 Though usually concerned by US activities, even R.M. Macdonnell noted that "in presenting this request, the United States Embassy made it clear that there was no question of interfering in any way with Canadian sovereignty. I think that their approach to the problem should reassure your minister if he is troubled by any thought of Canadian sovereignty in the Arctic being called into question by the United States." See Macdonnell to Camsell, 11 May 1946, LAC, RG 25, vol. 3347, file 9061-A-40.

29 See, for example, Macdonnell to Heeney, 3 November 1945, LAC, RG 25, vol. 3047, file 9061-A-40.

30 Ambassador in the United States to Acting Under-Secretary of State for External Affairs, 5 June 1946, in *DCER, 1946* (Ottawa: Queen's Printer, 1967), 1565–66.

31 Wrong to Heeney, 8 June 1946, LAC, RG 25, vol. 3347, file 9061-A-40.

32 Wrong to Abbott, 13 June 1946, and Wrong to Heeney, 8 June 1946, LAC, RG 25, vol. 3347, file 9061-A-40.

33 Memorandum attached to letter from Acheson to Clayton, 15 July 1946, NARA RG 165, entry 421, box 598. In 1951, the Department of State made this stance official, specifically addressing the question of sovereignty over ice in a policy decision written to inform American diplomats and consular officials. The relevant section read: "Nor could the Arctic seas, in our view, be made subject to 'territorial' sovereignty of any state even though they might contain ice areas having some characteristics of land ... The US position is that the Arctic seas and the air spaces above them, in so far as they are outside of accepted territorial limits, are open to commerce and navigation in the same degree as other open seas." See United States, Department of State, *Foreign Relations of the United States*, "Department of State Policy Statement," *Polar Regions*, vol. 1, 1 July 1951, 1724.

34 Stairs, "Realists at Work," 98–99.

35 We have found no evidence in the documentary record that Pearson received official permission to publish this article as a formal statement of government policy.

36 L.B. Pearson, "Canada Looks 'Down North,'" *Foreign Affairs* 24 (1946): 638–47.

37 Minutes of Second Meeting of Advisory Committee on Northern Development, 1 June 1948, *DCER, 1948* (Ottawa: Department of External Affairs and International Trade, 1994), 1523; extract from Minutes of Meeting of Advisory Committee on Northern Development, 10 March 1949, *DCER, 1949* (Ottawa: Department of Foreign Affairs and International Trade, 1995); and Grant, *Sovereignty or Security?*, 227.

38 See Lester Pearson, "Canada's Northern Horizon," *Foreign Affairs* 31, 4 (1953): 581–91.

39 Phillips to Clerk of the Privy Council, "Developments in the Arctic," 29 December 1952, *DCER, 1952* (Ottawa: Department of External Affairs and International Trade, 1990), 1196–200.

40 See Phillips, "Development in the Arctic," 1198. As Phillips explained, "I am not now worried by formal claims, since the US Administration has been entirely reasonable during the past six years that we have been working together in the Arctic."

41 R.J. Sutherland, "Strategic Significance of the Canadian Arctic," in Macdonald, *Arctic Frontier*, 271.

42 For the best analysis of the early legal theories concerning the sector and the notion of continuity, see Smith, *Historical and Legal Study*.

43 Defence Research Board, "Russian Activities on the Canadian Side of the Pole," 12 August 1954, DHH, file 2002/17.

44 "The Sector Theory and Floating Ice Islands in the Arctic," 30 August 1954, DHH, file 2002/17.

45 The file cited here quotes heavily from the cabinet decision. The original remains classified, as does much of the surrounding material. See Memorandum from Legal Division, 12 July 1968, LAC, RG 25, vol. 15729, file 25-4-1.

46 International Court of Justice, *Fisheries Case*, Judgment of 18 December 1951, ICJ Reports. The similarity of the Norwegian and Canadian Arctic baselines was, and remains, an issue of debate. See Pharand, *Canada's Arctic Waters*, 142–43.

47 Boyer to Léger, 16 November 1956, LAC, RG 25, file 10600-40.

48 Reference to these events is made in Beesley to de Blois, 5 April 1968, LAC, RG 25, vol. 15729, file 25-4-1.

49 Dave McIntosh, "Canada Will Ask UN for 12-Mile Limits," *Globe and Mail*, 17 August 1956.

50 Rewinkel to the Department of State, 7 September 1956, NARA, RG 59, Central Decimal File 1955–1959, box 3215, file 742.022.

51 Excerpt from unofficial transcript of press conference, 30 August 1956, NARA, RG 84, entry UD2195C, box 50.

52 Léger to Robinson, 9 January 1957, LAC, RG 25, file 9057-40.

53 See previous notes for evidence. Records of Pearson's interviews were taken from American State Department records.

54 House of Commons, *Debates*, 7 July 1958, 1963.

55 Carty to Robertson and Nutt, 24 July 1958, LAC, RG 25, vol. 6510, file 9057-40-pt.7.

56 "Populate Arctic Establish Canada's Claim, Pearson Urges," *Toronto Star*, 14 August 1958.

57 See statements by John Diefenbaker, House of Commons, *Debates*, 16 August 1958, 3652; and Alvin Hamilton, House of Commons, *Debates*, 14 August 1958, 3513.

58 Memorandum, "Canadian Sovereignty over Arctic Waters," in Minutes of the 54th Meeting of the ACND, 6 July 1959, LAC, RG2-B-2, vol. 6182.

59 Draft letter by Delisle to R.G. Robertson, 17 December 1958, LAC, RG 25, vol. 7118, file 9057-40-pt.8.

60 Adam Lajeunesse, *Lock, Stock, and Icebergs: A History of Canada's Arctic Maritime Sovereignty* (Vancouver: UBC Press, 2016).

61 The other bodies of water were the Gulf of St. Lawrence, the Bay of Fundy, Dixon Entrance, Hecate Strait, Queen Charlotte Sound, and Hudson Bay.

62 Cabinet Conclusions, 7 August 1963, LAC, RG 2, vol. 6245.

63 Memorandum, "Canadian Sovereignty over Arctic Waters," in Minutes of the 54th Meeting of the ACND, 6 July 1959, LAC, RG2-B-2, vol. 6182.

64 Deputy Secretary of Defence to Johnson, 16 September 1963, NARA, RG 59, Central Foreign Policy Files 1957–1966 (CFPF), Canada-US POL 33-4 1963.

65 Memorandum of conversation discussion of proposed extension of fisheries zone, 12 February 1964, NARA, RG 59, Central Foreign Policy Files (CFPF) 1957–66, Canada-US POL 33-4 1963.

66 Stairs, "Realists at Work," 112–13n9.

67 Memorandum for the Prime Minister from the Secretary of State for External Affairs, 2 March 1963, DHH, file 20044/79, file 35.

68 "Status of the Waters of the Canadian Arctic Archipelago," 9 March 1959, LAC, RG 25, vol. 7118, file 9057-40-pt.8.

69 Memorandum of conversation, 5 February 1964, NARA, RG 59, CFPF, POL 33-4 CAN-US; and Memorandum of conversation, 6 July 1964, NARA, RG 59 CFPF, POL 33-8, CAN-US.

70 Memorandum of conversation, NARA, RG 59, Central Files 1964–66, POL 33-4, CAN-US.

71 Cabinet Minutes, 2 March 1967, LAC, RG 2, vol. 6323.

72 Bruce Garvey, "Pearson Says We Should Assert Arctic Control," *Toronto Star*, 22 October 1969.

73 At the time, the political opposition and the media demanded a straightforward claim of sovereignty. For practical and legal reasons Trudeau was reluctant to do this. Instead, he adopted more functional powers with the Arctic Waters Pollution Prevention Act, leaving the legal question of sovereignty unresolved.

Maurice Jr. M. Labelle

8 Not So Nobel
Arab Perceptions of Lester Pearson and Canada

Canada's centennial anniversary, exemplified by Expo '67 in Montreal, offered Canadians and non-Canadians alike a rare space to collectively reflect upon the idea of Canada. For Prime Minister Lester Pearson, it was "a wonderful opportunity to celebrate our Canadian identity."[1] The world was invited to Canada, and Kuwait, alongside other Middle Eastern states such as Egypt, Israel, and Iran, accepted Ottawa's invitation. With Expo "passports" in hand, many Canadians encountered the Persian Gulf sheikhdom for the first time. Kuwait's pavilion on Île Notre-Dame told stories about its path to national development. Kuwait's "tribal modern" identity was on display,[2] as the "travels of the country's traditional coffee merchants [we]re contrasted with the routes of the country's modern airline system."[3]

Eight weeks into this intercultural exchange, Kuwait offered an unexpected glimpse into Middle Eastern politics when "fairgoers found two hand-lettered signs reading 'Closed' on the locked glass door" of its pavilion.[4] Expo '67, it turns out, facilitated the arrival of issues of Arab decolonization into the Canadian public sphere when Kuwait – unlike its Middle Eastern neighbours in Montreal – abruptly folded up its $200,000 tent to protest Canada's policy vis-à-vis the Arab-Israeli conflict. Worse yet, the Arab perspective critiqued a core myth within Canadian nationalism: Kuwait charged that Canada was far from a "friendly" peacekeeping nation.[5] Pearson's reluctance to defend Arab territorial integrity following Egypt's blockade of the Gulf of Aqaba to Israeli shipping in late May 1967 unearthed "Canada's hostile stand [towards] the Arab nations."[6] In a telegram sent directly to the Canadian prime minister and the speaker of Canada's Parliament, Foreign Minister Sheikh Sabah al-Ahmad al-Jabir denounced Ottawa's Middle East policy as detrimental to "the Arab states who are legitimately seeking to restore their usurped rights, liberate occupied Palestine and return it to their legitimate owners."[7]

To the chagrin of Pearson, Secretary of State for External Affairs Paul Martin, Expo '67 organizers, and fairgoers, the Kuwaiti pavilion remained closed. Yet Kuwait's timely critique of Canadian national identity loomed as the Arab-Israeli crisis of 1967 unfolded over Canada's centennial year and much of Pearson's remaining time at 24 Sussex Drive. Kuwait's withdrawal from Expo '67, moreover, represents an under-explored dimension of international relations: Arab perceptions of Canada.[8] The historiography of Canada-Middle East relations is in dire need of creative investigation as existing literature tilts towards bilateral relations between Israel and Canada, indirectly positioning Arab, Iranian, Turkish, and Kurdish voices on the margins of Canadian diplomatic history.[9]

This chapter explores Arab perceptions of Canada and Pearson during the Arab-Israeli crisis of 1967. The category of "Arab" here is best explained as a "transnational consciousness."[10] The Arab world and its myriad peoples, of course, are far from being socially, politically, and culturally uniform. But, as Eugene Rogan aptly explains, "They are one people and many peoples at the same time."[11] Arab distinctiveness in the Middle East and North Africa, as well as in the world, should not occlude a powerful, historical sense of interconnection cemented by common historical experiences with Western imperialisms, its Orientalist culture, national decolonizations, and postcolonalism, amidst other unifying factors such as religion and language.[12] And, as immigration historians contend, flows of peoples between continents failed to restrict cultural linkages as numerous bridges of global imaginaries engendered unique, often frustrating, experiences for migrant communities and their new-found societies.[13] The Arab *mahjar* (diaspora) in Canada was no exception. Arab Canadian objections to Pearsonianism (defined and discussed by Robert Bothwell in Chapter 1, this volume) connected Canada with the Middle East as, throughout 1967, Arab-initiated conversations regarding Canadian identity and Middle East policy rapidly criss-crossed multiple states, cultures, and geographies.

An Arab consciousness in the world indicted Canadian diplomacy and its Nobel Prize-winning architect. Pearson's policy in 1967, it argued, tragically deviated from Ottawa's culture of "impartiality," best exemplified by its noble stand during the Suez Crisis, which catapulted Canada, Pearson, and the national peacekeeping myth into Canadian and international imaginations. The Arab critique of Pearson's self-proclaimed "even-handedness," this chapter argues, embodied a transnational attempt to push Canadian Middle East policy in a more "balanced," humanitarian direction and pull it away from indirectly sponsoring Israeli settler colonialism at the expense of Arab human dignity, both in Canada and abroad.

Prior to the United Nations' creation in 1945, the Middle East and North Africa had been relatively disconnected from Canada – and vice versa – for most of the latter's national existence. It was only during the special session of the United Nations Special Committee on Palestine in 1947 that Ottawa – and Pearson – established direct, extensive contacts with newly independent Middle Eastern states, peoples, and perspectives. Both long-time Israeli diplomat Abba Eban and a handful of Canadian diplomatic historians contend that Pearson was central in the UN's controversial decision to partition British-mandated Palestine into "Arab" and "Jewish" states. His rapport with Arab delegates – "some of whom did not hesitate to tell [him] at the time what they thought of [his] views and the policy of [Louis St-Laurent's] government" – suffered as a result. Even as partition incited the first Arab-Israeli war and led to *al-nakbah* (the catastrophe), the passing of UN Resolution 181 cemented Pearson's reputation as a peacemaker.[14]

In fact, it is likely that few Middle Eastern and North African Arabs outside UN walls knew of or discussed Canada's involvement in Palestine's partition. Likewise, Pearson had few encounters with foreign Arab perspectives. Only following Ottawa's de jure recognition of Israel in early 1949 did Canada normalize diplomatic relations with some Middle Eastern states – an exception being Turkey, which exchanged ambassadors with Canada in 1944. After establishing official representation with Tel Aviv in the early 1950s, Ottawa forged formal cursory relations with Egypt, Lebanon, and Iran. And whereas Canada contributed financially to assuage the worsening plight of Arab refugees, it failed to consider Palestinian suffering as "a major issue" in Canada-Middle East relations.[15]

Back in Ottawa, however, Pearson gradually became acquainted with Arab "immigration foreign relations."[16] The Arab Canadian community numbered just 12,301 people and congregated mainly in Montreal, Toronto, and London. Its political presence within the Canadian public sphere was limited. According to Arab Canadian leader James Peters, "very little activity" existed "at the grass roots levels." That said, Arab Canadian activism focused predominantly on "the defence of the Arab name" and Palestine.[17]

The Middle East itself gained a special place in Canadian imaginations following the Suez Crisis of 1956–57, when Pearson was integral to creating a UN-implemented ceasefire and publicly pushed the formation of the United Nations Emergency Force. Middle Eastern and Canadian Arabs alike heralded the Israeli-British-French withdrawal as a victory over imperialism and celebrated Canada's dedication to global "peacekeeping." Sami Hadawi, a public relations officer for the Palestine Arab Refugee Office in New York City, later explained that "Canada's contribution ... was highly appreciated by the Arabs and its image as a nation of principle with no colonial or territorial ambitions was greatly enhanced." Arab Canadian leader Mohammad Said Massoud, upon hearing the news in 1957 that Pearson had won the Nobel Peace Prize for his role during the Suez Crisis, congratulated the Canadian minister for this "noble reward." Pearson's accomplishment led the League of Arab States to acknowledge Canada's importance in world affairs by establishing its first information office in Ottawa.[18] Ultimately, the Suez Crisis, the invention of the "peacekeeper," Pearson's Nobel Peace Prize, and ensuing global praise deepened Canadians' self-perceptions of their nation as an impartial middle power. The crisis exacerbated the myth of Canadian exceptionalism as the idea of the Middle East and the region itself became important spaces for Canadian national identity formation and Pearsonianism. Canadians perceived themselves as being antithetical to Americans and to fading imperial powers.

The establishment of formal relations between Ottawa and Middle Eastern states, plus the growth of Arab Canadian communities, coincided with Pearson's move to 24 Sussex Drive in 1963. Considered by Arabs as a welcome change to the pro-Zionist Tory leader John Diefenbaker, Pearson embodied Canadian exceptionalism. Canada's Middle East policy, many Arabs hoped, would abandon a pro-Israeli bias in favour of "impartiality." Pearson's government privately vowed to reassert Canada's "peacekeeping role" in the Middle East and "keep [its] skirts clean from Arab and Israeli mud." Yet, in fact, Pearson's policy was marred as Ottawa made "Israel's right to exist and prosper" *the* key tenet of Canadian diplomacy, even if this led many to declare that Canada was "3/4 impartial on the Israeli side." Pearsonianism, publicly boasting its so-called neutrality, chose *not* to grant equitable treatment to the Palestinian and Arab right to self-determination. Nor did it buttress the territorial integrity of Arab states against perceived Israeli expansionism; rather, Ottawa ardently defended Israeli security to the detriment of Palestine and decolonization more broadly.[19]

The partial nature of Canadian diplomacy revealed itself to Arabs in May 1967. Tensions had mounted along various Arab-Israeli frontiers given Israel's occupation of Palestinian border villages, mistreatment of Palestinian refugees seeking to recover their properties, and *fedayeen* raids from Syria into Israel. Following the development of a "Syrian syndrome," Israeli leaders opted to publicly humiliate Damascus by sending planes to visibly roam the skies over the Syrian capital and shoot down Syrian aircraft on the way home. Then, on 12 May, Israeli chief of staff Yitzhak Rabin declared: "We will carry out a lightning attack on Syria, occupy Damascus, overthrow the regime there and come back."[20]

This threat sounded Arab alarms, drew Soviet attention, and engendered the Arab-Israeli crisis of 1967. To prevent the global Cold War from turning hot in the Middle East, Moscow immediately fabricated a false report detailing Israeli troop mobilization along the Syrian border and passed it first to Damascus, which ignored it, and then to Cairo. An Egyptian diplomatic response, Soviet leaders hoped, would dissuade Israeli hawkishness. Egyptian *raïs* Gamal Abdel Nasser agreed. The much-heralded father of Arab nationalism could not sit idly on the sidelines when Arab territorial and moral integrity, not to mention his public image, were at stake. Like Israel, Nasser believed Arab states had a right to exist and live in security. Cairo, which had a defence pact with Damascus, needed to deter Tel Aviv from launching a third Arab-Israeli war in Syria. Nasser thus responded by mobilizing Egyptian forces in the Sinai Desert bordering Israel.[21]

On 16 May 1967, Nasser surprised the world by urgently demanding the removal of the seven-nation, 3,393-person UNEF force stationed along the Egyptian side of the Egypt-Israel border. UN *casques bleus*, Nasser contended, infringed upon Egyptian sovereignty. If Tel Aviv could reject peacekeepers on Israeli soil back in 1957, so could Egypt.[22] UN Secretary-General U Thant controversially respected the Egyptian request and initiated a withdrawal. Nasser's demand, given Canada's leading role in UNEF, drew much criticism from Ottawa. During a House of Commons debate, Martin proclaimed: "This will be a matter of the greatest regret, because we recall with pride that this force was setup as a result of the initiative, action and imagination of the present Prime Minister of Canada." The "whole concept of peacekeeping," Martin explained, was in jeopardy.[23] As Michael Carroll notes (Chapter 2, this volume), Nasser's move left many Canadians disillusioned with peacekeeping; but Canadian actions during the subsequent crisis left many Middle Easterners disillusioned with Canada.

Nasser aggravated matters on 22 May by shutting the Straits of Tiran to Israeli shipping, prompting many Canadians to fear the onset of a third Arab-Israeli war and its potential impact upon Israeli security. Egypt's decision coincided with Israeli president Zalman Shazar's visit to Canada "to celebrate Canada's centennial" and Israel National Day at Expo '67 on 23 May. In talks with Pearson, Shazar invoked Canadian exceptionalism by outlining Canada's centrality in resolving the Suez Crisis and urged another Pearsonian intervention. Heeding Shazar's request, Pearson turned to the UN. With covert US and British assistance, Canada's UN representative George Ignatieff co-sponsored an unsuccessful Security Council resolution with his Danish colleague Hans Tabor to urge "restraint" in the Middle East and to call for UN pacification.[24]

Canada's strident opposition to UNEF withdrawal and its desire to lead UN intervention in the Middle East incited Arab consternation. Egypt's UN representative, Mohammed Awad al-Kony, "launched into a bitter attack," accusing Ottawa of being partial towards Tel Aviv as Canada would not denounce Israeli threats against Syria let alone support Palestine's right to exist. Egypt, he lamented, was "the target of an ugly campaign of distortion and abuse." While he accused Canada of being an Anglo-American diplomatic disciple, Egypt's undiplomatic accusation was correct given Ignatieff's collusion with his US and British colleagues. As Ignatieff later recounted, they "met many times during the weeks leading up to the Six-Day War, and because of Canada's direct involvement in UNEF, [they] agreed that [he] should carry the ball for the three of [them] in the Security Council." Egypt's delegation told its Canadian counterpart privately that Canada's reputation in Egypt was suffering given its role in the proposed UN resolution. Cairo wished that Canada would resume its much-celebrated peacekeeping role by being "a 'bridge' for Western powers who are exercising threats" towards Egypt.[25]

The Egyptian-led Arab critique of Canadian diplomacy persisted. In a press conference held on 28 May 1967, Nasser singled out Pearson, who "won the Nobel Prize for peace." Ottawa's opposition to UNEF withdrawal, Nasser declared, "is a hostile, neo-colonialist action, because UNEF arrived in our country with our approval and could not ... continue when we withdraw this approval." Pearson's position, if anything, proved his collusion with the United States, whose special relationship with Israel endangered Arab decolonization. Ottawa had chosen Israel and settler colonialism over impartiality and decolonization, engaging in "a hostile action towards [Egypt] and all Arabs." As evidenced by its participation in Expo '67, Nasser reiterated Egypt's "friendly feelings toward the Canadian people." He was shocked, therefore, "by her prejudiced attitude as well as Mr. Pearson's in favour of Israel." Nasser lamented: "Our relations with Canada these days are not ... as cordial as they used to be."[26]

With increased Western naval traffic in the eastern Mediterranean breeding suspicions of a Suez-like international plot, Nasser demanded that Canada's UNEF contingent be withdrawn within forty-eight hours. As reported by Egypt's leading newspaper *Al-Ahram,* Pearson's "suspicious, belligerent, unjustified policy" had forced Nasser's hand. An affronted Pearson immediately sent a personal letter to Nasser protesting his "quite unfair and unjustified" allegations. His government "always tried to act objectively and without prejudice." Pearson's objective was to prevent another Suez, not reproduce it. Canada, contrary to Egyptian impressions, was a friendly nation. Thus, Pearson acquiesced to Egypt's request.[27]

As Canadian peacekeepers left the Middle East, Pearson defended Canada's peacekeeping identity. Unbeknownst to Nasser, Tel Aviv secretly approached Ottawa about partaking "in naval action *outside* the framework of the United Nations to maintain the freedom of innocent passage in the Gulf of Aqaba." Pearson refused, venting in his diary about the "unfair" Arab "charge" that Canada was "pro-Israel and anti-Arab." Arabs, he passionately remarked, "should be the first to know that we didn't help bring UNEF into being – or serve it faithfully for 10 years – because we were pro-Israel!" Canada, he insisted, "could have taken and shown deep offence at [Arab] remarks" and sided with Israel; instead, it offered a "balanced" position. Cairo's reference to Ottawa "as the cat's paw" of the United States was "completely unfounded."[28]

Pearson publicly clarified his position towards the brewing crisis. Declaring that Canadian policy towards the Middle East remained as noble as it had been in 1956, he affirmed: "I have no feeling of any kind in favour of one side or the other." Next he explained that global Zionism, contrary to popular Arab belief, did not dictate Canadian diplomacy. While Arab criticisms of Canadian peacekeeping were unjustified, Canada, despite harsh critiques, refused to get "sore." He saw the situation as a major challenge for so-called middle powers: "We have always been loved by everyone ... [u]ntil recently. But it's not anything to get too panicky about because we are being criticized and attacked by a particular country for the wrong reason, and I think without justification." If war ensued, Canada would align itself with the UN and hold the aggressor accountable, be it Arab or Israeli.[29]

Whereas Pearson's television appearance likely appeased many Canadians, Arab discomfort about Canadian diplomacy was far from mollified. Pearson's position, complained Canada's embassy in Cairo, remained a subject of Egyptian "misinterpretation." Writing to Izzat Tannous, the newly created Palestine Liberation Organization's (PLOs) permanent representative to the UN, Arab Canadian leader James Peters commented: "I am sickened by the biased presentation of the news. Occasionally, a flash of truth is allowed through, but it is soon buried beneath the Zionist lies, and the stereotyped and conventional thinking of all those using the media." Peters's Canadian Arab Friendship Society of Toronto issued a press release to counter the "claim that Arab resentment towards Canada is based on Arab misunderstanding of Canada's motive in her relations with the Arab states." The document encouraged Canadians to "realize that we have been rubbing the Arabs the wrong way for the last 20 years." Canada's Middle East policy was flawed for Canadian diplomacy "never was truly neutral in the dispute between the Arabs and the Zionists, both in and out of Israel." Ottawa, through its support for partition, "which was rejected by the Palestinian Arabs as unjust and oppressive"; its rapid recognition of Israel; its tolerance of Israel's forceful relocation of 900,000 Palestinians; and its siding with Zionist settler colonialism consequently belied Arab rights to self-determination. The Canadian state, society, and media, furthermore, continually represented "Arabs in a poor light ... while Israel [was] always portrayed as heroic, democratic, and progressive." Peters's organization lamented, "in no other country in the world outside Israel, has Zionism such freedom to propagandize and influence people with its lies as it enjoys in Canada." Canadians "have not been neutral, neither at the governmental nor at the popular level, while deceiving ourselves with our imagined self-image of neutrality." In Arab imaginations, as Canada had betrayed its "national mission" of peacekeeping, Canadians "should not be surprised at the cumulative reaction of the Arabs, nor at the growing mistrust of the non-aligned nations."[30]

Canada's opportunity to demonstrate impartiality came on 5 June 1967 with the outbreak of war between Israel and Egypt. Israel's UN representative immediately disseminated calculated misinformation when he informed the Security Council president "that Egyptian land and air forces [first] moved against Israel and Israeli forces were now engaged in repelling Egyptian forces." Israel was "acting in self defense," its sole aim being "to put an end to the Arab attempt to conquer Israel." Reifying a foundational Israeli myth, Israel's UN representative avowed David would outmatch Goliath: "Arabs had greater numbers but Israel though small was brave and would prevail." The Security Council, which included Canada, convened to halt hostilities as Cairo denied Israel's claims of Egyptian instigation and accused its foe of premeditation.[31]

As Israel quickly gained the military upper hand in the Egyptian-administered Gaza Strip and Sinai region, as well as in Jordan's West Bank, Pearson offered Ignatieff "a typically Pearsonian piece of advice ... 'Keep your head up, George' ... 'With your head down, you look bald and asleep.'"[32] Despite having declared on Canadian television that Canada would hold any aggressor accountable, he declined to reprimand Israel and saw an opportunity to exercise Pearsonianism. Ottawa collaborated with Washington and London at the UN to ensure Israel was not deemed "guilty of aggression." Indeed, Canada's delegation, based on US "suggestions," tabled a successful ceasefire resolution to the Security Council on 7 June, the third day of the war. By design, Israeli responsibility for instigating the conflict was absent from the Canadian resolution.[33]

Egypt and Jordan, admitting defeat, agreed to an immediate ceasefire with Israel, with Syria following suit on 10 June. Israel, having occupied the West Bank (including Jerusalem's Old City), the Gaza Strip, the Sinai, and the Golan Heights, now insisted that these territories be incorporated into *Eretz Yisrael*.[34] A permanent peace seemed elusive in the short term, at least for Pearson. After the guns fell silent, Pearson asked in his diary: "How are peace and security to be secured in the new situation created by the fact that Israel, after the quick and sweeping victory of its armed forces, now occupies strategic territory beyond its present borders?" Israel's refusal to return all occupied territories aggravated the Arab sense of defeat and caused most to question Tel Aviv's dedication to peace. Yet the former Canadian Nobel Peace Prize winner again made Israeli security his first priority. Land for peace, Pearson concluded, was the most viable means to solve the Arab-Israeli conflict. As Israel had the upper hand, Pearson hoped that it would "act with a wise consideration for her own long-range interests in the negotiations which will soon begin."[35]

Arabs urged Ottawa to demand Israeli withdrawal as a necessary first step in the so-called peace process. Albert Salloum, leader of the Arab community in southwest Saskatchewan, petitioned Pearson to have "Israel be condemned [as] the aggressor." Iraq's ambassador to Iran called on Canada "to support the withdrawal of all Israeli troops from conquered territory and to oppose the retention by Israel of any such territory." Arab perceptions of Canada and the future of Arab-Canada relations, he declared, were at stake. Canada, as a peacekeeper, must ensure that international law prevailed over settler colonialism and therefore must acknowledge Israeli aggression. Frustrating Canadian diplomats stationed in the Middle East, instead, Canada recognized Israel's "right of conquest" and called for Arab recognition of Israel's territorial existence as a prerequisite to peace talks. "Our relations with Arab countries have seriously deteriorated during the past few weeks," warned Canada's embassy in Cairo, "and are not likely to improve so long as we insist that Israel's right to exist is a fundamental proposition which Arabs must accept as a basis for a viable Middle East settlement."[36]

The Security Council's refusal "to demand the immediate and conditional withdrawal of Israeli troops from Arab territory occupied during the war" – thanks in part to Canadian diplomacy – prompted a General Assembly emergency session. The Security Council, however, unanimously adopted a cursory resolution, asking Tel Aviv "to facilitate the return of those inhabitants who ha[d] fled the areas [in] which military operations had taken place] since the outbreak of war."[37] Seeking to uphold Canada's benevolent reputation at home and globally, Pearson announced that Canada was dispatching "$2.5-million worth of relief food to the Middle East." Recent Palestinian victims – concerning which Tel Aviv falsely vowed to Ottawa "that at no time had [it] encouraged the movement of refugees from the West Bank to the East Bank of the Jordan" – would get "a million dollars of wheat flour," courtesy of Canada. In the name of humanitarianism, Pearson indirectly buttressed private Zionist initiatives to solve the Palestinian refugee problem via resettlement beyond Israel's new borders as early as 7 June 1967, despite Arab objections. Canada, Minister of Manpower and Immigration Jean Marchand told Pearson, "could realistically absorb" 100,000 Palestinians.[38]

Rather than demanding that Palestinian refugees be allowed to return to their former homes, Pearson backed Tel Aviv's desire to have the land without the people; or, as Israeli historian Avi Raz puts it, to have a dowry without the bride.[39] Whereas Middle Eastern public optics predominantly shifted away from Canada and the "West" and focused on the failed development of Arab societies in the wake of what Nasser called the Arab *naksah* (setback), Arab Canadians held Canadian diplomacy to be complicit in the ongoing humiliation of Arabs and fought to reorient Canadian exceptionalism. More specifically, Pearson's approach to Palestinian refugees had the adverse effect of belying Arab human dignity. A telegram sent to the prime minister on behalf of the Arab Canadian Community critiqued Pearson's "seemingly humanitarian offer to the Arab Palestinian refugees for resettlement in Canada." A more honest, humanitarian approach would be "to stop the migration of [Israeli citizens] to the lands of these refugees" and to "make plans to absorb the illegal occupants of the Arab homelands." Palestinian Canadian refugee Michel Haddad, in an op-ed for the Arab Canadian-operated *Canadian Middle East Journal,* called upon all Arabs in Canada "to help explain the Arab's point of view for the benefit of [his] countrymen" in Canada and Palestine.[40]

Meanwhile, the UN General Assembly debated the framework for peace. International divisions over condemning Israeli "aggression" and making an Israeli withdrawal from occupied Arab territories a first condition for settling the conflict remained entrenched. Ottawa, for its part, held firm. While insisting that Canada had "no direct national interest" in the Middle East and held no prejudice, Ignatieff told the

General Assembly that Canada could not condone any resolution that "restored the situation to what it was" prior to 5 June 1967. Israeli withdrawal, accordingly, should only come after key Arab concessions, not vice versa.[41]

Canada's embassy in Beirut, a week after Ignatieff's speech, received a three-page petition signed by sixty-eight Lebanese intellectuals. Seeking to "foster a better understanding" between Lebanon and Canada, the petitioners explained the logic behind the general Arab reluctance to recognize Israel. Above all, they asserted that the claim that Israel was strictly a "Jewish land" violated the individual and collective rights of Indigenous Palestinians. Zionism, by design, also jeopardized the human dignity and territorial integrity of neighbouring Arab nations. The Lebanese petitioners saw Arab recognition of Israel as "the Jewish state" as a means of effecting the "liquidation of Palestine" and of dispossessing Palestinians. This was why the Arab perspective demanded that Israeli withdrawal and the rightful return of Palestinians must be first steps in any peace process. Israel, by definition, could not and should not be strictly Jewish: Israel/Palestine was meant for Arabs, Jews, and others. Zionism thus jeopardized peaceful coexistence and Canada tragically lent it credence.[42]

The Arab-Israeli situation worsened on 28 June 1967 when Israel officially annexed Jerusalem's Old City and its suburbs. Arabs protested this illegal manoeuvre and the ensuing destruction of Palestinian properties, which contravened international law.[43] While privately expressing regret, Canada, accepting Israel's explanation that the initiative would guarantee basic "administrative" services to the local populace, refused to publicly condemn Israeli expansionism. Canada's embassy in Tel Aviv relayed Israeli minister of defence Moshe Dayan's controversial comments during a press conference. Dayan, a powerbroker in Prime Minister Levi Eshkol's government, declared: "[The] Gaza strip is Israel and I think it should become an integral part of the country ... I don't see any difference between Gaza and Nazareth any more ... [the] West Bank and Gaza enjoy the same status. I don't see any difference."[44]

The UN's inability to generate a legally sound framework for peace, to formally denounce Israel's annexation of Old Jerusalem, and to demand an immediate Israeli withdrawal from all occupied territories frustrated Arabs, especially those "who ha[d] tended to favour friendly relations with the West." Myriad "moderate" Arabs continued non-violent protests, including petitioning countries such as Canada. Middle Eastern church leaders – with the backing of global Christian organizations such as the World Council of Churches – conveyed to Canada's embassy in Beirut a pressing need "to bring the cutting edge of the Gospel and theological reflection to bear on political Zionism." These Arab "Churchmen" urged Canada "to understand the depth of agony that millions of Middle Eastern Christians will have to face (and are presently facing) if cut off from the Holy Lands and particularly Jerusalem." Arab opposition to Israel, they explained, was "often misunderstood in terms of threat of genocide ... What our leaders mean is that the State of Israel was unjustly created and should cease to exist *as a racial State*." Arabs, said the Christian representatives, "do not want to kill Jews, but do want the cessation of the racial State of Israel." Israeli society could not genuinely achieve peace if it chose to segregate itself from its Palestinian and Arab neighbours.[45]

Canadian diplomats, based in and outside the Middle East, engaged in "constructive" conversations about how to improve Arab-Canada relations at this time. Canada's image, many Arabs made clear, was "at an all-time low." Postcolonial Arabs, many "well-educated and cultured," equated Canada with imperialism, "thus lowering [Ottawa's] standing and effectiveness in the eyes of developing nations." Canada's ambassador to Egypt, John Starnes, explained: "[No] matter whether Arab attitudes towards us are fair or justified ... these attitudes exist." Perhaps the best way to showcase Canada's commitment to "even-handedness" would be to alter its position on Jerusalem and to separate an Israeli withdrawal from the greater "peace process." If Canada "appeared to take a pro-Arab stand over Jerusalem" at the UN, it could "achieve a better balance in [its] relations with the two sides." According to Starnes, "this [was] a price we could afford to pay."[46]

Whereas Canadian officials located in Ottawa, Tehran, and New York opposed this suggestion, those in Beirut said that Arabs were "not interested in any comprehensive settlement the main elements of which would be withdrawal of Israeli forces from part of their conquests on the one hand and Arab recognition of and negotiation with Israel on the other." They wanted decolonization, not Israeli neo-imperialism. "The fact remains that we are probably more criticized for what we have not said and what we have not done ... than for what we have said and done." Canada's ambassador in London, Geoffrey Murray, and his counterpart in Paris backed their colleagues in Cairo and Beirut. Canadian diplomacy must realize, Murray opined: "While it is true that Israel holds the strongest cards for bargaining and bluffing, the Arabs have one big joker in terms of world opinion, that is, 'aggression cannot be allowed to pay.'" Yet Ottawa held firm to Pearson's vision of the Middle East, establishing an overarching framework for permanent peace agreed upon by all sides. While peace remained elusive, in part due to Tel Aviv's refusal to vacate all occupied territories, Canada failed to intervene in or to denounce Israeli settlement building in East Jerusalem.[47]

Israel's dedication to the land but not to its Indigenous peoples generated further consternation in the Arab public sphere. A humanitarian crisis intensified on the East Bank of Jordan as Tel Aviv encouraged Palestinian flight and closed its borders to West Bank evacuees who sought to return. Succumbing to international pressure from the likes of the International Red Cross, Israel reluctantly agreed to monitor the return of some Palestinians within a strict two-week window. On the eve of the first day of repatriation, Jordanian officials reported, "more than 167,500 people had filled out the forms" for repatriation. Despite Amman's contention that it could repatriate "more than 5,000 daily," Israeli conditions restricted the flow of peoples across the "makeshift wooden bridge" atop the Jordan River to a mere fraction of Palestinian applicants. As the Israeli-imposed deadline of 31 August passed, only 14,439 Palestinians set foot in the West Bank. To the dismay of Jordanian officials, Israel set "several obstacles" to Palestinian return, such as severe restrictions based on age, time, and district of residence. Furthermore, Palestinian refugees registered with the United Nations Relief and Works Agency were automatically denied re-entry.[48]

Arabs also fought the prospect of Palestinian resettlement outside Israel. Canada's public commitment to solve the worsening refugee problem exacerbated critiques of Canadian policy in the Middle East. For Arabs in the world, the 1967 refugees served "as the concrete example of injustice." *Al Ahram* reported an Iraqi accusation, echoed in Lebanese and Syrian media, that Israel and Canada had concocted a "Zionist-imperialist plot" to pressure Palestinian refugees to relocate to Canada, as evidenced by long Arab line-ups at Canada's consulate in Tel Aviv and concomitant Canadian immigration recruitment in Arab states. The *Egyptian Gazette* alleged that Arab sources had information that Canada "was trying to attract the greatest number of Palestine refugees." Despite Ottawa's fervent denials, its official position on resettling Palestinian refugees outside the West Bank and Gaza made it easy to believe such exaggerated reports.[49]

Ultimately, Ottawa's policy towards the Arab-Israeli conflict remained unchanged. Canada, Britain, and the United States continued behind-the-scenes efforts at the UN to push through an Israeli-friendly Security Council resolution that contravened Arab rights and demands. UN Resolution 242 was passed on 22 November 1967 by an Arabless Security Council. In the words of Paul Martin, the resolution "contrived to please everyone, and therefore please no one." Israel rejoiced at Resolution 242's failure to demand an immediate military withdrawal from the West Bank, Gaza, Sinai, and the Golan Heights. Israeli UN representative Abba Eban bluntly told Martin prior to the vote that "Israel would not abide by a resolution making any reference to Israeli withdrawal." And so Pearsonian Ottawa, as it had done in early 1957 when negotiating UNEF positioning on the Egypt-Israel border, again acquiesced in the name of Israeli security and "peacekeeping." Canada and the international community thus cemented a flawed diplomatic framework – land for peace – that perpetuated the status quo post bellum and buttressed Israel's settler colonial determination to keep the dowry without the bride. On 1 January 1968, Israeli officials revealed a "stand-firm policy" regarding withdrawal when Israeli minister without portfolio Menachem Begin declared that the occupied territories "were integral parts of the land of Israel and [that] there [was] no question of returning them."[50]

In contrast to the much-acclaimed national celebration that was Expo '67 – which, according to Pierre Berton, made Canada's centennial anniversary "a special year – a vintage year ... It was a turning point-year" – the third Arab-Israeli war jarred Arab-Canada relations. Whereas Canada "was in love with itself,"[51] Arabs grew increasingly disenchanted as Canadian diplomacy in the Middle East betrayed the very idea of Canada. A foundational shift thus occurred within Arab perceptions of Lester Pearson and Canada's role in the world. A transnational Arab consciousness, distraught by Ottawa's role in injustices done to Palestinians and Arab decolonization, challenged Canadian exceptionalism. Canada's neutrality in the Arab-Israeli conflict, it insisted, was a homemade mirage. Canada was not as special as its Nobel Peace Prize-winning prime minister, Pierre Berton, and many other Canadians thought.

The Arab-Israeli crisis of 1967 tainted the legacies of Lester Pearson and UN peacekeeping in Arab imaginations. As the Palestinian plight worsened and observers proclaimed a "massive human problem" in the Middle East, Jordanian ambassador to the UN special committee on peacekeeping Dr. Mohammed al-Farra opined in December 1967 that international initiatives like that embodied by Pearson's peacekeepers provided a "palliative" option to political impasse, "not a cure." Just as Pearson announced that his tenure at 24 Sussex Drive was over, so, too, was international peacekeeping's attraction in the Middle East. According to Dr. al-Farra, Arabs sorely needed a "genuine will to deal with the basic issues which invite conflicts and lead to the threats to peace or acts of aggression." Pearson, as James Peters recollected in his private journal after the former's death in 1972, was far from being a noble statesman as he "used his great political power to put the Arabs down."[52]

The Arab-Israeli crisis of 1967 fundamentally changed relations between the Middle East and Canada. Arab demystification of the Canadian peacekeeping myth, despite its failure to alter popular Canadian perceptions of self, unearthed the fact that Arab-Canada relations mattered to both Canadians and Middle Eastern peoples and demonstrated the interconnectivity between these two disparate geographies. The Middle East, Arabs argued in 1967, served as a strategic space in which Canadians constructed a glorified self-image of their place in the world. The idea of impartiality, exercised through the UN, self-sanctioned a Canadian intervention in the Middle East. An Arab perspective highlighted the fact that, contrary to Ottawa's official line, Canada had a direct interest in Middle Eastern affairs – an interest that contravened the spirit of humanitarianism. The globalization of this perception consequently symbolized the Canadianization of Arab decolonization.

Notes

1 Lester Pearson, *Mike: The Memoirs of the Right Honourable Lester B. Pearson*, vol. 3 (Toronto: University of Toronto Press, 1975), 304.

2 Miriam Cooke, *Tribal Modern: Branding New Nations in the Arab Gulf* (Berkeley: University of California Press, 2014).

3 *Expo 67: Manuel d'information / Information Manual* (Montreal: Information Services, 1967), 2.

4 Clipping, 30 May 1967, LAC, RG 25, vol. 10501, file 55-7-3-MTL-ARAB PLACE-pt.3.

5 Tehran to DEA, 31 May 1967, LAC, RG 25, vol. 8757, file 20-1-2-kwait-pt.1.

6 Memorandum, 29 May 1967, LAC, RG 25, vol. 8757, file 20-1-2-kwait-pt.1.

7 Telegram, 31 May 1967, LAC, RG 25, vol. 10501, file 55-7-3-MTL-ARAB PLACE-pt.3.

8 Two notable exceptions are: Baha Abu-Laban, "Arab-Canadians and the Arab-Israeli Conflict," *Arab Studies Quarterly* 10 (1988): 104–26; and Jenna Hennebry and Bessma Momeni, eds., *Targeted Transnationals: The State, the Media, and Arab Canadians* (Vancouver: UBC Press, 2013).

9 David Bercuson, *Canada and the Birth of Israel: A Study in Canadian Foreign Policy* (Toronto: University of Toronto Press, 1985); Tareq Ismael, ed., *Canada and the Arab World* (Edmonton: University of Alberta Press, 1985); Zachariah Kay, *Canada and Palestine: The Politics of Non-Commitment* (Jerusalem: Israel University Press, 1978); Zachariah Kay, *The Diplomacy of Impartiality: Canada and Israel, 1958–1968* (Waterloo: Wilfrid Laurier University Press, 2010); Zachariah Kay, *The Diplomacy of Prudence: Canada and Israel, 1948–1958* (Montreal and Kingston: McGill-Queen's University Press, 1996); Michael Oren, "Faith and Fair-Mindedness: Lester B. Pearson and the Suez Crisis," *Diplomacy and Statecraft* 3 (1992): 48–73; and Elizabeth Tauber, *Personal Policy Making: Canada's Role in the Adoption of the Palestine Partition Resolution* (Westport, CT: Greenwood Press, 2002).

10 Akira Iriye, "Postwar Transnationalism," in *Global Interdependence: The World after 1945*, ed. Akira Iriye (Cambridge, MA: Belknap Press, 2014), 698–99.

11 Eugene Rogan, *The Arabs: A History* (New York: Basic Books, 2009), 11.

12 Edward Said, *Orientalism* (New York: Vintage, 1978).

13 Donna Gabaccia, *Foreign Relations: American Immigration in Global Perspective* (Princeton: Princeton University Press, 2012).

14 Bercuson, *Canada and Israel*, 229–30; Kay, *Canada and Palestine*, 169; and Lester Pearson, *Mike: The Memoirs of the Right Honorable Lester B. Pearson*, vol. 2 (Toronto: University of Toronto Press, 1975), 217.

15 Bercuson, *Canada and Israel*, 238–39; and Kay, *Diplomacy of Prudence*, 12–13 and 107.

16 Gabaccia, *Foreign Relations*, 1.

17 Baha Abu-Laban, *An Olive Branch on the Family Tree: The Arabs in Canada* (Toronto: McClelland and Stewart, 1980), 58; and "Notes for a Talk on the Origins of the Arab Immigrants to Canada," April 1984, LAC, James Peters Papers, vol. 2.

18 Memorandum, 3 March 1983, LAC, Sami Hadawi Papers. vol. 1; Sheikh Muhammad Said Massoud, *I Fought as I Believed: An Arab Canadian Speaks Out on the Arab-Israeli Conflict* (Montreal: Ateliers des Sourds, 1976), 443, 570, and 572; and Memorandum, 5 January 1957, LAC, RG 25, vol. 7061, file 7631-b-40-pt.2.1.

19 DEA to Beirut, 10 February 1965 and DEA to London, 11 March 1965, LAC, RG 25, vol. 10052, file 20-1-2-ME.

20 Shira Robinson, *Citizen Strangers: Palestinians and the Birth of Israel's Liberal Settler State* (Stanford: Stanford University Press, 2013), 113–52; "The President in the Middle East Crisis," 19 December 1968, Lyndon Johnson Presidential Library, Lyndon Johnson Papers, NSF, National Security Council Histories, Middle East Crisis 12 May–19 June 1967, box 17; Avi Shlaim, "Israel: Poor Little Samson," in *The 1967 Arab-Israeli War: Origins and Consequences*, ed. Wm. Roger Louis and Avi Shlaim (Cambridge: Cambridge University Press, 2012), 25–26; and Richard Parker, *The Politics of Miscalculation in the Middle East* (Bloomington: Indiana University Press, 1993), 15.

21 Shlaim, "Israel," 25–26.

22 Laura James, "Egypt: Dangerous Illusions," in Louis and Shlaim, *1967 Arab-Israeli War*, 59–61; *Mideast Mirror* 19, 20 (1967): 2–3; and Cairo to DEA, 29 May 1967, LAC, RG 25, vol. 10501, file 55-7-3-MTL-2-ARAB PLACE-pt.3.

23 House of Commons, *Debates*, 19 May 1967, 416–19.

24 Memorandum, 22 May 1967, LAC, RG 25, vol. 8601, file 20-1-1-14-pt.4; Can. Del. UN to DEA, 25 May 1967, LAC, RG 25, vol. 13438, file 25-3-2-ARAB-ISR-1-pt.1; Report, 21 November 1968, LAC, RG 25, vol. 10053, file 20-1-2-ME-pt.6; and *Mideast Mirror* 19, 21 (1967): 17–18.

25 Can. Del. UN to DEA, 24 May 1967 and Can. Del. UN to DEA, 25 May 1967, LAC, RG 25, vol. 13438, file 25-3-2-ARAB-ISR-1-pt.1; George Ignatieff, *The Making of a Peacemonger* (Toronto: University of Toronto Press, 1985), 228.

26 Cairo to DEA, 29 May 1967, and Cairo to DEA, 1 June 1967, LAC, RG 25, vol. 10501, file 55-7-3-MTL-2-ARAB PLACE-pt.3.

27 *Mideast Mirror* 19, 21 (1967): 4, 7; *The Arab World* 162 (1967): 8; Cairo to DEA, 29 May 1967, LAC, Lester Pearson Papers, vol. 255, file 845; Nasser to Pearson, 28 May 1967 and Cairo to DEA, 29 May 1967, LAC, RG 25, vol. 13438, file 25-3-2-ARAB-ISR-1-pt.1.

28 Emphasis added. Record of Cabinet Decision, 29 May 1967, LAC, RG 25, vol. 13438, file 25-3-2-ARAB-ISR-1-pt.1; Diary entry, 30 May 1967, LAC, Pearson Papers, vol. 8.

29 CBC transcript, 30 May 1967, LAC, RG 25, vol. 8602, file 20-1-1-14-pt.5.

30 Cairo to DEA, 3 June 1967, LAC, RG 25, vol. 10052, file 20-1-2-ME-pt.2; Peters to Tannous, 31 May 1967, LAC, Peters Papers, vol. 3; and press release, 2 June 1967, LAC, Peters Papers, vol. 3.

31 *Mideast Mirror* 19, 23 (1967): 4; Avi Raz, *The Bride and the Dowry: Israel, Jordan, and the Palestinians in the Aftermath of the June 1967 War* (New Haven: Yale University Press, 2012), 22; and Can. Del. UN to Ottawa, 5 June 1967, LAC, RG 25, vol. 13438, file 25-3-2-ARAB-ISR-1-pt.3.

32 Ignatieff, *Peacemonger*, 227.

33 House of Commons, *Debates*, 7 June 1967, 1254; Can. Del. UN to DEA, 5 June 1967, LAC, RG 25, vol. 13438, file 25-3-2-ARAB-ISR-1-pt.3; and Memorandum, 10 June 1967, RG 25, vol. 13438, file 25-3-2-ARAB-ISR-1-pt.4.

34 Shlaim, "Israel," 54; and Raz, *Bride and the Dowry*, 43.

35 Diary entry, 12 June 1967, LAC, Pearson Papers, vol. 8.

36 Salloum to Pearson, 14 June 1967, LAC, Pearson Papers, vol. 256, file 845; Tehran to DEA, 13 June 1967, LAC, RG 25, vol. 17628, file 20-KUWAIT-1-3; Beirut to DEA, 14 June 1967, LAC, RG 25, vol. 13438, file 25-3-2-ARAB-ISR-1-pt.3; Cairo to DEA, 15 June 1967, LAC, RG 25, vol. 10052, file 20-1-2-ME-pt.2; and Frigon to Pearson, 15 June 1967, LAC, Pearson Papers, vol. 256, file 845.

37 *Mideast Mirror* 19, 24 (1967): 4–5; and cited in Raz, *Bride and the Dowry*, 116.

38 Memorandum, 14 June 1967 and press release, 16 June 1967, LAC, Pearson Papers, vol. 8; Raz, *Bride and the Dowry*, 44–45; London to DEA, 31 July 1967, and Tel Aviv to DEA, 4 August 1967, LAC, RG 25, vol. 8897, file 25-3-2-ARAB-ISR-1-pt.5; Marchand to Pearson, 7 June 1967 and Pearson to Marchand, 12 June 1967, and Memorandum, n.d., LAC, Pearson Papers, vol. 8.

39 Raz, *Bride and the Dowry*, 3.

40 Canadian Arab Community to Pearson, 19 June 1967, Bodoloi to Pearson, 19 June 1967, and Farrell to Pearson, 22 June 1967, LAC, Pearson Papers, vol. 256, file 845; Michel Haddad, "A Refugee's Viewpoint about the Middle East Crisis," 20 July 1967, *Canadian Middle East Journal* 8.

41 *Mideast Mirror* 19, 25 (1967): 3; and Can. Del. UN to DEA, 16 June 1967, LAC, RG 25, vol. 13438, file 25-3-2-ARAB-ISR-1-pt.3.

42 *Arab World* 163 (1967): 10; and Open Letter to Canadian Embassy Beirut, 26 June 1967, LAC, RG 25, vol. 8931, file 20-ARAB-1-3-ISR-1-pt.2.

43 Raz, *Bride and the Dowry*, 110.

44 Ottawa to Tel Aviv, 4 July 1967, LAC, RG 25, vol. 8931, file 20-ARAB-1-3-ISR-1-pt.2; Memorandum, 12 July 1967, LAC, RG 25, vol. 8931, file 20-ARAB-1-3-ISR-1-pt.2; and Tel Aviv to Ottawa, 6 July 1967, LAC, RG 25, vol. 8897, file 25-3-2-ARAB-ISR-1-pt.5.

45 Beirut to Ottawa, 11 July 1967, LAC, RG 25, vol. 8931, file 20-ARAB-1-3-ISR-1-pt.2; and Rev. James Pierce to Canadian Ambassador to Lebanon, 10 July 1967, LAC, RG 25, vol. 8898, file 25-3-2-ARAB-ISR-1-pt.6, emphasis added.

46 Cairo to DEA, 17 July 1967 and Beirut to Ottawa, 31 July 1967, LAC, RG 25, vol. 10052, file 20-1-2-ME-pt.2; Cairo to DEA, 26 July 1967, LAC, RG 25, vol. 8897, file 25-3-2-ARAB-ISR-1-pt.5.

47 DEA to Cairo, 19 July 1967, LAC, RG 25, vol. 8931, file 20-ARAB-1-3-ISR-1-pt.2; Beirut to DEA, 31 July 1967 and Paris to DEA, 4 August 1967, LAC, RG 25, vol. 10052, file 20-1-2-ME-pt.2; London to DEA, 31 July 1967 and Tel Aviv to DEA, 28 August 1967, LAC, RG 25, vol. 8897, file 25-3-2-ARAB-ISR-1-pt.5.

48 *Mideast Mirror* 19, 26 (1967): 11; *Mideast Mirror* 19, 30 (1967): 20; *Mideast Mirror* 19, 33 (1967): 15; *Mideast Mirror* 19, 34 (1967): 6; and *Mideast Mirror* 19, 35 (1967): 6.

49 Cairo to DEA, 24 August 1967, LAC, RG 25, vol. 10052, file 20-1-2-ME-pt.2; DEA to Cairo, 25 August 1967, LAC, RG 25, vol. 10052, file 20-1-2-ME-pt.2; and Cairo to DEA, 5 September 1967, LAC, RG 25, vol. 8898, file 25-3-2-ARAB-ISR-1-pt.6.

50 Report, 21 November 1968, LAC, RG 25, vol. 10053, file 20-1-2-ME-pt.6; *Mideast Mirror* 19, 41 (1967): 8; Pearson to Martin, 13 November 1967, LAC, RG 25, vol. 13439, file 25-3-2-ARAB-ISR-1-pt.13; Paul Martin, *A Very Public Life*, vol. 2 (Toronto: Deneau, 1983), 569–71; Raz, *Bride and the Dowry*, 162–80; and

Tel Aviv to Ottawa, 8 January 1968, LAC, RG 25, vol. 8931, file 20-ARAB-1-3-ISR-1-pt.3.

51 Pierre Berton, *1967: Canada's Turning Point* (Toronto: Seal Books, 1998), 7–8.

52 *Mideast Mirror* 19, 50 (1967): 12; and *Jameel's Journal* 4 (1973): 3.

John Dirks

9 Friendly Noises but Distant Neighbours

Pearson, Latin America, and the Caribbean

The countries south of the Rio Grande were never Lester Pearson's highest priority. Politically and culturally remote to most Canadians, and encompassing a small fraction of Canada's foreign trade and investment, for Pearson their importance paled in comparison to the United States, the British Commonwealth, Western Europe, and even Asia. Yet by the time he became prime minister, he could not ignore the region. Not that he had entirely done so before – his long tenure as secretary of state for external affairs included the opening of several Canadian embassies in Latin America as well as expanding commercial ties with the region. Yet not once did he travel to Latin America as either prime minister or SSEA.[1]

Much had changed by 1963. The intervening John Diefenbaker government had made important symbolic gestures that had raised the profile of Canadian-Latin American relations, including the first official visits by an external affairs secretary and a prime minister. But it was the Cuban revolution, more than anything else, that drove Latin America to the top of the international agenda – probably for the first time since its countries became independent. Bringing the Cold War to the western hemisphere in earnest, this event catapulted Latin America to the top of American foreign policy priorities. Naturally, given its economic and military dependence on the United States, Canada also felt the impact. The Diefenbaker government acted to preserve Canadian interests in Cuba and adopted a notably more conciliatory posture than its neighbour. Yet, given Cuba's importance to the American government, Canadian-Cuban relations could not be simply bilateral as they affected Canadian-American relations. Since Fidel Castro sought to export his country's revolution across Latin America, antagonizing its governments and alarming the Americans, Canadian-Cuban relations also had broader hemispheric implications. Thus, as prime minister, the North Atlanticist Pearson was forced to pay the region greater attention than his inclinations would otherwise have dictated, and, for his duration in office, American concerns about Cuba and hemispheric communism cast their shadow and significantly influenced his hemispheric policy.

Both despite and because of the American factor, Pearson's approach to the hemisphere reverted to the minimalist one that he had followed while heading up the external affairs portfolio. For Latin America, this meant prioritizing commercial over political engagement, with a limited focus on larger or richer countries. With the exception of the Commonwealth Caribbean, an area for which he had more personal affinity, Pearson retained a hands-off posture, although he did not hesitate to assert his authority at any hint of friction with the United States. This was much to the chagrin of his SSEA, Paul Martin Sr., who strongly believed that Canada needed a bolder, more intentional policy in Latin America. Unconvinced, Pearson believed Canadian interests were best served by repairing recently strained relations with the United States, with Cuba being one bone of contention. Washington's strong sense of its regional "backyard" made the prime minister loath to ruffle the eagle's feathers over Latin America. For Pearson, despite his personal misgivings about American intrigue and the Monroe Doctrine's heavy-handedness, such concerns did not trump the Auto Pact and defence commitments. They were also secondary to volatile matters of far greater concern such as Cyprus, Vietnam, China, and the Middle East, all of which consumed much of his attention regarding foreign policy. Pearson's hemispheric strategy largely satisfied the Americans, although it disappointed many Latin American governments who expected more from Canada, and it did generate some criticism at home (albeit small in scale in comparison to the next two decades). While low key, Canada under Pearson's leadership still made some important strides forward in the hemisphere, particularly in the Commonwealth Caribbean and Mexico, paving the way for the more overt cementing of ties under Pierre Trudeau. But Pearson's hemispheric policy remained pragmatic to the core.

Prime Minister Pearson's approach to Latin America stemmed from his celebrated nine years as external affairs secretary. Then, for him the region was his lowest priority across the globe, lagging well behind other geographically and culturally distant but more prominent areas such as the Middle East, South Asia, and the Pacific Rim. Indicative of this fact is that, in his personal memoirs for those years, Pearson ignored relations with Latin America altogether, a neglect repeated in most of the leading secondary works on his career.[2] As SSEA, his one planned trip there – a 1951 visit to Mexico – was shelved when Ambassador C.P. Hébert advised his boss, then preoccupied with other international issues, to stay away unless he could give the Mexicans adequate time and attention.[3] Pearson eventually met President Ruiz Cortines at a 1956 tripartite gathering with US president Dwight Eisenhower in West Virginia, although that conversation did little to further Canadian-Mexican relations, focusing instead on US concerns about communism.[4]

Pearson's lack of formal engagement with Latin America as SSEA does not mean he was unaware of its growing importance. As a diplomat and official in the 1940s, Pearson witnessed Ottawa establishing missions with the region's largest countries, such as Argentina, Brazil, Chile, and Mexico, and he was very familiar with Canada's established connections through bankers, investors, insurance brokers, and missionaries.[5] As SSEA, Pearson continued this process for medium-sized countries such as Colombia and Venezuela, although at a slower pace, wanting assurances that a country met the minimum threshold of Canadian commercial and other interests to warrant the costs of an embassy.[6] Staffing these posts was another challenge. Not many Canadian diplomats clamoured for them save a few French Canadians who shared the region's Romance languages and Catholicism.[7] Some Latin American governments, predisposed to value formalized face-to-face diplomacy, found Ottawa's aloof approach off-putting, much to the embarrassment of diplomats such as Hébert, who complained that Canada showed "too little interest in Latin America" and who called for greater engagement and development assistance.[8] That the Liberal government's Latin American priority remained trade and investment was readily apparent when its most publicized regional initiative – a 1953 month-long trade and "goodwill" visit – was not led by Pearson but by Trade and Commerce Minister C.D. Howe, accompanied by an entourage of business leaders.[9] While touted as a success, statistics suggest the mission's actual results were disappointing. Latin America's portion of Canada's exports fell from 4.5 to 3.8 percent between 1950 and 1955, dropping another half percent by 1960. The corresponding figure for imports remained around 6.7 percent before falling almost by half in 1960, recovering modestly five years later.[10]

Politically, the prevalent hemispheric question for Ottawa was whether to join the Organization of American States. Since 1909, Latin American states had been waiting for Canada to occupy its empty chair set up in the OAS predecessor, the Pan American Union. Before passage of the 1931 Statute of Westminster, this vacancy was due to Britain's control of Canadian foreign policy; subsequently, the inhibiting factor was American scepticism regarding genuine Canadian autonomy. Initially favourable to joining the body, Prime Minister William Lyon Mackenzie King quickly soured on the idea, annoyed at the Americans' wartime ambivalence to Canada's increasing presence in Latin America. Washington's views changed after 1945 once the Cold War set in and a kindred regional partner became desirable.[11] In the 1950s, the United States actively courted Canadian OAS membership by appealing to its neighbour's multilateral foreign policy, of which King's successor Louis St-Laurent and Pearson were the architects. Yet, on the OAS, Pearson and other Canadian officials remained divided as this body was not deemed vital to Canadian interests, unlike the United Nations, NATO, and the Commonwealth. The secretary himself, and leading advisers, felt Canada's hands were sufficiently full and did not relish being caught between a hegemonic United States and Latin American states, and perhaps segments of the Canadian population that feared or resented the American colossus.[12] Conversely, Latin American experts at external affairs worried that its countries would interpret Canada's ongoing absence as indifference, and they nudged Pearson slightly towards accepting an OAS observer role.[13] No decision had been reached before the Liberals' electoral defeat by Diefenbaker's Progressive Conservatives in June 1957.

The new government made important symbolic gestures to raise the profile of Canadian-Latin American relations. Travelling to Brazil and Mexico in November 1958, Pearson's replacement Sidney Smith became the first SSEA to officially visit a Latin American country, reporting to Diefenbaker on the importance of closer economic and political ties and the potential for collaboration in the United Nations.[14] Smith's successor Howard Green followed suit in May 1960 with a five-country tour that also included Argentina, Chile, and Peru. Diefenbaker himself made the first such prime ministerial visit, travelling to Mexico in April 1960; in turn, he hosted President Lopes Mateo, Argentina's Arturo Frondizi, and the Brazilian and Venezuelan foreign ministers.[15] External affairs' departmental actions in those years attested further to the region's elevated profile. It established missions where they were still lacking, along with a dedicated Latin American division.[16] In 1961, Canada also joined the development-oriented UN Economic Commission for Latin America (ECLA), whose sphere also extended to the Caribbean islands.[17] This suited Diefenbaker and Pearson alike, both of whom were Commonwealth enthusiasts. Diefenbaker extended the 1950 Colombo aid plan to the British West Indies Federation and to its ex-members following its 1962 demise.[18] Yet, despite these forward gestures, Diefenbaker resisted OAS membership, sharing the Liberals' concerns about entanglements with the United States, a position reinforced by President John F. Kennedy's unexpected public call for Canadian membership during his May 1961 Ottawa visit.[19]

While committed from the outset to expanding Canada's hemispheric role, events in Cuba after 1959 really drew Diefenbaker's (and Pearson's) attention southward. Fidel Castro's revolution pulled Cuba out from under American hegemony to become the hemisphere's first communist state. While the revolution itself concerned both prime ministers alike, the greater concern was the United States' reaction to it. Both men deplored Castro's embrace of communism and the Soviet Union but also concluded that Washington's embargo and anti-Castro efforts did not serve Canada's interests and would ultimately fail. Canada's embassy in Havana thus remained open, and normal, nonstrategic trade with the island continued as before, to the dismay of official Washington and the ire of the American public, press, and many on Capitol Hill. After two years of testy discourse on the subject, the Kennedy administration conceded both that Ottawa's policies did not desire to spite the United States and that Washington gleaned useful intelligence and other advantages from Canada's ongoing presence in Cuba.[20] Still, Canada had to approach hemispheric issues warily. The communist presence in the hemisphere had sparked a resurgent US interventionism, which unnerved many Canadians and many more Latin Americans, and nearly ended in nuclear catastrophe in October 1962.

Defeating Diefenbaker electorally in April 1963, Pearson's highest priority, as he later confirmed in his memoirs, was to repair Canadian-American relations, then badly marred by the Kennedy-Diefenbaker rift and made even worse by the latter's seeming vacillations during the missile crisis.[21] Delighted at Pearson's election, Kennedy invited him to his seaside vacation home for informal talks only weeks after the prime minister took office, meetings that both leaders deemed a success. With the Castro regime still in power, on Moscow's side, and dedicated to revolution across the region, Latin America remained a preoccupation in the White House. Weighing only slightly below nuclear weapons and bilateral economic issues in their conversation, the president hammered home to Pearson his concerns not only about Cuba itself but also about its efforts to topple Venezuela's Romulo Betancourt, his favourite Latin leader, and the pro-Castro outlook of Cheddi Jagan, the emerging leader of the soon to be independent British Guiana. These were but two examples of countries that Kennedy and his successor Lyndon Johnson viewed as vulnerable to communism – others included Joao Goulart's Brazil, Guatemala, Chile, Haiti, and the Dominican Republic. Kennedy labelled Latin America "the most dangerous area in the world" and stressed to Pearson that the United States would not tolerate a second Castro.[22] New CIA covert action programs and military contingency plans were set up, all continued enthusiastically by Johnson.[23] It was abundantly clear to the prime minister that disregarding American sensitivities in this area would seriously hinder his bilateral objectives.

While Pearson did not share the extent of either president's alarm, he sympathized with their objectives of curtailing communism's spread in the hemisphere. Although disdainful of the caustic extremes of McCarthyism, Pearson was still a committed cold warrior and differed with Washington more over means than intentions.[24] Regarding Cuba, Pearson steadfastly refused to prevent normal Canadian trade and diplomacy but he promised both Kennedy and Johnson that he would neither help Castro politically nor permit any subversive activities on Canadian soil. Both presidents praised Canadian intelligence reports from Havana and other cooperative efforts, but they also quietly requested that Canada reduce its trade (especially spare parts) and civil air traffic with Cuba.[25] For the most part, Pearson kept these promises, at times personally intervening in diplomacy to ensure that they were honoured.

In setting a Canadian course for the region, the one Pearson charted was cautious and low key. He recognized that appearing to be too easily swayed by the United States would spark criticism at home as more Canadians doubted the wisdom or rightness of American foreign policy, especially concerning the developing world, and believed it had too much influence on Canada. With important economic and political matters still to resolve with the Americans, Pearson was determined not to impede their resolution by another row with Washington over a region of considerably greater importance to the United States than to Canada. He would walk in the Americans' general direction in the hemisphere, but at arm's length. He saw Canadian-American goals overlapping in many ways, including non-lethal trade, security, development aid, and the Commonwealth Caribbean. On trickier matters, such as OAS membership, the US Dominican intervention, or Washington's support for rightist military coups, Pearson remained circumspect and mostly silent, aware that such developments were viewed negatively at home. Mostly with Vietnam in mind, Pearson told the Canadian Club early in 1965: "Official doubts about certain United States foreign policies often should be expressed in private through official channels of diplomacy."[26] Following this approach, particularly on this side of the Atlantic, the prime minister mostly succeeded. He avoided major difficulties with the Americans on hemispheric matters, even though he was seen in some Latin American circles as too pro-American – a price he was largely willing to pay.

Nonetheless, Pearson could not entirely avoid bumping heads with the Americans over Latin America. As Washington's paramount regional concern, Cuban issues received disproportionate attention in Ottawa, and on that file, in order to avoid angering his neighbour, Pearson occasionally acted as his own foreign minister. His conversations on the subject with Kennedy and Johnson were sanguine enough; nonetheless, Pearson felt vulnerable on Cuba. At their January 1964 meeting, Johnson fumed aloud over British bus exports. Later that year, Secretary of State Dean Rusk confronted a defensive Paul Martin over a fourfold increase in Canadian exports to Cuba (mostly grain).[27] The potential impact of American pressure on Canadian businesses was readily apparent in July 1963, when Kennedy blocked all Cuban-connected financial assets in an effort to stop Castro's external activities – measures that reached extraterritorially into Canadian banks. Despite vigorous complaints about transgressing Canadian sovereignty, neither Pearson nor his successors ever persuaded the United States to revoke these controls, although, during the 1960s and 1970s, Ottawa usually succeeded in obtaining case-specific exemption licences, often by playing on Washington's concerns about igniting Canadian anti-Americanism.[28] The extraterritorial impact of US law regarding Cuba on US-owned businesses in Canada remained a bilateral irritant for decades to come and was never resolved in principle.

Pearson's promises not to aid Cuban subversion were tested on several occasions, and he went out of his way to squash potential American criticism. In November 1963, Venezuelan officials discovered that a Canadian-made outboard motor exported to Cuba had powered a weapons shipment to leftist guerrillas in that country. Embarrassed and fearful of negative American press, Pearson discreetly cooperated with a US-OAS investigation, one that spawned a July 1964 OAS resolution calling on its members to sever diplomatic and economic relations with Cuba. Only Mexico refused to comply, leaving it and Canada, as a non-member, as the only western hemisphere countries having embassies in Havana until the early 1970s.

That same year, the DEA's strongly anti-communist under-secretary Marcel Cadieux influenced his superiors to pressure Havana to find another host country for a pro-Castro Latin American solidarity organization's congress, originally scheduled for Montreal.[29] That same spring, Pearson allowed American sentiments to override Canadian interests in thwarting a visit by British Guiana's Cheddi Jagan, even though Diefenbaker had previously received him and had given his country $1.5 million in aid, accompanied by considerable private Canadian banking and mining investments.[30] Two years later, Pearson again narrowly escaped serious embarrassment after reneging on a commitment to the Soviet Union to allow Aeroflot Montreal-Havana onward flight rights, in the wake of direct American pressure – including two letters from President Johnson and two visits from veteran diplomat Averell Harriman, both vehemently objecting to such flights, seeing them as reinforcing Cuba's communist mission. Pearson, Martin, and even Cadieux rejected this premise but concluded the price in Canada-US relations was too high. In retreating, the prime minister dodged questions in Parliament and the press about American pressure. The full record of this episode remained unavailable for some decades.[31]

In 1967, Pearson again intervened directly to ensure that neither Fidel Castro nor Cuba's ceremonial president Oswaldo Dorticos visited

Expo '67, despite the latter having been officially invited to the world's fair. Fearing that much-needed American tourists might stay away in protest, the prime minister also had security on his mind. US-based Cuban exiles had firebombed Cuban diplomatic premises and ships in Canada, and Pearson impressed upon the Cubans that Ottawa could not guarantee their leaders' safety. Havana instead sent its trade minister to officially represent it.[32] Several weeks later, again fearing adverse American publicity, Pearson rejected Martin's suggestion that his parliamentary assistant, Gérard Pelletier, discreetly include a Cuba stop on his impending Latin American tour.[33]

Cuba was the leading, but not the only, hemispheric issue challenging Canadian-American relations. In April 1965, President Johnson landed marines in the Dominican Republic following a coup that had left a polarized country verging on civil war. The first such direct intervention in three decades, Johnson argued his action was necessary to prevent a communist takeover, a threat later proved to be exaggerated but that, at the time, was believed to be genuine.[34] Commencing unilaterally, the president sought greater international legitimacy by requesting OAS member force contributions. Pearson's response was muzzled. Both he and Martin held great reservations about the intervention and would not openly endorse it, a stance influenced by numerous critical letters from Canadians.[35] Pearson told his cabinet the US action held "serious and potentially long range implications" for the hemisphere, which would have spillover consequences for Canada. Ever the champion of multilateralism, Pearson was pleased to see other OAS states participating, although he nervously pondered his response should Johnson request Canadian assistance, even though Canada was a non-member.[36] To his relief, no such request was forthcoming.

While not endorsing the invasion, neither Pearson nor Martin would openly criticize it, especially with Johnson's celebrated tirade over Pearson's Vietnam speech in Philadelphia all too fresh in their memories.[37] In the House of Commons, Pearson thanked American forces for protecting Canadians on the island. More circumspectly, a few weeks later, the SSEA expressed Ottawa's internal division:

> It is easy to criticize countries which bear the brunt of responsibility when dangerous situations develop. Such criticism might best be directed at the imperfections of our international arrangements.

> Unilateral intervention, however, is bound to create anxiety, and it should be our object to work out arrangements that might make such unilateral action unnecessary in the future.[38]

American officials sought to reassure their Canadian counterparts that their concerns about communism were no mere smokescreen. In Santo Domingo, Ambassador Ellsworth Bunker opined to the newly arrived Canadian chargé d'affaires, Michel Gauvin: "Communism could be dealt with by constitutional means in [the] USA or Canada but not in Latin America. To prevent communism here is our main purpose. We have never concealed that this was our main objective."[39] Though sympathetic to the Americans, Gauvin was unconvinced, describing how they had "gone from one mistake to another" and were "blinded by the fear of the communist."[40] When the Dominican turbulence finally settled in 1966 with the establishment of Joaquín Balauger's government, Canadian officials privately decried American policy as a failure but, in keeping with the prime minister's wishes, publicly refrained from criticism.[41]

Cuba and the Dominican crisis brought home for Pearson the dilemmas Canada might face on joining the OAS, offering him little incentive to move forward. He told Kennedy in 1963, "if circumstances were very propitious [Canada] might accept" an invitation.[42] Perceiving the reality as anything but favourable, he reverted to his position of a decade earlier – Canada's international plate was sufficiently full, and OAS membership would mean facing uncomfortable choices among its American neighbour, Latin American states, and a critical Canadian public.[43] His old colleague Vincent Massey cautioned him, "we would be more or less geared to following American policy once we took this step."[44] Pulling in the other direction was Paul Martin. Genuinely interested in Latin America, for years he had favoured joining the organization, and he was particularly frustrated with Pearson's hesitancy on this issue and on others such as Chinese representation in the United Nations.[45] On the OAS, Martin admitted to Brazil's ambassador that he was "having to carry out 'an educational program' in that regard."[46] The SSEA had his supporters, notably Ambassador Arthur Irwin in Mexico City, who wrote a lengthy farewell assessment that concluded membership best served Canadian interests.[47] In response, Under-Secretary Cadieux canvassed other Canadian diplomats in Latin America. Presenting the findings to Martin, Cadieux reported in

January 1965 that "the consensus seemed to be against until the Latin Americans decided what kind of organization they wanted." The minister scribbled at the bottom: "noted with disagreement."[48]

Choosing a gradualist, middling approach, Pearson opted instead for a Canadian OAS liaison officer. Yet before he could get this decision through cabinet, the OAS had simplified the membership process, and Martin warned him that the Latin republics would view such half measures as another stalling tactic.[49] Pearson held firm, allowing Canadian participation in OAS affiliate bodies such as the Pan American Institute of Geography and History, the Inter-American Radio Office, and the Inter-American Statistical Institute, but not taking the full plunge.[50] The prime minister did not want Canada wedged between Latin American states and either the Americans or the British over Belize or the Falkland Islands, nor did he welcome the prospect of assuming collective defence obligations under the Rio Treaty. Further reinforcing his posture was the reticence of some OAS members to embrace non-Latin applicants such as Jamaica and Trinidad and Tobago, citing cultural differences and Commonwealth trade preferences; this hinted that Canada might face choosing between OAS and Commonwealth members.[51] Ottawa continued to receive mixed messages from the Latin Americans, which was partly a reaction to its ambivalent policies. They still wanted more engagement with Canada and yet, as Irwin's successor in Mexico Herbert Feaver reported, he had heard ECLA delegates describe Canada as economically and culturally dissimilar, pro-American in outlook, and unsympathetic to their protectionist trade policies.[52] Pearson thus sat tight on the OAS. As he told the Finnish ambassador in 1964, "Canada was making friendly noises" towards the organization, but that was as far as he would go.[53]

In cabinet, in January 1967, Pearson and Martin openly debated their differences on the OAS. Stating the case for membership, the secretary, reflecting his French Canadian heritage, emphasized the "strong religious and cultural bonds" between Canada and Latin America, and argued that, once the Commonwealth Caribbean states finally joined, as they were about to do, Canada would have even fewer excuses to stay out. Pearson repeated his doubts that membership was in the country's interests, and referred again to anticipated difficulties with Canada-US relations. Former finance minister Walter Gordon, now minister without portfolio, backed Pearson using another angle – that Canada might be embarrassed by being associated with American support for "extreme right wing groups."[54] Public correspondence suggested to Pearson that Canadians mostly opposed OAS membership.[55] Martin later conceded in his memoirs that internal disagreements and events such as the Dominican intervention dampened enthusiasm for the organization.[56] Canada would not have a regular observer until 1972, nor would it join until 1989. As Greg Donaghy makes clear (Chapter 4, this volume), the OAS was just one of several points of disagreement between Martin and Pearson, a relationship that would remain uncomfortable until both left their offices in April 1968.[57]

Mentioned frequently in the OAS discussions, the Commonwealth Caribbean was the one part of the hemisphere in which Pearson truly wanted to do more and envisioned a helpful Canadian role. In contrast to Latin America, where he neither travelled nor hosted any leaders, he welcomed Trinidad and Tobago's prime minister Eric Williams to Ottawa in 1964, and Pearson visited both his country and Jamaica late the following year. Pearson's affinity for the Caribbean stemmed from his long-standing commitment to the Commonwealth, from Canada's long history of purchasing its sugar, mining its bauxite, providing its banking and insurance services, and, increasingly, visiting its lovely beaches.[58] Continuing Diefenbaker's initiatives, the Liberals quadrupled aid to the region from $2 million to $9 million a year in 1964–65, with $3.5 million being outright grants.[59] The high-water mark was the July 1966 Ottawa conference of Commonwealth Caribbean prime ministers. Envisioning this meeting since 1963, Pearson personally took charge of its planning, trying to convince his somewhat sceptical ministers of the influential opportunity this initiative offered Canada. Some in external affairs sought to curb the prime minister's enthusiasm, advising against Canada replacing Britain as the latter cut its Caribbean colonies loose.[60] The conference proceeded with a broad agenda centring on trade and development but also including tourism, civil aviation, immigration, and defence. Canada committed itself to $75 million in aid to the region over five years, along with a tariff-free sugar quota and revisions to an antiquated 1926 arrangement that had required shipping Caribbean goods directly to Canada first as a precondition to gaining preferential market access. Ottawa also began revising its discriminatory immigration policy. The lasting legacies were future conferences and increases in both Caribbean immigrants to Canada and Canadian tourists seeking a tropical winter respite. Yet the tariff reductions fell short of the preferential access the Caribbean states actually wanted. Further, soon these gains would be offset by a proportional decline in their trade with Canada as other parts of the hemisphere finally began to gain Canada's attention.[61] The Caribbean countries turned elsewhere, notably to the United States, where their sugar access was helped by the Cuban embargo. Thus, while the 1966 conference was an important milestone in Canada's relations with the islands, what followed was a less "special" economic relationship than the one enjoyed in earlier times.[62]

While the Caribbean states gave the Ottawa conference a mixed evaluation, the United States was pleased with its neighbour's efforts in the region, while Pearson's belief that the anglophone Caribbean offered a natural theatre for greater Canadian influence resonated well in Washington. Dean Rusk shared his government's approval with Martin shortly after the meetings.[63] Reminded poignantly by National Security Adviser Walt Rostow that "the Caribbean is awfully close to home," President Johnson wanted the newly independent states inoculated against Castroism but did not want to devote much attention to them. Thus, he welcomed the British and Canadians acting as friendly American surrogates by means of agencies such as the proposed Caribbean Development Bank.[64] In contrast, Latin American governments were not enamoured by Pearson's Caribbean initiatives, believing that they came at their expense. Ambassador Feaver reported how Mexican observers at the Ottawa conference saw it as yet another reminder of Canadian aloofness towards Latin America or, worse, the genesis of a new Anglospheric bloc in the hemisphere.[65] As at ECLA a year earlier, the Ottawa conference confirmed for them that Canada's hemispheric interests were much more in line with US interests than with their own, an accurate reading given the Johnson administration's enthusiasm. Ottawa's lack of political engagement with them left Latin America's leaders frustrated and disappointed.

The absence of similar high-level meetings with Latin American leaders did not mean the Pearson government neglected trade or development assistance to their countries, although that, too, was both modest and selective in nature. Of the Latin republics, Canada's largest trading partners oscillated between Mexico and Venezuela, followed by Cuba. In 1967, external affairs officials reported that the previous year's $76 million in exports to Venezuela neared the figures for France, not to mention the fact that Venezuela provided roughly half of Canada's foreign oil.[66] Ottawa vacillated over which country deserved greatest priority. Democratic Venezuela, clearly valued for oil, was a natural candidate, and Jean Luc Pépin, minister of energy, mines and resources, made a five-day visit there in 1966, reciprocated the following year at Expo '67 by his Venezuelan counterpart.[67] However, Mexico was a much larger and North American country, one that shared Canada's position on issues such as Cuba and that was also then enjoying a 6 percent annual growth rate. While not receiving technical aid, Mexico consumed 60 percent of the $120 million in Canadian export credits then earmarked for Latin America.[68] Canadian visitors to Mexico nearly doubled in the Pearson years, from twenty-five thousand in 1963 to forty-six thousand in 1967, forcing external affairs to increase consular services to that country.[69] In late 1965, Foreign Minister Carrillo Flores suggested to the vacationing finance minister Mitchell Sharp that a joint Canada-Mexico committee be set up. Martin and Cadieux were favourable, but the initiative did not materialize until May 1968.[70] Pearson did invite Mexican president Diaz Ordaz to Canada, although that, too, would not occur before the prime minister's retirement. Nonetheless, a forward trajectory was set in motion for Canadian-Mexican relations that would bear fruit the following decade.

After trade, export credit financing and technical development assistance were the mainstay of mid-1960's Canadian-Latin American relations. Whenever the region was discussed in the Pearson cabinet, the conversation largely concerned exports of machinery or vehicles to individual countries, ranging from locomotives for Mexico, Buffalo aircraft for Brazil, engineering services and hardware for Caracas's mass transit system, or road construction equipment and nuclear reactors for Argentina.[71] Beginning late in 1964, Canada contributed $10 million to the Inter-American Development Bank (IADB) for soft loans to Latin American countries, with similar accruals forthcoming the next two years.[72] But the evaluations were mixed. By autumn 1966, External Aid Office director Maurice Strong reported that a third of Canada's IADB contributions covering twelve projects in nine countries remained unused and that a disproportionate amount was being channelled to smaller countries in which Canada had few interests.[73] External affairs officials debated in 1966–67 over which countries to prioritize for such assistance. Embarrassed at how minuscule Canada's technical assistance to the region was in comparison to Africa and Asia, Latin American division head Alfred Pick supported Strong's position that priority be given to larger countries – such as Brazil, Chile, and Peru – that could buy Canadian goods and advised Ottawa to avoid what he labelled "older end ring dictatorships" such as Paraguay or Nicaragua, or unstable countries such as Ecuador and Bolivia.[74] Aware of the advantages given to larger countries, fifteen of these smaller and poorer countries met in Guatemala late in 1967, demanding improved access to industrialized markets and technical assistance. Canada's chargé d'affaires noted that such views offered a "useful yardstick" to inform future decisions, but, in the meantime, cabinet had already sided with Pick, directing the Committee on External Aid to assist Brazil, Argentina, Chile, Colombia, and Peru but to discourage the remainder.[75]

Echoing Pick's commentary about dictatorships, many years later Martin wrote: "the steady trend towards military rule in Latin America dampened our enthusiasm to get too embroiled in the region's affairs."[76] The contemporary record suggests that neither Pearson nor Martin appeared overly concerned about dictatorships, coups, or human rights abuses in the region, despite the growing prevalence of both; indeed, as Jennifer Tunnicliffe makes clear (Chapter 6, this volume), human rights were largely an afterthought for Pearson.[77] In a June 1964 review of recent coups, Pick urged that departmental officials advise Martin on when to resume normal relations with a country following an undemocratic transition. To minimize embarrassment, he recommended that Canada act in tandem with the United States but preferably after other NATO and Latin American countries had already extended recognition. In his view, only the most contentious cases warranted a prime ministerial or cabinet decision, none of which occurred during Pearson's tenure.[78] Pick's memo betrayed a cynical belief that, however distasteful they might be to Canadians, military coups were then part of Latin America's political landscape. Officially preferring democracy, American officials signalled their approval of such coups if directed against the left. That same June, Thomas C. Mann, who oversaw Inter-American Affairs, hinted that post-coup relations would have to be considered "in light of circumstances."[79] Washington quickly recognized Brazil's junta that April and would do so after other rightist *golpes,* such as Argentina's in 1966. In both instances Ottawa followed Pick's strategy, continuing relations once the new regimes had secured control and were recognized by other states.[80] Not until late in the decade, as political violence and repression cascaded across the region, did concerns about human rights enter the mainstream Canadian consciousness, as churches, unions, journalists, and students brought them to light. By 1970, reports of torture in Brazil were raised in Parliament.[81] Over the next ten years, developments throughout Latin America would generate substantial public pressure on Ottawa and Canadian businesses regarding engagement with such regimes.[82]

Military takeovers did not damage Canada's normal trade or diplomacy with the region's countries; nor did they stop munitions sales. Manufacturers such as Canadair and De Havilland were anxious for new markets, and American republics seeking to upgrade their arsenals were willing buyers for their wares as well as for national defence surpluses of aging aircraft and ships. In June 1963, Pearson's cabinet renewed its predecessor's prohibition of arms sales to Cuba and required case-by-case approval for any such exports to Central American or Caribbean hotspots such as the Dominican Republic. The rest of Latin America was not deemed politically objectionable in this regard, but approval of the minister of trade and commerce, in consultation with external affairs and defence, was required for exports exceeding $10,000.[83] Ottawa had to contend with American opposition to selling sophisticated "prestige" weapons, such as supersonic aircraft, to the larger republics, as Under-Secretary of State George Ball articulated to NATO in 1965, warning that a regional arms race could divert funds away from economic development. Little was said in Ottawa or Washington about smaller arms, which the latter wanted Latin American governments to have to enforce internal order, even if this meant facilitating domestic repression.[84]

Washington's opposition to advanced weaponry sales created awkward moments for Canadian relations with Brazil and Argentina. In 1965, with Ottawa's blessing, Canadair executives travelled to South America and found willing buyers for CL-41 light trainers and CF-5 aircraft. Cadieux advised Martin to approve exporting CL-41s to eight South American countries, including Brazil and Argentina, as a good economic and political decision.[85] However, supersonic CF-5s were another matter. While Canadian-made, they were American-designed, and Ottawa was contractually obliged to seek American approval for third-country export.[86] Washington refused, forcing the government to decline Brazilian and Venezuelan orders, an action generating significant irritation in Brazil. Explaining its obligations, Canada instead offered Brazil CL-41 and De Havilland Buffalo aircraft; for the latter, the procurement did not go through.[87] Such scenarios again reinforced to Latin American governments that their interests in Ottawa would always remain subordinate to Canadian-American relations, thus perpetuating disappointment and distrust.

The year 1967 was a busy one for Pearson's government. With the centennial celebrations, Expo '67, the Six Day War, and Charles De Gaulle's controversial Quebec visit, the prime minister's attention was certainly not on Latin America. Once again, Paul Martin sought to give it the attention that he believed was long overdue, the distance reflected by the presence of only three Latin American pavilions at Expo – Mexico, Venezuela, and Cuba. The SSEA lamely sought to reassure the Inter-American Association in Ottawa that the region had not been forgotten, and it touted what had been accomplished in trade and development.[88] Unable to go himself that year, Martin informed Pearson that, in lieu, he was sending Gérard Pelletier.[89] Visiting nine countries over three weeks in September, Pelletier issued a detailed report describing how living standards had declined in several of the nations that he had visited as a young man in 1945.[90] Confirming Martin's suspicions, Pelletier reported how Latin American governments were frustrated with Canada's ambivalent and unfocused policy, adding that what they really wanted was cooperation and partnership rather than aid, which they found condescending.[91] Within weeks of Pelletier's report, Trade and Commerce Minister Robert Winters commenced plans for a spring 1968 goodwill mission.[92] Yet these plans were shelved when Pearson announced his impending retirement and Winters entered the Liberal leadership race, a contest he and Martin alike lost to Pierre Trudeau. New initiatives towards Latin America had to await the new government. Before 1968 was out, Martin's successor, Mitchell Sharp, undertook the mission, beginning a new and more eventful chapter in Canadian hemispheric engagement, one that broke with the Pearsonian tradition of ignoring Latin America in favour of paying more attention to regions in which Canada's interests seemed more apparent.

Notes

1 As Opposition leader, Pearson twice visited his son Geoffrey in Mexico (in 1961–62 when he was posted at the Canadian Embassy) and also attended a conference in Brazil in 1962.

2 See Lester Pearson, *Mike: The Memoirs of the Right Honourable Lester B. Pearson*, vol. 2 (Toronto: University of Toronto Press, 1972). Greg Donaghy, *Tolerant Allies: Canada and the United States, 1963–1968* (Montreal and Kingston: McGill-Queen's University Press, 2002); and John English, *The Worldly Years: The Life of Lester Pearson, 1949–1972* (Toronto: Knopf, 1992), only mention Latin America in terms of the Cuban Missile Crisis.

3 Hébert to Pearson, 24 July 1951, LAC, RG 25, vol. 6648, file 11563-2-40.

4 Canadian Embassy Washington Telegram, 601, 26 March 1956, in *Documents on Canadian External Relations* [*DCER*], *1956–1957,* vol. 23, pt. 2 (Ottawa: Department of Foreign Affairs and International Trade, 2002), doc. 4.

5 For an overview, see J.C.M. Ogelsby, *Gringos of the Far North* (Toronto: Macmillan, 1976).

6 Memorandum from Acting Head, Far Eastern and American Division, "Colombia," 21 July 1949, in *DCER, 1949,* vol. 15 (Ottawa: Department of Foreign Affairs and International Trade, 1995), doc. 1066.

7 Peter McKenna, *Canada and the OAS: From Dilettante to Full Partner* (Ottawa: Carleton University Press, 1995), 82.

8 Canadian Embassy Mexico Letter 19, 14 January 1953, in *DCER, 1953,* vol. 19 (Ottawa: Department of External Affairs, 1991), doc. 1049.

9 Comments, Canadian Inter-American Association, 1–31 March 1953, *DCER, 1953*, doc. 1089.

10 See appendix in James Rochlin, *Discovering the Americas: The Evolution of Canadian Foreign Policy towards Latin America* (Vancouver: UBC Press, 1994).

11 McKenna, *Canada and the OAS*, 75. For the US position, see "United States Objectives and Courses of Action in Latin America," NSC 144/1, 18 March 1953, in *Foreign Relations of the United States* (*FRUS*), *1952–1954*, vol. 4, doc. 3.

12 See Pearson to Washington Embassy Despatch X-1456, 18 September 1952, in *DCER, 1952*, vol. 18 (Ottawa: Department of External Affairs, 1990), doc. 1040.

13 See Léger's comments "Organization of American States," in *DCER, 1952*, vol. 18, doc 1090.

14 Smith to Diefenbaker, 5 December 1958, in *DCER, 1957–1958*, vol. 25 (Ottawa: Department of Foreign Affairs and International Trade, 2004), doc. 527.

15 "Visits Made to Latin America by Canadian Ministers and Other Senior Representatives since 1940," [May 1964, revised October], LAC, RG 25, vol. 10052, file 20-1-2-LAT AM-pt.1.

16 John Hilliker and Donald Barry, *Canada's Department of External Affairs: Coming of Age, 1946–1968* (Montreal and Kingston: McGill-Queen's University Press, 1995), 180.

17 Cadieux to Martin, 22 April 1965, LAC, RG 25, vol. 14245, file 35-20-ECLA-pt.1.

18 Cabinet Conclusions, 22 January 1958, 4 March 1958 and 21 May 1962, LAC, RG 2.

19 Asa McKercher, "Southern Exposure: Diefenbaker, Latin America, and the Organization of American States," *Canadian Historical Review* 93 (2012): 57–80.

20 See Don Munton, "Our Men in Havana: Canadian Foreign Intelligence Operations in Castro's Cuba," *International Journal* 70 (2015): 23–39.

21 Pearson, *Mike*, 3:117–19. For the difficulties, see Donaghy, *Tolerant Allies*, chap. 1.
22 Stephen Rabe, *The Most Dangerous Area of the World: John F. Kennedy Confronts Communist Revolution in Latin America* (Chapel Hill: UNC Press, 1999), 91.
23 See ibid., chaps. 2–3.
24 See English, *Worldly Years*, 256–57; Reg Whitaker and Gary Marcuse, *Cold War Canada: The Making of a National Insecurity State, 1945–1957* (Toronto: University of Toronto Press, 1994), 265.
25 Hyannis Port Telegram to Department of State, 11 May 1963, in *FRUS 1961–1963*, vol. 13, doc. 449.
26 Quoted in Donaghy, *Tolerant Allies*, 128.
27 Pearson, *Mike*, 3:122–23; and Sayre to Bundy, 15 September 1964, Lyndon B. Johnson Library (LBJL), National Security Files, Latin America, June-December 1964.
28 See John Dirks, "Managing a Cooperative Disagreement: Canada the United States and Revolutionary Cuba, 1959–1980" (PhD diss., University of Toronto, 2014), chap. 7.
29 Cadieux to Martin, "Second Congress for the Independence of the Peoples of America and Solidarity with Cuba – Montreal," 27 February 1964, LAC, RG 146, ATIP 2011-00248-pt.1.
30 Pearson to Georgetown, 15 May 1964, LAC, RG 25, vol. 10043, file 20-1-2-BRGU-pt.1.
31 Summarized from documents in LAC, RG 25, vol. 14857, file 42-8-3-1-USSR-pt.2.
32 See Pearson to Havana XL-355, 7 July 1967, LAC, RG 25, vol. 10502, file 55-7-3-MTL-2-CUBA-pt.2.
33 Martin to Pearson, 20 September 1967, LAC, RG 25, vol. 10093, file 20-CDA-9-LATAM-pt.1.2.
34 See Russell Crandall, *Gunboat Democracy: US Interventions in the Dominican Republic, Grenada and Panama* (Lanham: Rowman and Littlefield, 2006), chap. 2.
35 See examples in LAC, Pearson Papers, vol. 278, file 845/D67.
36 Cabinet Conclusions, 6 May 1965, LAC, RG 2.
37 Donaghy, *Tolerant Allies*, 129–30.
38 House of Commons, *Debates*, 28 May 1965, 1775–76.
39 Santo Domingo to DEA, 11 June 1965, LAC, RG 25, vol. 9130, file 20-1-2-DOM-pt.1.
40 Santo Domingo to DEA, 3 June 1965, LAC, Pearson Papers, vol. 274, file 840/D671 Conf.
41 Rochlin, *Discovering the Americas*, 55–56.
42 *FRUS, 1961–1963*, vol. 13, doc. 449.
43 "Statements Concerning Canada Joining the OAS Made at the Hyannis Port Meeting," 8 January 1964, LAC, RG 25, vol. 9130, file 20-4-OAS-4-1-pt.1.
44 Massey to Pearson, 6 May 1963, LAC, Pearson Papers, vol. 290, file 890 Pers and Conf.
45 Greg Donaghy, *Grit: The Life and Politics of Paul Martin Sr.* (Vancouver: UBC Press, 2015), 222–23.

46 Clark to Pick, 27 August 1964, LAC, RG 25, vol. 9030, file 20-1-2-BRA-pt.1.

47 Irwin Memorandum on Canada and OAS, 17 July 1964, LAC, RG 25, vol. 9130, file 20-4-OAS-4-1-pt.2.

48 Cadieux to Martin, 8 January 1965, LAC, RG 25, vol. 9130, file 20-4-OAS-4-1-pt.3.

49 Martin to Pearson, 14 February 1964, LAC, RG 25, vol. 9130, file 20-4-OAS-4-1-pt.2.

50 "Canada and the Organization of American States," 1 March 1966, LAC, RG 25, vol. 10052, file 20-1-2-LATAM-pt.1.

51 Montevideo to DEA, 2 April 1964, LAC, RG 25, vol. 9130, file 20-4-OAS-4–1-pt.2; and Mexico City to DEA, 6 October 1965, LAC, RG 25, vol. 11306, file 38-7-1-AMRICA LAT.

52 Mexico City Numbered Letters 231 and 233, both dated 28 May 1965, LAC, RG 25, vol. 14245, file 35-20-ECLA-pt.2.

53 Douglas Memo, 7 April 1964, LAC, RG 25, vol. 9130, file 20-4-OAS-4-1-pt.2/.

54 Cabinet Conclusions, 26 January 1967, LAC, RG 2.

55 For examples, see LAC, Pearson Papers, vol. 270, file 890.

56 Paul Martin, *A Very Public Life* (Toronto: Deneau, 1985), 666.

57 See Donaghy, *Grit*, 247–53, 280–81.

58 Brian Douglas Tennyson, "Canada and the Commonwealth Caribbean: The Historical Relationship," in *Canadian-Caribbean Relations: Aspects of a Relationship* (Sydney, NS: Centre for International Studies, 1990); Greg Donaghy and Bruce Muirhead, "'Interests but No Foreign Policy': Canada and the Commonwealth Caribbean, 1944–1966," *American Review of Canadian Studies* 38 (2008): 275–94.

59 "Assistance to the Commonwealth Caribbean," 23 September 1966, LAC, RG 25, vol. 10093, file 20-9-CDA-LATAM-pt.1.1.

60 Cabinet Conclusions, 28 June 1966, LAC, RG 2.

61 Donaghy and Muirhead, "Interests but No Foreign Policy," 288–89.

62 Tennyson, "Canada and the Commonwealth Caribbean," 57.

63 Washington to DEA, 26 July 1966, LAC, RG 25, vol. 10842, file 20-1-2-USA-pt.4.

64 Rostow to Johnson, "Caribbean Development Bank," 19 October 1967, LBJL, National Security Files, box 3.

65 Mexico City to DEA, 15 July 1966, LAC, Pearson Papers, vol. 2, file 004 Conf. Carib. Can.

66 Briefing documents for visit of His Excellency Jose Antonio Mayobre, Minister of Mines and Hydocarbons of Venezuela, 30 July–4 August 1967, LAC, RG 25, vol. 8801, file 20-1-2-VEN-pt.1.

67 Caracas to DEA, 7 October 1966, LAC, RG 25, vol. 10093, file 20-CDA-9-LATAM-pt.1.

68 Cadieux to Martin, 5 May 1966, LAC, RG 25, vol. 10053, file 20-1-2-MEX-pt.1/.

69 Summary Documents "Mexico," 20 June 1968, LAC, RG 25, vol. 10053, file 20-1-2-MEX-pt.2.

70 See Draft Memo for Cabinet, [January 1968,] LAC, RG 25, vol. 10053, file 20-1-2-MEX-pt.2/.

71 See numerous examples in Cabinet Conclusions, LAC, RG 2.

72 File Memorandum, 30 September 1966, LAC, RG 25, vol. 11306, file 38-7-1-AMRICA LAT.

73 Maurice Strong file memo, 31 October 1966, LAC, RG 25, vol. 11306, file 38-7-1-AMRICA LAT.

74 Pick to Cadieux, 29 April 1966, LAC, RG 25, vol. 11306, file 38-7-1-AMRICA LAT.

75 Guatemala City to DEA, 10 November 1967, and Memorandum to Committee on External Aid, 7 February 1967, LAC, RG 25, vol. 11306, file 38-7-1-AMRICA LAT.

76 Martin, *Very Public Life*, 666.

77 For an overview see Hal Brands, *Latin America's Cold War* (Cambridge, MA: Harvard University Press, 2010).

78 "Relations with New Governments in Latin America," 8 June 1964, LAC, RG 25, vol. 10052, file 20-1-2-LAT AM-pt.1.

79 Washington Telegram 2066, 8 June 1964, LAC, RG 25, vol. 8928, file 20-USA-1-3-LATAM-pt.1.

80 See LAC, RG 25, vol. 9030, file 20-1-2-BRA-pt.1; and LAC, RG 25, vol. 9408, file 20-22-5-ARG-pt.1.

81 See LAC, RG 25, vol. 10114, file 20-22-2-BRA-pt.1.

82 Rochlin, *Discovering the Americas*, 101–7.

83 Cabinet Conclusions, 25 June 1963, LAC, RG 2.

84 Can. Del. NATO Telegram 698, 2 April 1965, LAC, RG 25, vol. 13964, file 37-22-1-AMRICA LAT-pt.1.

85 Cadieux to Martin, 3 February 1965, LAC, RG 25, vol. 13964, file 37-22-1-AMRICA LAT-pt.1.

86 DEA to Rio de Janeiro, 10 February 1967, LAC, RG 25, vol. 13964, file 37-22-1-BRAZIL-pt.1.

87 Rio de Janeiro Telegram 105, 27 February 1967, LAC, RG 25, vol. 13964, file 37-22-1-BRAZIL-pt.1.

88 Paul Martin address to Canadian Inter-American Association, 31 May 1967, LAC, RG 25, vol. 11306, file 38-7-1-LATAM-pt.1.

89 Martin to Pearson, 29 May 1967, LAC, RG 25, vol. 10093, file 20-CDA-9-LAT AM-pt.1.2.

90 Gérard Pelletier, *Years of Choice 1960–1968* (Toronto: Methuen, 1987), 246–48.

91 "Rapport sur le voyage de Gérard Pelletier," 2 November 1967, LAC, RG 25, vol. 11306, file 38-7-1-LATAM-pt.1.

92 Cadieux to Martin, 18 December 1967, LAC, RG 25, vol. 10093, file 20-CDA-9-LAT AM-pt.2/.

Lara Silver

10 A Long Goodbye
Pearson and Britain

Lester Pearson's affinity for Britain was genuine and personal. In the First World War he trained in the Royal Flying Corps, but his service abruptly terminated when he was struck by a London bus in 1917. Afterwards he studied at Oxford for two years, where he enjoyed himself immensely. In the late 1930s, he returned to London with his wife and two children to take up a diplomatic position at Canada House. Like William Lyon Mackenzie King, Canada's prime minister, Pearson carried on a common mission of trying to serve as a linchpin in Anglo-American relations. This linchpin mission lasted throughout the Second World War and into the early years of the 1950s, but it ended during the 1960s due to Canadian disinclination. As the Anglo-Canadian relationship loosened – the result, in part, of changing immigration patterns and shifts in Canadians' cultural tastes – Prime Minister Pearson helped the process along, most notably with the creation of a new flag for Canada that did not showcase the Union Jack. Moreover, the British Empire's rapid dissolution and London's interest in joining the European Economic Community steered Britain in a new direction. By the mid-1960s, the Department of External Affairs, noticing a "general sensation of friction" in its relationship with the British government, tried to remedy it but to little avail. While old feelings of loyalty to Britain remained for some, Pearson was glad to leave the familiar ways behind. His attitude was all the more surprising given that he himself was a product of the "British world" –

a white, Anglo-Saxon, Oxford-trained Methodist.[1] Yet, despite his sentimental views of Britain, by the time he became prime minister, Pearson treated the mother country in pragmatic terms that recognized the reality of the empire's end.

Pearson had a long-standing willingness to play a special part in international affairs. In 1935, he began his work in London as first secretary in the Canadian High Commission. He worked alongside High Commissioner Vincent Massey, but their orders came directly from King in Ottawa. Pearson had to send pertinent British newspaper clippings to keep King abreast of how international events were reported and regarded overseas. Given the vital nature of the transatlantic relationship, King impressed upon Pearson that Canada's position was to serve as a linchpin in Anglo-American relations. King referred to this vocation as Canada's "manifest destiny," a role that provided a useful lamppost for Pearson.[2] During the early years of the Second World War, before the United States had entered the conflict, Pearson delivered speeches around England on the importance of the Anglo-American relationship and of Canada's usefulness in promoting "the friendliest possible relations between London and Washington."[3]

Even after Japan's December 1941 attack on Pearl Harbor incited American belligerence, Pearson continued to emphasize the same theme. He moved to Washington in June 1942 to work as minister-counsellor at the Canadian Legation. In this capacity, in November 1943, while addressing the English-Speaking Union in Chicago, Pearson emphasized his desire for Americans and Britons to think of him as a useful interpreter between the two sides. Notwithstanding the obvious fact that President Franklin Roosevelt and Prime Minister Winston Churchill did not need his or anyone else's services to interact with one another, he argued:

> There may be occasions in which we can help in this regard. Personally, I often find that when I argue with Americans about Anglo-American questions, I put forward the British side of the case; when I talk to Englishmen on the same subject, I talk like an American. That may mean merely that I am an argumentative and contrary fellow, or it may possibly be an illustration of a part that Canada can play on the international stage.[4]

He continued to offer this assistance when, in 1944, he became Canada's ambassador to Washington. In New York City in February 1945, he told an audience:

> I have had more than one opportunity of convincing the English friends that all Americans are not gangsters who speak out of one side [of] the mouth while chewing gum vigorously on the other. Similarly, I have in Washington more than once hazarded the opinion that an Oxford drawl and a passion for privacy and understatement does not necessarily make an Englishman an aloof bore and an oppressor of natives.[5]

Pearson believed in his – and Canada's – unique ability to convey the impressions of one side to the other across the Atlantic Ocean.

Cooperation in the "English-speaking world," as it was often called, was considered a first essential step towards world peace. As the first signs of the Cold War became evident, Churchill's March 1946 pronouncement that an Iron Curtain was splitting Europe in half was quickly taken up, becoming a fixed feature in the minds of many for decades. As an insurmountable barrier seemingly had divided East from West, this made it all the more important to nurture a "fraternal association of English-speaking peoples." Days before the famous Iron Curtain speech was delivered, Pearson had gone over the text with Churchill at the British Embassy in Washington, where the former wartime leader was residing. Churchill had invited Pearson to sit by his bedside to discuss the text, and the latter felt embraced in a moment of cordial tenderness. Their goal was clear, and Pearson launched himself into the postwar years having the same objective that had guided him over the previous decade. He became under-secretary of external affairs in September 1946, moving back to Ottawa to address the challenges facing the world.

In Britain, financial disability had pushed the Labour Party under Prime Minister Clement Attlee to move away from a sentimental attachment to empire. Over the span of one dramatic week, 14–20 February 1947, a series of decisions signalled that Britain was not the great power it once was. First, Britain withdrew from its mandate in Palestine and referred the issue to the United Nations. Second, it ended military and financial assistance to Greece and Turkey, a burden it could no longer afford. Third, the British announced their forthcoming departure from the prized colony of India. In withdrawing from these areas, Britain eased its responsibilities, but the departures created new problems. The desire for a national home for Jewish people led to the creation of the State of Israel and prompted unending violence in the Middle East. The cessation of military and financial aid to Greece and Turkey invited the United States to take on the responsibility, and the expansion of American influence into Europe wrestled that position away from Britain and, with it, a degree of great power status. Last, with India's independence, a Muslim Pakistan formed amidst much bloody intracommunal violence and ill will that has yet to dissipate.

Responding to crises brought forward to the UN, Pearson announced that Canada would align itself "almost unconsciously" with positions adopted by Britain and the United States, and that deviation from this set path would occur only if those two countries differed in opinion.[6] With King's retirement from public life in 1948, however, new possibilities emerged. Arnold Heeney, clerk of the Privy Council, did not want Canada to cling to its old role or have Canadians be misconstrued as a "race of Anglo-American hermaphrodites." As he emphasized at an address to the US National War College in October 1948, "we're rather tired of being 'interpreters' and 'links' and 'bridges.'"[7] In Pearson's elevated role as SSEA, he strove to seek out the "Canadian" position. But as Canadian delegates so frequently sided with the American and British positions at the UN – for example, on crises brought forward that year in Palestine, Kashmir, and Indonesia – it seemed that, in foreign policy, Canada was moving sideways, from being a British dominion to being an American satellite state. In a radio interview broadcast by the CBC in January 1949, Pearson tried to dispel notions that Canada was a "satellite state," saying simply: "we and our friends have common interests and ... we often agree about the way in which we should act."[8] The Anglo-American relationship, and soon afterwards the North Atlantic Alliance formalized through NATO, remained important constellations for Pearson.

Beneath the surface of diplomatic politeness lurked the desire to take on a more assertive, independent voice in external affairs. At the end of 1953, Heeney, as Canadian ambassador to Washington, invited the public to understand that Canada should not be regarded as "*merely the ham* in the trans-Atlantic sandwich – nor even the bridge, or the golden hinge, or the linchpin – dangerous passive similes."[9] But Heeney's words fell on some deaf ears. When an aged Churchill visited

Ottawa in the summer of 1954, again as British prime minister, he referred to Canada as "the master-link in Anglo-American unity." Canada's image as the eager third party in the Anglo-American relationship was entrenched in the minds of politicians both at home and abroad. Pearson eventually helped to form a new role for Canadians, but it meant stepping away from tradition and angering some Anglophiles in Canada.

The Suez affair brought the Anglo-Canadian relationship into sharp focus. British prime minister Anthony Eden had mistakenly assumed that he could rely upon Canada's support. Although Canadian Progressive Conservatives winced, Louis St-Laurent's Liberal government angrily reprimanded Britain and France for joining with Israel to attack Egypt. Speaking to the House of Commons in late November 1956, St-Laurent declared: "I have been scandalized more than once by the attitude of the larger powers, the big powers as we call them ... the era when the supermen of Europe could govern the whole world has and is coming pretty close to an end." Although Pearson wrote to Eden with a more pleading tone to make amends, he felt that London had not acted appropriately. John Holmes, a long-standing Canadian diplomat and, later, a historian, wrote a decade after Suez that the St-Laurent government's aim was not "anti-British" but rather an attempt to "rescue the old lady from an unfortunate and uncharacteristic aberration."[10] While Holmes's view of British conduct was exceedingly kind, Britain's policy to maintain authority over the Suez Canal by force was not a departure from its actions elsewhere in the world. London had an interest in maintaining the status quo – an interest that had developed over years of imperial supremacy – and, in the 1950s, it used force to quell indigenous uprisings in Iran, Malaya, and Kenya.

In some respects, British agility in dealing aggressively in world politics benefitted Canada's economy. For instance, British Guiana's bauxite exports provided 85 percent of that used by the Canadian aluminum industry, contributing to large profits ($29 million in 1951).[11] For the British to lose Canada's support during the Suez Crisis was a bitter blow to their friendship. The British were often condescending towards colonial Canadians, but, after Suez, familiar condescension was replaced with acute resentment. Many Britons believed that Canada should have been more supportive in the debacle. Even if the "Old Lady" had misjudged the situation, her age and experience still deserved deference.

The Progressive Conservative Opposition in Canada launched a polemical attack against the Liberal Party's stance on Suez. Howard Green (who became SSEA in June 1959) claimed that the month of November 1956 was "the most disgraceful period for Canada in the history of this nation" and that the government had knifed its best friend in the back.[12] His own morale low thanks to such criticism, Pearson believed that he had helped to both prevent a Commonwealth collapse and a general war in the Middle East. But receiving the Nobel Peace Prize for organizing the dispatch of peacekeeping troops to Egypt rescued Pearson from his melancholy. He accepted the prize on 11 December 1957, a date he probably noted with special satisfaction for it was twenty-six years to the day since, in 1931, the Statute of Westminster had granted Canada autonomy in its external affairs.

Surprisingly, Anglo-Canadian relations worsened after the Progressive Conservative Party won the Canadian election of 1957 – and Pearson could do little more than watch the downturn unfold from the Opposition benches. John Diefenbaker was sentimentally attached to the British connection, famously heading off to a Commonwealth prime ministers' meeting in London within days of assuming office in June 1957 and then announcing his intent to divert 15 percent of Canadian imports from American to British suppliers. Britain needed a boost in revenue, but it did not come from Canada. Prime Minister Harold Macmillan was determined to proceed with rapid decolonization in Africa in light of economic losses and burgeoning nationalist uprisings that were too costly, politically and economically, to subdue. As he announced in July 1957: "Nationalism, which a few years ago was but a ripple, has become a tidal wave surging from Asia across the ocean to the shores of Africa on one side and the Caribbean on the other." He requested an economic report be conducted on the colonies to determine which colonial possessions were liabilities and which were assets. The Conservative Party, the "Party of Empire," according to its campaign manifesto back in 1951, sought a new road to economic recovery, but it was a painful path for those nostalgic for the old ways.

Diefenbaker's staid attachment to tradition and his own personal sense of righteousness put him against the British Conservative Party in a time of challenging decision making and change. Diefenbaker was not naturally affable, even to the British, whom he held in such high regard. In a telling encounter in London in July 1957, he refused a special drink of cognac offered by Churchill as he was a "teetotaller."

Churchill had to adjust his hearing aid to understand what Diefenbaker meant, and when it became clear that Diefenbaker was not a "prohibitionist," Churchill replied, "Ah, I see, you only hurt yourself."[13] As Diefenbaker would not let go of his principles, during his time in office he aggravated Canada's relationships with the United States and Britain. As Churchill had prophetically noted, these wounds were self-inflicted.

As part of his Progressive Conservative revivalism, Diefenbaker sought to bring Canadians closer to their monarch in the form of a royal tour over the summer of 1959. Queen Elizabeth II made a forty-five-day trek across the provinces, a demanding and tiring schedule that drew criticism from those especially protective of her well-being, especially when news broke that she was pregnant.[14] Trying to convince Canadians that Elizabeth was the Queen of Canada, not just the British monarch, was an ambitious task as Diefenbaker felt that forces were at work to shake off the country's monarchial heritage. The royal tour's lavish cost raised questions, while the use of the Red Ensign and "God Save the Queen" drew attention to the absence of a truly Canadian flag or national anthem. The anti-monarchial forces present in Canada worried Diefenbaker for the entire British Commonwealth seemed under siege.

At the same time, the Commonwealth was expanding with the independence of Malaya and Ghana in 1957; Nigeria in 1960; and Cyprus, Sierra Leone, and Tanganyika in 1961. But it also contracted, thanks to South Africa's departure in 1961 over the apartheid issue. The Sharpeville massacre in South Africa the previous year had embittered many against Hendrik Verwoerd's regime, including a critical Diefenbaker. The sense that the Commonwealth faced real jeopardy was accentuated by Britain's decision to apply for membership in the European Economic Community, thereby abandoning the preferential imperial trading practices in effect since the Ottawa Agreements of 1932. Diefenbaker, asserting that Canada "could not be sanguine" lest the Commonwealth cease to exist altogether,[15] was publicly obstinate over the duration of Britain's negotiation proceedings and lamented anticipated losses of Canadian revenue, even though Britain suffered from a serious balance-of-payments problem.

When Pearson won the election of 1963, a collective sigh of relief was likely heard in Washington and London. The John F. Kennedy administration was pleased to have a government in Ottawa that it could work with amicably and that would enable it to finalize the basing of nuclear weapons on Canadian soil. Macmillan was eager to meet with Pearson immediately, doing so on 30 April, although they had shared pleasant conversations years earlier. Pearson felt there was little of significance to discuss aside from questions of nuclear weapons and defence, but he enjoyed spending five days in London and stayed for one night at Windsor Castle at the Queen's invitation. The trip was meant to establish a good personal relationship, and in this Pearson succeeded. But "closeness" can have dangerous consequences diplomatically, as Pearson later noted in his memoirs.[16] The Liberal Party's domestic critics in Quebec looked unfavourably upon the "Anglo-Saxon establishment," and the Front de libération du Québec, established earlier that year in February 1963, escalated its militancy in the following months. Although having only thirty-five members around that time, the underground initiative gained young sympathizers who angrily demonstrated against the province's oppression and class exploitation. Graffiti, arson, and dynamite were used, followed by guerrilla actions in the form of armed holdups, burglaries, and theft of arms later that year.[17] The group was the most extreme outgrowth of a larger, growing Québécois nationalism, a sentiment that Pearson would spend much of his premiership trying to placate.

The FLQ was encouraged by the rise of anti-colonial movements globally. As radical movements were surfacing in Algeria, Cuba, and in the United States among militant African Americans, Quebec discontent played heavily on Pearson's mind. As he told a concerned citizen in April 1964, "if we do not find fair and satisfactory solutions to these problems, our Confederation – and hence Canada – is not likely to survive."[18] His determination to bring out a new Canadian flag without a Union Jack formed a major part of his strategy to appeal to French Canadians. The emotive and divisive flag debate that ensued in 1964 angered Anglophile Canadians who lamented the loss of tradition, but 70 percent of francophone Quebeckers polled backed a new flag. Pearson, inasmuch as he held a deep love for London and a special fondness for the Royal Family, believed a new flag could placate Quebec. When Queen Elizabeth visited in October 1964, she was jeered and booed by a crowd in Quebec. The ceremonial unfurling of the Maple

Leaf on 15 February 1965 prompted cheers, but there were funereal aspects to this for those paying respects to the old flag, with Diefenbaker's tears flowing freely down his cheeks.[19]

Political change made the 1960s a particularly turbulent decade. While matters of national unity had centre stage in Canada, the British government grappled with its own crises. Harold Wilson's newly elected Labour Party concentrated on resolving the financial crisis over the pound, which necessitated American assistance at an awkward time. Wilson's sense of Britain's economic insecurity overwhelmed his political thinking, which is understandable given his former life as lecturer in economics at Oxford. In his diplomatic efforts with President Lyndon Johnson over Vietnam, the pound's precariousness meant that Wilson needed to court American favour for bailouts. But his refusal to provide military commitments despite intense US pressure badly embittered London's relations with Washington. The Johnson administration's Operation Rolling Thunder launched in March 1965, an aerial bombing campaign against North Vietnam, continued despite mounting criticism from American allies and from within the United States itself. Domestic British public opinion being what it was, Wilson could not offer moral support. Besides, he may have revealed his true sentiments in May 1954 when he publicly denounced the "lunatic fringe" in the American Senate, which was determined to wage a holy crusade against communism. A series of British "peace initiatives" over the summer of 1965 was fruitless. Johnson lamented that entanglement in Vietnam dominated his presidency, and he explained to the world that the American military was preventing the spread of communism. As Johnson commented on 28 July 1965, "we did not choose to be the guardians at the gate, but there is no one else." As Greg Donaghy notes (Chapter 4, this volume), Pearson, like Wilson, was concerned by Vietnam, but, even as Canada, too, launched its own quiet peace initiatives, there was no coordinated effort between London and Ottawa to dissuade the Americans.

Britain had its own problems in the Commonwealth, notably in Rhodesia, where racial supremacists presided over a police state. Following Rhodesia's unilateral declaration of independence on 11 November 1965, Wilson became so obsessed with that nation that his cabinet colleagues referred to it as "his Cuba," comparing it to President Kennedy's test of strength in 1962.[20] Unfortunately for Wilson, the crisis did his reputation no good. He complained to Pearson during a meeting on 19 December 1965 that he had a four-dimensional audience listening to him: the Rhodesians, the British public, the Commonwealth with its African members, and the diverse UN. Being difficult, if not impossible, to satisfy all these players, Wilson asked Pearson if RCMP personnel could help guard the Kariba Dam, which powered neighbouring Zambia. Stating that there was a shortage of RCMP officers, Pearson suggested using guards administered by the UN instead. Pearson might have been put off by Wilson's confidential suggestion that a saboteur with a pair of pliers could snip the power cable and deny power to Rhodesia.[21] More concerning than an independent Rhodesia governed by a white minority was the possibility of Rhodesia joining the Union of South Africa as a fifth province. Not only would such a step badly undermine race relations in former British Africa, it could also damage Britain's economic prospects as negative repercussions might include an interruption of Zambian copper for British industry.

In the case of another Commonwealth crisis, this one in Cyprus, Canada took on a helpful peacekeeping role. As Donaghy, Adam Chapnick, and Michael Carroll each note in their contributions to this volume (Chapters 4, 3, and 2, respectively), the Canadian role in the Cyprus crisis – working to create and then staff a UN force to interpose itself between warring Turk and Greek Cypriots – was much appreciated in both London and Washington. Herein lies an example of the Pearsonian "helpful fixer" role being played out, but it was something that was becoming less frequent.

As for economic issues, Pearson, unlike Diefenbaker, was unwilling to stand in the way of British movement towards Europe. As SSEA Paul Martin told his British counterpart in 1966, while Canada might suffer economically from Britain's Common Market membership, the move had "long term political benefits."[22] Yet Anglo-Canadian relations suffered over the price of raw materials, notably Canadian copper, and over an imbalance in Anglo-Canadian trade that had Canada outselling Britain more than two to one. Such "gloomy facts" were made public by Peter Allen, chair of the British Committee for Exports to Canada, in an open letter to the *Glasgow Herald* in March 1966. Touting Canada's wealth, steady expansion, and great potential for growth, he encouraged British exporters to sell to Canada as "Britain [could] gain an appreciably larger share of this lucrative market."[23] A booklet entitled *Selling to Canada*, written by Kenneth McGregor, former senior

British trade commissioner in Ottawa, was designed to help British manufacturers. A drive to showcase British manufactured products in Canada was planned for the country's centennial year, 1967. Two exhibitions of British industrial and consumer goods were to be organized in Toronto and Vancouver, respectively, in May, with a "British Week" in Toronto the following October. The Canadian market was being targeted as it was the world's largest importer of manufactured goods, well ahead of Britain, the United States, and Japan.

Canada's bright economic future contrasted with Britain's gloomier outlook, an unhappy reality that dampened relations. But there was more to it – namely, a lack of intimate contact, feelings of ungratefulness thanks to the long shadow of Suez, and a sense of divergence in the paths that lay ahead. By mid-April 1966, Marcel Cadieux, the Canadian under-secretary of state, wrote to Geoffrey Murray, Canada's deputy high commissioner in London, to request Canada House's analysis of Anglo-Canadian relations. Further, by month's end, a confidential memo circulating within the Department of External Affairs drew attention to the "present deterioration of Anglo-Canadian relations" and sought opinions from within the DEA on the "general sensation of friction" with Britain. Divisions were requested to provide comments, observations, or specific areas "where the British have reasonable grievances which might have been avoided."[24] The resulting reports exposed the ambivalence of mid-1960s' Anglo-Canadian relations.

In the view of the DEA's Latin American Division, Anglo-Canadian relations were "satisfactory" but not "particularly close." Moreover, if the relationship *had* "deteriorated, this [was] probably a reflection of the decline of Britain as a world power in both the economic and political sense and the progressive weakening of the Commonwealth through its miraculously flexible evolution to the point where there [was] little left but the grin of the Cheshire cat."[25] The rapid disintegration of the British Empire in the 1960s certainly marked a shift in Britain's reputation. As more of the Old Lady's children gained independence, with Kenya in 1963 and Malta in 1964, the Commonwealth became a looser familial arrangement. Thus, British interests would be met only if the newly independent countries agreed to do so.

In its own submission, the Defence Division noted a "general coolness" in relations and, more specifically, pointed out that "Canada may have created unnecessary friction" over the British proposal for an allied nuclear force, from which the Canadian government backed away and left "an unhappy legacy."[26] The British expectation of Canadian compliance came at the wrong time as divisive forces and a watchful Quebec electorate made it exceedingly difficult to cooperate openly. Some believed that Britain took Canada for granted in matters of a political nature. Regarding Rhodesia, for instance, London provided views and information to Ottawa rather than seeking out Canadian assessments and opinions. As the DEA's irritated staff in the Division of African and Middle Eastern Affairs noted, the British tended to "assume in the field of Rhodesia and other Southern African questions, in particular, that we would follow the British lead reasonably automatically."[27] If Wilson struck an agreement with Rhodesia that appeased white settler demands, Canada would be in the uncomfortable position of having to criticize or even dissociate itself from British policy.

After examining the nature of the Anglo-Canadian relationship from his position in London, Murray sent his report to Cadieux in May 1966. He emphasized that both countries were "at a crossroads," grappling with new identities, roles, and goals in international affairs. For Britain, its "agonizing experience of the post-war period," as it became a second-class power, was only now being slowly accepted by Britons. Britain's economic problems were at the forefront, and its trade deficit with Canada was blamed for causing unnecessary hardship. Citing British opinion, Murray concluded that "if Britain could overcome or substantially narrow its trade gap with Canada, the general British problem would be well on the way to solution." For instance, undisguised bitterness had followed Canada's purchase of French fighter aircraft rather than of British planes. The impetus to "buy British" was not sufficiently strong in Canada. Murray concluded his observations as follows:

> More often than not, in Britain Canadian representatives are faced with such questions as: "What has happened to Canada?, What is happening in Canada?, What does Canada stand for?, Why is Canada going downhill?, Where is Canada going in world affairs?" Most of these questions are posed not by critics but by well intentioned and worried friends of Canada – British people who have had long association with Canadians.
>
> In large part perhaps the questions derive from a fear, or even an awareness, that Britain itself has lost its place and direction in

> the rapidly changing world of the Sixties. In part the questions may be a reflection of the shock of Suez or the disappointments of the Diefenbaker years. In part they may be simply symptomatic of a broader dismay about the disintegration of old ideas, old values, old relations and an old order of things.[28]

Pearson had grown up in a Canada bound within the British Empire. He was a veteran of the First World War, an Anglophile, and a nationalist. His former political dictum of trying to "interpret" the British to the Americans and vice versa was part of the "old order of things." That lamppost had dimmed. By the mid-1960s, Wilson and Johnson were not on good personal terms, and Pearson did not try to reconcile them. He may have been preoccupied with domestic matters, but Pearson also recognized that Canada deserved a bright future free from any subservience. When contemplating the reasons behind the deterioration in the Anglo-Canadian relationship, in mid-June 1966, SSEA Paul Martin suggested that "one of the problems arises from the fact that the Commonwealth Office and not the Foreign Office is their main body of contact."[29] The British tendency to reach out to Canada through the old channels of bureaucracy was considered by some to be a serious faux pas, emblematic of the divergence that existed between British expectations to carry on dealing with Canada as it had in the past and a growing Canadian distaste for reminders of colonialism. The merger of the Foreign Office and the Commonwealth Office in 1968 seemed to many Canadian diplomats to be a worthy, if not long overdue, move.

As for the matter of Britain's trade imbalance, it was to be dealt with sympathetically. Robert Winters, Canada's trade minister, had a meeting with Douglas Jay, president of the British Board of Trade, and they announced their decision to establish a joint committee on trade and economic problems to urgently search for solutions.[30] Relations were sufficiently warm for Pearson and Wilson to meet on 29 July 1966 in Montreal after Wilson met with Johnson in Washington. Wilson found Montreal more convenient than Ottawa as he, just briefly passing through, stayed but ninety minutes. Pearson intended to talk to him about Vietnam, Britain's defence policy east of Suez, plus Rhodesia and Zambia, but limited time meant that little could be said. Perhaps this is how they both wanted it, or perhaps, given the list of things Pearson wished to discuss, Wilson was freezing out his Canadian counterpart.

There would be much time for political romping over the duration of Canada's Centennial year. Expo '67 brought over 50 million Canadian and foreign visitors to Montreal from April to October 1967. There was much good cheer and fanfare, and Canada impressively showcased itself to the world. Britain also put its own stamp on Expo: the Britain Today Pavilion brought the swinging style of Carnaby Street to Montreal,[31] while in July, the Queen and Prince Philip enjoyed a ride over the Expo grounds on the mini-rail. Celebrating Canada's Centennial marked a milestone in the country's growth towards adulthood, and, for Pearson, the occasion had to be combined with a shedding of the old clothes. In his address on 3 July 1967, in which he welcomed the Royals to Expo, he said good-naturedly: "No longer is our national costume a union jacket worn with star striped trousers!"[32] Canada's personality on the world stage remained a work in progress, but Canadians could look forward to the future without fear of being stuck in the past.

At year's end, Pearson announced his resignation as prime minister. His successor was a young bachelor, enviously bilingual, and more playful than politically shrewd. The baby-boomers were now a powerful voting body, and they enjoyed the intellectualism of Pierre Trudeau plus his eagerness to challenge accepted dogma and ruffle some feathers.[33] In the heady atmosphere of Trudeau's election victory the following April 1968, the *London Times* reported that there was "a surging, if often fuzzily defined, desire for change on the part of many Canadians and the recognition by many more that change [was] essential and inevitable."[34] The new prime minister was willing to jettison previous labels describing Canada's global role. A classified report reviewing foreign policy indicated a disinclination towards the old way: "More often than not the would-be 'interpreter' or 'honest broker' soon finds himself working willingly or otherwise for one side or the other."[35] Pearson knew this, but with no other role on offer, he worried about how peace and security could be achieved in a very different world. The British Empire had disintegrated, fewer Canadians thought affectionately of the Queen, and Britain was not looked upon for leadership as it had been when Pearson was young. Certainly some still cherished the British connection, but Trudeau was not among them.

Hardly a product of the British world, Trudeau, even more than Pearson, saw Britain in pragmatic terms.

Notes

1 See Phillip Buckner and R. Douglas Francis, *Canada and the British World: Culture, Migration and Identity* (Vancouver: UBC Press, 2006); and C.P. Champion, "Mike Pearson at Oxford: War, Varsity, and Canadianism," *Canadian Historical Review* 88 (2007): 263–90.

2 King used the phrase "manifest destiny" during the Second World War to highlight Canada's role in bringing together Britain and the United States. See W.L.M. King, *Canada at Britain's Side* (Toronto: Macmillan, 1941), 173–74.

3 Pearson, Address, "United States-Canada Relations," Nottingham University, 31 January 1941, LAC, Pearson Papers, vol. 1, file Speeches.

4 Pearson, Address to the English-Speaking Union, Chicago, 1 November 1943, LAC, Pearson Papers, vol. 1, file Speeches.

5 Pearson, Address to the Canadian Society Dinner in New York, 3 February 1945, LAC, Pearson Papers, vol. 1, file Speeches.

6 Pearson, Address, "Some Principles of Canadian Foreign Policy," 21 June 1948, LAC, Pearson Papers, vol. 1, file Speeches.

7 A.D.P. Heeney, Address, "The Kingdom of Canada," 25 October 1948, LAC, A.D.P. Heeney Papers, vol. 11, file Speeches 1946–1953.

8 Pearson, Broadcast delivered over the Trans-Canada Network of the CBC, 20 January 1949, LAC, Escott Reid Papers, vol. 7.

9 Heeney, notes for an address, "Some Canadian Reflections on Anglo-American Friendship," 10 December 1953, LAC, Heeney Papers, vol. 11, file Speeches 1953–1954, emphasis in original.

10 John Holmes, "The Anglo-Canadian Neurosis: A Mood of Exasperation," *Round Table* 56 (1965–66): 256.

11 Mark Curtis, *Web of Deceit: Britain's Real Role in the World* (London: Vintage, 2003), 348.

12 Lester Pearson, *Mike: The Memoirs of the Right Honourable Lester B. Pearson*, vol. 2 (Toronto: University of Toronto Press, 1973), 273.

13 John Diefenbaker, *One Canada: Memoirs of the Right Honourable John G. Diefenbaker – The Years of Achievement, 1957–1962* (Toronto: Macmillan, 1976), 191.

14 Phillip Buckner, "The Last Great Royal Tour: Queen Elizabeth's 1959 Tour to Canada," in *Canada and the End of Empire*, ed. Phillip Buckner (Vancouver: UBC Press, 2005), 85.

15 Diefenbaker, *One Canada*, 203.

16 Lester Pearson, *Mike: The Memoirs of the Right Honourable Lester B. Pearson*, vol. 3 (Toronto: University of Toronto Press, 1975), 101.

17 Bryan Palmer, *Canada's 1960s: The Ironies of Identity in a Rebellious Era* (Toronto: University of Toronto Press, 2009), 332.

18 Pearson, *Mike*, 3:244.
19 Jose E. Iguarta, *The Other Quiet Revolution: National Identities in English Canada, 1945–71* (Vancouver: UBC Press, 2006), 190.
20 Ronald Hyam, *Britain's Declining Empire: The Road to Decolonisation, 1918–1968* (Cambridge: Cambridge University Press, 2006), 365–68.
21 Discussions between Prime Ministers Pearson and Wilson, 19 December 1965, LAC, RG 25, vol. 10042, file 20-1-2-BRIT-pt.2.
22 Record of meeting between Paul Martin and George Brown, 18 December 1966, LAC, RG 25, vol. 10042, file 20-1-2-BRIT-pt.2.
23 Peter Allen, "Transatlantic Exports Made Easy," *Glasgow Herald*, 30 March 1966.
24 Commonwealth Division, "Survey of Anglo-Canadian Relations," 26 April 1966, LAC, RG 25, vol. 10042, file 20-1-2-BRIT-pt.2.
25 Latin American Division to Commonwealth Division, "Survey of Anglo-Canadian Relations," 27 April 1966, LAC, RG 25, vol. 10042, file 20-1-2BRIT-pt.2.
26 Defence Division to Commonwealth Division, "Survey of Anglo-Canadian Relations," 6 May 1966, LAC, RG 25, vol. 10042, file 20-1-2BRIT-pt.2.
27 African and Middle Eastern Division to Commonwealth Division, "Survey of Anglo-Canadian Relations," 10 May 1966, LAC, RG 25, vol. 10042, file 20-1-2BRIT-pt.2.
28 Murray to Cadieux, "Britain and Canada 1966," 27 May 1966, LAC, Basil Robinson Papers, vol. 13.
29 Cadieux to Martin, "Relations with Britain," 14 June 1966 and Martin minute, LAC, RG 25, vol. 10042, file 20-1-2-BRIT-pt.2.
30 "Joint Canada-UK Cabinet Committee on Trade Problems to Be Established," *Montreal Gazette*, 18 June 1966.
31 Elizabeth Darling, "'Britain Today' at Expo," in *Expo 67: Not Just a Souvenir* ed. Rhona Richman Kenneally and Johanne Sloan, 47–60 (Toronto: University of Toronto Press, 2010).
32 Lester Pearson, *Words and Occasions* (Toronto: University of Toronto Press, 1970), 275.
33 Nearly half of the electorate in 1967 was under the age of thirty-five. See Paul Litt, "Trudeaumania: Participatory Democracy in the Mass-Mediated Nation," *Canadian Historical Review* 89 (2008): 27–53.
34 *Times*, 5 April 1968.
35 Memorandum to the Minister, "Foreign Policy Review," 5 April 1968, LAC, Heeney Papers, vol. 5.

Part 3:

Pearson the Idealist

Timothy Andrews Sayle

11 A Cold Warrior? Pearson and the Soviet Bloc

In his Nobel Lecture, Lester Pearson reminded his audience that he – and they – had lived since 1945 "in a period of cold war."[1] In December 1957, few needed reminding. Months before his speech, the Soviet Union had launched its *Sputnik* satellite, opening up a new chapter in the nuclear arms race. This was the high Cold War. And yet, half a decade later, with Pearson now prime minister, Canada's Cold War seemed a thing of the past for Canada's relations with the Soviet Union and its Eastern European satellites from 1963 to 1968 were anything but the stuff of high drama. The list of public events in Soviet-Canadian relations during Pearson's time as prime minister is long but mundane: trade agreements, civil aviation links, student exchanges, and Telex connections. A Soviet parliamentary delegation visited Medicine Hat, where they were excited to see real live cowboys.[2] And the Soviet Union outspent all other states in its gargantuan contribution to Expo '67. At first blush, it seems difficult to sustain the argument that the Cold War was the "essence" and not just the "context" of Pearson's foreign policy towards the Soviet Bloc.[3] But Pearson's Cold War policy would not have been Pearsonian if it had not had an element of paradox, blending an immediate, realist pragmatism with a long-term, idealist vision.[4]

Certainly, the remarkable normality, even banality, of Canada's good relations with the Soviet Union in the mid- and late 1960s resulted from many forces, some beyond Canadian control. First was the lessening of international tensions after the crisis years of the early 1960s.

Second were twin Soviet efforts to engage with NATO countries in an effort to weaken alliance cohesion and to obtain wheat and other products from the West.[5] Third was a Canadian desire for new markets and to protect Canada's balance of payments from American tax measures.[6] All of these forces might even lead to the mistaken assumption that "Pearson's Canada" belonged to no side of the Cold War but lay somewhere "between East and West."[7]

But Pearson's Canada was never "between" East and West. The Soviet Union, to Pearson, was a "massive and fearful force, alien and menacing to many of the things we take for granted in our way of living."[8] In his memoirs, he singled out Soviet aggression as causing the Cold War and blasted revisionist historians who sought to cast blame any other way.[9] Robert Bothwell sums up Canada's Cold War in a style that fits Pearson, too: for reasons of history, geography, and ideology, there was never any question that Canada "would take its place among the nations resisting communism."[10] This resistance required not only diplomacy but also defence. Pearson was convinced that the Soviets would treat with the West only if they were properly deterred.[11] All of Pearson's policies towards the Soviet Bloc – as Isabel Campbell notes (Chapter 13, this volume) – rested on preserving NATO's firm foundation. He expected that if NATO could balance the military strength of the Red Army, and if Western diplomats persevered in dogged diplomatic efforts to engage Moscow in dialogue, the two sides could avoid the mutual destruction that seemed always to be lurking around the corner.

But this story does not account for the essence of Pearson's beliefs and the repugnance with which he viewed the Soviet political system. He was, after all, not only a Liberal but a liberal, fundamentally opposed to totalitarianism or despotism. The end goal of Pearson's policy towards the USSR was not simply peaceful co-existence, though he knew this was difficult enough to achieve and was worth every effort in its own right. His efforts to contain and engage the Soviet Union were accompanied by a deeper faith that the Soviet system was untenable in a world of lessened international tension.[12] Pearson agreed with and pronounced as well George Kennan's inversion of Karl Marx: the Soviet Union contained within it the "seeds of its own decay."[13]

But unlike so many Cold Warriors of his vintage, Pearson recognized that any overt effort – and most covert efforts were painfully overt – to challenge the Soviet regime would, in fact, strengthen it. Pearson understood that the Cold War was the greatest source of the Kremlin's power both at home and abroad; ratcheting down the global confrontation would both lessen the chance of accidental conflict and weaken the elements of the Soviet state that made it so dangerous. But Pearson's acknowledgment of the complexities of Soviet power brought him into conflict with those statesmen who had, alongside Pearson, established the postwar system of Atlantic security cooperation. In 1966, for instance, the former American Secretary of State Dean Acheson, worried his Canadian colleague had gone soft on communism, complained: "Mike Pearson is one of the leading frauds of our day."[14] Despite Acheson's acid words, Pearson's efforts to engage the Soviet Union diplomatically offered the best way to encourage the Soviet bloc to abandon its revolutionary pretences on the international stage. And by using diplomacy to open opportunities for exchanges between people – diplomats, businesspeople, tourists, and students – Canada and the West could help, modestly, to encourage Soviet society to move away from a social model that Pearson both disliked and thought dangerous.

In the Second World War's waning days Canadian officials understood that the need for security trumped all other concerns in the war-ravaged Soviet Union. Still, Canadians in the Department of External Affairs and parliamentarians concerned with events in Europe were shocked by the "brutal treatment" the Red Army and Soviet security services meted out to social democrats, resistance members, and Jews. Pearson was hardly alone in finding these actions morally reprehensible.[15] Soviet brutality at war's end only confirmed Pearson's instincts that the Soviet Union was on the wrong side of history. Pearson was no expert on Soviet affairs, but few Western officials were in 1945. He had had no opportunity or reason to develop a special appreciation for the Russian people, unlike the handful of Canadians who served in the Soviet Union and spoke and wrote warmly of its peoples – if not its leaders.[16]

As he conceded in his diary in 1945, Pearson did not know what to think of the Soviet Union, stating succinctly: "[The USSR is] a force which we simply do not understand."[17] What quickly became clear was that the USSR was an active force seemingly intent on challenging the interests of its wartime allies in the Balkans, Iran, and Manchuria. In March 1946, Winston Churchill told an American audience that an "Iron Curtain" had split Europe. The speech electrified Washington. Pearson, as ambassador to the United States, was obliged to report the mood of the country to which he was accredited, not to analyze Churchill's logic. He reported to Ottawa that American officials and congressmen were now speaking of the Soviet Union, alarmingly, as a new enemy. While Pearson knew Washington's denizens were prone to "exaggerations and verbal irresponsibility," he found their attitude "depressing if not dangerous."[18]

Pearson's reporting on Churchill's speech – in fact, his reporting on the American reaction to Churchill's speech – is instructive. In the 1940s, and for the rest of his public life, Pearson would not separate his analysis of the Soviet Union from his understanding of Soviet-American relations. To Pearson, much of the threat emanating from the Kremlin was the threat of a collision between Washington and Moscow. As ambassador to the US, Pearson worried about the Americans, fearing that they would bluster and then shrink back, tempting Moscow to "push ahead" even further. He did not go in for theories of a Soviet horde forever on the march, and he acknowledged that Soviet policy "may well be ... fundamentally defensive; an effort to exploit a fluid postwar situation ... in the interest of their own domestic security." Nonetheless, whatever the Soviets' motives, their policies were dangerous and the Americans might compound the problem. Pearson wrote to Ottawa proposing a solution along the lines of the wartime "Big Three" conferences. Britain, the United States, and the USSR must meet and lay "*all* the cards ... on the table" and face "*all* the issues" in a "genuine effort ... to resolve them."[19] Hume Wrong, the associate under-secretary of state for external affairs, disagreed. The Soviets were too secretive, too devious, to ever show their hand. The only solution was "substantial modification" of the Soviet regime.[20] Dana Wilgress, Canada's ambassador in Moscow, agreed with Wrong's assessment that diplomacy seemed impossible with "Generalissimo Stalin" in charge.[21]

By 1946's end, Pearson was back in Ottawa and he had adopted a grimmer appreciation of Soviet designs. Writing to the prime minister in November in an effort to put the fear of the early Cold War into William Lyon Mackenzie King, Pearson asked rhetorically: "Is it possible for the western democratic world to work out, if not a friendly, at least a tolerable relationship with a state, organized on a police basis, governed by ruthless despots, inhabited by millions of fighting men to whom life is hard and cheap, and with a dynamic communist ideology?"[22]

In 1954, Pearson would again ask this same question. But, in 1946, he warned King that the USSR was "ultimately bound to come into open conflict with western democracy" if the Soviets did not change.[23]

The Czech coup in 1948 – by then, Pearson was under-secretary of state – seemed to confirm the inability of East and West to co-exist. The coup, to Pearson, was not some clever manoeuvre but the product of the Kremlin's "bound and stultified" policies.[24] There was little point in looking for a diplomatic solution to tensions with Moscow until the USSR underwent some transformation and was freed from "the iron hand of one of the most ruthless tyrants of all time."[25]

Still, American attitudes towards the Soviet Union continued to worry Pearson as he and his subordinates doubted whether Washington could conceive and execute a careful Cold War policy.[26] American officials seemed remarkably sensitive to slights – real and perceived – in any dealings with the Soviets. Inexperience in world affairs, especially as a superpower, was to blame. Their inexperience and sensitivity seemed matched only by the Soviets themselves, who were short of qualified diplomats and generally lacked exposure to the outside world.[27] All of this increased the chance for misunderstandings and miscalculations, and thus for war.

In late spring 1948, after the Czech coup, Pearson worried that the West was in the calm before the storm. He wrote to Wrong that the Western powers needed to organize, that it was necessary to establish the "basis for a supreme war council, or some such body" that could help organize the West in case of a military showdown with the Soviets. But Pearson did not want decisions to rest with Washington. After seeing the gargantuan American war machine at work, he recognized its effectiveness at destroying enemies. But he had "more confidence in the wisdom" of the Europeans on political issues. It was essential that the West's supreme council include "governments which have wisdom and maturity," prerequisites, he implied, that precluded the US acting alone.[28] Here were some of the seeds, which, sowed by different men on both sides of the Atlantic, and fertilized with various nutrients, would grow NATO. Pearson supported institutionalized Western cooperation, with the Korean War soon both confirming the need to build up Western defences and offering a warning of the devastating effects that occur when "emotionalism" drives American Cold War policy.[29]

Western policy was in stasis by the end of 1952 as there seemed no way out of the deadly East-West struggle. Stalin ratcheted up international tensions by directing Soviet diplomats to take uncompromising positions at various international conferences, issuing terse diplomatic notes, and denouncing Western states in the various propaganda organs of the USSR, only then to make conciliatory noises and slight retreats. The Canadians believed this frustrating diplomatic style was "practically a requisite for the Soviet system," used by Stalin to maintain strength and authority at home and as a tactical ploy to gain advantage in any dealings with the West. Robert Ford, the chargé in Moscow, warned Pearson that this hot-and-cold approach would soon exasperate the Americans and might lead to the escalation of minor clashes into "something more serious." Though the West had stopped Soviet expansion, there had been no "fundamental change of heart on the part of the Russians." If the West continued to bolster its defences and strengthened NATO, perhaps the Soviets would re-examine the premises underlying their Cold War policies. But perhaps not.[30] The answer to Pearson's question to King about the prospects for a tolerable relationship with Moscow still seemed rhetorical. Conflict appeared if not inevitable, then highly probable, and if not by design, then perhaps by accident.

Suddenly, in 1953, Stalin was dead.[31] The new ruling group in Moscow sent out dozens of diplomatic feelers. Was this the change the Canadians had been waiting for? Ford urged the West not to press for any large concessions or to seek the regime's collapse. "Perhaps this" – significant change – "will come in due course," he wrote, but the new Soviet leaders could not cede too much, yet.[32] The Canadians urged the United States to take a moderate line with the new Soviet leaders.[33] Still, they worried that if Stalin's successors raised hopes of peace but did not follow through, Americans might be convinced there was nothing left to do but fight; the "dangers of war" would increase.[34]

In July 1954, Pearson asked Ford, now head of the DEA's European Division, to write a report in response to one question: "How could we find a stable relationship with a hostile regime?"[35] This was, in literal terms, similar to the question Pearson had posed to King. But now it was a genuine puzzle. As he had admitted in 1945, Pearson did not have all the answers; almost ten years later he remained ready to listen to others' ideas and weigh them carefully.

Ford began his memorandum by stating flatly that the "conclusion that there is no way to solve this impasse save by an eventual recourse to arms is unwarranted." It was a remarkable sign of the times that Ford had to begin by disputing the claim that war was inevitable. Knowing that American officials were insisting that "peaceful coexistence is impossible," Ford deemed this view as not only "unduly pessimistic" but "positively suicidal." The only alternative was to live "with the Russians on a more or less peaceful basis" and to "try to live in a divided world."[36] Ford's answer to Pearson's question was not a happy one. It was, he warned, "a *de facto* recognition that communism ha[d] conquered a large portion of the world." It required "abandoning the peoples of Eastern Europe to their fate" and the "admission of a division of the world into two spheres." Still, in such a world, there was "just a chance that developments inside the Soviet bloc [would] tend towards a maturing of Soviet society."[37]

Pearson accepted Ford's premise.[38] The notion that peace was possible, and that a period of peace offered the best opportunities for improving the world situation according to Western preferences, resonated with him. So, too, did the underlying argument that all of the moral outrage in the world could not change realities in the Soviet bloc; indeed, it could make things worse. Events in the following years bore out Ford's analysis. War did not come to Europe but the Cold War continued. The Federal Republic of Germany's accession to the North Atlantic Treaty in 1955 and the subsequent establishment of the Warsaw Pact guaranteed a military stalemate in Europe that perversely pushed Cold War antagonisms into new spheres of activity and different parts of the world.

Beginning in late 1954, the Soviets initiated several new diplomatic ventures. Canadian diplomats figured that it was not the end of the Cold War but, rather, a new way of fighting it. The Soviets were trying to shift the focus of the conflict away from the military showdown towards a "peaceful contest of the allegiance of Europe."[39] This might undermine support for NATO, and so this new Soviet offensive – using diplomats rather than soldiers – was a formidable challenge. Still, as Ford wrote to Pearson, "[the] Russians are now acting in the fashion we have always hoped they would."[40] Moscow had decided negotiations and compromise concessions were essential to their policy. They were coming closer to playing by Pearson's rules.

In 1955, the Soviet Union invited Pearson to visit. Some time before, Pearson had told the Soviet ambassador in Ottawa that he would like to one day visit Russia; the comment had been dutifully reported back to Moscow. When, in July 1955, the Soviet foreign minister was seeking to demonstrate the "peace-loving" nature of the post-Stalin regime, he remembered Pearson's request and invited him to visit.[41] Pearson detected that the invitation was a political manoeuvre, and, as the first NATO foreign minister to visit the USSR, he had to be cautious that his trip did not aid Soviet efforts to weaken NATO's cohesion. Pearson's trip had little fanfare, and he avoided loading it with the ramifications Harold Macmillan or Charles de Gaulle would attach to their later visits to Moscow. But given the premium Pearson put on diplomacy and engagement, it would have been an even more curious event if he had refused the invitation.

To Pearson, it was obvious – even through the haze of vodka plied by the Soviets – that the Soviet leadership remained committed to the Cold War showdown. Pearson found "not much indication of peaceful policies," and he assumed Soviet moves towards co-existence were efforts to gain Soviet advantage.[42] Nikita Khrushchev said as much, bragging to a Canadian correspondent that the USSR had the toughness, discipline, and patience to outlast the West.[43] Pearson called this a "game of patience between east and west," and it was a game he was willing to play.[44]

During Pearson's visit the Soviets sought to sow dissension in NATO's ranks by offering to buy Canadian wheat if Canada would overlook restrictions NATO had set on the sale of specific goods to the Soviet bloc.[45] Though the Canadians refused to accede to this demand, the Soviets nonetheless agreed to a massive wheat purchase. They also tried to catch Pearson up in a gaffe. In one of many toasts, Khrushchev toasted "to peace." Pearson was not to be caught up by this loaded phrase; he instead toasted to "peace and security."[46] Such were the nuances of the times.

In Pearson's account of his trip given to the cabinet upon his return, he hinted at his emerging hope that real change was under way in Soviet society. Stalin's reign of terror was slowly being repealed. While specifics were unclear in late 1955, Pearson thought that the "Russian people were being given more freedom."[47] Indeed, Soviet society in the 1950s was undergoing a rapid modernization and a broader cultural thaw, including an end to Stalin's ban on foreign tourists in the Soviet

Union and also allowance for more Soviet citizens to travel abroad.[48] Hence, Pearson said it was "just possible that a process had been started which would be difficult to interrupt or change."[49]

Pearson's visit strengthened his expectation that a policy of co-existence would undermine the Soviet system. Just before his trip, he elucidated his basic Cold War policy in a memorandum to the prime minister. Pearson – aided partly by Ford's analysis – claimed the Cold War had entered a new stage. And now that a "process of evolution" was under way in the USSR, "we should ... try to speed it up in every way possible." What Pearson was seeking was no less than a "basic alteration of the Soviet system." Pearson's plan did not repeat American designs to "rollback" Soviet occupation of the satellites or to foment unrest as he knew well that such overt efforts would force the return of Stalinist paranoia and an "armed, embittered and xenophobic despotism."[50] Instead, Pearson's plan was much more subtle. He wished to look for compromises and to encourage the Soviets to permit visitors, official and unofficial, to enter the USSR, and for Moscow to send delegations abroad. Any "light which we can help to let in," by encouraging visits and visitors, "will have a cumulative effect over the years out of all proportion to the number of individuals actually affected." These exchanges would only be possible by diplomatic effort and maintaining NATO's strength. But the ultimate result, achieved by "a long period of détente," would be to "weaken the [Iron] Curtain piecemeal."[51]

The gradual changes in the Soviet Union, DEA officials wrote to Pearson after his trip, were the very "evolution which was dimly foreseen in the policy of containment." The communist world, they argued, faced a deep and broad crisis.[52] Indeed, the changes that Khrushchev had initiated in the Soviet Union – those that Pearson had sensed during his visit – were becoming clear to Western officials when Khrushchev's 1956 speech to the Twentieth Congress of the Communist Party of the Soviet Union was leaked. At the Congress, Khrushchev had attacked Stalin's personality cult. The effect was to "put the entire ideological and propaganda apparatus" of the Soviet Union into "a state of paralysis."[53] The speech, Pearson told St-Laurent, marked "a milestone in Soviet history as important in its way as the death of Stalin."[54]

Pearson knew the Soviet leadership was riding a tiger by dismantling the Stalinist legacy and relaxing an oppressive state system. In the short run, perhaps the Soviets could control, and even harness, the changes in Soviet society. Still, he believed that "Khrushchev and company [were] exposing themselves to very real dangers in the long run." By telling the Soviet people they had been lied to for decades, they were "surely planting a very big grain of doubt and scepticism in the minds of the people about future propaganda." There would be no sudden and dramatic "revolution." But like the light that visitors could bring to the USSR, the Congress speeches were a "new wind" blowing "through the musty corridors of intellectual thought in Russia." This was dangerous for the regime as the limited changes under way were "impossible to turn back."[55] Although Khrushchev, according to a foremost historian of Soviet affairs, "had neither the vision nor the intellectual ability to foresee the consequences of this speech," they were apparent to Pearson and his officials.[56]

Changes in the USSR led Ford to conclude that it was time for Canada to stop treating the satellites as just "appendages."[57] While the Americans remained rigid, refusing to abandon their rhetoric of liberating the captive peoples, the European allies hoped to engage Eastern Europe "in order to promote increased contacts ... and possibly to modify internal conditions in the satellites." Ford summed up the dual nature of Canadian policy, noting: "Naturally, we agree in private with the hope for 'peaceful liberation' of the satellites." Yet, "we have attempted to avoid policies which are unduly provocative and self-defeating."[58]

Pearson continued to urge that Canada and its allies exploit the changes in the Soviet Union not by facing off against the Soviets in a moral showdown, but by bringing them "more, if not into our confidence, at least into consultation." They should be treated "more as a member of the *group* of great powers."[59] The plan for the satellites was similar. Diplomatically, Canada would treat Eastern European states as independent nations. Perhaps Canadian diplomats could talk with their Polish colleagues on Indochina or with Czech diplomats on Egypt. Canada could also increase trade with the satellites with any eye to reducing economic dependence on Moscow. Economic exchange could bring commercial advantages for Canada but also might draw the satellites from their Soviet orbit. In an effort to encourage the independent, national identities of the citizens of the satellite states, they should be "the target of commercial and technical exchanges, and the exchange of sports, films, radio and artists."[60] The trick was to treat the Soviet bloc not as a bloc at all.

Change came more quickly than expected. The readiness of students and others to take up the anti-Stalinist message showed the limits of Moscow's efforts at indoctrination. Still, Ford warned that the West must abandon "both privately and publicly ... any hope of effecting liberation within the foreseeable future." It was essential that the West "cease to foster any false hopes" that the satellites would be liberated by force or other assistance.[61] Pearson and the Canadians recognized that rhetoric demanding the satellites' independence from Moscow's diktats would provoke just the opposite. The contrast with Washington is striking. The Republican Party had ridden to power in 1952 on a wave of support from Eastern European immigrants. Such support, the Canadians surmised, led to American public statements about liberation that Ford worried risked "sparking a hopeless revolt."[62]

Indeed, 1956 witnessed revolts against Soviet dominance in East Germany, Poland, and, most dramatically, in Hungary. Khrushchev's speech fuelled Hungarian dissent, but the Hungarians also received misleading signals from Washington. The American response to the revolt was nil, although the US, like Canada and other NATO allies, accepted Hungarian refugees. Scholars have criticized American policy for not focusing "on the calm pursuit of partial gains," a phrase that sums up Pearson's policy rather tidily.[63] Still, Khrushchev's speech and the internal dissent indicated to the Canadians that Soviet policies were "out of date" both in the USSR and in its satellites. They showed the "failure of Russian policy," the "absurdity of Soviet claims" to unity, and the "real character of the Muscovite security system."[64] And all of this had been the work of the Soviets themselves with Khrushchev's de-Stalinization campaign. After the Hungarian uprising, Pearson told St-Laurent that the Soviets "ha[d] gone too far down this road in internal policies to revert to full Stalinism."[65] After Hungary, Moscow sought to return to the emerging pattern of peaceful co-existence, and Pearson did not want to go back to the high Cold War.[66] The Canadians accepted the Soviet brutality as a harbinger that change would come to the Soviet bloc.

In 1959, Pearson, now leader of the Official Opposition, published a collection of his speeches delivered in a prestigious Tufts University lecture series. The book offered, in the words of one reviewer, Senator John F. Kennedy, to "map out the terrain of modern statecraft."[67] The main contours of this landscape were still those of the Cold War. Pearson stuck to his convictions: there would be no "easy and quick solutions" to Cold War problems; resolution would not be achieved "either by sentimentalizing or slugging" but by "hard-headed, realistic negotiations." Even if "the Communist diplomat" often frustrated his counterpart, the risk and cost of war was so great that one must engage to maintain peace. For now, Pearson wrote, this would allow the NATO allies and the Soviet bloc to live together out of "mutual self-interest" and perhaps, later, out of "good will."[68] But underlying this recipe for improved East-West relations, Pearson remained convinced that the arrangements for co-existence were not permanent. He did not advocate directly challenging the Soviet Union for he thought it unnecessary and counterproductive. The Soviet system, he wrote, had an Achilles' heel. While the USSR had great strength in international affairs, communist society "[bore] within itself the seeds of its own decay."[69] Those seeds could only grow in peace, and they had to grow on their own.

By 1963, Pearson was prime minister. As he would acknowledge, "the world of 1963 was not the world of 1948," and the world was free from the "over-hanging and immediate threat of a powerful, aggressive, monolithic communist conspiracy, centred in Moscow and controlled by Stalin."[70] Almost every historian who has studied Pearson's prime ministership has skipped over Canada's relationship with the Soviet bloc, and for good reason: there were far more exciting things going on at home and abroad. Domestically, Canadian unity reached a crisis point. Vietnam consumed any oxygen left for international affairs.

By the time Pearson became prime minister, the nearly catastrophic crises over Cuba and Berlin had ushered in a new era of the Cold War. By the end of his first calendar year as prime minister, Pearson told the UN that superpower relations, and the Cold War, were "a little less frigid."[71] But Pearson never lost sight of the challenges posed by the Soviets, or of the formula that he, along with Ford, had come up with when he was SSEA and that he had trumpeted while in Opposition. As prime minister, he put it into practice: he approached the Soviet Union as a state to be treated as an equal among states, and he put the satellites on the same plane, not as appendages but as equals. There were real benefits for Canada in treating with these states, and, at the same time, the Soviet system could not, over the long term, withstand such normality.

Starting in 1964, Canada and the Soviet bloc states entered into a torrent of agreements. In January, Ottawa and Moscow agreed to exchange information on atomic power and research reactors.[72] Midyear, Canada and Hungary struck agreements on outstanding financial claims,[73] establishing the first Canadian-Hungarian postwar trade agreement, a three-year deal to sell wheat and to exchange most favoured nation (MFN) status. Minister of Trade and Commerce Mitchell Sharp called it "yet another step in the development of closer trade links between Canada and the countries of Eastern Europe," coming as it did after the renewal of longer-standing trade relations with Poland and Czechoslovakia.[74] In 1965, Canada sent its first ambassador to Hungary, and, in 1966 and 1967, it established diplomatic relations with Bulgaria and Romania, respectively.[75] There were visits by Czech parliamentary delegations and the Czech foreign minister in 1966, and a Canadian delegation was sent in return the next year.[76] Arthur Laing, minister of northern affairs and national resources, travelled to the USSR to see advances in building on permafrost.[77] In 1966, Canada and the USSR signed the largest commercial contract for a fixed quantity of Canadian wheat and flour ever concluded, and they continued their exchange of MFN status.[78]

Throughout Pearson's years as prime minister, Canada sent graduate students on exchange to Moscow. The Canadian Press sent a resident correspondent to Moscow in 1964, soon followed by more Canadian journalists. Telegraphic and telex services were established the same year. Direct air service linking Montreal and Moscow was inaugurated just in time for Expo '67, and the Montreal consulate opened in April 1967. The Soviet Union was the largest foreign participant in Expo '67, marking the "high point" in Soviet-Canadian relations.[79]

Canadian-Soviet relations were encouraged, and aided, by a Canadian public that was ready to forget the Cold War. But only two years before Expo, Canadian officials described the relationship with Moscow as having reached a "low point," and it nearly foundered.[80] That it did not reveals that the pattern of agreements between Ottawa and Moscow was not simply a reflection of that amorphous craving for détente that lurched, in fits and starts, onto the world scene in the 1960s. It was, instead, the product of wagers, made by both sides, about the power of their respective systems of governance.

In spring 1965, Canada declared two commercial officers of the Soviet embassy persona non grata for spying. The move might have brought a chill reminiscent of the one that descended on Canadian-Soviet relations in 1946 after the defection of the Soviet cypher clerk

Igor Gouzenko the previous year. Canadian officials, knowing Moscow's penchant for reacting harshly to actions against Soviet embassies, waited for the other shoe to drop. Yet, to the surprise of Ford, now Canadian ambassador to Moscow, there was no commensurate expulsion of Canadian officials and no significant escalation. This, Ford reported, was a clear signal that Moscow had calculated that it was in the Soviet interest not to imperil the emerging pattern of productive Soviet-Canadian relations. The most pressing concern for Moscow was the drastic failure of Soviet agriculture and a need for wheat. While the Canadian Wheat Board's rates were expensive, the Soviets found it easier to deal with Canada than with the Americans, Australians, or Argentines. At the same time, the Soviets wished to encourage a genuinely independent Canadian policy, hoping to wean it from the United States and to aid Moscow's broader Cold War goals.[81]

Pearson, also for reasons of national interest, worked to restore the relationship with Moscow. He knew well that "there was such a thing as Kremlin-directed communist subversion."[82] He certainly wished for the RCMP to prevent such subversion, but he was unhappy with how the police had handled the well-publicized 1965 case. Nor did he want to prejudice Soviet participation in Expo '67. But his "primary concern" was to find a buyer for what was likely to be the "biggest wheat crop in Canadian history," and the Soviets were the answer.[83] Pearson, given the importance of the pending wheat deal, authorized the early return from Moscow of a naval attaché about whom the Soviets had made accusations. The DEA also avoided making an issue of the disparity in the freedoms of Canadian diplomats in the USSR as compared to Soviet diplomats in Canada, letting the matter lie. Finally, to bolster the faltering relationship, Pearson sent Soviet premier Alexei Kosygin a letter stressing the benefits of mutual cooperation. Pearson did not pull any punches; he referred to the continued disagreements between Canada and the USSR, made inevitable by "the differences between our political and economic philosophies and the structure of our societies."[84] Still, the letter was a sign that the Canadians, like the Soviets, wished to get over the bump of 1965.

There were obvious domestic benefits for Canada – and for Pearson in the election year of 1965 – to making a deal on wheat. Further, Ford had advised Pearson that better relations between the East and the West would allow Canada to develop its "independent personality" and to "avoid the natural American tendency to overwhelm us in their friendly embrace."[85] This might have been attractive to Pearson as questions of Canadian identity reached a fevered pitch. But, Ford told Pearson, there were still Cold War politics at play. The "important revolution" in the Soviet Union that Ford and Pearson had identified in the preceding years continued, and it was crucial that Canada encourage these "forward liberal trends." Now, more than ever before, Canada had "a very significant role to play" in this effort because the Soviets were indeed willing to exchange goods and people with Canada. Ultimately, Ford reported, Canada "must never lose sight of the basic incompatibility between the Soviet system and our own," remaining aware that Moscow was seeking friendly relations with Ottawa to further its own ends.[86]

The Canadians saw evidence of this incompatibility in Soviet espionage and subversion efforts, both of which increased in periods of détente.[87] The DEA reported, in the lead-up to Expo '67, that Moscow was "using Expo as a pretext to break down our security measures and that ... it would be difficult to recover all the ground we have lost even after Expo is over."[88] There was "no doubt" that a Soviet Intourist office in Montreal, planned to accompany Expo, "would serve intelligence functions."[89] The proposed Soviet consulate in Montreal, too, was deemed a "security threat" that would "strain further the overstretched resources of the RCMP." Indeed, the Soviets requested visas for so many known and potential intelligence officers that Canadian officials occasionally granted such visas just to avoid embarrassing strings of refusals. Despite the security challenges, the government weighed the risks and allowed the tourism office and consulate because of the benefits from "growing exchanges and trade" between the countries, and the impending Expo.[90]

Soviet participation in Expo was, as Ford described it, a "little short of overpowering." Millions of visitors saw the enormous Soviet Pavilion, with its bust of V.I. Lenin and Yuri Gagarin's spacecraft. The Bolshoi Opera made its North American debut, and the Moscow Circus and the Red Army Choir performed. About six thousand Soviet citizens visited Expo, which, while tiny compared to the overall international attendance, was "fantastically high" given Soviet travel restrictions. The result was that a large number of Soviet elites and "tourist groups" (stuffed with area experts and Soviet citizens rewarded for "good behaviour") took in not only Montreal but also (usually) Ottawa, Toronto, and Niagara Falls. Here was another opportunity to nurture liberal trends in the USSR. Ford admitted that any impact on Soviet society would be difficult to judge and that Expo would not, in itself, change the Soviet Union. But, he noted, Expo '67 marked "the first time [that] really massive numbers of Soviet[s] ... had been exposed to a new and very different way of life, and it [was] hard to believe that some ideas ha[d] not penetrated."[91]

This was the trade-off Pearson accepted: both sides would try to exploit the new relationships, with Pearson confident that Canada would come out on top.[92] The Soviets might send spies, but Canada would send wheat along with "light" and "fresh winds" into the dark and musty corridors of the Soviet Union, a precursor, the prime minister hoped, to more and greater change in both Soviet foreign policy and the Soviet political system. Here we see Pearson's pragmatism married to his idealism.

Since Pearson's visit Moscow in 1955, Canada remained "half-a-step ahead of the Americans in promoting the relaxation of East-West tensions" in each of the political, trade, and cultural realms.[93] Indeed, as J.L. Black and Norman Hillmer point out, the Canadian-Soviet détente lasted longer than that between the larger powers, surviving until the Soviet invasion of Afghanistan in 1979.[94] This relationship was good for Canada as it provided economic benefits and greater opportunities for Canadians. But its fundamental engine was Pearson's paradoxical approach to the Cold War: the best policy was to treat the USSR and its satellites as states equal to any other even if he believed that the basis of their power was artificial and thus untenable. Pearson fully expected co-existence to be a long, drawn-out process. But his policy towards the Soviet bloc was remarkable both in that he identified the changes occurring within it and their ultimate implications. In a broad sense, the unpredictable tiger Mikhail Gorbachev unleashed in the Soviet Union in the 1980s was the same one Pearson thought Khrushchev was riding in the 1960s.

Pearson's policy had much in common with that of his Cold War allies, but he borrowed only the best parts. Many European and American statespeople shared his belief that the West must maintain sufficient strength to deter the Soviets. Pearson knew the crucible for this cohesion was fear of Soviet aggression, and he recognized that détente somewhat undercut this policy; as Isabel Campbell (Chapter 13, this volume) stresses, he believed that one of the greatest challenges was to keep NATO together during periods of calm, which, by the 1960s, meant having to convince growing numbers of Canadians of the necessity of NATO membership. The best, and perhaps most painful, case in point was Pierre Trudeau, Pearson's successor as prime minister. Trudeau wished to build on Pearson's legacy of conducting good relations with the USSR, but, at least initially, he did not understand the importance of NATO to ensuring peaceful co-existence.[95]

Diplomats during the early Cold War had been quick to recognize that the problem with achieving containment would be continuity. In 1947, Frank Roberts, a British diplomat in Moscow, judged George Kennan's containment thesis as "excellent for the British, but impossible for the Americans." While London, by temperament and experience, could wait twenty-five years for the results of such a policy, he believed that the United States would demand results in five. Pearson could wait too, even if his version of containment favoured more engagement, or co-existence, than some Americans preferred. The trajectory of his own career ensured continuity. And many of his colleagues had their own long tenures; Ford, for instance, served as ambassador to the Soviet Union for an incredible sixteen years, becoming dean of the diplomatic corps in Moscow.

Pearson also sought to sever his policy from the vagaries of domestic politics. He avoided the temptation to charge his foreign policy with the support of immigrants to Canada from the Soviet bloc, especially the vocal Ukrainian Canadians.[96] In 1957, Diefenbaker unwisely toyed with supporting Ukrainian independence until Moscow threatened to raise matters related to Quebec. A decade later, during Expo '67, the Soviet delegation refused to stir the pot, even after given a chance by Quebec premier Daniel Johnson.[97]

Although Pearson found the Soviet system immoral and unacceptable, he sought to "resist the Anglo-Saxon tendency to make a moral issue of every political problem."[98] Hence, he accepted Ford's grim prognosis in the 1950s that Eastern Europeans must be abandoned to their indeterminable fate. This policy outlasted Pearson; in 1968, with Trudeau as prime minister, Soviet tanks crushed the Prague Spring. The invasion, wrote Ford, had to be "swallowed as part of the price of coexistence with the Soviet government." Canada did not move to end the détente by breaking relations with Moscow but, instead, sought to increase exchanges of all sort. "Life," Ford said, "had to go on."[99] This attitude represented not so much callousness on the part of Pearson and other Canadians as Pearson's sense of the limits to what Canadian policy, and that of the Western allies generally, could achieve in the Cold War. In an era of tremendous hubris, Pearson's humility was the handmaiden of wisdom. He recognized that both Canadian and broader Western efforts could only do so much to change the Soviet Union. Time, and human nature, he believed, would have to do the rest.

Notes

1 Lester Pearson, *Diplomacy in the Nuclear Age* (Cambridge, MA: Harvard University Press, 1959), 93.
2 R.A.D. Ford, *Our Man in Moscow: A Diplomat's Reflections on the Soviet Union* (Toronto: University of Toronto Press, 1989), 94.
3 This draws a broader point from the argument in Denis Stairs, "The Political Culture of Canadian Foreign Policy," *Canadian Journal of Political Science* 15 (1982): 676.
4 Barbara Ward, "That Shrewd yet Visionary Voice," in *"Freedom and Change": Essays in Honour of Lester B. Pearson*, ed. Michael Fry (Toronto: McClelland and Stewart, 1975), 244. See also the introduction to this volume.
5 Ford, *Our Man in Moscow*, 92, 105.
6 Robert Bothwell, Ian Drummond, and John English, *Canada since 1945: Power, Politics and Provincialism*, rev. ed. (Toronto: University of Toronto Press, 1989), 295.
7 Costas Melakopides, *Pragmatic Idealism: Canadian Foreign Policy, 1945–1995* (Montreal and Kingston: McGill-Queen's University Press, 1998), 67.
8 Lester Pearson, "After the Paris Debacle," *Foreign Affairs* 38 (1960): 538.
9 Lester Pearson, *Mike: The Memoirs of the Right Honourable Lester B. Pearson*, vol. 2 (Toronto: University of Toronto Press, 1973), 25.
10 Robert Bothwell, "Canada's Moment: Lester Pearson, Canada, and the World," in *Pearson: The Unlikely Gladiator*, ed. Norman Hillmer (Montreal and Kingston: McGill-Queen's University Press, 1999), 24.
11 See Lester Pearson, "After Geneva: A Greater Task for NATO," *Foreign Affairs* 34 (1955): 14.
12 "National despotism is in greatest danger when the international atmosphere is calm," Pearson told an audience in 1959. See Pearson, *Diplomacy in the Nuclear Age*, 55.
13 "X" [George F. Kennan], "The Sources of Soviet Conduct," *Foreign Affairs* 65 (1947): 580; Pearson, *Diplomacy in the Nuclear Age*, 85.
14 Acheson to Stikker, 11 July 1966, Yale University Archives, Dean Acheson Papers, General Correspondence, box 29, fol. 375.
15 John Holmes, *The Shaping of Peace: Canada and the Search for World Order, 1943–1957* (Toronto: University of Toronto Press, 1982), 23; John English, *Shadow of Heaven: The Life of Lester Pearson* (Toronto: Lester and Orpen Dennys, 1989), 310–11.

16 Robert Ford, head of the European Division and former chargé in the USSR, wrote that, while "capable of the most atrocious barbarities," the Russian people were also "one of the most likeable, human and kind peoples in the world." See "Relations with the USSR: A Re-Assessment," Memorandum by European Division, November 1954, *DCER, 1954* (Ottawa: Minister of Public Works and Government Services Canada, 1997), 1590. A distinction between a loveable Russian people and a despicable Soviet regime was a common device used by Western diplomats writing about the USSR. See, for example, J.L. Gaddis, *George F. Kennan: An American Life* (New York: Norton, 2011).
17 English, *Shadow of Heaven*, 264.
18 Canadian Ambassador to United States to SSEA, 11 March 1946, *DCER, 1946* (Ottawa: Department of External Affairs, 1977), 2043–46.
19 Ibid. Emphasis in original.
20 Associate Under-Secretary of State for External Affairs (USSEA) to Canadian Ambassador to United States, 23 March 1946, *DCER, 1946*, 2052.
21 Canadian Ambassador to Soviet Union to SSEA, Despatch 110, 21 March 1946, *DCER, 1946*, 2047–50.
22 English, *Shadow of Heaven*, 300.
23 Ibid.
24 USSEA to Chargé d'Affaires in Soviet Union, 30 March 1948, *DCER, 1948* (Ottawa: Minister of Supply and Services, 1994), 1786.
25 Pearson, *Mike*, 2:25.
26 Denis Stairs, "Realists at Work: Canadian Policy Makers and the Politics of Transition from Hot War to Cold War," in *Canada and the Early Cold War, 1943–1957*, ed. Greg Donaghy (Ottawa: Department of Foreign Affairs and International Trade, 1998), 111.
27 Second Secretary, High Commission to United Kingdom, to Assistant USSEA, 26 February 1948, *DCER, 1948*, 1783.
28 USSEA to Canadian Ambassador to United States, 21 May 1948, *DCER, 1948*, 1794–95.
29 Pearson quoted in John English, *The Worldly Years: The Life of Lester Pearson, 1949–1972* (Toronto: Knopf, 1992), 56, 53.
30 See Chargé to SSEA, 9 October 1952, *DCER, 1952* (Ottawa: Minister of Supply, 1990), 1486–94; and Chargé to SSEA, 27 October 27, *DCER, 1952*, 1494–1500
31 Melvyn Leffler, *For the Soul of Mankind: The United States, the Soviet Union, and the Cold War* (New York: Hill and Wang, 2007), 84–150.
32 Chargé to SSEA, 31 March 1953, *DCER, 1953* (Ottawa: Minister of Supply, 1991), 1459.
33 See Louis St-Laurent's remarks to Dwight Eisenhower recounted in Dale Thomson, *Louis St. Laurent: Canadian* (Toronto: Macmillan of Canada, 1967), 347.
34 Deputy USSEA to SSEA, 2 May 1953, *DCER, 1953*, 1465–67.
35 Charles Ruud, *The Constant Diplomat: Robert Ford in Moscow* (Montreal and Kingston: McGill-Queen's University Press, 2009), 26–27.
36 "Relations with the USSR: A Re-Assessment," November 1954, *DCER, 1954*, 1586–87, 1570.

37 Ibid., 1589–90.

38 Holmes, *Shaping of Peace,* 382–84; John Hilliker and Donald Barry, *Canada's Department of External Affairs: Coming of Age, 1946–1968* (Montreal and Kingston: McGill-Queen's University Press, 1993), 112.

39 Memorandum by Head, European Division, 30 May 1955, "Soviet Policy in Europe," *DCER, 1955* (Ottawa: Minister of Supply and Services, 1999), 1147.

40 Ibid., 1145.

41 SSEA to Canadian Ambassador to Norway, 8 July 1955, *DCER, 1955*, 1160–61.

42 Extract from Cabinet Conclusions, 16 November 1955, *DCER, 1955*, 1173.

43 Norman Smith, "Pearson, People, and Press," *International Journal* 29 (1973–74): 18.

44 Extract from Cabinet Conclusions, 16 November 1955, *DCER, 1955*, 1173.

45 Ruud, *Constant Diplomat*, 36–37.

46 English, *Worldly Years*, 99–100.

47 Extract from Cabinet Conclusions, 16 November 1955, *DCER, 1955*, 1173.

48 Vlad Zubok, *A Failed Empire: The Soviet Union in the Cold War from Stalin to Gorbachev* (Chapel Hill: University of North Carolina Press, 2009), 163–91.

49 Extract from Cabinet Conclusions, 16 November 1955, 1173.

50 "Canadian Policy in the Light of Soviet Tactical Changes since Geneva," attached to Memo from SSEA to PM, 29 September 1955, *DCER, 1955*, 1158.

51 Ibid.

52 Memorandum from Head to USSEA, 17 January 1956, *DCER, 1956–1957*, pt. 2 (Ottawa: Department of External Affairs, 2002), 983.

53 Zubok, *Failed Empire*, 112–13. Quote on 168.

54 Memorandum for the Prime Minister, 27 March 1956, *DCER, 1956–1957*, pt. 2, 911.

55 Ibid., 911, 914.

56 Zubok, *Failed Empire*, 168.

57 Memorandum from Head to USSEA, 17 January 1956, *DCER, 1956–1957*, pt. 2, 860.

58 Ibid., 862–64.

59 Memorandum for the Prime Minister, 27 March 1956, *DCER, 1956–1957*, pt. 2, 915, emphasis in original.

60 Memorandum from Head to USSEA, 17 January 1956, *DCER, 1956–1957*, pt. 2, 864–76.

61 Memorandum from Head to USSEA, 12 June 1956, *DCER, 1956–1957*, pt. 2, 868–76.

62 Memorandum from Head to USSEA, 17 January 1956, *DCER, 1956–1957*, pt. 2, 863.

63 Charles Gati, *Failed Illusions: Moscow, Washington, Budapest, and the 1956 Hungarian Revolt* (Washington, DC: Woodrow Wilson Center Press, 2006), 112.

64 Memo from USSEA to SSEA, 27 November 1956, *DCER, 1956–1957*, pt. 2, 970.

65 Memo from SSEA to PM, 26 October 1956, *DCER, 1956–1957*, pt. 2, 952.

66 See Memo from Head to SSEA, February 1957, *DCER, 1956–1957*, pt. 2, 890 and Pearson's marginalia in n103.

67 John Kennedy, "The Terrain of Today's Statecraft," *Saturday Review*, 1 August 1959, 19.
68 Pearson, *Diplomacy in the Nuclear Age*, 58.
69 Ibid., 85.
70 Lester Pearson, *Mike: The Memoirs of the Right Honourable Lester B. Pearson*, vol. 3 (Toronto: University of Toronto Press, 1975), 117.
71 "Some Elements of Canadian Foreign Policy," *External Affairs* 15 (1963): 346.
72 "USSR-Canada Nuclear Agreement," *External Affairs* 16 (1964): 118.
73 "Canadian-Hungarian Relations," *External Affairs* 16 (1964): 329–31.
74 Ibid.; and "Wheat Sales behind the Iron Curtain," excerpt of 14 July 1964 announcement, *External Affairs* 16 (1964): 404.
75 "Canadian-Hungarian Relations," 370; "Diplomatic Relations between Canada and Roumania," *External Affairs* 19 (1967): 183; "Canada's Relations with Bulgaria," *External Affairs* 18 (1966): 331.
76 "Canada-Czechoslovakia Contacts Increase," *External Affairs* 10 (1967): 55.
77 "Tour by Minister of Northern Affairs and National Resources," *External Affairs* 17 (1965): 373.
78 "Canada-USSR Wheat Pact Renewed," 20 June 1966, *External Affairs* 18 (1966): 302.
79 "Mr. Polyansky Visits Canada Again," *External Affairs* 10 (1967): 425; "Air-Link between Canada and the USSR," *External Affairs* 18 (1966): 322; quote in Ruud, *Constant Diplomat*, 82–83.
80 Cadieux to Pearson, "Your Message to Mr. Kosygin," Cadieux, 22 September 1965, LAC, RG 25, file 20-1-2-USSR-pt.2.
81 Moscow to External 1516, 11 November 1965, LAC, RG 25, file 20-1-2-USSR-pt. 1. The Soviets believed Canada created fewer shipping problems for the USSR than other suppliers and offered the surest supply in case of an agricultural disaster in the Soviet Union.
82 Pearson, *Mike*, 3:166.
83 Ford to Cadieux, 27 July 1965, LAC, RG 25, file 20-1-2-USSR-pt.1.
84 Pearson to Kosygin, 6 August 1965, LAC, RG 25, file 20-1-2-USSR-pt.1.
85 Moscow to External, tel. 1740, 18 December 1965, LAC, RG 25, file 20-1-2-USSR-pt.1. See also Ruud, *Constant Diplomat*, 58.
86 Moscow to External 1740, 18 December 1965, LAC, RG 25, file 20-1-2-USSR-pt.1.
87 Crean to Seaborn, 12 January 1967, LAC, RG 25, file 20-1-2-USSR-pt. 4.
88 European Division to Cadieux, "The Impact of Expo on Our Security," 4 May 1967, LAC, RG 25, file 20-1-2-USSR-pt.5.
89 Cadieux to Martin, "Soviet Request for Intourist Office – Montreal," 27 April 1967, LAC, RG 25, file 20-1-2-USSR-pt.1.
90 Cadieux to Martin, "Soviet Consulate in Montreal," 10 May 1966, LAC, RG 25, file 20-1-2-USSR-pt.2.
91 Moscow to External 3947, 2 November 1967, National Archives of the United Kingdom, FCO 28, 347.
92 "Canadian Policy in the Light of Soviet Tactical Changes since Geneva," 29 September 1955, *DCER, 1955*, 1159.
93 Aloysius Balawyder, ed., *Canadian-Soviet Relations, 1939–1980* (Oakville, ON: Mosaic Press, 1981), unpaginated introduction.

94 J.L. Black and Norman Hillmer, "Canada and the Soviet Union as Neighbours," in *Nearly Neighbours: Canada and the Soviet Union,* ed. Norman Hillmer and J.L. Black (Kingston: R.P. Frye, 1989), 10.

95 Ruud, *Constant Diplomat*, 94.

96 Black and Hillmer, "Canada and the Soviet Union as Neighbours," 7; Ford, *Our Man in Moscow*, 101–4; Adam Bromke, "Canada's Relations with the USSR and Eastern Europe," in *From Mackenzie King to Pierre Trudeau: Forty Years of Canadian Diplomacy, 1945–1985*, ed. Paul Painchaud (Quebec: Presses de l'Université Laval, 1989), 302; J. Petryshyn, "The 'Ethnic Question' Personified: Ukrainian Canadians and Canadian-Soviet Relations, 1917–1991," in *Re-Imagining Ukrainian Canadians: History, Politics, and Identity*, ed. R.L. Hinther and J. Mochoruk (Toronto: University of Toronto Press, 2011), 240–41.

97 During Expo '67, Dmitri Polyansky, a rising star in the Soviet Politburo, met with Quebec premier Daniel Johnson for a formal banquet. Johnson, in his speech, spoke of Quebec's desire for its own world role, but Polyansky avoided this point in his own speech. When the two men met privately, Polyansky told Johnson that the USSR was administered by a strong centre – an indication he had no wish to encourage or champion Quebec's desire for greater independence from Ottawa. Ford suggests this restraint was the result of geopolitical machinations: a fragmented Canada would, ultimately, lead to American expansion. See Ford, *Our Man in Moscow*, 101–4.

98 Pearson, *Diplomacy in the Nuclear Age*, 58.

99 Ford, *Our Man in Moscow*, 105.

Ryan Touhey

12 Commonwealth Conundrums
Canada and South Asia during the Pearson Era

Well before he became prime minister in 1963, South Asia mattered to Lester Pearson as both a senior diplomat in the Department of External Affairs and then as secretary of state for external affairs. As SSEA, Pearson spent much time and effort engaging India and Pakistan, becoming a key architect of some of the most creative approaches in early Cold War Canadian diplomacy that sought to align the newly independent states of India and Pakistan with the West. When he became prime minister, South Asia again tested Pearson's diplomatic mettle, but his ability to navigate various diplomatic problems relating to South Asia was often found wanting in contrast to his earlier days as SSEA, when he approached South Asia with optimism and interest influenced by currents of idealism and realism. As prime minister, Pearson appeared more uncertain, and at times aloof, about how to engage the subcontinent on regional security issues and important matters affecting Canada's bilateral relations with India and Pakistan, and this had profound consequences, particularly for his successor. This chapter brings a long neglected area of Pearson's international record – namely, his time as prime minister – into clearer focus.[1]

Years before Britain's withdrawal from South Asia in August 1947, Pearson lobbied Prime Minister William Lyon MacKenzie King to craft foreign policy and dispatch personnel to a region that Ottawa knew little about. Compared to Japan or China, Canada had a small missionary and trade presence in South Asia. Anticipating decolonization, Pearson saw the opportunity to play a unique role in nurturing links between India and Pakistan and the West, hoping Canada might act as a bridge to the region as the Cold War began.[2] Archival evidence suggests that Pearson was the first in the DEA to believe that a shared inheritance of empire provided Canadian officials with common ties to South Asia elites through the English language, similar legal codes, and a similar political evolution. The partition of the subcontinent in August 1947, inciting horrific sectarian violence and mass refugee movements, created India and Pakistan. Both countries immediately had to learn the machinery of government, alleviate rampant poverty, and integrate millions of traumatized refugees. Bilateral tensions, already fraught, worsened further as Pakistan disputed India's possession of Muslim-dominated Kashmir. Shortly after independence the two countries fought their first war over Kashmir.

As the Cold War escalated, Pearson grasped the need to keep India and Pakistan in the British Commonwealth even if that meant accepting India's becoming a republic. The possibility that either country could succumb to communism concerned diplomats in Ottawa. As the perceived threat of Soviet machinations in South Asia intensified, Canadian officials thought that the Commonwealth forum could provide "an important link between the peoples of Asia" and the West.[3] Pearson represented Canada at the London Commonwealth Prime Ministers Conference in April 1949, while Prime Minister Louis St-Laurent was on the hustings. With St-Laurent's blessing, Pearson collaborated with British officials to craft the constitutional means to keep republican India in the Commonwealth, so long as Canada's interests were unaffected. That conference, meeting India's constitutional aspirations in a manner satisfactory to most participants, recast the Commonwealth as a multiracial organization dominated demographically by South Asians. Pearson's helpful role did not go unnoticed by India's prime minister, Jawaharlal Nehru.

In October 1949, Ottawa hosted Nehru following his visit to the United States. The Indian leader impressed Pearson and St-Laurent with his thoughtful interpretation of global events, including the recent communist victory in China. The Canadians also impressed Nehru. By comparison, Nehru's trip to Washington had been a disaster. India's embrace of non-alignment disturbed American policy makers, while Nehru dismissed Washington's fixation on the communist threat as simplistic and wrong. Ottawa's assessment differed. India's geographic size and population, and Nehru's rising prominence as a statesman, made it the predominant democracy in Asia. Shortly, India became an area of interest for Ottawa, and much of that was due to Pearson. Although Nehru seemed determined to pursue a foreign policy of non-alignment between East and West, Canadian officials were initially tolerant, content that India remained connected to the West through the Commonwealth and its economic and political relations with Britain.

Two months after Nehru's state visit, Pearson became the first senior Canadian diplomat to travel to South Asia, attending the January 1950 Colombo Conference of Commonwealth foreign ministers. That conference inspired the Colombo Plan under which Canada directed billions of dollars of aid to India and Pakistan over the next three decades. Following Colombo, Pearson visited India and Pakistan. Both visits attracted and repelled him. Nehru again struck Pearson as a statesman of considerable talent whose views on international affairs must be considered by the West. Likewise, Pearson found his meetings with the Pakistanis fruitful and educational, although he recognized that Pakistan had no leader akin to Nehru. Witnessing brutal poverty of the likes he had not previously encountered, such extremes in wealth, economic opportunity, and even sanitary conditions startled Pearson. He left South Asia convinced of Canada's vested interest in participating in the embryonic aid plan. In February 1951, nearly a year after the Korean War's onset, Pearson persuaded the St-Laurent cabinet to aid India and Pakistan. This was not an easy feat despite the initial meagre sum as government finances faced new strains with a decision to rearm due to Korea and a decision to deploy forces to Western Europe as part of Canada's NATO commitments. Pearson had to overcome the scepticism of Finance Minister Douglas Abbott, who suspected that aid monies would fuel the simmering Indo-Pakistani feud over Kashmir – a feud Canada sought to keep at arm's length despite participating in the UN mission monitoring it. Nonetheless, Canada's role in the Colombo Plan was unprecedented. Granting aid in various innovative forms to South Asia had been unimaginable just over a year earlier. Such support demonstrated Canada's interest in promoting stability and good relations with the region. Pearson, with support from key colleagues in the DEA and government, managed a complex matter with aplomb. Ottawa's Colombo commitment became a precedent for future Canadian foreign aid roles.

The diplomatic courtship of Nehru continued as Ottawa and New Delhi consulted with each other at the United Nations, in Commonwealth meetings, and through their high commissioners on ways to end the Korean War. Pearson spent much of autumn 1952 at the UN working with India's delegation to craft a compromise deal on the question of prisoners of war. Though that process proved arduous as the Canadians sought to reconcile competing American and Indian proposals, a successful outcome led Pearson to express his "appreciation" to Nehru "for the close and friendly collaboration between our two delegations at this Assembly."[4] During that time, Ottawa dispatched one of its most talented and mercurial diplomats to India as high commissioner. Pearson wanted Escott Reid to cultivate close ties with India, to bolster democracy in the country, and to capitalize Canada's unique advantage by pressing its own interests, and that of the West, with New Delhi.[5] Reid's ambitions for the bilateral relationship closely resembled those of his SSEA. While flickers of differences subtly lurked because Nehru's international assessments did not entirely match those of Pearson or Ottawa, those glimpses seemed innocuous at the time. The SSEA continued to respectfully seek and consider Nehru's views.

Ottawa's perception of Nehru and non-alignment failed to mirror the strident criticisms from Washington. By 1953, the United States, exasperated with non-alignment, chose Pakistan as its key regional ally. American military aid flowed into Pakistan much to India's ire. Reid sympathized with New Delhi's reaction and reported on it to Ottawa. Pearson did not oppose the American decision despite India's anger with Washington. Ottawa's quiet political support did not mean that Pearson favoured a Canadian strategic partnership with Pakistan; rather, Pearson understood the need for strong Western allies in a region straddling the Middle East and Asia.[6] Pursuing close ties with India did not prevent the DEA from recognizing Pakistan's worth. Pakistan had no predominant leader, and it was smaller and poorer than India (it could not afford to open a post in Ottawa until 1949). While Pakistan determined its place in world affairs and its role in the Commonwealth, Canadian officials believed by 1949 that Pakistan had "great strategic importance in the event of a war with the Soviet Union," with its defence being "of great value to the Western world." Based on this assessment, the DEA thought "Canada could do its share in maintaining and strengthening the Western influences in Pakistan."[7] While Nehru's stature and India's influence overshadowed the Pakistani leadership and nation, Pearson believed that Pakistan had an important role to play in strengthening Western interests in Asia, particularly that country's willingness to embrace the West more effusively than India. Canada's first high commissioner in Pakistan, David Johnson, observed that, as Nehru's "immense prestige" drew more international visitors in these early years of independence, Pakistan felt "neglected by foreign countries."[8] Johnson's observations resonated in Ottawa. The Canadian government welcomed the Pakistani prime minister, Liaquat Ali Khan, to Ottawa at the end of May 1950. It was Khan's first visit to a Commonwealth country outside of South Asia, a noteworthy signal that Canada mattered to Pakistan. Canada emerged as the second largest aid donor to India and Pakistan behind the United States. By the mid-1950s, Ottawa's policy towards South Asia was balanced, thoughtful, and creative in seeking to draw the two enemies closer to the West. Pearson was a key architect of that policy.

Pearson's early diplomatic successes are noteworthy for he knew little about South Asia. However, two key foreign policy decisions supported by Pearson reaped bitter fruit during his later years as prime minister. First, in June 1954, Canada, India, and Poland agreed to serve on the International Commission for Supervision and Control in Indochina (ICSC), which monitored the ceasefire after France's withdrawal from this troubled region. Second, Ottawa decided to export nuclear technology to India as part of the Colombo Plan, despite signals the two countries viewed the question of safeguards differently. On each file, Pearson lent his support as close and friendly relations with India rendered both initiatives worthwhile. And on each file Pakistan lurked uneasily in the background.

Although an unexpected request, Ottawa consented to serve on the Indochina commissions in part because of its ties with India. Years later, Reid assessed this occasion as another example of the ongoing Indo-Canadian cooperation and further evidence of his thesis that a "special relationship" existed between the two countries, while Pearson's biographer described the summer of 1954 "as the glorious summer of Indo-Canadian harmony."[9] Pearson believed, fundamentally, that Canada and India had similar objectives in Indochina. While Pearson was not alone in thinking this was the case, he was soon proven to be mistaken. As Robert Bothwell and Michael Carroll show (Chapters 1 and 2, respectively, this volume), Pearson defined Canada's goal in Southeast Asia as promoting security and stability, and he expected full

Indian cooperation.[10] Pearson misread New Delhi's willingness to sympathize with Hanoi and underestimated North Vietnam's ability to emphasize its regional and colonial bonds with India.[11]

Ottawa's frustration towards Indian foreign policy bubbled to the surface given India's take on non-alignment, decolonization, and the ICSC. The working relationship on the Indochina commissions had not gone according to plan. To the surprise of senior DEA officials, Arthur Menzies and Marcel Cadieux, the Indians seemed sympathetic to Hanoi and disdainful of Saigon. Cadieux, one of the first Canadian diplomats to serve in Indochina and a critic of Indian foreign policy, questioned the depth of Western values among the Indians and judged their self-proclaimed neutrality as hypocritical given their behaviour in Indochina. "Indian neutrality or non-alignment may be the expression of basic Indian and spiritual moral attitudes which may be the result of geographical and historical factors," but Cadieux concluded that this meant that Indians did not approach matters in "a scientific, objective Western way."[12] And here lay a fundamental problem with Pearson's original expectation that Canada could link India with the West. One of the key assumptions underpinning this concept of tangible links was an idealistic belief that Canada and India, enjoying entrenched commonalities thanks to a shared imperial past, approached geopolitical questions similarly. Instead, senior Canadian officials, including Pearson, gradually concluded that India did not see events through a pro-Western lens. Nehru's explicit support for non-alignment in April 1955 at the Bandung Conference underscored this point.

As senior DEA officials increasingly questioned Indian foreign policy, they sought comparisons with Pakistan and revisited their assessments of the region. In November 1955, Pearson travelled to India and Pakistan. While his discussions with Nehru were friendly, he was not as enamoured as he had been six years earlier. Critical of India's non-alignment, Pearson recorded in his diary: "People here are morbidly sensitive about their independent position, satisfied with, even proud about their 'neutralist' stand ... At times, this makes them unreasonable and self-righteous, as does their occasional assumption of superior virtue vis-à-vis the west."[13] By contrast, Pearson's description of the Pakistanis reveals the stark differences he observed between the two countries while illuminating the lingering cultural unease that he and many of his colleagues experienced towards India:

> It is surprising, the difference in the atmosphere between India and Pakistan. The people of the latter country – or at least West Pakistan – seem much easier to talk to, more like ourselves, than the Indians. They seem franker and more straightforward, more vigorous ... finally, the Pakistanis seek, and very often secure, your sympathy as the smaller state ... anyway we seem to like the Pakistanis.[14]

Pearson's annoyance with the Indians soon leapt from his diary pages into his communications with Reid. Pearson was livid with the warm reception Soviet premier Nikita Khrushchev received during his visit to India in December 1955, the generous Indian press coverage given to the visit, and Moscow's public offer of aid. Pearson lashed out at Nehru in correspondence to Reid for the Indian leader's willingness to publicly fete Soviet aid while failing to credit the larger Western aid program to India.[15] Pearson's original hope that Canada could act as a bridge to non-aligned India suffered as DEA officials accused India of pursuing a double standard: accepting Western aid but criticizing the West's policies at the same time as it ignored Soviet abuses, notably Moscow's brutal quelling of Hungary's revolution. This concern manifested itself weeks before Nehru's December 1956 visit to Ottawa. Various DEA divisions were asked to consider Canada's relationship with India and Reid's suggestions about how Canada might reach out to India in a post-Suez Crisis world. Few DEA officers responded positively to India's influence at the UN or its pursuit of non-alignment. The DEA politely dismissed Reid's proposals.[16]

Canadian attitudes towards Indian and Pakistani foreign policy changed as those countries neared the end of their first decade of independence. Canadian policy makers had overestimated their ability to coax India Westward. New Delhi's adherence to non-alignment led gradually to India's being placed on the periphery of Canadian interest in Asia as well as a modest adjustment to the importance Canadian policy makers placed on pro-Western Pakistan. Whereas India disdained NATO and welcomed Soviet leaders to New Delhi, Pakistan joined the American-led SEATO in 1954 and the Baghdad Pact in 1955. Accordingly, Pakistan, not India, emerged as the West's central military and political ally in South Asia. A sense had also emerged that the Pakistanis possessed a different and better character than did India's leaders. In early 1957, Morley Scott, one of the first Canadians posted to New Delhi ten years earlier, prepared to leave Pakistan for Canada after serving as high commissioner for three years. In a final letter to Pearson, he concluded that Pakistan had become increasingly important as "[the country's] foreign policy, at the moment, is the most to our liking of any of the nations in these parts, and it is worth a real[,] and even painful, effort to keep it so."[17] Pearson concurred. In one of his last missives as SSEA, he sharply suggested to Reid that "Asian membership and Asian policies" in the Commonwealth prompted "increased concern; a concern as to whether the Commonwealth can exist in its present form ... and spirit when there are such growing divergences of policy and approach and feeling between the Asian and other members." Despite the blanket reference to "Asia," Pearson more precisely objected to India's "ambiguous" UN role, "one which has at times caused both irritation and impatience, even in friendly delegations like the Canadian. The tendency to indulge in moralizing at Western expense" and to "adopt a double standard" while protecting their "national interests," exasperated the SSEA.[18] However, by June 1957, John Diefenbaker's Progressive Conservative government was directing relations with India and Pakistan.

Political differences aside, Diefenbaker's assessment of South Asia resembled Pearson's. Canada's Colombo aid continued and modestly expanded, and, despite ongoing frustration, Canada remained on the ICSC. Unlike Pearson, the Progressive Conservative leader cultivated a stronger friendship with Ayub Khan, Pakistan's first military leader. A strong proponent of the Commonwealth and stridently anti-communist, Diefenbaker was keen that India and Pakistan be connected with the West. Like Pearson, his aspirations for the region were challenged.

Diefenbaker visited India and Pakistan in November 1958. He worried that economic offensives directed from Moscow and Peking threatened the freedom and independence of developing nations. He also wanted to gain first-hand experience "of the problems, and personal acquaintance with the leaders, of the non-white Commonwealth countries in Asia."[19] Diefenbaker's visit cemented in his mind which countries and which leaders could be regarded as pro-Western counterweights to Moscow's efforts in South Asia. Even before arriving in India, Diefenbaker found New Delhi lacking in this regard. And while talks with Nehru were amicable, they lacked the easy atmosphere

Diefenbaker felt in Pakistan. Such views were long-lasting. Following Sino-Indian border clashes in 1959, Diefenbaker wondered how Nehru could not now recognize "the dangers of a neutralist policy."[20] In contrast, Khan reaffirmed to Diefenbaker his pro-Western bona fides and both leaders bonded over shared distrust of India.[21] Relationships matter in diplomacy, and Diefenbaker's relationship with Khan was one of mutual respect and was of importance to him. But soon enough, Diefenbaker was out of office.

Cabinet splits over Diefenbaker's ability to govern and his mounting political unpopularity incited the fall of the Progressive Conservative minority government. In April 1963, Canadians elected a Liberal minority government led by Pearson. As SSEA, Pearson had defined internationalism like no other Canadian before him. The Indians had appreciated his efforts. As Pearson had "spectacularly presented the national policy" of Canada "to the outside world," India favoured his election victory, hoping for a fresh change in a bilateral relationship that appeared to be waning.[22]

Indian and Pakistani officials observed Pearson's win closely. New Delhi realized that relations had slipped during the Diefenbaker era. The Pakistanis, hoping to reap rewards for their loyalty to the West, sought to establish friendly ties with Pearson. But to what extent did India and Pakistan matter to the new prime minister's foreign policy? While in office from 1963 to 1968, Pearson never travelled to the region. Ottawa's international priorities quickly became apparent to Canadian and foreign observers alike as Pearson soon visited his British, American, and French colleagues. There were no plans to travel to Asia or to meet with Nehru. Had Pearson made the trip, he would have encountered a physically weakened Nehru. Undoubtedly, India's severe military defeat in a short border war with China in 1962 had accelerated the decline in his health. Still, Nehru warmly congratulated Pearson on his victory and invited him to India, an offer that Pearson side-stepped.[23] Further encouragement to visit India from Chester Ronning, Canada's high commissioner, received little consideration.

Despite this reluctance, the Pearson government continued a Diefenbaker program – started during the Sino-Indian War in 1962 – to export some armaments to India to help rebuild that nation's shattered army so that it could defend its mountainous border with China. More significantly, Canada approved the sale of a CANDU nuclear reactor to India in 1963. Ottawa had entered into preliminary negotiations for the CANDU in late 1962, and negotiations progressed after the election. Atomic Energy Canada Limited (AECL) aspired to cultivate international markets for Canadian nuclear technology. India was a key market for AECL as it sought to build on the initial transfer of the Canada India Reactor (CIR) donated to India in 1956. The CIR became operational in 1960, but the negotiation process had been difficult as both countries disagreed on reactor safeguards.

Neither the decision to export the reactor nor the decision to extend modest military shipments was evidence that Ottawa aspired to "reset" relations with India. Frustration with non-alignment remained and political relations lagged. Indeed, Pearson did not connect the reactor sale or continued military aid, however meagre, to any grand political ambitions in the bilateral relationship. Neither decision was made with an assessment of what Ottawa sought to achieve with India or with a sense that Pakistani sensibilities might be considered.

Decisions by Canberra, London, Ottawa, and Washington to send military aid to India, then news of another Canadian reactor sale, provoked consternation in Rawalpindi. Pakistan's alignment with the West came with a quid pro quo. The Pakistanis yearned for Western support over Kashmir, an aspiration that intensified with Pearson's election victory. Pearson, however, did not pursue the friendly relationship that Diefenbaker had cultivated with Khan, and he declined to be drawn into a regional squabble despite Pakistan's fear that Ottawa was bolstering India's defence capabilities. The Pakistanis expressed frustration that their close ties with the West, especially with Ottawa, had not won them greater support.

Initially, Pakistan could take some solace in the fact that Pearson pursued a line with India similar to that followed by Diefenbaker. Bilateral ties between Canada and India continued to atrophy at the political level. Conversely, however, Ottawa dismissed Pakistan's security concerns regarding military exports and nuclear cooperation. When SSEA Paul Martin met with Pakistan's foreign minister, Zulfikar Ali Bhutto, the latter wanted the exports discontinued. He also used the opportunity to point out that, in contrast to Indian "unfriendliness toward western nations," Pakistan "had been firmly aligned with the West." While Bhutto's tactic might have appealed to Diefenbaker, it failed with Martin and Pearson. Martin countered that Ottawa had received "strong assurances" from India that Canadian materials would not be used against Pakistan, comments that did nothing to reassure

Bhutto.[24] Meeting with Bhutto, Pearson, like Martin, refused to criticize or to halt military assistance to India; rather, he relayed to Bhutto his comfort in dealing with Pakistani officials and his considerable sympathy for Pakistan's concerns.[25] But as Canadian words did not translate into notable deeds, for Bhutto this was confirmation that Canadian support was fickle, and he returned home with the standard platitudes. For Pearson and Martin, it was an early hint that South Asian affairs would be more difficult than had been initially anticipated.

One of those tests remained the ICSC as the Vietnam War affected Canada-India relations. Canadian frustration at ICSC inaction and reporting became increasingly vocal.[26] Frustrations bubbled to the surface in early 1965 through a frank exchange between Martin and Swaran Singh, his Indian counterpart in the Indian Ministry of External Affairs, after an ICSC commission report admonished South Vietnam. While the Canadians acknowledged the report's contents, they fumed at its speedy preparation, reinforcing a long-standing belief in the DEA that India moved quickly when chastising Saigon or Washington but dithered in matters involving Hanoi. By March 1965, senior DEA officials persuaded Martin to direct Roland Michener, Canada's high commissioner in New Delhi, to severely caution the Indians on their "continuing unwillingness ... to have the Commission produce balanced reports and – more important – conclusive judgments reflecting what we all know to be shortcomings on both sides of the agreement." The inability to get objective reporting led Ottawa to question the ICSC's impartiality and usefulness.[27] Michener told Pearson that Singh carefully read Martin's message but questioned its content and underlined Indian impartiality. Michener countered Singh's claim with an assertion "that on [a] large number of items before [the] commission it was not being impartial and that in fact it was not doing anything at all."[28] In his response to Martin, Singh brushed aside Canadian concerns. Admitting that differences occasionally existed between Canada and India on the commission, he reaffirmed his country's impartiality and stressed the "very good cooperation between our two countries." Still, the Canadians pushed too far in their objections: "Within its limited terms of reference, the Commission cannot, correctly speaking, attempt a general political commentary on the complicated situation in Vietnam."[29] However, a letter distributed to the Indian prime minister's secretariat acknowledged that both countries "seemed to be speaking with different voices" about the ICSC. The point would be raised when Nehru's successor, Lal Bahdaur Shastri, visited Ottawa in June 1965.[30]

The fundamental changes to Indian defence policy post-1962 and the subsequent idiosyncrasies of non-alignment dominated the prime ministerial talks. The leaders emphasized the Indochina commissions, nuclear assistance, and possible military sales to India. Pearson and Martin discussed their misgivings about specific Indian policies on the ICSC, as advised. The Canadians intended the exchange to re-establish the previous close cooperation that had existed when both countries pursued "our common objectives." Whether either nation had genuinely pursued such objectives on the ICSC is debatable. Nonetheless, the Canadians saw the commissions "as one of the most important ventures in international peace-keeping yet undertaken."[31]

The Indians asked to discuss "defence aid," but, unlike with nuclear assistance issues, policy makers in the DEA's Defence Liaison (1) Division turned their masters against any undertakings that would lead to substantial military assistance or sales to India.[32] India sought Canadian equipment, particularly Caribou aircraft, but Ottawa declined direct military assistance.[33] Although the threat of another conflict with China had receded, tension between Pakistan and India had escalated. Canada refused to favour one Commonwealth country over the other for that would have threatened the meaningful aid that Canada had poured into the Indian subcontinent to enhance regional stability. Finally, Pearson and Martin could rightly argue that Canada's substantial aid assistance and loans freed Indian funds for defence purchases.[34]

The bilateral talks had been cordial and mostly candid. But the meetings did not solve the differences concerning the ICSC. Pearson and Martin chose a softer tone on the ICSC during the meetings with Shastri, despite DEA briefs recommending a firm line. A British official in Ottawa observed: "The bitter frustrations which the Canadians have been experiencing over Indian tactics in the Commission over the past year were not allowed to protrude above the smooth surface of this ministerial visit."[35] While the decision to avoid a confrontational tone provided an amenable meeting environment, it also enabled tensions to swell. A steady stream of young Canadian diplomats arriving to work on the ICSC developed their own frequently jaded perspective on Indian conduct.

Shastri returned home to an unsettled security situation. Spring 1965 saw border skirmishes between Pakistani and Indian patrols along the desolate Rann of Kutch. Though tensions cooled, the fighting gave the Pakistanis a sense they had managed to get the better of an Indian military that perhaps had not recovered from its war with China. Both Pearson and Martin considered whether Canada might mediate between the two hostile neighbours. Martin asked John Hadwen, a diplomat seconded to his office, what "we were doing to be peacemakers ourselves," seeking ideas from both the DEA and from the Canadian high commissions in India and Pakistan.[36] Hadwen, informing Martin that Ottawa's efforts might not be required, suggested to USSEA Marcel Cadieux that Britain might "attempt to discourage us from intervening in a matter on which they appear to be willing to carry the ball."[37] That is exactly what occurred, possibly to Pearson's relief. Martin appears to have taken the lead to seek Canadian intervention, asking the DEA for suggestions and meeting with the Indian and Pakistani high commissioners in Ottawa. Such an initiative was subtly discouraged by the DEA, which advised that "there was limited scope for third parties."[38] Pearson did not push Canadian involvement. The matter went unmentioned when Shastri met with him the following month in Ottawa.

Fighting resumed in September 1965, forcing Pearson and the DEA to manage a bizarre turn of events during the Second Indo-Pakistan War. A confident Ayub Khan, believing that Shastri was a weak leader, decided to test India's mettle in Kashmir in August. Thousands of Pakistani soldiers gradually infiltrated the border to seize strategic points and foment insurrection among Kashmir's majority Muslim population. India responded on 6 September with an armoured invasion directed towards Lahore.

Pakistani hopes quickly suffered. Ottawa contemplated a response in the early days of the 1965 federal election. Unlike the previous spring, Britain, much to India's fury, ceded the position of mediator by condemning the Indian attack. Pearson appears to have flirted with a more direct role. During a cabinet meeting on 8 September, he "expressed deep concern" as the new conflict could place Asia "on the verge of a bloody catastrophe," and he announced that he had "offered his services to both governments as a mediator." Though both Khan and Shastri had rejected the offer, Pearson told his cabinet he was willing to "fly out immediately" if either country or the UN thought he might be "useful and effective." How sincere was Pearson's mediation offer? Previously, he had avoided entanglement in the Kashmir dispute; this offer would undermine that effort. And neither India nor Pakistan accepted responsibility for the conflict. It is revealing that, prior to the cabinet meeting, Pearson met with the Indian high commissioner, B.K. Acharya, who downplayed mediation. Afterwards, Pearson mused, "having now a good idea of the position of the two parties in response to his [Lester Pearson] offer of good offices, we need do no more for the time being except support the United Nations effort as appropriate."[39] Mere hours after that meeting, Pearson genuinely feared a "bloody catastrophe." But his comments suggest he embellished his concern to his cabinet colleagues.

Martin encouraged cabinet to adopt tough export restrictions that prohibited the shipment of any commodities, even those connected to foreign aid, with "military potential."[40] In his memoir Martin discussed the Kashmir War in a single though revealing paragraph. Pearson, the cabinet, the DEA, and the Department of National Defence were peripheral players. Martin implied that he took the lead on the Kashmir file in Ottawa and at the UN. According to Martin, within the span of a week, Canada agreed to provide "the commander and the nucleus of a UN force to oversee the withdrawal of Pakistani and Indian troops from Kashmir. This done, [he] could begin canvassing in [his] constituency."[41]

If only it were that simple. Once India gained the military upperhand in the conflict, a ceasefire emerged. Ottawa agreed to a UN request at the end of September to assist the United Nations India-Pakistan Observation Mission (UNIPOM), dispatching a major-general to command the mission with a small unit of military observers and an Air Transport Unit to service up to eight RCAF aircraft.[42] The decision to support the UN request reflected a desire to maintain a policy of "strong and loyal support for UN peacekeeping." Ottawa also hoped to assist in "a lasting settlement" between the two quarrelling Commonwealth members.[43] Before supporting the UN effort, though, Pearson had responded cautiously by agreeing that Ottawa could play a key role in shaping a new ceasefire force. Still, the Kashmir dispute remained a festering bilateral sore in South Asia, with Moscow offering to broker peace talks between the two troubled nations in January 1966. The unwillingness of the West, including Canada, to explicitly side with Pakistan prompted a new challenge for the Pearson government at the same time that it was working with the UN to solve the crisis.

As the Pakistani army faced defeat, Khan's regime assailed Western diplomatic establishments and their staff. The Canadians were no exception. During the brief war, the Canadians endured numerous Pakistani diplomatic slights – some bizarre, some serious – to make it clear that the West, including Canada, had let Pakistan down. Communications between Ottawa and its posts in Pakistan were deliberately interrupted for an extended period during the conflict. An anti-Western riot in Karachi led to Canada's new flag being ripped down and rioters stoning the Canadian mission. Pakistani annoyance also prompted delayed clearance approval for RCAF aircraft to evacuate Canadians and to delay landing permission for RCAF UN-related flights in September and again in December.[44] Marcel Cadieux met with the Pakistani high commissioner to express Ottawa's displeasure at these slights in the hope that a polite but firm discussion could resolve the matter. This episode, in conjunction with the broader context of the Kashmir dispute, was a watershed. The positive comparisons made between Pakistani and Indian foreign policy vanished, as did discussion of Canada's viewing Pakistan as a pro-Western outpost in Asia.

At first glance, Ottawa's handling of the Kashmir War seems a classic case of Pearsonian helpful-fixer diplomacy. Ottawa offered to mediate but was far more comfortable with the UN taking the lead; Ottawa then promptly acted when called upon to provide personnel and material support to UNIPOM. Importantly, unlike the hostile security environment Canadian peacekeepers encountered in the Congo, or the case of Suez in which the Canadian UNEF contingent was expelled in 1967, or the tense and ongoing peacekeeping commitment in Cyprus, UNIPOM appeared to achieve its main objective: ensuring the integrity of the ceasefire while Pakistani and Indian forces withdrew – and the mission ended in March 1966. However, obvious shortcomings existed. In the war's aftermath, Ottawa returned to its traditional hesitation to mediate between its Commonwealth counterparts, and tensions over Kashmir continued to plague the subcontinent. The Canadian role also earned little goodwill with Pakistan as Rawalpindi increasingly viewed diplomatic relationships through

Kashmir's prism. Similarly, India pursued policies, particularly on the ICSC and non-alignment, that irritated Canadian officials.

A troubling issue arose in Pearson's final years as prime minister, a problem that bedevilled Canadian policy makers well into the 1970s, indeed becoming one of the major problems of Canadian foreign policy in the second half of the twentieth century. Selling Canadian nuclear technology abroad remained a keen ambition for the AECL and Ottawa. In 1966, Ottawa and New Delhi discussed selling a third Canadian reactor to India. At the same time, multilateral discussions occurred in Geneva to frame the eventual Non-Proliferation Treaty (NPT). In addition to backing a nuclear test ban – an issue covered by Norman Hillmer, Daniel Macfarlane, and Michael Manulak (Chapter 15, this volume) – Ottawa supported a robust nuclear non-proliferation treaty. During the NPT negotiations, India accused the nuclear powers of nuclear apartheid. New Delhi insisted that the nuclear "haves" must treat the have-nots equitably and with mutual obligations. India desired a treaty that obliged nuclear and non-nuclear weapon states to stop production of nuclear weapons and any related delivery mechanisms. The nuclear powers opposed that position. Despite concerted lobbying from Ottawa and the Canadian High Commission in New Delhi, India refused to sign the NPT in 1968, creating uncertainty as to how Canada could cooperate with an NPT non-signatory. Although that phase occurred in the early months of the Pierre Trudeau government, Pearson knew of both the firm Indian position during the NPT negotiations and India's reluctance to embrace stricter safeguards for its new Canadian reactor.

A frustrated and angry Pakistan watched the new round of nuclear export discussions between Ottawa and New Delhi. Pakistani officials bitterly commented that, safeguards or not, Canada was giving India the ability to produce a nuclear bomb.[45] The Pakistanis also objected to stronger IAEA-sanctioned safeguards on any Canadian reactor deal that they pursued with Ottawa. Rawalpindi insisted that any reactor purchase should receive the exact same safeguards as those India had negotiated with the Canadians with the 1963 Rajasthan Atomic Power Project (RAPP I) CANDU reactor sale. That reactor had stricter safeguards than did the original 1956 CIR deal, but in the years after 1963 the International Atomic Energy Agency (IAEA) pressed for enhanced safeguards, which Ottawa supported. As was the case with earlier Canadian military exports to India, Pakistan expected a quid pro quo or the cessation of nuclear discussions with India. By August 1966, the acting Canadian high commissioner, James Weld, cited Canada's nuclear cooperation with India as "a festering sore." Pakistani officials, believing that they faced discriminatory treatment, appealed that India was using the CIR reactor to produce weapons-grade plutonium.[46] Ottawa appreciated the concerns raised, but barring a dramatic change in Indian actions, it refused to modify its policies to placate Pakistan.[47] Negotiations with India to purchase the RAPP II continued, with the Indians determined to avoid upgraded IAEA safeguards. Pakistan increased its lobbying efforts against the reactor sale, alleging that India was set to explode a nuclear device.

The allegations, made in late July, occurred just as the Liberal government entered into cabinet debate over the proposed RAPP II reactor sale. On 27 July, cabinet agreed to finance the second phase of RAPP II if India accepted appropriate safeguards as accorded to RAPP I. Martin wanted more stringent safeguard requirements, even though he suspected the Pakistani allegations were unfounded. The "best intelligence assessment," he informed Pearson, "is that the Indians have no present intention to explode a 'peaceful' nuclear device." Nonetheless, he and his DEA advisers believed it was imperative to push India to accept IAEA safeguards. Given Ottawa's desire to see the IAEA succeed and to obtain the most stringent safeguards possible, it was critical that India accept. This was particularly so while Ottawa was simultaneously developing its nuclear relationship with Pakistan. The Pakistanis, perhaps hoping to drive a wedge between Ottawa and New Delhi, were willing to adhere to IAEA safeguards. Ideally, Martin hoped to push the Indians onto the same track, but Pearson remained circumspect. Though he agreed with his minister's desire, he wrote on the memorandum: "How can we do this now – after having made other arrangements with India?"[48] Martin was uncertain whether the Indians would accept a stricter approach, but he surmised that the chances of successfully reaching an agreement had improved. Pearson disagreed: the chances of India's making a nuclear bomb had "probably improved," but Pakistan's charges had not helped. He saw "little chance" of successfully linking the financing of the reactor to the IAEA safeguards and cautioned, "if we persist now we are likely to get into serious trouble with India."[49]

Martin's memorandum was generated, in part, by a letter that Indian prime minister Indira Gandhi had sent to Pearson in June. She had written Pearson hoping to exchange views on matters of bilateral interest and had invited him to India. Martin supported accepting Gandhi's invitation, hinting that Pearson should make the visit as "no Canadian Prime Minister ha[d] been in Asia since 1958 and visits of Canadian Cabinet Ministers ha[d] been few and far between."[50] Declining the Indian invitation, Pearson agreed with Martin that a response concentrating on Indochina and the commission problems, atomic energy, and development assistance should be sent.[51] The DEA prepared a draft letter, but, in light of the recent emphasis on the Indian nuclear program, Martin and his advisers decided that they would not discuss "controversial issues of interest to ourselves and the Indians," such as the ICSC. The authors thought it best to emphasize relatively non-controversial problems, "except for the urgent matter of atomic safeguards."[52] Pearson agreed. This tactic suggests that the relationship between the two countries was far less open than many Canadians would have suspected. It also illuminates Pearson's passive approach to handling differences with India.

Meanwhile, the Indians thought that they had conceded too much in terms of RAPP I safeguards. At most, they would accept the same conditions for RAPP II as they had for RAPP I. They objected, on both technical and political grounds, to Ottawa's push that New Delhi accept additional IAEA safeguards.[53] An agreement in principle was reached. The solution was to treat the RAPP II agreement similarly to the RAPP I agreement. Cadieux believed that discussions had led to "a rather extensive paper which incorporate[d] the essential provisions of the IAEA safeguards."[54] The IAEA would be asked to apply safeguards to both RAPP stations no later than one year after a reactor in each station became critical, but there would be no safeguards on future Indian-produced fissionable materials. Martin agreed that Indian acceptance of the same safeguards for RAPP II as existed for RAPP I, with limited IAEA inspections, was likely the best deal that could be secured.

Cabinet endorsed the proposed agreement on 10 November.[55] On 15 December, an order in council confirmed the RAPP II agreement. Canada would contribute $38.5 million to construction as well as technical support from AECL. Robert Winters, the minister of trade and commerce, later hailed the agreement, stating, "the sale confirmed Canada's position as one of the leading international suppliers of nuclear power stations."[56] So, at a critical juncture concerning international nuclear safeguards, the Indian nuclear program benefitted enormously from Canadian cooperation and patronage.

At this late stage there appears to have been little input on the nuclear file from either Pearson or Martin. One cannot help but wonder if they were simply swept along by events or whether the intricacies of a new Liberal leadership race, sparked by Pearson's December 1967 decision to retire, was a distraction. In one of his last formal decisions on the India file and on whether Ottawa should continue to lobby India on the NPT, Pearson commented: "I think we should be careful about bringing pressure to bear on this matter."[57] Indeed, Canadian policy had been overtly careful as aid was never used to pressure the Indians to modify their position; instead, Ottawa quietly pursued diplomatic channels to persuade India of the logic of signing the NPT. Security trumped Canadian reasoning. From New Delhi's perspective, Canada could afford to sign the NPT and act on its principles for geography and the American strategic umbrella protected it. On 5 April 1968, Gandhi confirmed publicly that India would not sign the NPT. If, she reasoned, some countries cut aid as a result it would be "the first real step towards self-sufficiency." Self-interest and domestic considerations would guide India on this matter.[58]

In stark contrast to his time as SSEA, Pearson's ability to reconcile thorny diplomatic problems concerning India and Pakistan proved mixed during his time as prime minister. While some may argue that Paul Martin was the appropriate point person to deal with diplomatic files on a region like South Asia, Pearson – as Greg Donaghy points out (Chapter 4, this volume) – occasionally overruled and questioned his SSEA. He remained briefed on South Asian affairs, making key decisions on the ICSC and nuclear reactor sales. The complexities of the India-Pakistan relationship tested Ottawa's patience and goodwill in a way they had not during Pearson's time as SSEA. Compared to relations with the United States and Western Europe, Canada's ties with South Asia had declined since their peak in the 1950s. Yet various India-Pakistan issues that confronted Pearson and Martin involved more than just bilateral ties: they affected security in South Asia and Indochina, and they entailed questions pertaining to international nuclear safeguards. Towards both countries, Pearson's government adopted nonchalant policy positions that were baffling and, at times, contradictory. Robert Bothwell, in his fine study of the ICSC, suggests: "For Pearson, good relations with India were still a major consideration, and he was willing to accommodate Indian sensitivities even on issues to which Canada attached a great deal of importance, such as controls over nuclear materials."[59] Perhaps so, but this does not fully explain Pearson's handling of either topic. Fundamentally, Pearson comes across as aloof and uncertain in his decision making about the ICSC and on how to persuade India to accept tougher safeguards on Canadian-purchased reactors and to accede to the NPT. While Ottawa sought to curtail military exports to both countries, it pressed ahead with nuclear reactor sales to India and entered into similar negotiations with Pakistan at a time when relations between the two neighbours were volatile. Just as puzzlingly, discussions to sell reactors to India and Pakistan occurred as Ottawa's political ties with those countries were deteriorating. Canadian nuclear cooperation with India expanded despite signals that both countries differed on nuclear safeguards and despite reports that India sought a nuclear bomb. Not surprisingly, continued cooperation with India had a negative impact on Ottawa's relations with Rawalpindi as it urged Ottawa to ideally scrap the deal or to put strict safeguards on reactors sold to India.

Tensions with India on the ICSC heightened and remained unresolved. Yet Pearson refused to withdraw Canada from the ICSC or to confront Indian leaders on the matter. Thus, the ICSC continued to erode bilateral ties until it concluded in 1973. In the meantime, a generation of young diplomats serving on the ICSC returned to Ottawa to influence policy making towards India in the Trudeau era, blocking efforts to enhance bilateral ties with India proposed by a small group of pro-Indianists in the DEA.[60] It is, therefore, questionable whether good relations with India was a major consideration for Pearson. Pearson declined requests from Nehru, Shastri, and Gandhi to visit India and ignored suggestions from Ronning and Martin that he visit India. Knowing that USSEA Marcel Cadieux loathed Indian foreign policy, Pearson kept him in place to speak bluntly to the Indians when required. Yet a bizarre environment emerged in which political ties declined but India remained the main recipient of Canadian foreign aid and its most prominent nuclear export market. The one notable success, albeit limited, occurred through the UN. Following renewed conflict in Kashmir in September 1965, Canada contributed the core of a new peacekeeping force after the UN arranged a ceasefire between

India and Pakistan, a classic peacekeeping case study associated with the mythology of Pearsonian internationalism. However, that case has been largely forgotten, and it did not earn Ottawa much credit in the region as the two leading South Asian states created multiple conundrums for Canada. The end of the Pearson era saw Canada's relationship with Pakistan deteriorate, partly because Pearson chose not to embrace Pakistan as firmly as did Diefenbaker and partly due to Pakistan's inability to persuade Ottawa to side with it against India. Likewise, bilateral relations with India shifted to the periphery of Canadian foreign policy interests, completing the trajectory that began during the last years of Pearson's time as SSEA, when questions related to Indian non-alignment soured Pearson's earlier idealism about having Canada act as a bridge between South Asia and the West. Tensions within the ICSC and nuclear cooperation with India and Pakistan remained troublesome well into the 1970s, when they had to be addressed by the Trudeau government.

Notes

1 Only recently have Canadian historians begun to analyze the Canada-India relationship: Ryan Touhey, *Conflicting Visions: Canada and India in the Cold War World, 1946–1976* (Vancouver: UBC Press, 2015); Ryan Touhey, "Dealing in Black and White: The Diefenbaker Government and the Cold War in South Asia, 1957–1963," *Canadian Historical Review* 92 (2011): 429–54; Duane Bratt, *The Politics of CANDU Exports* (Toronto: University of Toronto Press, 2006); Greg Donaghy, "'The Most Important Place in the World': Escott Reid in India, 1952–57," in *Escott Reid: Diplomat and Scholar*, ed. Greg Donaghy and Stéphane Roussel, 67–84 (Montreal and Kingston: McGill-Queen's University Press, 2004); Hector Mackenzie, "An Old Dominion and the New Commonwealth: Canadian Policy on the Question of India's Membership, 1947–49," *Journal of Imperial and Commonwealth History* 27 (1999): 82–112

2 This "bridge" concept to the decolonizing world has been illuminated by Hector Mackenzie and David Webster, who have highlighted a tendency among Canadian officials to portray Ottawa as uniquely able to play a role as conciliators and friends to decolonizing states. This belief that Canada could be a linchpin had deep roots in the North Atlantic Triangle, with many Canadians convinced that Canada could promote good Anglo-American relations.

3 Memorandum for the SSEA, "India and the Commonwealth," 16 March 1949, LAC, RG 2, vol. 248, file I-13.

4 Chairman, Delegation to the General Assembly of the United Nations, to SSEA, Telegram 385, 27 November 1952, in *DCER, 1952* (Ottawa: Minister of Supply, 1990).

5 Wilgress to Reid, 12 November 1952, LAC, RG 25, vol. 3660, file 4900-E-40-pt.1.

6 Robert McMahon, "US Policy toward South Asia and Tibet during the Early Cold War," *Journal of Cold War Studies* 8 (2006): 131–44.
7 Escott Reid, "Canadian Representation in Pakistan and Ceylon," 4 February 1949, LAC, RG 25, vol. 6292, file 11493-A-40-pt.1; Heeney to SSEA, 13 October 1949, LAC, RG 25, vol. 3985, file 9908-BK-1-40-pt.1; Letter of Instruction to Kirkwood, 9 January 1952, LAC, RG 25, vol. 3661, file 4900-M-40-pt.1.
8 Johnson to Acting SSEA, 25 January 1950, LAC, RG 25, vol. 6255, file 9678-40-pt.1.
9 Reid, *Envoy to Nehru*, 69; John English, *The Worldly Years: The Life of Lester Pearson, 1949–1972* (Toronto: Knopf, 1992), 94.
10 Pearson to Lett, 22 August 1954, LAC, RG 25, vol. 4629, file 50052-A-40-pt.1.
11 Mark Atwood Lawrence, "The Limits of Peacemaking: India and the Vietnam War, 1962–67," *India Review* 1 (2002): 39–72.
12 Cadieux to file, 29 June 1955, LAC, RG 25, vol. 7127, file 9126-40-pt.8.1.
13 Pearson, Journal of His Asian Trip, November 1955, LAC, Escott Reid Papers, vol. 9, file 1.
14 Ibid.
15 Reid, *Envoy to Nehru*, 130.
16 Touhey, *Conflicting Visions*, 110–12. Reid's proposals encouraged Ottawa to move quickly as British prestige in India declined post-Suez. His ideas ranged from encouraging Ottawa to share information with India on foreign affairs, enhancing Canadian cultural diplomacy initiatives in India, increased economic assistance, and increased sympathy for Indian views on colonial issues in Asia and Africa.
17 Scott to Pearson, 6 February 1957, LAC, Lester Pearson Papers, vol. 32, file Heads of Mission Appointments.
18 Pearson to Reid, 8 March 1957, LAC, Reid Papers, vol. 10, file 34.
19 Basil Robinson, *Diefenbaker's World: A Populist in Foreign Affairs* (Toronto: University of Toronto Press, 1989), 71.
20 Robinson to Commonwealth Division and USSEA, 30 November 1959, LAC, Basil Robinson Papers, vol. 2, file 14.
21 See Diefenbaker Canada Centre, University of Saskatchewan, Diefenbaker Papers, file: MG 01/XII/A/270, Correspondence with Field Marshall M.A. Khan, 1960–61.
22 Venkatachar to Ministry of Indian External Affairs, Subject: Annual Political Report for the Year 1959, Ottawa, 25 February 1960, National Archives of India (NAI), file F.4(2)-P/60/A-59.
23 Nehru to Pearson, 17 June 1963, LAC, RG 25, vol. 5034, file 1617-40-pt.5.
24 CANDELNY to DEA, D-1297, 30 September 1963, LAC, RG 25, vol. 10555, file 20-1-2-PAK-pt.1.
25 Memorandum – Summary of conversation between the Prime Minister and Z.A. Bhutto, 1 October 1963, LAC, RG 25, vol. 10555, file 20-1-2-PAK-pt.1.
26 Robert Bothwell, "The Further Shore: Canada and Vietnam," *International Journal* 56 (2000–01): 107.
27 Rogers to USSEA, 19 March 1965, LAC, RG 25, vol. 10098, file 20-1-2-India-pt.2.

28 Michener to DEA, D-298, 23 March 1965, LAC, Pearson Papers, vol. 279, file 845/I41V666.
29 Singh to Martin, 30 May 1965, NAI, Indian MEA, AMS, 1965.
30 L.K. Jha to C.S. Jha, 21 April 1965, NAI, file 315-Dir., AMS, 1965.
31 Visit of Prime Minister Shastri, Briefing Book, LAC, RG 25, vol. 3494, file 18-1-H-IND-1965.
32 Menzies to Robinson, 4 June 1965, LAC, RG 25, vol. 10417, file 27-20-5-India-pt.2.
33 Martin to Pearson, 16 August 1965, LAC, Pearson Papers, vol. 264, file 802/I39.
34 Menzies to Robinson, 4 June 1965, LAC, RG 25, vol. 10417, file 27-20-5-India-pt.2/.
35 Quoted in Bothwell, "Further Shore," 108–9.
36 Hadwen to Cadieux, 8 May 1965, LAC, Paul Martin Papers, vol. 225, file 225-4.
37 Ibid.
38 Martin to Pearson, 30 April 1965, LAC, Pearson Papers, vol. 275, file 840, I39.
39 Cadieux to SSEA, 9 September 1965, LAC, RG 25, vol. 10121, file 21-13-UMOGIP-pt.1.1.
40 Cabinet Conclusions, 8 September 1965, LAC, RG 2, vol. 6271.
41 Paul Martin. *A Very Public Life*, vol. 2 (Toronto: Deneau, 1985), 492.
42 Record of Cabinet Decision, Meeting of 27 September 1965, LAC, RG 25, vol. 10121, file 21-13-UMOGIP-pt.1.1.
43 Memorandum to the Cabinet, 24 September 1965, LAC, RG 25, vol. 10121, file 21-13-UMOGIP-pt.1.2.
44 Cole to Commonwealth Division, 12 January 1966, LAC, RG 25, vol. 10055, file 20-1-2-PAK-pt 1.1.
45 Ibid.
46 Weld to DEA, D-448, 12 August 1966, LAC, RG 25, vol. 10055, file 20-1-2-Pak-pt.1.2.
47 DEA to Rawalpindi, K-397, 19 September 1966, LAC, RG 25, vol. 10055, file 20-1-2-Pak-pt.1.2.
48 Martin to Pearson, 29 July 1966, LAC, Martin Papers, vol. 225, file 225-4 Commonwealth 1965–67.
49 Ibid.
50 Martin to Pearson, 11 July 1966, LAC, RG 25, vol. 10098, file 20-1-2 India-pt.2.
51 Pearson to Gandhi, 2 August 1966, LAC, RG 25, vol. 10098, file 20-1-2 India-pt.2.
52 Martin to Pearson, 29 July 1966, LAC, Martin Papers, vol. 225, file 225-4 Commonwealth 1965–67.
53 Robert Bothwell, *Nucleus: The History of Atomic Energy of Canada Limited* (Toronto: University of Toronto Press, 1988), 365–66.
54 Cadieux to Martin, 4 November 1966, LAC, Martin Papers, vol. 225, file 225-4 Commonwealth 1965–67.
55 Cabinet Conclusions, 10 November 1966, LAC, RG 2, vol. 6321.
56 Department of Trade and Commerce News Release 24/67, 28 February 1967, LAC, RG 20, vol. 1672, file 3-51-1-pt.2.
57 George to DEA, D-1186, 5 April 1968, LAC, RG 25, vol. 10099, file 20-1-2-India-pt.4.

58 George to DEA, D-1187, 6 April 1968, LAC, RG 25, vol. 10099, file 20-1-2-India-pt.4.
59 Bothwell, "Further Shore," 104.
60 See Touhey, *Conflicting Visions*, chap. 10.

Isabel Campbell

13 Pearson's Promises and the NATO Nuclear Dilemma

This chapter traces the key changes and ambiguities in Lester Pearson's views on nuclear weapons from the moment the first atomic bomb exploded in 1945, when he was a senior diplomat, until 1968, when he stepped down as prime minister in the era of détente. Pearson and other leaders faced difficult dilemmas, stemming from the UN's failures and NATO's acrimonious disputes over strategic needs and nuclear weapons. Both John Diefenbaker and Lester Pearson could offer astute, sophisticated strategic judgments, but neither delivered decisive leadership on alliance, defence, and nuclear issues during their terms as prime minister. Similarly, while Pearson lacked Pierre Trudeau's charisma, he, too, performed sub rosa and wobbly pirouettes on nuclear weapons and alliance commitments.

Given his diplomatic training, Pearson scrutinized all aspects of any issue: the atomic bomb was no exception. Canada had supported its development during the Second World War and Pearson took an intense interest in its effect on postwar peace and security. In late 1945, fearing an arms race, he idealistically advocated UN control of atomic weapons, yet he found American and Soviet negotiators inflexible and so his diplomacy achieved little.[1] Pearson was already mired in contradictions for while he endorsed UN control, Canada's defence policy promoted American nuclear deterrence.[2] These two clashing and intertwining threads – the diplomatic push for UN control and Canada's reliance upon American atomic weapons for its security – created contradictions in foreign and defence policies in the years ahead. In November 1949, Pearson (now secretary of state for external affairs) neatly summed up the situation:

> We do not trust the Russians enough to agree to destroy our atomic weapons ... until we are in a position to satisfy ourselves, by international inspection and control of their facilities, that they do not secretly stockpile atomic bombs. The Russians, for their part, are not willing to entrust to an international atomic development authority, which they claim would be under Anglo-American domination.[3]

By this time, the Soviets had exploded an atomic weapon and the nuclear arms race had begun.

Although Pearson's speech implied he was in charge of NATO and nuclear weapons, Canada had no atomic weapons and a limited voice in negotiations. His conflation of American, NATO, and his own views fostered a powerful myth of alliance, solidarity, and personal influence while masking bitter allied disputes, Canada's lack of power, and his own inner qualms. As the alliance lacked conventional force, he participated in discussions in 1955 leading to the adoption of massive retaliation and calling for members to arm their forces with American nuclear weapons.[4] Yet the subsequent growth in strategic and tactical nuclear weapons troubled him. To counter NATO's nuclear focus, he pushed for a North Atlantic community of nations with close economic and political ties in the "Three Wise Men" report of 1956. His confident public addresses concealed growing private doubts about NATO's future even as a limited military pact.[5] The Suez Crisis later that year exposed British and French arrogance and bred fears that the United States might abandon Europe. In its aftermath, France assembled its own atomic arsenal and refused American nuclear weapons, while the European Economic Community (EEC) adopted high tariffs, blocking American, British, and Canadian trading efforts.[6] When Diefenbaker took power in June 1957, Canadian influence, never great, had waned, and NATO faced a decade of volatile disputes ahead.

To support massive retaliation and to reassure European allies, American general Lauris Norstad, supreme allied commander Europe (SACEUR), asked Diefenbaker's recently elected Progressive Conservative government to acquire nuclear-armed aircraft for a new strike and reconnaissance role and Honest John surface-to-surface missiles for Canada's army brigade in Europe. After an initial refusal, a reluctant cabinet opted in June 1959 to replace eight Sabre squadrons with Lockheed F-104G Starfighters to fulfill the offensive atomic air role.[7] In 1960, Canada agreed to procure six Honest John launchers.[8] When Defence Minister George Pearkes announced the new role for Canada's air division in Europe in July 1959, over the course of several days in the House of Commons, Pearson (now leader of the Opposition) debated the pros and cons of nuclear arms for Canadian forces in light of the overlapping complexities in nuclear strategy and alliance politics. He understood that "if the Canadian forces were deprived of these weapons ... their morale could hardly be expected to remain very high if they were serving alongside NATO forces which had these tactical nuclear weapons."[9] This common-sense argument likely explained why Canadian public opinion favoured access to nuclear weapons.[10] Some, like journalist Peter C. Newman, insisted that Canadian forces must have nuclear weapons or withdraw from Europe as their allies and enemies would have them too.[11] However, Pearson's outlook was never that stark or that simple.

Instead, Pearson explored meandering and contradictory ideas. Who, he wondered, would control these nuclear weapons: Canada or the United States? Because Canada's defence contributions seemed "very often to be ignored or merely lumped with the British or American effort," he insisted that nuclear weapons "must be under Canadian control and operation" for reasons of national prestige and influence and to counteract Anglo-American nuclear dominance in the alliance.[12] Dependence upon nuclear arms damaged cohesion, he argued, observing that "the stronger the deterrent" the less incentive there was for the European allies to develop the conventional forces needed for "limited war."[13] General Maxwell Taylor had just resigned as army chief to protest President Dwight Eisenhower's massive retaliation strategy and to promote conventional forces and flexible response. Pearson was aware of these objections and new concepts, and he pushed for a reassessment of alliance strategy.[14] Thus, during parliamentary debate in early July 1959, the Liberal leader appeared to accept Progressive Conservative proposals to give Canadian forces nuclear arms, although he insisted upon national control of the weapons and protested the strategy and the lack of conventional forces that had created this requirement. Given his pragmatism, he undoubtedly realized that Canada alone could not alter these factors.

By 1961, Pearson's views transformed. Ottawa should promote disarmament and economic assistance to developing states for "if she became a nuclear power" Canada "would have far less influence and authority at the United Nations than she has had in the past."[15] Now he called for nuclear weapons for NATO forces under alliance, not American, control.[16] Although he must have realized that his proposal contravened American law, he insisted: "I see no military security in national defence alone; only in *collective defence* with *collective forces* under *collective control*."[17] He had come a long way from his 1959 insistence upon Canadian control. If some perceived idealism in his disarmament stand, others sensed political ambition in his complicated attempts to satisfy opposing views. Although he stressed NATO's need for conventional strength, he gave no credit to Diefenbaker, who had recently increased forces in Europe in reaction to the Berlin Crisis. Over the next year, Diefenbaker struggled to win a minority election and to hold his cabinet together in face of the 1962 Cuban Missile Crisis and profound disagreements over nuclear weapons, which delayed negotiations with the Americans.[18]

Pearson watched for a chance to defeat Diefenbaker while alliance difficulties mounted. In December 1962, after cancelling the Skybolt nuclear missile promised to Britain, US president John F. Kennedy met with Prime Minister Harold Macmillan at Nassau to negotiate giving the British submarines American Polaris nuclear missiles as compensation. Although Washington spun this decision as part of a new NATO multilateral (nuclear) force (MLF), Macmillan trumpeted the pact's bilateral nature, provoking European ire over its Anglo-American nuclear exclusiveness.[19] Partly as a result, in January 1963 French president Charles De Gaulle angrily vetoed Britain's entry into the EEC and struck a friendship pact with West Germany. The MLF was intended to discourage independent European nuclear forces, but American proposals, especially a Kennedy initiative for nuclear-armed naval surface forces, created havoc. Many agreed with a German newspaper's assessment that such MLF surface forces were "swimming nuclear coffins." Worse, American satirical singer-songwriter Thomas Lehrer mocked the MLF in a lullaby that warned "one of the fingers on the button will be German" and hoped Brezhnev would be "half as scared as I."[20]

Ignoring the widespread protests against these American initiatives, Liberal defence critic Paul Hellyer returned from a NATO parliamentary conference in December 1962 to tell Pearson that Canada was almost a "laughing stock" for failing to honour its nuclear commitments.[21] Pearson was already reconsidering his nuclear stand when Norstad paid a farewell visit to Ottawa on 3 January 1963 and pronounced that, by failing to negotiate for access to nuclear weapons, Canada was failing to fulfill its NATO commitments.[22] Pearson believed that Progressive Conservatives had hesitated too long. He shocked his own party on 12 January by announcing that, if elected, he would "equip our forces with nuclear weapons under joint control with the US and *afterwards* discuss with our allies" a more realistic defence role without these weapons.[23] This public address was widely (and incorrectly) interpreted as a sudden reversal on nuclear issues, and many Liberals were dismayed.

Party insider Tom Kent had advised Pearson to negotiate first and to accept nuclear weapons only if a different role could not be obtained.[24] Kent thought Pearson had bungled matters, but he believed Pearson's misleading statement that "to reject nuclear weapons of all kinds [was] to withdraw from the alliance."[25] This was untrue as Denmark, Norway, and Portugal remained firm members of the alliance while refusing nuclear arms: Canada could have done the same.[26] Where was Pearson's 1959 recognition that supporting American nuclear dominance might injure cohesion, widening the chasms among the allies rather than narrowing them? The revised nuclear stand lost him modest support in the subsequent election. While public opinion backed nuclear weapons, some considered his promise to honour Canada's commitment to acquire access to nuclear weapons and then negotiate his way out of nuclear roles a poor election platform.[27] Pearson's assessment of his decision, however, rings true:

> We were members of NATO. NATO had an arsenal of nuclear weapons for collective defence, even if these were under American control. These weapons formed a part of NATO strategy. We had accepted that strategy and hence accepted responsibility for the use of nuclear weapons as a part of that strategy. Even more, we supplied most of the uranium to make these nuclear bombs. If we were immoral, we had been immoral from the beginning.[28]

While his anti-nuclear arguments had drawn upon a sincere, idealistic concern over the proliferation of nuclear arms, Pearson's stand had never been doctrinaire; rather, his consideration of every side of the question produced paradoxical inconsistencies, and his attempt to claim high moral ground by restoring Canada's international reputation and its commitments lost its shine, appearing to be a politically motivated reversal.

On 25 January 1963, Diefenbaker rose in the House of Commons to counter Pearson's new nuclear stand and to justify his own delays in negotiating nuclear weapons agreements: "Delivery of the F-104G has commenced, but the strike reconnaissance role has been placed under doubt by the recent Nassau declaration concerning nuclear arms." He suggested re-evaluating allied defence plans at the forthcoming NATO meetings in Ottawa in May.[29] Although mired in indecision, Diefenbaker clearly grasped the strategic situation and the path ahead. He was correct that the Nassau decision to assign Polaris missiles to a multilateral submarine force (as well as US flexible response initiatives) had altered the strategic requirement for the Canadian Starfighters, but his words fell on deaf ears. A week later, Pearson disputed Diefenbaker's interpretations, chiding him for alleged inaccuracies and concluding that the prime minister had either released confidential information or lied – a reference to Diefenbaker's additional revelations about secret talks with the Americans on nuclear warheads for air defence systems in Canada.[30] The State Department, outraged by Diefenbaker's indiscretion and delays, had issued a press release belittling ongoing discussions as merely exploratory. At the same time, it stated that Diefenbaker was wrong about Nassau.[31] However, the Polaris missiles provided a *second strike* capability that changed NATO's strategic picture. This crucial capability rendered tactical nuclear forces, including the RCAF's strike and reconnaissance roles, less relevant.

A classified defence analysis endorsed Diefenbaker's argument. It also explained that prior NATO thinking assumed that conventional forces and tactical nuclear weapons were interchangeable. Now some strategists judged that tactical nuclear weapons might lead to strategic escalation and so might be useless in minor confrontations or in the early days of a war.[32] Given this operational analysis, Diefenbaker's hesitations made sense. Canadian diplomats observed that General

Lyman Lemnitzer, the new SACEUR, would not likely admit the nuclear-armed air division was ineffective despite its obvious vulnerability.[33] By contrast, Polaris-equipped nuclear submarines could lurk undetected under ocean layers, launching strikes at vulnerable targets.

The Americans, exasperated by Canadian wavering, were oblivious to the allied strategic and operational confusion that they had created. Given a new strategic situation and changing NATO plans, Canada should have re-evaluated its needs before completing nuclear negotiations. Diefenbaker was right, but his government fell.

Pearson won a minority in the subsequent election. Briefing the incoming prime minister and Defence Minister Hellyer, Air Marshal Frank Miller (chairman of the Chiefs of Staff) contended that most alliance members favoured the proposed MLF. To counter separate European nuclear forces, he championed substantive Canadian participation in the MLF with continued American control over NATO nuclear weapons, concluding that Canadian participation would make this force palatable to others.[34] Pearson's subsequent visits to Macmillan and then Kennedy reinforced this questionable argument. All three leaders fretted about a break with France but hoped that the MLF proposal would counter European outrage.[35] In the unlikely event of a Soviet attack, Macmillan called for the immediate use of tactical nuclear weapons, while Pearson worried that even one atomic bomb would result in escalation. Clearly, neither prime minister understood precisely what flexible response entailed. Although Pearson doubted the MLF's operational viability, he promised Kennedy to make "good noises" about it, neglecting to mention his 1959 worries that Canada's nuclear decisions might reinforce American hegemony, damaging cohesion and the building of European conventional forces. He also seemed unaware that his own foreign visits reinforced the appearance of a privileged Anglo-Saxon inner circle.[36]

At the North Atlantic Council meetings in Ottawa in May 1963, Pearson welcomed American proposals to recast nuclear policies, disregarding European objections. Then he stood aside as Paul Martin, Canada's SSEA, angered the French by clumsily seeking to smooth Franco-American relations.[37] Though the French and the Americans regarded these interventions as impertinent, Martin continued and Pearson failed to stop him. In a futile measure to repair relations, the

North Atlantic Council assigned Britain's bomber force and three Polaris missiles to SACEUR.[38] Concurrently with the meetings, Canadians discovered that the MLF was associated with West German access to nuclear weapons when a CBC documentary, *The Balance of Terror*, juxtaposed Belsen death camp photos with footage of German troops discussing Bonn's plans to gain access to nuclear weapons.[39] Pearson immediately backed away from a public endorsement, declaring in Parliament that Canada would not participate in the MLF.[40] Less than three months after he took office, Pearson's first pirouette was complete, and he was about to discover why Diefenbaker had hesitated in his nuclear commitments.

George Drew, Canada's high commissioner in London, alarmed Pearson with reports that Canada was the only NATO nation with a Starfighter aircraft modified for a nuclear-only role. Lemnitzer was devising a new military concept that envisioned a period of several days to a month of conventional fighting if war came, and so Drew asked: Would Canadian fighters be "sitting ducks" while American and West German aircraft were conducting conventional operations?[41] He urged Pearson to adopt a dual conventional-nuclear role and also questioned the value of the Honest Johns, which posed a danger to allies and enemies alike.[42] Soon after, Pearson met secretly with Lemnitzer to ask for a dual conventional-nuclear air role, but Lemnitzer hedged, warning of the high cost and difficult training involved.[43] Pearson had already set up a parliamentary special committee on defence in May 1963, but, in their testimony, Hellyer and the service chiefs defended tactical nuclear roles.[44] Several West German officials also argued that if Canada withdrew from the nuclear role, then West Germany would have to fill it.[45] The few criticisms of the nuclear role came from retired military personnel and those with no stake in defending resources or political platforms.[46] Drew exhorted Pearson again, sending him an article announcing the conventional pause and reiterating warnings about the nuclear-only role.

Soon after, Paul Martin advised NATO that Canada was reviewing its defence policy and would likely adjust its air force contribution in Europe. However, the Department of External Affairs and the Department of Defence quarrelled over the wording of the subsequent announcement. The DEA's draft declared that, "with SACEUR's concurrence," two squadrons of aircraft would be transferred from France to West

Germany. These two, plus four other squadrons in Germany, would have a dual capability strike role. Two remaining RCAF squadrons in France would carry conventional arms only for reconnaissance and ground attack.[47] Air Marshal Miller protested the phrase "SACEUR's concurrence" because Lemnitzer might object that he had merely been consulted. Miller preferred "the Canadian government intends" reducing the aircraft committed to SACEUR from 144 to eighty-eight, as a means of evaluating allied reactions.[48] Cabinet implemented the necessary changes, but the DEA's continued desire for SACEUR's approval impeded future negotiating efforts, impinged on Canada's sovereign rights, and put Lemnitzer in an awkward spot. If he endorsed Canada's cuts, how could he press other allies to fulfill their goals?

Drew had also fretted over public reaction to German access to nuclear arms, a possibility many called "madness." Too rushed to read Drew's letter carefully, Pearson merely agreed that it was folly to give Germans nuclear weapons – which was not the point.[49] Many Canadian and other anti-nuclear activists wrote to the prime minister, framing objections to the MLF by linking German militarism with the perils of atomic weapons. Pearson avoided this controversial issue, ignored most of his protest mail, and left it to his staff to respond vaguely about Canada's refusal to back the MLF. Some anti-nuclear advocates praised this measure, but most criticized Ottawa's agreements with Washington.[50] Overworked in September 1964, Pearson relied upon Hellyer to explain government plans to reduce its nuclear role.[51]

Yet, behind the scenes, Pearson tightly controlled the defence portfolio, ordering a complete rewrite of Hellyer's draft *White Paper on Defence* in February 1964. With specific measures to strengthen conventional forces, including weapon systems with lead times of eight to ten years, Hellyer had tried to produce a "nice, new, shining defence policy all neatly put together and packaged for the next ten years."[52] An appalled Pearson opposed the specifics, demanded versatility, and suggested that, in time, Canadian forces in Europe could be removed altogether or used elsewhere. Only months before, the prime minister had reassured West Germany's foreign minister that Canada would not pull back its forces as a result of its defence review.[53] Thus, the White Paper had to be sufficiently vague to allow forces to be withdrawn, cut, or reassigned while reassuring allies of their continued presence. Pearson's practice of placating NATO leaders, combined with internal directions to pursue different options, impeded coherent defence planning. Hellyer patiently noted that "the *White Paper* was to open the door to re-negotiation of Canada's defence commitments."[54]

Under Pearson, Canada's military leaders did exactly that, successfully reducing the air contribution and secretly exploring other changes in the land role. The final White Paper directed acquiring aircraft capable of undertaking roles "from ground attack to air surveillance" in close collaboration with Canada's army brigade. The brigade, protecting a vulnerable point in West Germany, would stay due to its importance to NATO solidarity.[55] Two brigades in Canada would train for mobile service and rotation to Europe; another brigade would be air-portable. Pearson wisely left it to Hellyer to implement this controversial unification proposal. Savouring the limelight, Hellyer defended his modernization by declaring Canada's military "the best dressed, best fed, best paid but poorest equipped military force in the world."[56]

Ignoring these controversies, Pearson engaged closely with UN and selected defence matters. For example, while the White Paper was being finalized, and as Michael Carroll, Adam Chapnick, and Greg Donaghy discuss in Chapters 2, 3, and 4, respectively (this volume), Pearson sent Canadian forces to Cyprus under UN auspices, dispatching an advance party before receiving parliamentary approval.[57] That operational success, averting a civil war between NATO partners Turkey and Greece, reinforced Pearson's and Hellyer's notions about strategic mobility and flexibility. In the short term, the *White Paper on Defence* justified organizational reforms to reduce personnel and to increase expenditures on equipment, allowing the brigade to improve its firepower and ground mobility. As these improved defence capabilities were especially critical to West German security, Pearson wooed Chancellor Ludwig Erhard in June 1964. Together, they issued a joint communiqué stressing the importance of Western military strength combined with détente measures that might lead to peaceful German reunification.[58] Yet such modest Canadian efforts paled against American flash.

In December 1964, McNamara grabbed headlines at the NATO meeting by announcing more than eight hundred intercontinental ballistic missiles for the protection of Europe, more than one hundred Polaris missiles, and hundreds of bombers. Hellyer complained that these statements made him wonder "How much of our effort should be put into nuclear strike forces for Allied Command Europe if we are told their value is marginal?"[59] That was a question that Pearson and Hellyer should have asked in early 1963. Pearson's weariness and indecision were evident by early 1965.[60] In a draft of a speech he did not deliver, he proposed reducing expenditure on Canadian forces and NATO in order to offer defence aid to emerging countries like Kenya, Zambia, and Nigeria. "What is the minimum force we should leave in Europe?" he wondered.[61] This line of thinking was critical for, as several chapters in this volume attest, by the 1960s, with the emergence of the Third World and decolonization, Pearson's focus turned increasingly to the Middle East, Asia, and Africa. Western Europe had recovered economically and Central Europe seemed stable and therefore less important than it had been before. Canada could cut defence, reducing its expensive voluntary forces while improving social programs. As a result of these trends, in February, Pearson alarmed Canada's allies by asking the Europeans to defend their side of the Atlantic, leaving North American forces on the other side, supported only by the alliance clause for mutual assistance in the event of an attack.[62] These words strained cabinet relationships – already frayed, as Greg Donaghy notes (Chapter 4, this volume), by Martin's close diplomatic engagement in American affairs in Vietnam. Some cabinet members, including the francophones, remained unhappy with Canada's continued nuclear role. When Finance Minister Walter Gordon protested American dominance in the alliance, Pearson agreed with him, but he was not ready to make a firm stand.[63]

At the May 1965 NATO meetings, McNamara shocked the allies again, tossing agreed force goals aside for new efficient mobile forces. The West Germans protested this move and the shift to conventional defence,[64] but Hellyer seized upon this mobile force concept to rationalize Canada's defence posture, apparently not comprehending that strategic mobility would be too costly to implement.[65] In 1965, Canadian forces established Mobile Command, leaving one mechanized brigade for rotation to Europe, two air-portable brigades for rapid deployment, and a newly formed airborne regiment. In May, Hellyer compelled a reluctant military to acquire CF-5 tactical aircraft despite Miller's warning that the aircraft did not support strategic mobility.[66] Pearson seemed uninvolved in defence details, but Canada's military leaders tried to implement his political guidance for new, flexible roles in Europe, while hampered by the DEA's fears of upsetting European allies, inadequate funding, and the procurement of equipment which the military leaders had advised against.

In late 1965, Miller asked Lemnitzer to assess the impact of withdrawing the brigade from Europe and removing the divisional reinforcement commitment. Unsurprisingly, Lemnitzer opposed these changes. Miller then asked about switching the brigade to a light air-portable role to reinforce NATO flanks rather than its current role along the intra-German border.[67] Lemnitzer refused to recommend the change as he was also facing American, British, and European cuts.[68]

International tensions fell. West German leaders pursued *Ostpolitik* – the normalization of relations with Eastern Europe, especially East Germany – and signed a nuclear non-proliferation treaty, but they insisted that North American forces stay close to the intra-German border as a security guarantee. These circumstances created even greater *political* significance for Canada's brigade role, but Canada's military leaders continued to explore alternatives, eventually negotiating a mobile force option on the flanks to replace the divisional reinforcement commitment.[69]

Meanwhile, Pearson did not stop Martin, who angered the Americans again by criticizing their doomed MLF proposals at a December 1965 NATO meeting in a misguided effort to woo France, a topic covered by Brendan Kelly (Chapter 14, this volume). By March 1966, when De Gaulle demanded that foreign forces leave French soil and withdrew French forces from NATO's integrated command, rumours of the decision had been circulating for months.[70] De Gaulle assured Lemnitzer of continued French military cooperation, but this measure did not satisfy Pearson.[71] At the Atlantic Awards dinner later that year he bitterly acknowledged that "we should have acted earlier." Trying to grope his way to a new concept, he pushed for "unifying political institutions." The Europeans were strong enough to have a "rightful share" in alliance policies, but "only de Gaulle ha[d] translated it into policy and action."[72]

Pearson told Martin and Hellyer that the Americans should replace one or two American divisions with European divisions, reducing US personnel to custodial teams to guard the nuclear weapons. Martin assessed Pearson's proposal as producing American "hostages in the event of war" – a phrase Pearson enthusiastically endorsed with a handwritten "yes." Canada might also cut its forces in Europe – presumably leaving a few hostages behind as well.[73] In July 1966, Pearson's cabinet approved cutting the air division down to four strike and two reconnaissance squadrons located on two bases in Germany, forecasting that the Europeans would assume more responsibility to "permit a gradual reduction, by agreement, in the level of North American military commitments in Europe."[74] Importantly, as Timothy Andrews Sayle concludes (Chapter 11, this volume), by this point Canadian relations with the Soviets had warmed, with large wheat sales and cultural exchanges. Thus, under Pearson, détente inched forward with plans to decrease Canadian forces in Europe – in parallel with the US over the next decade.

In December 1966, to resolve nuclear issues, NATO formed a nuclear planning group. While Pearson acknowledged that Canada would be one of seven NATO members serving on the committee for eighteen months, he argued that participation "in no way increase[d] Canada's involvement in nuclear matters" and refused to provide Parliament with details on Canada's withdrawal from nuclear roles.[75] The next summer, when cabinet secretly approved storing NATO nuclear anti-submarine weapons for US naval forces in Newfoundland, several ministers, including Walter Gordon and Jean Marchand, reminded the prime minister of his election promise to drop nuclear roles. Available cabinet records show no discussion of missile-carrying submarines operating off Canada's coasts or of the Soviet fishing fleet off Newfoundland and Labrador, which hindered detection of submarines. Rather than risk debate over why the Americans requested storage of these weapons on Canadian soil, Pearson merely assured his cabinet that it was not possible to get out of the commitment. The decision, belying Canada's changing political climate, was kept secret from Parliament and the public.[76]

By the mid-1960s, nuclear war seemed far-fetched and pressure built for Canada to seek alternative roles, such as the light mobile force to reinforce NATO's flanks or, as Michael Carroll notes (Chapter 2, this volume), service in peacekeeping missions elsewhere in the world. The Americans, British, and Europeans had reduced their forces near the intra-German border, but, as West German leaders noted, European forces remained close by. The Americans had an impressive airlift capability, but Canada's remained inadequate. Although building airlift forces was costly, in early 1967 New Democratic Party defence critic Andrew Brewin endorsed proposals for a "highly mobile" force that might be "far more important than the massive, tactical nuclear confrontation in Central Europe."[77] Members of Pearson's own cabinet, Walter Gordon, and new ministers Donald Macdonald, Jean Marchand, Gérard Pelletier, and Pierre Trudeau, also criticized the NATO commitment. Trudeau opposed the alliance's nuclear weapons policies while all considered neutralism as a viable option to increase Canadian independence from the United States.[78]

Ignoring these wider concerns, Pearson wrote to Martin and Hellyer, bitterly denouncing the "inflexibility of our position regarding Canadian forces in NATO." Given the problems in Vietnam, financial issues, and a declining threat in Europe, the United States and Britain planned to redeploy forces. Surely Canada could do the same. Martin agreed to reduce the air division and to terminate the nuclear role by the mid-1970s but insisted on maintaining the brigade and assigning mobile battalions to SACEUR's mobile force.[79] When cabinet convened on 1 June 1967, Joe Greene, the minister of agriculture, argued that "the European Economic Community had developed into a very tough and self-centred organization" while trade with the Soviet Union had grown "very considerably." He wondered whether "continued Canadian contribution in Europe through membership in NATO" was in the "national interest."[80] Other ministers insisted on a reappraisal of NATO membership. European capabilities had changed. The French launched their first ballistic missile submarine in March 1967. By the autumn, the British launched theirs, while the Americans and Soviets met to discuss parity of nuclear weapons and arms reductions.[81] Cabinet therefore directed a "gradual disengagement achieved through an improvement in East-West relations," or détente. The mechanized brigade would stay, while military leaders worked on a concept for assigning forces in Canada to Europe.

Martin, anticipating American pressure for costly increased Canadian peacekeeping activities in Vietnam, hoped that NATO would use American, British, and other cuts to negotiate Soviet reductions. Pearson did not support European withdrawal "when the future of peacekeeping operations looked particularly bleak," a reference to the evacuation of UNEF from Egypt – an issue covered by Maurice Jr. M. Labelle, Michael Carroll, and Adam Chapnick (Chapters 8, 2, and 3, respectively, this volume) – but warned that Canada would have to decide between becoming "completely non-committed" or remaining allied. Martin responded by trying to marshal cabinet support for NATO.[82] Gordon accompanied him to NATO meetings later in June but continued to demand cuts to Canada's forces in Europe. Soon after, Dalton Camp, a Progressive Conservative MP, endorsed shifting defence funds to foreign aid. A small group in his party agreed with him as Camp pushed for disarmament and non-proliferation.[83]

During the summer of 1967, Canada's military leaders explored possible future roles. Lemnitzer's new defence posture for post-1972 recommended more mobile reserves in Europe, strategic reserves in home countries, and fewer units at the intra-German border. While reducing the controversial nuclear strike role, he called for additional close air support of ground forces. Canada's vice chief of the defence staff, Air Marshal Frederick Sharp, therefore proposed a switch to a close air support role in Europe, while making two Canadian-based brigades air-portable for peacekeeping duties. As the tank-heavy brigade in Europe and its replacement in Canada were not air-portable, Sharp recommended that Canada pursue a NATO mobile reserve role, eliminating the need to replace the tanks and giving the two mechanized brigades air mobility. These recommendations, dependent upon SACEUR plans and expensive new equipment, would have allowed the brigade to withdraw from the intra-German border, but Hellyer did not present them to cabinet.[84]

Instead, on 12 September, Hellyer proposed keeping the mechanized brigade in Europe and substituting the air portable brigade in Canada (earmarked for SACEUR's mobile command) for the divisional commitment. The air division would be reduced to four squadrons. Martin supported Hellyer's case, arguing that the present effort increased Canada's influence at little cost. NATO could not decrease forces any further because the Soviets refused to cut their forces in Europe until Vietnam was resolved. Gordon demanded further cuts, but Pearson refused, insisting that the present contribution was "the minimum price for club membership." Without Canada's military contributions, NATO might become "dominated by the United States and Germany, with the United Kingdom acting as a junior partner and France withdrawing completely." He wearily agreed to review the matter further in December.[85] After cabinet approved Hellyer's force recommendations for the next four years, Pearson asked retired diplomat Norman Robertson to review Canadian foreign policy.[86]

In the meantime, faced with inflationary pressures, the new defence minister, Léo Cadieux, and military leaders struggled to stay within the budget and proposed closing bases and other drastic measures to cut costs, while studying Sharp's expensive new proposals.[87] Though this planning occurred in secret, rumours made their way to the opposition parties. T.C. Douglas, head of the New Democratic Party, proposed bringing Canada's European forces home and shifting defence funds to Medicare. When pressed by Douglas in Parliament in December 1967, Pearson denied any "radical" changes to military roles. Progressive Conservative MP Davie Fulton pressed again, asking if Canada might withdraw any NATO components unilaterally. Pearson's answer – that decisions "should be discussed and if possible agreed to" – hinted at future changes ahead.[88] Then, he announced his retirement from politics.

Days later, Cadieux proclaimed NATO's approval of flexible response. After 1968, Canada would reduce air division numbers further and substitute one air-portable brigade (which might be used for other requirements) for the two brigades in Canada earmarked for NATO. Cadieux also revealed the participation of a destroyer in the multilateral Standing Naval Force Atlantic. While former Progressive Conservative defence minister Douglas Harkness bemoaned these reductions, pointing to NATO's call for firm deterrence in the face of Soviet naval advances in the Mediterranean, Brewin endorsed the plans. Under questioning, Cadieux admitted that the brigade in Europe would cut its numbers, but he failed to mention Canada's internal decision to eliminate two of the four Honest John launchers.[89]

Pearson was still prime minister in February 1968 when Cadieux initiated a study for the reduction, withdrawal, or major change in Canada's European forces over the next four years.[90] Major General Jean Allard, chief of the defence staff, hesitated to recommend an expensive mobile role given consideration of withdrawal,[91] but once again Canadian military officers approached SACEUR for a brigade role on the flanks or as a mobile reserve to be co-located with air units.[92] Ross Campbell, Canada's ambassador to NATO, thought the proposal made sense,[93] but Basil Robinson at the DEA warned: "General Lemnitzer should not erroneously conclude that the Canadian Government has taken a firm decision on a change of role and a change of location."[94] After more diplomatic cautions, Canadian officers suggested that SACEUR study their proposals until they could be given firm guidance.[95] Lemnitzer reluctantly agreed to investigate the implications of assigning Canadian forces to a different command and moving boundaries.[96]

Canadian diplomats feared widening the chasms between Europe and North America, though arguably Pearson's nuclear decisions had done just that by enhancing American dominance. Canadians who attended the Atlantic Policy Advisory Group in April 1967 reported that Belgium objected to a non-proliferation treaty because it prolonged the United States' near monopoly over NATO's nuclear weapons. The dual-key nuclear system that Canada and others (including the Belgians) had adopted increased this perception. When some Europeans suggested concentrating upon conventional forces, leaving nuclear arms to the Americans, the Belgians proposed a European, an American, and a Canadian grouping, which, the Canadians pointed out, put Canada in an impossible, isolated position.[97] However, after much discussion, the NATO Council approved a revised *Report of the Council on the Future Tasks of the Alliance* in December 1967. It called for balancing force reductions and strengthening détente and German *Ostpolitik* while maintaining a defensive posture.[98] Canadians could count this report as a small triumph at the end of a decade of acrimony – a time when many people questioned NATO's very existence.[99]

During Pearson's tenure as prime minister, Canadian military leaders cut forces and secretly explored alternative NATO roles, including expensive air lift proposals. Because this planning remained secret, the Trudeau era seemed a grand departure. It was not. Pearson implemented air division changes and reductions, and his 1964 White Paper discussion points included the measures implemented by Trudeau. Pearson privately contemplated withdrawal from Europe, though, by September 1967, he had changed his mind on this point. It was his last pirouette. Cadieux, Allard, Sharp, and other military leaders implemented Pearson's suggestions – they had even unilaterally cut the two Honest John launchers – but budgetary and inflationary constraints coupled with inadequate equipment restricted the options. DEA's concerns and allied focus on intra-German defence also hampered military negotiations.[100] With the Czech Crisis in the summer of 1968, the opportune moment for reducing forces on the Central Front passed.[101]

NATO had achieved much since 1949, providing forums for strategic discussion, creating stability for economic growth, integrating the West Germans into Europe, and, finally, promoting détente. Pearson had contributed to these successes while turning his attention to unrest elsewhere in the world. However, by 1968 his long NATO association smacked of collusion in the nuclear arms race and Western elitism rather than world peace. His 1963 decision to negotiate access to American nuclear weapons exacerbated underlying alliance tensions, with Canada missing its chance to re-evaluate roles that changing strategy and plans had rendered almost irrelevant. Pearson was no more responsible for NATO's convoluted dynamics than was Diefenbaker, but neither PM provided decisive leadership. Pearson's wavering on nuclear and other issues rendered coherent defence planning impossible, while his insistence on secrecy impeded public debate on key issues. Trudeau would take up the gauntlet, implementing ideas that Pearson and Diefenbaker had considered, only to be stopped by firm cabinet opposition and allied outrage, the very factors against which his predecessors had also run aground.

Notes

Thanks to William Johnston, Matthew Trudgen, Katherine Morrow, the editors, and readers for helpful comments. The article reflects the author's opinions, not those of the Department of National Defence.

1 J.A. Munro and A.I. Inglis, "The Atomic Conference 1945 and the Pearson Memoirs," *International Journal* 29 (1973–74): 90–101; Albert Legault and Michel Fortmann, *The Diplomacy of Hope: Canada and Disarmament, 1945–1988* (Montreal and Kingston: McGill-Queen's University Press, 1992), 56–60.

2 Douglas Abbott, "Atomic Energy and National Defence" ca. February 1946, LAC, Douglas Abbott Papers, vol. 15, file 2.

3 House of Commons, *Debates*, 19 November 1949.

4 "Priorities within NATO. A digest of a memorandum prepared for ministers attending the NATO Council meeting," December 1955, DHH, 2002/17, 17, series 2, box 6, file 89. In May 1957, Pearson approved MC 14/2, which called for nuclear weapons to be the principal element in NATO's strategy.

5 Lester Pearson, *Mike: The Memoirs of the Right Honourable Lester B. Pearson*, vol. 2 (Toronto: University of Toronto Press, 1973), 90–97.

6 Isabel Campbell, *Unlikely Diplomats: The Canadian Brigade in Germany, 1951–64* (Vancouver: UBC Press, 2013), 80–82.

7 Cabinet Conclusions, 19 June 1959, LAC, RG 2.

8 Cabinet Defence Committee Record, 25 March 1960, DHH, 73/1223, file 2522.

9 House of Commons, *Debates*, 2 July 1959, 5358–59, 5414–45.

10 An early 1959 poll revealed that 46 percent supported nuclear weapons for Canadian forces, 20 percent were opposed, and 34 percent were undecided. See Patricia McMahon, *Essence of Indecision: Diefenbaker's Nuclear Policy, 1957–1963* (Montreal and Kingston: McGill-Queen's University Press, 2009), 92.

11 Peter Newman, "Canada's Final Agonizing Choice on Nuclear Arms," *Maclean's,* 17 December 1960, 14.
12 House of Commons, *Debates*, 2 July 1959, 5358–59.
13 Ibid., 3 July 1959, 5420.
14 Ibid., 2 July 1959, 5367.
15 Lester Pearson, "My Hopes for Peace," *United Church Observer*, 15 October 1961.
16 *Montreal Star,* 10 January 1961; *Montreal Gazette,* 10 January 1961; Liberal Party Rally, 1961, Queen's University Archives (QUA), Tom Kent Papers, box 6. Earlier, Pearson had promoted storing nuclear weapons for Canadian NORAD forces in House of Commons, *Debates,* 23 August 1958, 4012.
17 Pearson, "My Hopes for Peace." Emphasis in original.
18 See McMahon, *Essence of Indecision*.
19 Andrew Priest, *Kennedy, Johnson and NATO: Britain, America and the Dynamic of Alliance* (London: Routledge, 2006).
20 Thanks to Robert Bothwell, who brought these lyrics to my attention.
21 Tom Kent, *A Public Purpose: An Experience of Liberal Opposition and Canadian Government* (Montreal and Kingston: McGill-Queen's University Press, 1988), 188–89.
22 McKercher, *Camelot and Canada*; Lester Pearson, *Mike: The Memoir of the Right Honourable Lester B. Pearson*, vol. 3 (Toronto: University of Toronto Press, 1971), 71.
23 Kent, *Public Purpose*, 191, emphasis in original.
24 Kent, *Public Purpose*, 191.
25 Pearson, Statement, 21 February 1963, LAC, Pearson Papers, vol. 42, file Nuclear-Defence, 1956–63.
26 Iceland and Portugal rejected nuclear weapons on their soil, and Denmark refused weapons for its forces. Norway acquired Starfighter aircraft but ruled out a nuclear role in 1963. See Vojtech Mastny, Sven G. Holtsmark, and Andreas Wenger, eds., *War Plans and Alliances in the Cold War: Threat Perceptions in the East and West* (London: Routledge, 2006).
27 Kent, *Public Purpose,* 191–94; Pearson, *Mike*, 3:217.
28 Pearson, *Mike*, 3:71.
29 House of Commons, *Debates*, 25 January 1963, 3125–37.
30 Ibid., 31 January 1963, 3303.
31 The American Nassau analysis was accepted by Canadian historians. See Andrew Richter, *Avoiding Armageddon: Canadian Military Strategy and Nuclear Weapons, 1950–63* (Vancouver: UBC Press, 2002), 100–1; McKercher, *Camelot and Canada*.
32 Boulton to High Commissioner, 25 April 1963, LAC, George Drew Papers, vol. 400, file Correspondence and Memoranda, 1963.
33 J.H. Taylor and G. Ignatieff, "Immediate Canadian Defence Problems as They Affect NATO," ca. February 1963, LAC, Drew Papers, vol. 400, file Correspondence and Memoranda, 1963.
34 Miller to Pearson, 26 and 30 April 1963, LAC, Paul Hellyer Papers, vol. 74, file 13.

35 Drew's handwritten meeting notes, LAC, Drew Papers, vol. 400, file Correspondence January-March 1963. Telegram from Hyannis Port to Department of State, 11 May 1963, *Foreign Relations of the United States, 1961–1963, Western Europe and Canada*, 449, https://history.state.gov/historicaldocuments.

36 Although visiting Macmillan and Kennedy immediately upon taking office, Pearson delayed an autumn visit to De Gaulle for months.

37 Pearson to the NATO Ministerial Meeting, Ottawa, 22 May 1963, LAC, Pearson Papers, vol. 9; Greg Donaghy, *Grit: The Life and Politics of Paul Martin Sr.* (Vancouver: UBC Press, 2015), 224.

38 Legault and Fortmann, *Diplomacy of Hope*, 255. The US president retained a veto.

39 Bonn to DEA, 23 August 1963, LAC, RG 25, vol. 5406, file 10935-B-40-pt.7.

40 House of Commons, *Debates*, 7 June 1963, 790.

41 Drew to Pearson, 11 July 1963, LAC, Pearson Papers, vol. 7, file 23. Cabinet approvals did not indicate a sole nuclear role. See Cabinet Decisions, 19 June 1959, 2 July 1959, LAC, RG 2, vol. 2745. RCAF draft documents called for an aircraft capable of delivering conventional and nuclear weapons. See "Future Role and Re-equipment of No. 1 Air Division, RCAF," 21 January 1959, DHH, 73/1223, file 363.

42 Campbell, *Unlikely Diplomats*, 11, 165, 172–23, 176–77, 183.

43 Extract, report of General Lemnitzer's meeting with PM [Pearson], 23 July 1963, LAC, Drew Papers, vol. 400, file Correspondence, 1963.

44 House of Commons, Parliamentary Special Committee on Defence, *Minutes of Proceedings and Evidence*, 27 June 1963 (Ottawa: Queen's Printer, 1963).

45 House of Commons, Parliamentary Special Committee on Defence, *Minutes of Proceedings and Evidence, Confidential Supplement B*, 18 November 1963 (Ottawa: Queen's Printer, 1963).

46 Ibid., Testimony of Guy Simonds and Charles Foulkes, 17 and 22 October 1963. Simonds called the idea that troops were better supported with nuclear weapons "a complete hallucination."

47 Leaving a total of eight squadrons. The four CF-100 squadrons in Europe had disbanded; External Affairs, draft announcement, n.d. DHH, 73/1223, file 365.

48 Miller to Campbell, 31 January 1964 in DHH, 73/1223, file 118; and Dunlap to Minister, 20 November 1963, DHH, 73/1223, file 365.

49 Drew to Pearson, 8 October 1963 and Pearson to Drew, 14 October 1963, LAC, Drew Papers, vol. 74, file 9.

50 Correspondence files, LAC, Pearson Papers, vol. 273, file 832.6.

51 Groos to Pearson, 24 September 1964, and Pearson to Groos, 13 October 1964, LAC, Pearson Papers, vol. 273, file 832.6.

52 Kent to Pearson, 21 February 1964, QUA, Kent Papers, box 3, File Correspondence, February 1963.

53 Martin to Pearson, 16 May 1963, LAC, RG 25, vol. 5406, file 10935-B-40-pt.7.

54 Hellyer's handwritten note, emphasis in original, 15 February 1964, LAC, Hellyer Papers, vol. 74, file 5.

55 Canada, Department of National Defence, *White Paper on Defence* (Ottawa: Queen's Printer, 1964).

56 "A Business Approach to Defence," *Montreal Gazette*, 16 January 1965.
57 John Hilliker and Donald Barry, *Canada's Department of External Affairs: Coming of Age, 1946–1968* (Montreal and Kingston: McGill-Queen's University Press, 1995), 281–83.
58 Roy Rempel, *Counterweights: The Failure of Canada's German and European Policy, 1955–1995* (Montreal and Kingston: McGill-Queen's University Press, 1996), 42–43.
59 Report on NATO Ministerial Meeting, 16 December 1964, LAC, Hellyer Papers, vol. 1, file 86.
60 Kent, *Public Purpose*, 214.
61 Draft speech, 25 January 1965, LAC, Pearson Papers, vol. 7, file 21.
62 Lester Pearson, "Extracts from an Address to the Canadian Club of Ottawa, 10 February 1965," Department of External Affairs, *Statements and Speeches*, 65/3.
63 Donaghy, *Grit*, 224–25, 252–53.
64 Ingo Trauschweizer, *The Cold War US Army: Building Deterrence for Limited War* (Lawrence: University Press of Kansas, 2008), 172.
65 Lee to Westell, 12 April 1965, LAC, Hellyer Papers, vol. 74, file 6.
66 Miller to Hellyer, 7 May, 1965, LAC, Hellyer Papers, vol. 74, file 9.
67 Miller to Lemnitzer, 18 January 1966, DHH, 73/1223, file 2526A.
68 Lemnitzer to Frank, 22 February 1966, DHH, 73/1223, file 2526A. The Americans lobbied the British to keep forces in Germany, encouraging Bonn to make offset payments to London.
69 Sean Maloney, "Global Mobile II: The Development of Forces Mobile Command, 1965–1972," *The Army Doctrine and Training Bulletin* (2001): 7–23, emphasis added.
70 House of Commons *Debates*, 22 February 1966.
71 Pearson to Martin, 20 April 1966, LAC, Pearson Papers, vol. 9, file NATO Memoranda.
72 Address by Pearson to the Atlantic Union Award Dinner, 11 June 1966, LAC, Pearson Papers, vol. 9, file NATO Pearson Statement and Addresses, 1958–1966.
73 Pearson to Martin, 20 April 1966 and Martin to Pearson, 6 May 1966, LAC, Pearson Papers, vol. 9, file NATO Memoranda.
74 Cabinet Decision, 11 July 1966, DHH, 73/1223, file 2526A.
75 House of Commons, *Debates*, 15 December 1966, 11150–51. The Nuclear Planning Committee was open to all members of NATO, nuclear armed or not.
76 Cabinet Conclusions, 26 July 1967, LAC, RG 2; John Clearwater, *US Nuclear Weapons in Canada* (Toronto: Dundurn, 1999), 200.
77 House of Commons, *Debates*, 1 February 1967, 12546–49.
78 John English, *Just Watch Me: The Life of Pierre Elliott Trudeau* (Toronto: Knopf, 2009), 58–63.
79 Martin to Pearson, 6 May 1967, in LAC, Pearson Papers, vol. 9, file NATO Memoranda.
80 Cabinet Conclusions, 1 June 1967, LAC, RG 2.
81 Julian Lindley-French, *The North Atlantic Organization: The Enduring Alliance* (Brighton, UK: Routledge, 2015), 34–35.

82 Cabinet Conclusions, 1 June 1967, LAC, RG 2.

83 Thomas Hockin, "The Foreign Policy Review and Decision-making in Canada," in *Alliances and Illusions: Canada and the NATO-NORAD Question*, ed. Lewis Hertzman, John W. Warnock, and Thomas Hockin (Edmonton: Hurtig, 1969), 112–14.

84 Memorandum to CDS, 14 June 1967, DHH, 73/1223, file 2526A. CDS Jean Allard, Colonel Robert Raymont, and others supported this concept. See Ray Stouffer, *Swords, Clunks and Widowmakers: The Tumultuous Life of the RCAF's Original 1 Canadian Air Division* (Trenton: Royal Canadian Air Force, 2015), 156–57.

85 Cabinet Conclusions, 12 September 1967, LAC, RG 2.

86 Hilliker and Barry, *Canada's Department of External Affairs*, 407–10. Robertson's independent review, completed by the next spring, endorsed the current commitments.

87 Planning Guidance, 17 October 1967, DHH, 73/1223, file 1022.

88 House of Commons, *Debates*, 7 and 14 December 1967, 513, 5404.

89 House of Commons, *Debates*, 18 December 1967, 5520–21, 5528; Clearwater, *Canadian Nuclear Weapons*, 172–73.

90 Cadieux, *Policy Guidance, 1968/1974*, 8 February 1968, DHH, 73/1123, file 1022.

91 Allard to Minister, 14 February 1968, DHH, 73/1123, file 2531.

92 Allard to Lemnitzer, 14 February 1968, DHH, 73/1123, file 2531.

93 Campbell to Allard, 27 February 1967, DHH, 73/1123, file 2531.

94 Robinson to Allard, 21 February 1967, DHH, 73/1123, file 2531.

95 Allard to Wilson-Smith, 13 March 1968, DHH, 73/1123, file 2531.

96 SACEUR to CDS Canada, 21 April 1968, DHH, 73/1123, file 2531.

97 Report, 9th meeting of Atlantic Policy Advisory Group, 19–22 April 1967, 6 July 1967, DHH, 73/1223, file 2526A.

98 Helga Haftendorn, "The Harmel Report and Its Impact on German *Ostpolitik*," in *The Making of Detente: Eastern Europe and Western Europe in the Cold War, 1965–1975*, ed. Wilfried Lothe and Georges-Henri Soutou, 103–16 (New York: Routledge, 2008).

99 Hilliker and Barry, *Canada's Department of External Affairs*, 382–83; Robert Bothwell, *Alliance and Illusion: Canada and the World, 1945–1984* (Vancouver: UBC Press, 2007), 271–73, 275, 282, 333.

100 Cadieux, *Policy Guidance*, DHH, 73/1223, file 1022.

101 NATO Council endorsed balanced force reductions on 24–25 June 1968 just as Trudeau came to power and before the Soviets invaded Czechoslovakia.

Brendan Kelly

14 Pearson, France, and Quebec's International Personality

In 1963, confronting a dynamic new nationalism in Quebec, Lester Pearson's incoming government turned to France to strengthen Canadian unity. Ottawa promised French Canadians a foreign policy reflecting the country's bicultural reality in which relations with Paris would be as close as those with London and Washington. But in July 1967, as Canadians celebrated their nation's centenary, this dream turned nightmarish. While addressing a boisterous crowd from the balcony of Montreal's City Hall, French president Charles de Gaulle shouted the separatist rallying cry "Vive le Québec libre!" Prime Minister Pearson publicly declared de Gaulle's conduct "unacceptable," prompting his abrupt departure from Canada. What had been implicit for several years was now clear: France, embodied by de Gaulle, was renewing its kinship with Quebec and abetting its "freedom," a concept embracing everything from an improved place in Confederation to complete independence.

The provincial administrations of Jean Lesage and then Daniel Johnson welcomed France's support. Driven by the Quiet Revolution, Quebec's relationship with Paris allowed it to make a constitutional point: that a province could have an international legal personality, one traditionally associated with sovereign states. The minority Pearson government, weakened by crises and scandals, was ill-prepared to counter the combined assault of Quebec and an ostensibly friendly foreign power. Far from strengthening the nation, Canada's bizarre relationship with France by 1967 posed a serious threat to national unity. Vulnerable as the Pearson government was, two constants defined its response between 1963 and 1968 to the Quebec-France alliance: defending its constitutional prerogative in the field of foreign affairs, and crafting a foreign policy that represented the interests of both English and French Canadians. More specifically, the legal approach of the Department of External Affairs to Quebec's international ambitions set the tone for the Pearson government's response. The DEA made concessions on substance but resisted any on form since the form of Quebec's international activities mattered most in both international and constitutional law.

Lester Pearson was a late convert to the gospel of a bicultural foreign policy. The DEA he joined in 1928 was distinctly British in character. Many departmental luminaries, Pearson included, had been educated at Oxford, and, like most Canadians, they viewed the world through the prism of London and Washington, capitals to which "Mike" was posted early in his career. While there were senior French Canadians in the DEA, men like Jean Désy and Pierre Dupuy had a well-known chronic aversion to work at headquarters, the federal civil service being an exclusively unilingual institution. By 1941, the DEA boasted a coterie of promising young francophones, including Jean Chapdelaine, Jules Léger, and Marcel Cadieux. But in the East Block the only French they heard was what they spoke to each other. Pearson, as his biographer notes, found this situation neither "unusual" nor "deplorable."[1]

This attitude typified the widespread "cultural blindness in Ottawa," which, according to another historian, was "an unconscious expression of the English-Canadian view of Quebec as a land of happy (if slightly disloyal) peasants, notaries, and priests."[2] In 1954, six years after entering politics as secretary of state for external affairs, Pearson and Prime Minister Louis St-Laurent chose Léger as the DEA's first francophone under-secretary. Though the minister and his deputy were never close, the appointment shows that Pearson was becoming more attuned to Quebec, whose massive support of the Liberal Party ensured its dominance. He also took under his wing Jean Lesage, a new francophone member of cabinet, and invited him to write to him in French, a language Pearson cursed himself for never having learned.[3] As secretary of state for external affairs (SSEA) in the 1950s, however, his main focus lay abroad, primarily Britain and the British Commonwealth, the United States, and the Western alliance in the Cold

War. In 1956, he helped to defuse the Suez Crisis. But while Britain, one of its culprits, emerged chastened from the experience, the equally culpable France, feeling betrayed by its friends, increasingly became the enfant terrible of the North Atlantic Treaty Organization. Such cracks in Western solidarity were not Pearson's to repair as the Liberals were replaced by John Diefenbaker's Progressive Conservatives in June 1957.

When Pearson came to power in 1963, everything had changed. As prime minister, his first priority was national unity and that meant Quebec, where the federal Liberals had failed to re-establish their supremacy. Since 1960, under Premier Lesage, who had left Ottawa for Quebec City two years before, the clerical, conservative, and defensive nationalism of the late Maurice Duplessis's Union Nationale was giving way to the secular, liberal, and aggressive nationalism of the Quiet Revolution. The new regime insisted that French Canadians be masters of their destiny. Quebec nationalized its English-owned electricity companies, wrested control of health and education from the Roman Catholic Church, and greatly increased budgets and bureaucracies to support these and other initiatives. Federal-provincial relations were also affected. Reflecting a wider trend towards decentralization as Canada's provinces reacted to Ottawa's wartime centralization, Quebec, no longer content simply to defend its autonomy, wished to expand it. In this heady atmosphere, token gestures such as the Diefenbaker government's bilingual federal cheques, simultaneous translation in the House of Commons, and a $300,000 development assistance program for French-speaking Africa did not appease the province. In an age of crumbling empires and decolonization, some Quebeckers called for secession. In 1963, a violent minority, the Front de libération du Québec, began detonating bombs to achieve it.

Unversed though he was in Quebec culture, society, and politics, Pearson knew that his government must act. It made good on its promise in 1962 to establish a Royal Commission on Bilingualism and Biculturalism, it promoted a formula to amend and thus to patriate the country's nearly century-old Constitution, and it pursued closer relations with France. After lobbying by the DEA's ailing under-secretary, Norman Robertson, in 1964 the prime minister chose as head of the department Marcel Cadieux, a key architect of the Pearson government's response to Quebec's attempt to forge closer relations with France. DEA manoeuvres under Cadieux's direction sought to define the legal parameters of the province's international activities. A proud Canadian and Quebecker, the tough new deputy minister welcomed as overdue the Pearson government's commitment to a less Anglocentric foreign policy. In words that seem ironic today, Cadieux once rhapsodized that he loved France more than any foreign country.[4] His friend, Jules Léger, an even greater Francophile, became Canada's ambassador to Paris in the same year.[5] Both appointments addressed the widespread malaise among the DEA's francophones (detected by the French Embassy in Ottawa in late 1963) that had, in part, been created by the departure of some federal civil servants for Quebec's expanding bureaucracy.[6] Not surprisingly, Pearson entrusted the France file to his SSEA, Paul Martin. Of French descent on his mother's side, Martin could speak the language. However, as France's ambassador to Canada, Raymond Bousquet, cynically remarked, it was only after the Liberals had returned to power that Martin suddenly embraced his roots and began making speeches in somewhat ungrammatical French.[7] But he was genuinely enthusiastic about the new policy and began courting his French counterpart, the suave Maurice Couve de Murville.

Strengthening Canada's relations with France presented a challenge. Led by the imperious de Gaulle, Paris pursued an independent policy of *grandeur*. The motivation was clear: France's international prestige had never recovered from its ignominious defeat in 1940, the Suez debacle, and the postwar loss of its colonial empire. *Grandeur*, therefore, would restore the country's place in the sun. To this end, de Gaulle distanced France from its traditional "Anglo-Saxon" allies, replacing, for example, what he saw as its failed link to Britain with a close relationship with West Germany. He was sceptical of the United Nations and suspicious of NATO, preferring multilateral organizations like the European Common Market, which he could dominate. De Gaulle upheld the nation-state – not a supra-national one – as the highest ideal, opposed the concept of two implacably hostile Cold War blocs, and above all resisted anything that smacked of American hegemony.[8]

The contrast between Gaullism and Pearsonianism – which elevated multilateralism almost to a dogma – was stark. As Adam Chapnick and Isabel Campbell make clear (Chapters 3 and 13, respectively, this volume), Pearson and Martin felt most at home in the UN General Assembly or among friends in the North Atlantic Council, postwar Canadian foreign policy having been defined by those venerable bodies. Nor were these men inclined to criticize the United States, to which Canada was intricately linked. Rather, they opted to repair harm done to Canadian-American relations by Diefenbaker. As Greg Donaghy asserts (Chapter 4, this volume), Martin even considered the possibility that Canada might foster a dialogue between Washington and Paris. While the idea met with polite American and French interest, it was not taken seriously. Pearson was apprehensive about visiting France and its embassy knew it, reporting that this Canadian believer in an "Atlantic community" dreaded the prospect of a *tour d'horizon* with de Gaulle.[9] Their eventual encounter in the Elysée Palace in January 1964, on the surface, was satisfactory. De Gaulle expressed support for Canada-France rapprochement and denied any intention of intervening in Canadian affairs. But his worldview did not appeal to Pearson, who, days later, remarked at the White House that the general was confident, inflexible, and a century-and-a-half out of date.[10]

From the start the Pearson government's new relationship with France was hobbled by problems. Ottawa bought American-made instead of French-made aircraft for Trans-Canada Airlines. It also sold uranium with no strings attached to both London and Washington but not to Paris, which was building up its own nuclear arsenal. Making these early problems especially vexing was the increasing closeness between France and Quebec. Their reconciliation initially seemed innocent enough. De Gaulle's global vision predisposed his administration to favour this island of French speakers. Quebec naturally looked to the former metropole for inspiration in building its state. In 1961, the Lesage government opened a Maison du Québec in Paris, one which was subsequently renamed a Délégation générale. In 1963, Quebec made arrangements with the Association pour l'organisation des stages en France (ASTEF), a semi-governmental agency, which the federal government then sanctioned. When another provincial initiative, this one to send civil servants from Quebec to study at the prestigious École nationale d'administration (ENA) in Paris, was subsequently presented to the DEA by Bousquet as a French offer open to all Canadians, Ottawa, taking him at his word, reserved two places for its own bureaucrats.[11] As a result, Quebec, which claimed the remaining eight spots, made it known to the press – in what Cadieux termed a "poisonous leak" – that federal officials were opening mail and interfering in Quebec's relations with France.[12] The impression that Ottawa was meddling in the province's business was further strengthened by the fact that the ENA program was authorized by an exchange of letters between Martin and Couve de Murville during Pearson's 1964 visit to Paris.

When Cadieux, anxious to maintain contact with Quebec City, went there in February to discuss a new federal program for cultural relations with French-speaking European countries, he was told by one senior bureaucrat that Ottawa should simply cut Quebec a cheque for the amount it planned to spend on cultural exchanges with France and that there was no need for Ottawa to project itself into this field as it had done with the ASTEF and ENA agreements.[13] Meeting with France's ambassador that June, Cadieux stressed that Paris should deal with federal authorities before provincial ones. Agreeing, or so it seemed, Bousquet volunteered that Paul Gérin-Lajoie, the minister of Quebec's newly formed Department of Education, had approached him about educational exchanges with France. Did Ottawa wish, the ambassador asked, to extend this initiative to other provinces and to its federal agencies?[14] It did indeed, but meanwhile Ottawa scrupulously avoided interfering in the Quebec-France negotiations. In fact, Pearson's government was prepared to sanction them by an exchange of notes with France. All it asked, Martin informed Gérin-Lajoie in a letter, was that the arrangement be considered temporary, pending its insertion into a future general framework agreement to be concluded between Ottawa and Paris. In what became an increasingly common Quebec tactic during these years, the missive went unanswered.

Pearson's government was neither strategically positioned nor eager to fight Quebec on its developing relationship with France. Having made that country a foreign policy priority, Ottawa could hardly object when its French province drew closer to it. Furthermore, the government was publicly committed to "cooperative federalism," which promised harmony over confrontation. Thus, in a decision that was later regretted, Ottawa prevailed upon France in late 1964 to improve the status of Quebec's delegate general in Paris by conferring on him certain privileges and immunities. The immediate beneficiary was Jean Chapdelaine, who, leaving the DEA, became Quebec's representative in France. Henceforth his relations with his old colleagues were ambiguous, though some of them took his departure, probably rightly, as the product of ambition rather than ideology. But if the federal government formally approved of the increased Franco-Québécois contact, it also wanted to see the rest of Canada benefit and the federal prerogative in foreign affairs recognized. The DEA prepared an *accord cadre* to be signed with Paris, authorizing any province to pursue cultural relations with France.

In January 1965 Cadieux sent a draft of this agreement to Claude Morin, Quebec's powerful deputy minister of federal-provincial affairs. Once again, there was no response. About the same time, Morin informed Cadieux that Quebec wanted its program of educational exchanges and cooperation with France termed *un accord*. The request triggered a negative reaction from Cadieux, who proceeded to give his interlocutor "a brief telephone course in international law." Morin then proposed the word *une convention,* but Cadieux balked again, noting that Quebec was not a sovereign state. Finally, Morin advanced the term "joint declaration." As before, since such precise legal terminology struck Cadieux as a small step by Quebec towards international recognition, he advised Martin to oppose it. Ultimately, Cadieux and Morin agreed on the term "entente," which, being less precise, proved acceptable.[15] No doubt to avoid provoking Quebec, Ottawa had decided not to include a reference to the future *accord cadre* in the exchange of letters covering the provincial arrangement.[16] In Paris in late February to sign the entente – Quebec's first with a French government department – Gérin-Lajoie trumpeted it as a major precedent, a view enthusiastically echoed by Quebec's nationalist press. Cadieux later tersely summed up the provincial strategy: "Always the battle for autonomy. The public is made aware of the conflict. There is debate in the press and in the universities. Nationalist opinion must be aroused and Ottawa's intervention circumscribed."[17] In the province's negotiations with France, Gérin-Lajoie declared publicly, the federal government had been nothing more than a "consenting observer." He downplayed the fact that only the letters exchanged between Martin and the French Embassy on the same day gave the entente legal validity.

In this charged atmosphere the conclusion that month of the preliminary report of the Royal Commission on Bilingualism and Biculturalism – that "Canada, without being fully conscious of the fact, is passing through the greatest crisis in its history" – was not helpful. In early April, François Leduc, France's new ambassador to Canada, sent a telex to Paris in which he quoted Pearson (in French) as making the following remarkable statement: "'I am willing to accept an Austria-Hungary,' the prime minister told [Leduc], 'but not independent states

– and yet the independence of Quebec would certainly please other provinces which want nothing more than for it to leave the federation – and so this is why the Quebeckers must not go too far.'"[18] Since Austria-Hungary was effectively two nations, one wonders if Pearson, seemingly overwhelmed by events, grasped the full implications of his comment.

As the rest of Canada asked itself what Quebec wanted, the Lesage government offered an answer. Emboldened by his education entente, Gérin-Lajoie, a constitutional lawyer, argued in a speech to Montreal's Consular Corps in April that Canada had a dual international personality. In 1937, the British Judicial Committee of the Privy Council, then Canada's final court of appeal, had ruled that the federal government could not implement treaties whose subjects fell under the domestic jurisdiction of the provinces. Since only the latter could carry out such agreements, and since the 1867 Constitution was technically silent on the power to make them in the first place, Gérin-Lajoie felt that the provinces could negotiate and sign treaties in areas of their legislative competence. Nor did Quebec accept that Ottawa could supervise or control its external dealings. What became known as the "Gérin-Lajoie doctrine" – that provincial responsibility at home was provincial responsibility abroad – was a bold constitutional gambit. By stating one of its demands so directly, Morin believed, Quebec was serving notice to Canada about the kind of new constitution it wanted.[19] Unsurprisingly, the DEA was aghast, viewing the proposal as fundamentally unworkable and contrary to both constitutional and international law. Martin's public response was firm: "The constitutional position in this country on the question of treaty-making is clear. Canada has only one international personality in the community of sovereign states." He remained willing, though, to use the federal prerogative to help provinces meet their international goals.[20]

This was a small gesture towards bonne entente. Pearson was even more conciliatory. In early May, joined by several ministers, he met with Lesage and Gérin-Lajoie in Ottawa for a wide-ranging discussion in which the treaty power issue was raised, albeit briefly. Without compromising on the constitutional and international legal issues, the federal representatives agreed to explore "practical and mutually acceptable procedures" with Quebec. Days later, the two sides met again in Montreal in talks that were akin to "negotiations between representatives of two foreign countries," a development that greatly disturbed Pearson.[21] While acknowledging the federal government's overall responsibility for Canada's foreign policy, neither Lesage nor Gérin-Lajoie, who were accompanied by Morin, accepted that Ottawa alone had constitutional power to conclude international agreements and legal capacity in international law. Setting aside their doctrinal differences for the moment, the Canadian representatives proposed – and those from Quebec revised – some procedural arrangements to govern the conclusion of international agreements in fields of provincial jurisdiction. Both Lesage and Pearson agreed to submit the scheme to their respective cabinets for consideration but, in the latter's case, not before the ministers and officials concerned, in particular Martin and Cadieux, had studied it.[22]

Until now, what was discussed in Montreal has largely been a mystery.[23] Hidden in plain view, as it were, the document in question sat in the DEA files consulted by this writer. It outlined the points of a federal proposal that was first revised by Quebec and then revised again by both sides.[24] While the Montreal proposal is too long to quote here, its subsequent analysis by Allan Gotlieb, a rising star in the Legal Division of the DEA, and Cadieux, its former legal adviser, makes clear that it marked a major retreat for Ottawa. First, and crucially, it implied that Quebec could sign international agreements in its own right since a clause in the original federal draft, indicating that their "validity in international law" would derive from the exchange of notes between Canada and the foreign country involved, had vanished from Lesage's counter-proposal. Second, this diplomatic exchange would follow rather than precede or be simultaneous with the provincial signature, a process that raised the question of whether this important procedure could occur at all if the federal government were not one of those "concerned." Third, a clause in the original draft obliging the province to keep Ottawa "informed" of its negotiations with a foreign power had been removed by Quebec, which preferred merely to "consult" the central authorities. Fourth, an assumption that such provincial arrangements were generally agreements binding in public international law and only exceptionally private contracts was the opposite of what the normal rule should be: that on rare occasions Ottawa might give international legal effect to private law contracts between Quebec and a foreign entity.[25] Curiously, two of these flaws, specifically the timing of the exchange of letters and the statement about private international law, appeared in Pearson's original proposal.

Never one to mince words, Cadieux warned Martin that the formula's various parts, if combined, represented "an abandonment of the federal position," "an unauthorized amendment of the Canadian Constitution," and "a degree of acceptance of 'associate state' status for Quebec." Above all, by appearing to confirm that the province could enter into international agreements, it tacitly recognized the "principle of independent nationhood for Quebec." As Cadieux predicted, it would not be seen as "the final step of the evolution of Quebec's status but as the beginning of this process."[26] Martin, a lawyer with training in international law, agreed with Cadieux's analysis and urged Pearson to quietly "disengage" from the formula.[27] On 20 May, at a meeting of the cabinet committee on federal-provincial relations chaired by Pearson, the decision was made to do so.[28]

What remains unclear is Pearson's own attitude towards the Montreal proposal. One hint that he may have supported it, at least initially, was his comment to cabinet that discussions with Lesage had focused on "practical procedural arrangements" that would not bring "the constitutional and legal aspects of the problem into question," to which he added that "a good deal of progress had been made in this pragmatic approach."[29] As Cadieux and Gotlieb had shown, however, far from being an innocuous modus vivendi, the formula had dangerous constitutional and legal implications.

Gérin-Lajoie's speech and the Pearson-Lesage meetings seriously affected developments in the Canada-Quebec-France triangle. On 13 April, the day after Gérin-Lajoie's broadside, the DEA decided to amend its draft *accord cadre* by making it voluntary for any province that preferred the existing exchange-of-letters procedure.[30] This fateful choice, sacrificing the federal aim of bringing the Quebec-France relationship under its umbrella, was perhaps the only realistic option. As Pearson's cabinet learned later that month, the ominous silence from Quebec on the *accord cadre* was an obstacle to its conclusion with Paris. For this reason, "and in the spirit of 'co-operative federalism,'" an "opt-out" or "opt-in" clause had been added to it. The alternative, abandoning the arrangement altogether, was unacceptable, given that a retreat might be regarded "as the successful use of a provincial veto and the tacit acceptance by Ottawa of much of the Gérin-Lajoie constitutional thesis."[31] In Montreal in May, the Quebec spokesmen resigned themselves to the amended *accord cadre* but rejected Ottawa's proposal that a federal official attend meetings of the Quebec-France *commission mixte* created by the education entente and that a Quebec official sit in on the same committee planned for in the Canada-France agreement. In other words, the province brooked no interference in its programs with France and refused to be associated with Ottawa's.[32] Pearson's government subsequently authorized the completion of negotiations on the *accord cadre* and increased its budget for cultural relations with French-speaking countries to $1 million.[33]

Following Gérin-Lajoie's speech, Ottawa had two main goals: putting its cultural relations with France on a firmer, pan-Canadian basis, and protecting its exclusive constitutional authority to enter into international agreements. Recent scholarship has detailed how Paris, increasingly sympathetic to Quebec City, weakened the *accord cadre*'s consultative provision so that France simply had to notify Ottawa of its negotiations with the provinces. That spring it also began talks with Quebec on a cultural entente, discussions that the DEA learned of only belatedly. Such actions frustrated Ottawa and augured badly for Canada-France relations.[34]

Yet in November 1965, when both the *accord cadre* and Quebec's cultural entente were signed, Ottawa was reasonably pleased. Its constitutional prerogative, boldly challenged by Gérin-Lajoie and destined to be undermined had the Montreal formula been accepted, was safe. Specifically, the letters accompanying the *accord cadre* contained not only the provincial opt-in clause but also a critical statement (which, ironically, had been suggested by the French and which Cadieux and his legal advisers had initially advised removing for fear that it would be interpreted by Quebec as a blanket endorsement of the federal legal position) that the "capacitation" of provinces to conclude cultural or educational ententes stemmed either from their reference to the agreement and its annexed letters or from the "consent" given to them by the federal government. What is not known, despite its great consequence, is that, in response to a letter from Pearson enclosing a copy of the *accord cadre*, Jean Lesage acknowledged, without qualification, this statement of federal authority. Thus, Quebec had seemingly retreated from its position on the legal aspect of the question, the one most vital to Ottawa.[35] It is possible that Lesage, less nationalistic than some of his ministers and officials, brought them in line.

Less important, but still relevant, was the fact that the DEA could claim – and did through a reference to tripartite discussions in the exchange of letters sanctioning Quebec's cultural entente – that Ottawa had been kept informed of Quebec's negotiations with France since Morin had periodically discussed drafts of the text that fall with Cadieux. This assertion, which conveniently ignored how belatedly the DEA had been apprised of those talks, was significant given that Quebec's obligation to keep Ottawa informed of its negotiations with a foreign power had gone unmentioned in the revised Montreal formula. More important, Laporte would not be able to say, as Gérin-Lajoie had at the signing of his education entente, that Ottawa had merely been a consenting observer in the most recent negotiations. Revealingly, the French unsuccessfully tried to have this reference to Ottawa removed from the exchange of letters at the eleventh hour.[36]

Finally, the federal government not only signed the *accord cadre* before Quebec did its new entente – a symbolic victory that reinforced its public stance on treaty-making power – but also ensured that the exchange of letters authorizing the provincial action preceded (not followed, as the Montreal formula would have mandated) the signing ceremony in Quebec City. While it is true that the cultural entente made no reference to the *accord cadre*, the fact that the latter came first strengthened Ottawa's position vis-à-vis Quebec by making clear that provincial authority stemmed rather than derogated from federal power. This was because the exchange of letters accompanying the federal agreement had established the procedure to be followed in the case of any entente not concluded under its aegis.[37] The Pearson government's legal and public position in November 1965 was therefore stronger than it had been in February.

This analysis minimizes neither Quebec's achievement of a second entente with France, one more formal and intergovernmental in character, nor its developing ties with that country.[38] What it emphasizes, however, is that, at the end of 1965, both the Lesage and Pearson governments got what they wanted most: for Quebec City, the strengthening of its direct relationship with Paris; for Ottawa, the preservation of its exclusive authority to sign agreements binding in international law.

While the federal cover given to the two provincial ententes was, as a key Canadian diplomat from the period defined it, a "legal fig leaf," it still protected the central government's position that it alone had an international personality.[39] As Quebec and France coordinated their efforts in 1965, the wisest course open to Ottawa was to ensure that no constitutional precedent was set. The alternatives – either playing no part at all in the ententes or, conversely, refusing to authorize them

– were unthinkable. Naturally, the federal government had sought stronger supervisory control over France's dealings with Quebec. Yet, wanting neither to jeopardize its *accord cadre* with Paris nor to risk a new confrontation with Lesage, it could not insist upon it. Permissiveness, not inflexibility towards Quebec, was the Pearson government's philosophy between 1963 and 1965, thus allowing the province to opt out of certain national programs, including the new pension scheme, in order to build its own. While Ottawa had survived a first challenge to its international personality, it still remained vulnerable.

Exploiting weakness was de Gaulle's specialty, his military training having coloured his approach to politics. Impressed with Quebec's new dynamism, he increasingly lavished attention on it rather than on Canada.[40] For example, he snubbed the Canadian ambassador but not, tellingly, the provincial delegate general. He met with Quebec cabinet ministers at the Elysée but ignored federal ones. He angered his alleged friend, Governor General Georges Vanier, by refusing to receive him as a head of state, yet he treated visiting Quebec premiers as dignitaries. De Gaulle's fascination with Quebec, home to the globe's second largest group of French speakers, was shared by a growing Quebec lobby in Paris, which included politicians and bureaucrats.[41] Consequently, while bilateral cooperation between Canada and France proceeded slowly, cooperation between Quebec and France flourished. The US Embassy in Ottawa reported in mid-1966 that, while Ottawa treated de Gaulle with "great tolerance and conciliation," Cadieux was "downright caustic" in his belief that the general was using Quebec to attack the United States.[42] As Cadieux knew, however, Ottawa was in a bind.

Pearson and Martin tried to court Paris, not on such issues as the Vietnam War, the Third World, or the Middle East, where Gaullist foreign policy was simply too independent, but on NATO. As Isabel Campbell recounts (Chapter 13, this volume), Canada pushed for the alliance to re-examine its goals and tasks and echoed French opposition to the American-inspired Multilateral Nuclear Force. After France announced in March 1966 that it would withdraw from NATO's integrated military command structure, Canada urged alliance restraint. This last project was dear to Martin, who succeeded in delaying an alliance-wide decision to relocate NATO from Paris to Brussels, exasperating both his closest allies and even his own officials – a point Greg Donaghy covers in his chapter. While Martin put great faith in his friendship with Couve de Murville, the evidence suggests that the former was not a particularly effective advocate. As the Quai d'Orsay's North American desk officer remarked to an American diplomat, the meetings between the two foreign ministers were "always one-sided," with the Frenchman dominating the conversation and the Canadian listening "in evident awe."[43] Cadieux took a more charitable view of the Couve-Martin relationship, but he knew it could not contain the Quebec-France problem. The real issue was his chief's refusal to acknowledge that this problem was serious.[44] Indeed, two weeks before de Gaulle's July 1967 "Vive le Québec libre!" Martin, encouraged by a friendly encounter with the French president the previous month, remained strangely in denial about his intentions. As Cadieux bluntly told Martin, he could continue to close his eyes and plug his ears, but the French were up to no good.[45] Cadieux was right.

After de Gaulle's *cri du balcon,* France greatly increased cultural, economic, and technical assistance to Quebec. In September, French ministers went to Quebec City to discuss new areas of cooperation with provincial authorities but, on de Gaulle's orders, avoided Ottawa. A Quebec-France intergovernmental organization, established on a basis of parity, was created, and regular bilateral ministerial meetings at the "highest level" were announced, an arrangement de Gaulle had resisted with Canada when Pearson had proposed it in 1964. Plans were also made for a Quebec-France office for youth exchanges, yet another federal scheme originally, and both sides agreed to explore joint action in the economic and telecommunications fields. While these initiatives (and future ones) were carefully tied to the ententes of 1965, the link was sometimes tenuous. Impatient to see Quebec fulfill the destiny he had charted for it, de Gaulle spoke at a late November press conference about its becoming a "sovereign state," a brash intervention that embarrassed Quebec's government just as it was meeting with the other provinces to discuss the "Confederation of Tomorrow." More appreciated was France's key role in securing Quebec's invitation, but not Canada's, to an international meeting of French-speaking education ministers in Gabon, a major defeat that led Ottawa to suspend relations with Libreville. When the second half of the conference opened in Paris that April, Quebec was present again. Pearson's government appeared helpless to prevent the province from acquiring an international personality.

The Quebec-France relationship must be seen as the central element in a much broader provincial campaign. After all, Gérin-Lajoie's doctrine applied to every country, not just France. Similarly, the Montreal formula would have permitted legally binding ententes with every foreign capital, not just Paris. Nor were these goals unique to Lesage's Quebec Liberal Party. Daniel Johnson's Union Nationale, which won the June 1966 provincial election, was just as determined to entrench constitutionally Quebec's international status. Equivocal and opportunistic, Johnson oscillated between the poles of the title of his 1965 book, *Equality or Independence*. Equality, of course, meant securing more powers from Ottawa and, in fact, the creation of a binational state. Yet the Pearson government's stance towards the province was hardening. The November 1965 federal election had brought to the fore new politicians from Quebec who had no sympathy for the province's unending demands. Jean Marchand, Gérard Pelletier, and Pierre Elliott Trudeau, plus Marc Lalonde, who joined the Prime Minister's Office in 1967, had Pearson's ear. Their general analysis of the political situation echoed Cadieux's specific one in the field of foreign affairs: Quebec City's challenge to Ottawa demanded a commensurate response. Although naturally conciliatory, Pearson could not help but be influenced by what he heard.[46]

The DEA, still the lead opponent of Quebec's international activities, pursued a two-pronged approach to limit their constitutional significance. Basing itself on Pearson's rejection of outside interference in his public statement on de Gaulle's speech in Montreal, the DEA put firm but discreet pressure on France. While Ottawa had preserved its legal authority to sign treaties and agreements in 1965, the two provincial ententes that it had approved were now being exploited by Quebec and France to legitimize the former's quest for an international personality. Such conduct, by an allied country no less, was outrageous, but it could not easily be stopped. It became imperative, then, to protest, if only for the record, as silence implied acquiescence in the broader provincial campaign. Pushed by Cadieux, the DEA increasingly expressed its displeasure to the French Embassy in Ottawa, to the Quai d'Orsay, and, when Martin met with him, to Couve de Murville. These approaches essentially took the form of a series of questions. Would France continue to interpret unilaterally what it could and could not do with Quebec? Would it continue to flout international practice and protocol by sending its ministers to a subdivision of a country without informing its national government about goals and programs? Would it continue to keep Ottawa in the dark about its relations with Quebec even when those relations exceeded prescribed limits or encroached on areas of federal jurisdiction?

Despite the diplomatic wording of these tough queries, the answers Pearson's government received were unsatisfying. But that was beside the point. Having been put in an intolerable situation by France, Canada had to protect its legal position by asserting it.[47] This strategy annoyed Ambassador Léger, who advised Ottawa simply to bide its time until de Gaulle left the political stage. Yet what if by then the Constitution was in shreds? Clearly, French provocations could not last, but as long as they did it was incumbent upon Ottawa to voice its concerns. Just how loudly became an issue in the Liberal leadership race to succeed Pearson, who, in December 1967, announced his intention to retire. While Martin was the favourite in a crowded field, in February 1968 Trudeau, fresh from a dramatic (and triumphant) confrontation with Premier Johnson at that month's constitutional conference, declared his own candidacy. Martin understandably sought to differentiate himself from his new challenger's aggressive stance on Quebec, but he did so in peculiar ways. For example, he publicly declared that the Gabon affair was overblown and that Canada would not break relations with France if it acted similarly. This statement weakened Ottawa's decision to suspend relations with Gabon, one aimed more at Quebec City and Paris than at Libreville. Pearson was indignant.[48] He was not alone. In a revealing aside, the US Embassy reported that it was "small wonder" that, even among his own officials, Martin was "nobody's candidate."[49]

The second way the DEA tried to parry Quebec's international thrust was through firmness on issues over which it had more control and over which France had little influence. Four of its more notable strategies deserve mention. First, uncomfortable with the way the Quebec-France relationship was developing, Ottawa ensured that another francophone country, Belgium, whose ambassador had been approached early on by Quebec about a cultural entente, signed such a deal with the federal government instead. Belgium did so in May 1967.[50] Second, while unable to sever the links being forged between Quebec and France, the DEA impressed on the provinces and instructed its missions around the world that it alone was the proper channel for provincial activities abroad.[51] While such a policy was impossible to enforce, despite the creation in 1967 of a DEA coordination division partly for this purpose, in time it had an educative effect on both foreign governments and international organizations. Similarly, disturbed by Quebec's penchant for communicating directly with foreign ambassadors in Ottawa, the DEA issued a circular to heads of mission in December 1966, reminding them of the stipulation in the Vienna Convention on Diplomatic Relations that the sending state shall conduct official business only through the Ministry of Foreign Affairs of the receiving state.[52] This policy, though also hard to apply, was a necessary legal response to Quebec's pretensions. Third, the DEA resisted surrendering administrative control of certain aspects of its aid program in French-speaking Africa to Quebec, which retaliated by offering its own assistance to some countries. Ottawa refused to be intimidated: it persuaded Tunisia not to accept the funds and when Rwanda did, it neutralized the act's legal significance.[53] Fourth, while the DEA explored ways to increase provincial participation in international conferences in areas under their domestic jurisdiction, it insisted that there be only one delegation and that it speak in one name only – Canada's.[54]

It is true that Quebec and France tried to undermine this principle in Gabon and in the emerging international organization of la Francophonie. The concessions the DEA was forced to accept in that narrow field would not be extended, however, to the broader one, despite Quebec's hope to achieve a distinct presence and voice on Canadian delegations to such bodies as the World Health Organization, the International Labour Organization, and the United Nations Educational, Scientific and Cultural Organization.[55] While the architects of Ottawa's resistance to Quebec's international advances were Cadieux and his close advisers, Martin deserves more credit than he has hitherto received for supporting them. There is no doubt, given his strong legal background, that he understood the principles at stake. But by early 1968, as he eyed the leadership prize that had previously eluded him, he was reluctant to defend them forcefully. For instance, on the recommendation of Cadieux and other senior government officials, the DEA prepared a White Paper entitled *Federalism and International Relations,* which was uncompromising in its insistence that only the federal government had international status. When Martin hesitated to table the report at the February 1968 constitutional conference, where it would achieve maximum effect, Pearson ordered its distribution.[56] This was a nod to the man the prime minister had conspicuously seated at his side during the conference and whom he would come to favour to succeed him: Pierre Trudeau.[57]

Although it was the constitutional threat posed by France and Quebec that mainly preoccupied Pearson's government, there were positive developments as well. For the first time in its history, Canada was expressing its bicultural heritage through its actions in the world. In 1947, Louis St-Laurent, Pearson's predecessor as SSEA and Liberal Party leader, had declared national unity to be the first principle of Canada's foreign policy. After two divisive world wars, the federal government naturally sought to avoid any external provocation that might upset the balance between English and French Canadians. Confronted by a turbulent Quebec in the 1960s, however, it was no longer enough for Ottawa simply to tread carefully on the world stage – it had to actively find ways to strengthen Canada.

Pearson's government proved up to the challenge. It inaugurated and then supported the annual program for cultural relations with francophone European countries. It financed the expansion and renovation of the cash-strapped Maison des étudiants canadiens in Paris. It also approved, at the cost of about two diplomatic missions, building a cultural centre in the French capital. Put simply, cultural diplomacy had arrived in Ottawa with a vengeance, as evidenced by the creation in 1966 of a special DEA division to coordinate it.[58] This was no small achievement for a department whose budget for cultural affairs in 1963 had been only $8,000.[59] The Pearson administration also substantially increased development assitance to French-speaking Africa from a paltry $300,000 in 1961 to $12 million in 1967–68, and pledged to be more generous in future.[60] While Canadian assistance to Commonwealth countries still dwarfed that to French-speaking Africa, and while the second program was handicapped by a lack of both bilingual personnel in the External Aid Office and resident missions in the recipient countries, Ottawa had nonetheless changed its image both overseas and at home. To this end, and despite the DEA's strained personnel resources, it also established embassies in Tunisia and Senegal. Behind the scenes, officials planned an even greater expansion into the French-speaking world.[61] Finally, the federal government took an early and eager interest in la Francophonie. In all these endeavours the Pearson government arguably was more pragmatic than principled. It knew full well that if it failed to act, Quebec might fill the void. But it also wished to counter the damaging impression, fostered by some Quebec nationalists and Gaullist France, that Quebec City was the government of French Canada and Ottawa that of English Canada. By demonstrating that the federal government represented *all* of Canada, it changed Canadian foreign policy forever.

In Chapter 5 (this volume), Stephen Azzi highlights a dichotomy between Pearson's chronically weak government and its major lasting successes. This contrast can also be seen in its handling of the Quebec-France problem. Though the DEA was ridiculed by its critics for being hopelessly legalistic, the intellectual inspiration and support for the Gérin-Lajoie doctrine, which no federal government has ever accepted, came from Quebec nationalists with expertise in constitutional and international law. In short, a legal challenge required a legal response. To be sure, the damage done to Canadian unity by Quebec and France, whose special relationship would endure, was real, causing Cadieux to remark as Pearson prepared to leave office that, while it still stood, the federal house was in bad shape.[62] And even though after 1970 France never again intervened in Canadian affairs so directly, in an interconnected world where local issues were increasingly matters of global concern, the province would find new outlets for international engagement. But, in the end, the Pearson government did far more than simply provide for its successors a modus operandi for handling provincial initiatives: prompted by the passionate advocacy of Quebec nationalists, it finally made Canadian foreign policy a more faithful reflection of Canada itself.

Notes

1 John English, *Shadow of Heaven: The Life of Lester Pearson, vol. 1: 1897–1948* (Toronto: Lester and Orpen Dennys, 1989), 149.

2 J.L. Granatstein, *The Ottawa Men: The Civil Service Mandarins, 1935–1957* (Toronto: Oxford University Press, 1982), 6.

3 John English, *The Worldly Years: The Life of Lester Pearson, vol. 2: 1949–1972* (Toronto: Knopf, 1992), 84.

4 Marcel Cadieux, *Embruns* (Ottawa: Le Cercle du Livre de France, 1951), 62.

5 On Cadieux and Léger, see Robin Gendron, "Advancing the National Interest: Marcel Cadieux, Jules Léger, and Canadian Participation in the Francophone

Community, 1962–1972," in *In the National Interest: Canada's Department of Foreign Affairs and International Trade, 1909–2009*, ed. Greg Donaghy and Michael Carroll (Calgary: University of Calgary Press, 2009), 121–35.

6 Raymond Bousquet to MAE, 24 December 1963, Archives du Ministère des Affaires étrangères (MAE), Séries B, Amérique, Sous-séries Canada, 1952–1963, file 134.

7 Bousquet to Maurice Couve de Murville, 31 December 1963, MAE, Séries B, Amérique, Sous-séries Canada, 1952–1963, file 137.

8 On de Gaulle's foreign policy, see Maurice Vaïsse, *La grandeur: Politique étrangère du général de Gaulle, 1958–1969* (Paris: Fayard, 1998).

9 Bousquet to Louis Roché, 16 October 1963, MAE, Séries B, Amérique, Sous-séries Canada, 1952–1963, file 204.

10 Memorandum of Conversation between George Ball and Lester Pearson, 22 January 1964, NARA, RG 59, Central Foreign Policy Files (CFPF), 1964–66, box 1990, file POL CAN-US.

11 Cadieux, Memorandum to File, 25 June 1964, LAC, RG 25, vol. 10098, file 20-1-2-FR-pt.2.1.

12 Cadieux to Arnold Smith and F.G. Hooton, 24 December 1963, LAC, RG 25, vol. 10097, file 20-1-2-FR-pt.1.1.

13 Cadieux to Information Division, 25 February 1964, LAC, RG 25, vol. 10098, file 20-1-2-FR-pt.1.2.

14 Cadieux, Memorandum to File, 25 June 1964, LAC, RG 25, vol. 10098, file 20-1-2-FR-pt.2.1.

15 Claude Morin, *L'art de l'impossible: La diplomatie québécoise depuis 1960* (Montréal: Boréal, 1987), 26; Cadieux to SSEA, 19 January 1965, LAC, RG 25, vol. 10492, file 55-3-1-FR-QUE-pt.2.1; Dale Thomson, *Vive le Québec Libre* (Toronto: Deneau, 1988), 139.

16 European Division to Cadieux, 23 December 1964, LAC, RG 25, vol. 10492, file 55-3-1-FR-QUEBEC-pt.1.

17 Marcel Cadieux, *Le Général et la campagne du Québec, 1963–1968* (unpublished manuscript, 1980), 100. I am grateful to Cadieux's sons for providing me with a copy of this work.

18 François Leduc to MAE, 1 April 1965, MAE, Séries B, Amérique, Sous-séries Canada, 1964–1970, file 198. Given its importance, the following is exactly what Leduc reported: "'Je veux bien d'une Autriche-Hongrie,' m'a dit le premier ministre, 'mais pas d'états indépendants – et pourtant l'indépendance du Québec ferait bien plaisir à d'autres provinces qui ne demandent qu'à le voir quitter la fédération – c'est pour cela qu'il ne faut pas que les Québécois aillent trop loin.'" To my knowledge, David Meren was the first historian to cite Pearson's Austria-Hungary parallel, which he translates as "Austro-Hungarian solution," but he omits the prime minister's statement that Quebec's secession from Canada would please other provinces. See David Meren, *With Friends Like These: Entangled Nationalisms and the Canada-Quebec-France Triangle, 1944–1970* (Vancouver: UBC Press, 2012), 113.

19 Morin to Jean Chapdelaine, 21 April 1965, Bibliothèque et Archives nationales du Québec (BANQ), E42, 1990-09-002/405.

20 Press Release by SSEA, 23 April 1965, LAC, RG 25, vol. 11572, file 30-1-4-pt.1.

21 Cabinet Conclusions for 4 and 11 May 1965, LAC, RG 2, vol. 6271.

22 Draft Memorandum to Cabinet, 18 May 1965 and DEA to Cadieux (in London), 11 May 1965, LAC, RG 25, vol. 11585, file 30-5-1-pt.2.

23 The mystery was still unsolved in 2005, when two of Cadieux's contemporaries advanced very different interpretations of what was agreed to in Montreal. See Allan Gotlieb, "Only One Voice Speaks for Canada," *Globe and Mail*, 5 October 2005; Tom Kent, "Pearson Never Compromised on Who Spoke for Canada," *Globe and Mail*, 11 October 2005.

24 "Federal-Provincial Procedures to Govern the Conclusion of International Agreements in Fields of Provincial Jurisdiction," 9 May 1965, LAC, RG 25, vol. 11585, file 30-5-1-pt.2.

25 Cadieux to SSEA, 14 May 1965, LAC, RG 25, vol. 11572, file 30-1-4-pt.2. See as well Draft Memorandum to Cabinet, 18 May 1965, LAC, RG 25, vol. 11585, file 30-5-1-pt.2.

26 Cadieux to SSEA, 14 May 1965, LAC, RG 25, vol. 11572, file 30-1-4-pt.2.

27 SSEA to Pearson, 17 May 1965, LAC, RG 25, vol. 11572, file 30-1-4pt.2.

28 Cadieux to SSEA, 1 December 1965, LAC, RG 25, vol. 11585, file 30-5-1-pt.3.

29 Cabinet Conclusions, 11 May 1965, LAC, RG 2, vol. 6271.

30 European Division to Legal and Information Divisions, 23 April 1965, LAC, RG 25, vol. 10492, file 55-3-1-FR-pt.1.

31 Memorandum to Cabinet, 27 April 1965, LAC, RG 25, vol. 10492, file 55-3-1-FR-pt.1.

32 DEA to Cadieux (in London), 9 May 1965 and Draft Memorandum to Cabinet, 18 May 1965, LAC, RG 25, vol. 11585, file 30-5-1-pt.2.

33 Cabinet Conclusions, 11 May 1965, LAC, RG 2, vol. 6271.

34 For a fuller discussion see Meren, *With Friends Like These*, 216–21.

35 Cadieux to Pearson, 12 October 1965, LAC, RG 25, vol. 10492, file 55-3-1-FR-pt.2; Lesage to Pearson, 23 November 1965, LAC, RG 25, vol. 14625, file 30-10-FR-2-pt.3; Cadieux to SSEA, 1 December 1965, LAC, RG 25, vol. 11585, file 30-5-1-pt.3.

36 Cadieux to SSEA, 17 November 1965, LAC, RG 25, vol. 11644, file 30-14-QUE-pt.1; Gotlieb, Memorandum, 25 November 1964, LAC, RG 25, vol. 10492, file 55-3-1-FR-QUEBEC-pt.2.2.

37 Cadieux to SSEA, 1 December 1965, LAC, RG 25, vol. 11585, file 30-5-1-pt.3.

38 It is interesting to note, for example, that the original Montreal formula stated that any agreement between Quebec and a foreign country would be signed "at the appropriate technical level," a clause that the province removed in its counter-proposal. In November 1965 it got its way: the cultural entente was signed between the Quebec and French governments.

39 Max Yalden, interview with the author, 7 November 2012, Ottawa. On the DEA strategy of form over substance, see J.L. Granatstein and Robert Bothwell, *Pirouette: Pierre Trudeau and Canadian Foreign Policy* (Toronto: University of Toronto Press, 1990), 117.

40 As early as 1963, de Gaulle was convinced that Quebec would become an independent state. See Eric Roussel, *De Gaulle* (Paris: Gallimard, 2002), 832.

41 Granatstein and Bothwell, *Pirouette*, 115. On the Quebec lobby, see Jean-Pierre Fournier and Paul-André Comeau, *Le Lobby du Québec à Paris: Les précurseurs du Général de Gaulle* (Montreal: Québec-Amérique, 2002).

42 Memorandum of conversation between Cadieux, Walton Butterworth, and Rufus Smith, 13 May 1966, NARA, RG 59, CFPF, box 1990, file POL CAN-D.

43 US Embassy Paris to State Department, 30 April 1965, NARA, RG 59, box 1988, fol. POL 18 CAN.

44 Journal intime, 8 December 1966, LAC, Cadieux Papers, vol. 12, file 10.

45 Journal intime, 12 July 1967, LAC, Cadieux Papers, vol. 8, file 15.

46 I am not implying that Pearson suddenly became a hawk on Quebec. Indeed, as Cadieux's diary makes clear, he often greatly disappointed his French-Canadian collaborators, notably in September 1966, when he failed to object to Premier Johnson's meeting alone with Couve de Murville in Quebec City.

47 Journal intime, 19 February 1968, LAC, Cadieux Papers, vol. 8, file 14. As Cadieux wrote: "For legal reasons, I believe that we must continue to protest. If we do not protest our silence gives an increased legal validity to Quebec's actions."

48 Journal intime, 10 March 1968, LAC, Cadieux Papers, vol. 8, file 14; Cadieux to Paul Tremblay, 14 March 1968, LAC, Paul Tremblay Papers, vol. 4, file 13.

49 Butterworth to Dean Rusk, 18 March 1968, NARA, RG 59, CFPF, box 1949, file POL CAN-GABON.

50 On Quebec's approach to Belgium, see Cadieux, Memorandum to file, 1 July 1964, LAC, RG 25, vol. 10041, file 20-1-2-BELG-pt.1.

51 See, for example, Circular Document A 6/66: "Co-ordination of Provincial Activities Abroad," 26 September 1966, LAC, RG 25, vol. 11588, file 30-6-pt.1.

52 Circular Note L-961, 5 December 1966, LAC, RG 25, vol. 10140, file 30-2-1-pt.1.

53 See Robin Gendron, *Towards a Francophone Community: Canada's Relations with France and French Africa, 1945–1968* (Montreal and Kingston: McGill-Queen's University Press, 2006), 104–15.

54 Robertson to Pearson, 13 April 1967, LAC, RG 25, vol. 11572, file 30-1-5-pt.2. As Cadieux remarked in 1966: "If it cannot be fully understood in advance with the provinces and with provincial participants in Canadian delegations that they will not be taking part as representatives of provincial governments but as representatives of the Canadian Government, there will be no provincial participation in those delegations." See Cadieux to A.E. Ritchie, 15 February 1966, LAC, RG 25, vol. 11572, file 30-1-5-pt.2.

55 On this Quebec goal, see Chapdelaine to Morin, 8 January 1969 and Maurice Héroux to Morin, 24 November 1969, BANQ, P776, 2001-01-006/3.

56 Cadieux to SSEA, 29 May 1967, LAC, RG 25, vol. 10140, file 30-2-1-pt.1; Journal intime, 7 February 1968, LAC, Cadieux Papers, vol. 8, file 14; Paul Martin, *Federalism and International Relations* (Ottawa: Queen's Printer, 1968).

57 Pearson, who wanted a francophone successor, preferred Jean Marchand, who declined to run and suggested Trudeau instead, a choice Pearson supported. See English, *Worldly Years*, 382–84.

58 John Hilliker and Donald Barry, *Canada's Department of External Affairs: Coming of Age, 1946–68* (Montreal and Kingston: McGill-Queen's University Press, 1995), 318.

59 Meren, *With Friends Like These*, 74.

60 Before handing over the reins to Trudeau, Martin and Pearson decided to double the amount of development assistance for French-speaking Africa to over $23 million. See Gendron, *Towards a Francophone Community*, 134.

61 "New posts," 26 February 1968, LAC, RG 25, vol. 8824, file 20-1-2-2-pt.1.

62 Cadieux to Tremblay, 29 February 1968, LAC, Tremblay Papers, vol. 4, file 13.

Norman Hillmer, Daniel Macfarlane, and Michael W. Manulak

15 Pearson and Environmental Diplomacy

Lester Pearson was an environmental diplomat, although the description would have been foreign to him. During his long tenure in the Department of External Affairs prior to entering politics, he learned that the practitioners of his craft frequently dealt with the everyday issues of fisheries, waterways, and resources.[1] While secretary of state for external affairs in the Louis St-Laurent government, Pearson had a key role in the negotiations leading to the St. Lawrence Seaway and Power Project, one of the major instances of bilateral environmental diplomacy.[2] And within weeks of becoming prime minister, he met with US president John F. Kennedy to discuss an agenda packed with items having an environmental aspect, such as the Columbia River Treaty and the continental relationship in oil and gas.[3]

Trade in natural resources and joint projects that modify ecosystems on a grand scale have been a vital part of Canada's international business. Fisheries were at the front of John A. Macdonald's mind when he waded into the negotiations that resulted in the 1871 Treaty of Washington, and much of North American relations has revolved around the natural world, whether forests and resources, lakes and rivers, or the air the two countries breathe. An underappreciated aspect of Canada's external existence are those issues that can be captured by the term "environmental diplomacy" – international relationships that target the management of natural resources (such as the handling of a trans-border water body) or that have a pronounced impact on the environment (such as fossil fuel extraction).[4]

When Pearson entered office in April 1963, the dangerous impacts of post-Second World War North American industrial and technological developments were accumulating, as was a consciousness of widespread pollution, rampant waste and consumerism, and threatened ecosystems that were everywhere to be seen by those who would see them.[5] Canadians were reading the best-selling *Silent Spring,* Rachel Carson's epic indictment of the practice of dumping chemicals into the water, land, and air, with the power, she wrote, "to still the song of birds and the leaping of fish in the streams, to coat the leaves with a deadly film, and to linger on in soil."[6] Carson had an immediate influence: the noxious pesticide DDT, about which she wrote so eloquently, was banned by Montreal's city arborist and the Toronto parks commissioner.[7] The Pearson government, possibly also as a response to Carson, set up a House of Commons and an interdepartmental committee on pesticides.[8] But environmentalism was yet to come.[9] Canada's Gallup polling organization did not register environmental concerns in the period that Pearson was prime minister.[10]

In the United States, too, public opinion about environmental degradation moved slowly in the 1960s. Even at the decade's end, polls demonstrated that only nuclear fallout and DDT prompted anxiety. Washington, however, was ahead of the national mood. President Kennedy appointed an activist secretary of the interior, Stewart Udall, who matched Rachel Carson with a book of his own, warning that a "quiet crisis" of "pollution and noise and blight" required the might of the American federal government to defeat it. Like Kennedy, President Lyndon Johnson imbibed Carson's messages. Johnson allied with Congress to extend his Great Society program to include the environment, while his wife led a campaign to beautify highways and promoted the cleaning up of urban slums. During the Johnson presidency, over three hundred laws were passed to protect the environment. "Dirty water and black snow pour from the dismal air to ... the putrid slush that waits for them below," the president declared when he signed the 1967 Air Quality Act. "Now that is not a description of Boston, Chicago, New York, or even Washington, DC. It is from Dante's *Inferno* ...but doesn't it sound familiar?"[11]

Prime Minister Pearson gave no such speech. He was eloquent about the dangers to the planet of the testing of nuclear weapons, a concern he shared with his wife and her colleagues in the Voice of Women (VOW).[12] His government created the Science Council of Canada and established tax incentives for companies to purchase equipment to reduce pollution and, late in his second term, began work on a Canada water act.[13] Nevertheless, Pearson was apt to view the environment through the lens of the development and utilization of natural resources and the freest possible flow across the Canadian-American border of oil, gas, strategic metals and minerals, and electricity.[14] He was a diplomat by training, experience, and expertise. It seemed natural that the engagement that he and his government had with the environment played primarily into relationships with other states, particularly the United States. What follows is an examination of four cases in the Pearson government's diplomacy of the environment – the Columbia River Treaty; the management of North American water resources; radioactive fallout and test ban negotiations; and the law of the sea, ocean politics, and fisheries.

Columbia River Treaty

The Columbia River, the fourth largest on the continent, has its headwaters in British Columbia though the bulk of its watershed is in the United States. Schemes to harness it for flood control and hydroelectricity dated to the early twentieth century, and the US built power stations at Bonneville and Grand Coulee, as well as on a number of Columbia tributaries, prior to the Second World War. But the Columbia's full potential for US electrical development and flood control could only be unlocked if the upper parts of the river situated in Canada were also dammed to provide storage reservoirs. As Canada was eager to develop hydro facilities on the Columbia in its territory, in 1944 Ottawa and Washington requested that the International Joint Commission (IJC) – the bilateral body created by the 1909 Boundary Waters Treaty to handle border waters questions – determine whether it would be advantageous to develop the Columbia River system.[15]

The IJC, and both countries, undertook engineering studies and plans that would continue well into the 1950s. In 1954, BC premier W.A.C. Bennett struck a deal with the American firm, Kaiser Aluminum and Chemical Corporation, to develop a large storage dam on the upper Columbia River. In return for a fifty-year water licence, BC would get 20 percent of the electricity generated downstream. Canada's federal government, however, was opposed for a variety of reasons, including the fact that the Kaiser plan would interfere with ongoing IJC studies for the river's overall rationalization. In 1955, the St-Laurent government passed the International River Improvements Act, stipulating that a federal licence was necessary to dam an international river. Since the IJC had still not made a recommendation, the St-Laurent government and the Dwight Eisenhower administration began active negotiations about developing the Columbia. With John Diefenbaker's Canadian election victory in 1957, negotiations accelerated.

After considering three different plans, the negotiators settled on a scheme that involved three dams in Canada, including a high dam for the Arrow Lakes. In compensation for the downstream benefits, Canada would receive cash and half of the extra US electricity that the control dams made possible. Based on these terms, the Columbia River Treaty was signed in January 1961 and ratified by the United States. In addition to the three Canadian dams (Duncan, Mica, and Keenleyside), another (Libby) would be built on the Kootenay River in the US, whose reservoir would extend upriver into Canada. The Canadian dams would benefit downstream American power and flood control interests, but they could also generate electricity in their own right.

The treaty signing had been rushed, since Eisenhower was leaving office and Canada's government believed that it had the BC government's concurrence. But it soon became apparent that Premier Bennett was opposed, not only because Ottawa's interference annoyed him but also because the treaty's terms interfered with his "two rivers" scheme, which aimed to simultaneously replumb the Columbia and Peace Rivers for hydro development. Bennett wanted to sell the resulting power to American entities on a long-term basis. However, such sales contravened the long-established federal policy of allowing the export of electric power only on a non-permanent basis.

The 1961 Columbia Treaty was readily portrayed as a capitulation to Washington, an unpopular proposition in an era of incipient Canadian nationalism.[16] There were complaints that Canada received few benefits and arguments that alternative development proposals would put less Canadian territory, such as the Arrow Lakes Valley, under water; would allow for more hydro generation in Canada; and would give Canada much greater control over the future use and diversion of Columbia waters.[17] A vociferous treaty opponent, General A.G.L. McNaughton, chaired the IJC's Canadian Section. Building on his recent experience with the St. Lawrence Seaway and Power Project negotiations, during which he actively promoted an all-Canadian plan, he recommended diverting the Kootenay River into the Columbia to create greater water flows so that more hydro dams could be built entirely on the Canadian side.[18] As leader of the Opposition, Pearson favoured a renegotiation of the 1961 treaty to gain more favourable terms, promising that "all BC interests, particularly those of the Water Resources Committee of Nakusp Chamber of Commerce, will be consulted by a new Liberal government before a final decision is reached."[19]

At the Pearson-Kennedy meeting in May 1963, the prime minister explained Canada's problems with the proposed treaty. If favourable changes could be made to the agreement, Canada would authorize the sale of downstream power benefits over a long period. This was a significant change from Ottawa's long-standing ban on permanent electricity exports. Pearson proposed that the Columbia matter be settled by a protocol established through an exchange of notes rather than through a new treaty. Reflecting improvements in the bilateral relationship with Diefenbaker's departure, Kennedy was willing to consider this method if Pearson could get Premier Bennett on board.[20]

Bennett was amenable now that the sale of long-term downstream benefits was on the table. He and Pearson met in June, and Secretary of State for External Affairs Paul Martin Sr. was tasked with negotiating with the Americans and dealing with Parliament.[21] An elaborate series of triangular negotiations between the BC, Canadian, and American governments took up much of 1963, dealing with sticking points such as downstream benefits and the forming of an integrated continental electricity grid.[22] The governments of Canada and British Columbia reached an agreement in July 1963.[23] Though a range of competing political, economic, and technical interests were still in play, by early 1964 these had mostly been reconciled in a second Canada-BC agreement. Martin wrote the following assurance to McNaughton in January 1964: "I am satisfied that the agreement which has been reached will be of great benefit to Canada and will fully protect our sovereignty."[24]

On 22 January 1964, Canada and the United States agreed to a protocol that modified the 1961 Columbia River Treaty and governed its implementation. The revised terms included new procedures for the operation of flood control; reaffirmation and clarification of Canada's rights to divert water for consumptive and other uses; and the increase in Canada's entitlement to downstream power benefits.[25] The siting of the three Canadian dams remained unchanged. The Americans would send Canada half the power generated in the United States made possible by the Canadian works, while Canada would sell its downstream benefits for $254 million for thirty years to a group of American utilities and pass on these proceeds to British Columbia. Either country could terminate the treaty after sixty years with ten years' notice (2014 was the earliest point at which either side could signal plans to renegotiate or withdraw). By the summer, a sales contract had been negotiated. On 16 September 1964, the Columbia River Treaty, with its new protocol, was ratified by Canada and the United States.[26]

To its promoters, then and now, the Columbia River Treaty serves as one of the most successful examples of a transboundary water treaty. It is lauded for equitably sharing the benefits of an international river system and for its durability and flexibility, allowing for both significant flood control and hydro-electric development.[27] Yet environmental activist Donald Waterfield, who fought the treaty from the beginning, labelled Pearson's handling of the treaty a "pusillanimous surrender" and was joined by others who saw the Columbia projects as evidence of the American empire's appetite for Canadian natural resources.[28] Nationalist detractors condemned the Columbia project for integrating the two countries' power grids and preventing the formation of an all-Canadian grid.[29] Moreover, the "important downstream environmental and social costs were at best undervalued and in some cases ignored by the parties that crafted the final agreement."[30] John Shurts and Richard Paisley recently labelled the treaty an "anachronism" since, from a contemporary vantage point, "the most obvious substantive elements missing from the treaty are fish and wildlife, water quality, and other environmental and ecosystem benefits."[31]

The perspective of years passed and experience gained makes the utility and impact of the Columbia megaproject – and thus the treaty that enabled it – more open to question than it was to its 1960s' critics. It is unfair to hold Pearson's government to the environmental ethos of later decades; the intergovernmental disputes surrounding the Columbia Treaty centred on the benefits that would flow from it, not on how it would alter or damage the environment. The Pearson government united different viewpoints and political jurisdictions and brought an end to a difficult political and diplomatic situation.

Continental Water Resources

The Great Lakes-St. Lawrence water basin was a significant concern during the Pearson era, as it would be thereafter. Beginning in the 1950s, while various American states had urged the IJC to investigate pollution in the lower Great Lakes, a comprehensive agreement was stalled for years by protracted discussions and disputes involving a long list of North American jurisdictions. From 1954 to 1963, there was a stalemate between Ontario and Ottawa, the former in particular dragging its feet over which level of government should pay to address pollution.

The election of the Pearson government quickly led to a 1963 cost-sharing agreement between Ottawa and the province of Ontario. This allowed Canada to join with the US in 1964 to refer pollution in the lower lakes to the IJC, which created joint investigative boards for Lake Erie, Lake Ontario, and the St. Lawrence River. The IJC issued reports, the first in 1965, identifying the toxic combination of chemicals, sewage, and detergents that was contaminating the waters, and it made recommendations to address municipal and industrial pollution and to immediately reduce phosphates in detergents.[32] The 1972 Great Lakes Water Quality Agreement (GLWQA) was a product of the IJC's 1965 reference. The agreement established a non-binding framework for cooperative management of water quality in Lakes Ontario and Erie. Both nations developed common water quality objectives and regulatory standards for several types of pollutants, chiefly connected to excess nutrient loading, and implemented programs to achieve these goals. For example, the US spent $10 billion on improvements in municipal sewage treatment between 1972 and 1978. In 1978, the two countries arrived at a new agreement, building upon the 1972 version. The 1978 agreement was amended in 1983 and a subsequent protocol was signed in 1987. The GLWQAs, among the most important North American environmental accords, led to significant improvements for the Great Lakes ecosystem.[33]

At the same time as the Pearson and Johnson governments referred lower lakes pollution to the IJC in 1964, they also assigned to it another Great Lakes water issue. This was about water *quantity*, however, not water *quality*. Great Lakes water levels had reached new highs in the 1950s, but by the mid-1960s they were headed towards new lows. In the spring of 1964, much concern was expressed in the

House of Commons about low water levels in the Great Lakes. When questioned by Opposition leader John Diefenbaker, Prime Minister Pearson responded that he appreciated "the seriousness of this situation that seems to be cyclical on the great lakes" and promised to look into it. Two days later, Pearson tabled a statement from the IJC about the Great Lakes basin and assured the House "the government is very much concerned about this matter and will adopt all measures open to it which will help to minimize these extremely low water levels."[34] The IJC was then tasked with determining whether measures could be taken to regulate the water levels to reduce extremes. Though the final report did not arrive until the 1970s, interim reports indicated that lake level fluctuations primarily resulted from natural causes, a crucial finding that spawned further studies and investigations, including consideration of how climate change was affecting the lakes.[35]

In 1964, the American and Canadian governments asked the IJC to study causes of pollution in the Red River. This river begins in the United States before flowing into Manitoba and Lake Winnipeg. Major and frequent floods had attracted IJC attention, but water quality was the most pressing bilateral issue. The Red River drains one of the most fertile agricultural regions of North America, and nonpoint source pollution (that which does not emanate from an identifiable "point," such as a pipe) from runoff fouled the waterway, affecting local food processing (e.g., potatoes and sugar beets).[36] The two countries accepted the IJC's recommendations for water quality objectives and monitoring, creating the International Red River Pollution Board.

The Canadian and American governments also moved on the issue of air pollution in the Port Huron-Sarnia and Detroit-Windsor regions. They asked the IJC in 1966 to determine the extent of this pollution, identify its sources, and suggest remedial measures. The Pearson air pollution reference was a key step on the path to the 1991 US-Canada Air Quality Agreement (commonly known as the Acid Rain Treaty).[37]

The American-Canadian Niagara Water Diversion Treaty of 1950 had allowed the two countries to remake Horseshoe Falls, diverting up to three-quarters of the water around the falls to downstream hydroelectric stations, preventing erosion, and ostensibly improving the great cataract's scenic appearance. Following this project's successful completion, a campaign began in the mid-1960s to remove the "unsightly" rock talus that had formed at the base of the American Falls and to prevent further erosion and rockslides. In 1967, Ottawa and

Washington asked the IJC to investigate and report on measures necessary to preserve or enhance the beauty of the American Falls and, specifically, to deal with the talus. The US Army Corps of Engineers undertook studies and tests, including the dewatering of the American Falls in 1969, but it concluded that removal of the talus might weaken the rockface and, facing an estimated $26 million cost, the IJC recommended against further artificial measures to prevent rock erosion at the American Falls, a view both countries accepted. This represented an important shift in North American state attitudes towards large-scale technological modifications to the environment.[38]

During the 1960s, several proposals were also made to divert water on a continental scale. The largest may have been the North American Water and Power Alliance (NAWAPA), a scheme first presented in 1963 by engineering consultants Ralph M. Parsons and Co. It involved diverting water from major rivers in Alaska, British Columbia, and Yukon to a vast reservoir in the Rocky Mountain Trench (the damming of rivers such as the Columbia and the Peace meant that some of this reservoir had been achieved). From there it would be redirected for consumption in western North America, with the arid US southwest envisioned as a prime beneficiary. This mass diversion was studied by the US Army Corps of Engineers and received some political support. Hostile reaction from the Canadian government and the question of feasibility (in 1963, NAWAPA's total cost was estimated at about $100 billion with construction taking about twenty years) damned the idea, though it has resurfaced from time to time since. Fears about these massive diversions led to later attempts in the Great Lakes basin to prevent such schemes.

The IJC commissioners of the Pearson era presided over a rebirth of the IJC, transforming it into a proactive and positive force, a development that, in part, may be attributed to the commissioner appointments made and the mature Canadian-American relationship established by the Ottawa government.[39] Until the Second World War, the IJC had focused mainly on apportioning water resources. Yet, for much of that period, the IJC had not operated efficiently, sometimes splitting along national lines or failing to make timely recommendations. The IJC's politicization was apparent in several large-scale endeavours, affecting its work on the St. Lawrence Seaway and Power Project, Niagara remedial works and hydro developments, and the Columbia River Treaty. Furthermore, the IJC supported or influenced activities that tended to be unsustainable and ecologically harmful, though much of that was obvious only in hindsight. It was only in the 1960s that the IJC became a leader in addressing Great Lakes water quality and pollution issues. Though the commission's scope and authority are limited by its mandate, the IJC has achieved success and public trust through its joint fact-finding, objectivity, independence, and role as a forum for public participation.[40]

Radioactive Fallout and the Test Ban Negotiations

Although environmental issues were not then known or categorized as such, they influenced the Pearson government's multilateral diplomacy. Most notable among these was a global ban on nuclear testing. When Pearson took power in 1963, talks surrounding a test ban agreement were intensifying. After the Partial Nuclear Test Ban Treaty (PTBT) came into force later that year, the need to make the treaty comprehensive became a focus for Canadian policy makers. On nuclear testing issues, the Pearson government was a committed, if cautious, participant in United Nations disarmament negotiations.

The issue of a global nuclear test ban reached the international agenda after a March 1954 American thermonuclear test near the Marshall Islands irradiated Japanese fishers. Shortly thereafter, Indian prime minister Jawaharlal Nehru called for a "standstill" in nuclear testing.[41] Twenty-nine African and Asian governments backed this position at the April 1955 Bandung Conference, touting the UN as the most suitable vehicle for realizing nuclear disarmament.[42] Concern over the effects of atomic radiation on human health became increasingly widespread. While Canada's anti-nuclear movement was in its infancy, public concern over the dangers associated with radioactive fallout was mounting.[43]

Despite growing support for an international test ban agreement, there remained uncertainty concerning the impact of nuclear tests on human health and the world environment. In November 1956, for instance, officials in Canada's Department of External Affairs judged the evidence on the effects of nuclear testing to be incomplete, and expert advice conflicted.[44] On a global scale, it was not clear, for instance, whether nuclear test explosions would increase concentrations of ionizing radiation to dangerous levels. To avoid "extensive and inconclusive debate among non-experts," Canada's delegation to the 1956

General Assembly was instructed to avoid discussion of the scientific rationale for a limitation of nuclear tests.[45] Continued testing was, moreover, deemed vital to Western defence. Given the Soviet Union's overwhelming superiority in conventional forces, officials within Canada's Department of National Defence regarded the nuclear deterrent as essential to Western security.[46] Hence, Canadian diplomats advocated agreements on the limitation and the registration of nuclear testing through the General Assembly in the late 1950s, but these initiatives were in part designed to assuage Afro-Asian countries.[47] During Pearson's tenure as Canada's foreign minister, the evidence of the deleterious environmental effects of testing was not sufficiently conclusive to persuade officials of the need for a test ban.

The research linking nuclear testing to serious global environmental contamination began to grow rapidly through the mid- to late 1950s.[48] The UN Scientific Committee on the Effects of Atomic Radiation's (UNSCEAR) 1958 report concluded that "the cessation of contamination of the environment by explosions of nuclear weapons" would "act to the benefit of human health."[49] Given increased scientific clarity, the Diefenbaker government took a more aggressive tone concerning the environmental effects of nuclear fallout. Diefenbaker's foreign minister, Howard Green, was especially forceful in his pursuit of nuclear disarmament. In addition to staunchly opposing Canadian possession of nuclear weapons, Green was willing to overlook technical obstacles to the verification of a potential test ban agreement.[50] He used Canada's membership on the Eighteen Nation Committee on Disarmament to push aggressively to terminate nuclear experimentation. On occasion, as at the 1960 and 1962 General Assembly sessions, Green's principled stand drew the ire of Canada's allies and embarrassed Canadian officials.[51]

Green's anti-nuclear zeal contributed to indecision on vital national security questions and to a cabinet crisis that led to a public perception of incompetence that factored into the eventual defeat of Diefenbaker's government. As Pearson assumed the prime ministership in 1963, there was an appetite among many leading Canadian policy makers, including Canada's under-secretary of state for external affairs, Norman Robertson, for greater realism in Canada's nuclear policies. Though the new government was committed to greater pragmatism, the fundamentals of Canadian policy remained the same. While Pearson accepted nuclear weapons as a means of meeting Canada's alliance obligations, his government endeavoured to renegotiate these commitments to ensure that Canadian forces would not be required to use nuclear weapons.[52]

On international disarmament questions, the Liberals encountered a greater degree of scientific certainty than had existed when they last held office. In 1962, UNSCEAR was able to reach more definitive conclusions than had been possible in 1958. Combined with the increased incidence of somatic disease and the possibility for multi-generational genetic damage, the committee documented "the world-wide contamination of the environment with short- and long-lived radio-nuclides from weapons tests." UNSCEAR concluded its report by emphasizing "the need that all forms of unnecessary radiation should be minimized or avoided entirely," including through "a final cessation of nuclear tests," which, the report continued, "would benefit present and future generations."[53] Undoubtedly provoked by growing scientific knowledge about the environmental effects of nuclear testing, General E.L.M. Burns, Canada's chief disarmament negotiator, emphasized the environmental effects of continued testing in his fall 1962 statement to the UN General Assembly's First Committee. Before decrying the "fouling of the atmosphere," Burns highlighted the "incalculable effects [of continued testing] on future generations." Unless states reached an immediate test ban, "this generation would ... perpetrate a grave moral wrong on posterity."[54]

Armed with growing scientific support, Pearson's government resolved to advance the nuclear test ban cause.[55] Quietly but vigorously, Canadian diplomats advocated a test ban agreement within the Western camp. This work was significantly advanced when the world's major nuclear powers – the United States, the Soviet Union, and Britain – reached agreement on a partial nuclear test ban treaty in August 1963. This Moscow Treaty ended nuclear testing in the atmosphere, outer space, and underwater. Because of US-Soviet disagreement over verification procedures for underground tests, the treaty did not cover them. Thus, the treaty was not comprehensive. Washington insisted that onsite inspections would be required to distinguish underground tests from earthquakes. The Soviets opposed onsite inspections, citing fears of Western espionage.

Canada was among the first states to sign and ratify the new test ban treaty. At the 1963 General Assembly, Pearson welcomed the PTBT, noting its immense value "in putting an end to the poisoning of the atmosphere which sustains all life on our planet."[56] Foreign

Minister Paul Martin noted with satisfaction the paragraphs in the Moscow Treaty that expressed the desire of the three nuclear powers to extend the PTBT to include underground tests. These negotiations, Martin maintained, should be pursued through the Eighteen Nation Committee on Disarmament.[57] The Canadian delegation also sought to draw attention to the effects of atomic radiation on human health and environmental systems by promoting a General Assembly resolution on the subject.[58] Resolution 1896 called on governments and UN specialized agencies to provide UNSCEAR with support to conduct its evaluations and urged the World Meteorological Organization to proceed with its scheme for monitoring atmospheric radiation.[59] The resolution provided additional political backing for the scientific committee's often contentious work.

With the PTBT entering into force, the international community had adopted measures to slow the introduction of radiation from test nuclear explosions into the world environment.[60] The fight against nuclear testing shifted to the need to extend the PTBT to include underground tests, the issue that had prevented a comprehensive test ban agreement. Heading into the 1963 General Assembly, cabinet passionately debated the degree to which Canada should push publicly for a comprehensive agreement. On 12 September, Pearson expressed dissatisfaction with the cautious line proposed by the Department of External Affairs. With cabinet support, he urged the department to explore the possibility of a Canadian diplomatic initiative in pursuit of a comprehensive agreement. Martin agreed to act, while doubting the advisability of a public initiative.[61]

Martin's more cautious line was reinforced strongly by Norman Robertson. In a memorandum for Martin, Robertson noted that a Canadian initiative on disarmament matters should only be pursued within the context of a wider negotiating strategy agreed to in advance by Canada's Western partners. Wary of disarmament initiatives after years of diplomatic overreach under Green, Robertson questioned the advisability of public advocacy, given the apparently intractable divide between Washington and Moscow on the verification of underground tests.[62] The DEA line held. Though supporting a comprehensive test ban, Canadian negotiators restricted their public advocacy to reminders of the need to extend the PTBT. In addition, Canadian representatives backed the work of UNSCEAR.[63] At the General Assembly session in 1966, Canada introduced a resolution commending the scientific committee's work and encouraging its ongoing activities.[64] Ottawa's officials also supported international cooperation on seismological research that could distinguish between underground nuclear tests and earthquakes.[65]

Although it would not have described its participation in UN nuclear negotiations as environmental diplomacy, this is exactly what the Pearson government was doing by promoting a comprehensive test ban and supporting scientific research on the effects of atomic radiation. Global security imperatives were clearly at the head of the agenda, but concerns over atmospheric contamination and a sense of intergenerational environmental obligation were also important. The PTBT has rightly been called the first global environmental treaty.[66]

Law of the Sea, Ocean Politics, and the Fisheries

Ocean and offshore fishing concerns were environmental diplomacy issues that received the Pearson government's prolonged attention. These questions mainly involved the assertion of national control over the area off Canada's coasts, rather than the protection of resources in a manner that would now be described as sustainable development.[67]

After the Second World War, maritime jurisdiction increasingly attracted the attention of Canadian diplomats, particularly after Newfoundland and Labrador joined Confederation in 1949. The St-Laurent government explored ways to strengthen the existing three-mile territorial sea limit and extend it to offshore fisheries up to a twelve-mile limit. At the 1958 and 1960 United Nations conferences on the Law of the Sea, which sought to codify the use of ocean resources, the Diefenbaker government promoted international cooperation but also aggressively pursued Canada's interests as a coastal state. Ottawa pushed unsuccessfully for control of fisheries and continental shelf resources to twelve miles offshore but was able to prevent limitations in the length of straight baselines – the drawing of straight lines from headland to headland, constituting a way to shut off from foreign exploitation areas of particular interest to Canada. Following the two Law of the Sea conferences, several states moved unilaterally to protect their coastal interests, although Canada still sought a multilateral agreement.[68]

In June 1963, responding directly to a representation by the Canadian fishing lobby, Prime Minister Pearson announced that his government had decided "to establish a twelve-mile exclusive fisheries zone along the whole of Canada's coastline ... and to implement the straight baseline system at the same time as the basis from which Canada's territorial sea and exclusive fisheries zone shall be measured."[69] A year later, as the legislation to effect the change was before the House of Commons, Foreign Minister Martin explained the government's reasoning. There was, he said, no prospect of an international agreement on a twelve-mile zone, and meanwhile the fisheries were being depleted and ever-larger foreign fleets were moving nearer Canadian shores.[70]

The Pearson government's 1964 Territorial Sea and Fishing Zones Act abandoned the effort to reach international agreement and, in its place, set out a national strategy that claimed Canada's right to establish its own exclusive fisheries. Yet eight countries had existing rights to fish in the areas that had been declared off-limits. These rights could not be overridden without the agreement of foreign governments or unless Ottawa took drastic steps that it was unwilling to contemplate, not least because aggrieved parties would undoubtedly have brought Canada before the International Court of Justice. Nor did the Territorial Sea and Fishing Zones Act spell out the coastal baselines that lay at the heart of the legislation. The government instead entered into a lengthy, and ultimately futile, process of diplomatic negotiation and public relations to obtain international recognition for its baseline scheme.[71]

Caught between unilateralism and internationalism, the prime minister and his colleagues could not and would not escape their Pearsonian commitments to an interdependent world and the rule of law. The Territorial Sea and Fishing Zones Act was a failure. It fell to the next government, more intent on declarations of raw national self-interest and conscious of growing threats to and sensitivities about the environment, to take another approach. An innovative 1970 amendment to the 1964 act created a twelve-mile territorial sea (rather than twelve-mile fishing zones) and used fishery-closing lines (rather than straight baselines) to cut certain other areas off from foreign intrusion.[72]

Conclusion

The Pearson era record on environmental diplomacy, and on the environment more generally, was mixed. His government's international policies dealt with a range of problems with an environmental component. Ocean politics and the fisheries made for a bumpy road, but much was done in the Great Lakes and the International Joint Commission, and in delicate negotiations to complete the Columbia River Treaty and to restrict nuclear testing. A small start was also made to clean up Canadian water and air. Yet the government was not fully sensitive to emerging concerns about environmental challenges and the ecological impacts of its actions, or to the advances that were being made and the alarms that were being raised by leading politicians in the United States. This doubtless reflected generational perspectives that were not fully informed about planetary limits[73] and the lack of conclusive scientific research on environmental decline and damage.[74]

Environmental diplomacy preceded Canadian environmentalism. The historian Ryan O'Connor asserts that the key moment in the rise of Canadians' environmental understanding came late in the Pearson period with the 1967 CBC television documentary *The Air of Death.* This Canadian version of Rachel Carson's *Silent Spring,* O'Connor argues, galvanized public concern about pollution and led to the formation of environmental groups, particularly Pollution Probe in 1969.[75]

As a new decade began, action on the environment was notable in the 1971 Department of the Environment Act and the 1972 Great Lakes Water Quality Agreement, the latter a direct descendant of Pearsonian environmental diplomacy. These initiatives, and events such as the first Earth Day in 1970, revealed apprehensions that had been percolating when Pearson was prime minister and that he expressed vividly after he left office. The planet, he warned, could not long survive "half slave, half free, half engulfed in misery, half careering along toward the supposed joys of almost unlimited consumption." The chilling fact was "that man can now destroy his world by nuclear explosion or ecological erosion."[76] If he had stayed on as prime minister into the 1970s, Pearson might well have made environmental policies synonymous with his reputation as a forward thinking citizen of the world who transformed the life of Canadians.

Notes

For their indispensable assistance in the research for and shaping of this chapter, the authors express their gratitude to Stephen Azzi and Theresa LeBane. We also thank Joanna Dean and Nicole Marion.

1 See Norman Hillmer, *O.D. Skelton: A Portrait of Canadian Ambition* (Toronto: University of Toronto Press, 2015), 168.

2 Daniel Macfarlane, *Negotiating a River: Canada, the US, and the Creation of the St. Lawrence Seaway* (Vancouver: UBC Press, 2014), chaps. 2–3.

3 Tammy Nemeth, "Canada-US Oil and Gas Relations, 1958 to 1974" (PhD diss., University of British Columbia, 2007), 165; John F. Kennedy, "Joint Statement Following Discussions with the Prime Minister of Canada," 11 May 1963, *Public Papers of the Presidents: John F. Kennedy, 1963* (Washington: US Government Printing Office, 1964), 394–96.

4 Though environmental diplomacy sometimes involved conservation prior to the 1960s, during and after that decade the term also came to signify external relations that were concerned with environmental preservation and protection. Preservationists contended that nature should be protected for its own sake, while conservationists wished to maximize nature's utility for humanity's benefit. For a historiographical consideration of environmental diplomacy, see Kurk Dorsey, "Crossing Boundaries: The Environment in International Relations," in *The Oxford Handbook of Environmental History*, ed. Andrew C. Isenberg, 688–715 (New York: Oxford University Press, 2014).

5 For a pioneering Canadian case in scepticism about science and emerging environmental awareness, see Catherine Carstairs and Rachel Elder, "Expertise, Health, and Popular Opinion: Debating Water Fluoridation, 1945–80," *Canadian Historical Review* 89 (2008): 345–71.

6 Rachel Carson, *Silent Spring* (Boston: Houghton Mifflin, 1962), 7. See also G. Calvin Mackenzie and Robert Weisbrot, *The Liberal Hour: Washington and the Politics of Change in the 1960s* (New York: Penguin Press, 2008), 184–86, 198–203. *Silent Spring* has attracted a wide scholarship, for example: Ralph Lutts, *And No Birds Sang: Rhetorical Analyses of Rachel Carson's Silent Spring* (Carbondale: Southern Illinois University Press, 2000); Priscilla Coit Murphy, *What a Book Can Do: The Publication and Reception of Silent Spring* (Boston: University of Massachusetts Press, 2005).

7 Joanna Dean, "Seeing Trees, Thinking Forests: Urban Forestry at the University of Toronto in the 1960s," in *Method and Meaning in Canadian Environmental History*, ed. Alan MacEachern and William Turkel (Toronto: Nelson, 2009), 245.

8 House of Commons, *Journals*, 1963, 286; House of Commons, *Debates*, 17 February 1965.

9 On the evolution of Canadian environmentalism, see Janet Foster, *Working for Wildlife: The Beginning of Preservation in Canada* (Toronto: University of Toronto Press, 1978); Jennifer Read, "'Let Us Heed the Voice of Youth': Laundry Detergents, Phosphates and the Emergence of the Environmental Movement in Ontario," *Journal of the Canadian Historical Association* 7 (1997): 227–50; George Warecki, *Protecting Ontario's Wilderness: A History of Changing Ideas and Preservation Politics, 1927–1973* (New York: Peter Lang, 2000); Tina Loo, *States of Nature: Conserving Canada's Wildlife in the Twentieth Century* (Vancouver: UBC Press, 2006); Darcy Ingram, *Wildlife, Conservation, and Conflict*

in Quebec, 1840–1914 (Vancouver: UBC Press, 2013); Ryan O'Connor, *The First Green Wave: Pollution Probe and the Origins of Environmental Activism in Ontario* (Vancouver: UBC Press, 2014).

10 In April 2015, the authors consulted the *Canadian Gallup Poll* datasets dating from April 1963 (#302) to February 1968 (#327). These polling materials are no longer available online. See also Marilyn Dubasak, *Wilderness Preservation: A Cross-Cultural Comparison of Canada and the United States* (New York: Garland, 1990), 54.

11 Mackenzie and Weisbrot, *Liberal Hour*, 197, 215.

12 On Maryon Pearson, the VOW, and the hazards of nuclear fallout, see Tarah Brookfield, *Cold War Comforts: Canadian Women, Child Safety, and Global Insecurity* (Waterloo: Wilfrid Laurier Press, 2012), 71–72, 88, and 91; and Nicole Marion, "Canada's Disarmers: The Complicated Struggle against Nuclear Weapons, 1959–1963" (PhD diss., Carleton University, 2017). Pearson left the VOW during the election campaign that brought her husband to power: "Pearson's Wife Quits Peace Group," *Toronto Star*, 5 March 1963.

13 On a Canada Water Act "to conserve water resources and combat pollution," see Greg Connolley, "Divorce Law and Hanging Key Reforms," *Ottawa Citizen*, 9 May 1967; Rob Andras-Mitchell Sharp exchange in House of Commons, *Debates*, 12 December 1967. The Canada Water Act became law in 1970. See William McGucken, *Lake Erie Rehabilitated: Controlling Cultural Eutrophication, 1960s–1990s* (Akron: University of Akron Press, 2000), 103. On the Science Council of Canada, which the author argues was responsible for "a state-sponsored environmentalism" in the Pierre Trudeau years, see Henry Trim, "Experts at Work: The Canadian State, North American Environmentalism, and Renewable Energy in an Era of Limits, 1968–1983" (PhD diss., University of British Columbia, 2014), 7.

14 Lester Pearson, "Good Neighborhood," *Foreign Affairs* 43 (1965): 257.

15 On the IJC, see Kenneth M. Curtis and John E. Carroll, *Canadian-American Relations: The Promise and the Challenge* (Toronto: Heath and Company, 1983), 51–57.

16 Norman Hillmer, "Reflections on the Unequal Border," *International Journal* 60 (2005): 334.

17 Donald Waterfield, *Continental Waterboy: The Columbia River Controversy* (Toronto: Clarke, Irwin, 1970), 39.

18 See ibid.; Macfarlane, *Negotiating a River*, 215.

19 Pearson to Waterfield, 13 April 1962, in Waterfield, *Continental Waterboy*, 107.

20 Neil A. Swainson, *Conflict over the Columbia: The Canadian Background to an Historic Treaty* (Montreal and Kingston: McGill-Queen's University Press, 1979), 252.

21 On Martin's role, see Greg Donaghy, *Grit: The Life and Politics of Paul Martin Sr.* (Vancouver: UBC Press, 2015), 200–3.

22 On a transborder grid in the Pacific Northwest, see Paul Hirt, *The Wired Northwest: The History of Electric Power, 1870s–1970s* (Lawrence: University of Kansas Press, 2012).

23 For this and other documents relating to the treaty, see Canadian Departments of External Affairs and National Resources, *The Columbia River Treaty, Protocol, and Related Documents* (Ottawa: Queen's Printer, 1964).

24 Waterfield, *Continental Waterboy*, 187.

25 Chris W. Sanderson, "The Columbia River Treaty after 2024," in *The Columbia River Treaty Revisited: Transboundary River Governance in an Age of Uncertainty*, ed. Barbara Cosens, 249–70 (Corvallis: Oregon State University Press, 2012).

26 Robert Sandford, Deborah Harford, and Jon O'Riordan, *The Columbia River Treaty: A Primer* (Victoria: Rocky Mountain Books, 2014), 17.

27 Province of British Columbia, Ministry of Energy and Mines, "US Benefits from the Columbia River Treaty – Past, Present and Future: A Province of British Columbia Perspective," 25 June 2013, https://engage.gov.bc.ca/app/uploads/sites/6/2012/07/US-Benefits-from-CRT-June-20-13-2.pdf.

28 Waterfield, *Continental Waterboy*, 116; Joy Parr, *Sensing Changes: Technologies, Environments, and the Everyday, 1953–2003* (Vancouver: UBC Press, 2008), 123.

29 Jeremy Mouat, "The Columbia Exchange: A Canadian Perspective on the Negotiation of the Columbia River Treaty, 1944–1964," in Cosens, *Columbia River Treaty Revisited.*

30 Sandford, Harford, and O'Riordan, *Columbia River Treaty*, 43. See also Tina Loo, "People in the Way: Modernity, Environment, and Society on the Arrow Lakes," *BC Studies* 142/3 (2004): 161–96; Tina Loo with Meg Stanley, "An Environmental History of Progress: Damming the Peace and Columbia Rivers," *Canadian Historical Review* 92 (2011): 399–427; Parr, *Sensing Changes*, 103–35.

31 John Shurts and Richard Paisley, "The Columbia River Treaty," in *Water without Borders? Canada, the United States, and Shared Waters*, ed. Emma Norman, Alice Cohen, and Karen Bakker, 147 (Toronto: University of Toronto Press, 2013).

32 Laurel Sefton MacDowell, *An Environmental History of Canada* (Vancouver: UBC Press, 2012), 193–94; and see Ronald Shimizu "Evolving Institutional Arrangements for Water Quality Management in the Great Lakes," in *Institutional Arrangements for Water Management: Canadian Experiences*, ed. Bruce Mitchell, 45–80 (Waterloo: Department of Geography, Faculty of Environmental Studies, University of Waterloo, 1975). Lake Erie was pronounced a "dying sinkhole" in 1969, and "the public outcry was loud and widespread." See McGucken, *Lake Erie Rehabilitated*, 2.

33 Lee Botts and Paul Muldoon, *Evolution of the Great Lakes Water Quality Agreement* (East Lansing: Michigan State University Press, 2005), 13–15.

34 House of Commons, *Debates*, 15 and 17 April 1964. Jack Davis (Pearson's parliamentary secretary) raised the need for long-term planning of Canada's water resources, suggesting that Canadians might adopt "a broad continental approach to water development." See House of Commons, *Debates*, 4 May 1964.

35 International Joint Commission, *Report on Further Regulation of the Great Lakes: An IJC Report to the Governments of Canada and the United States* (Washington, DC: The International Joint Commission, 1976).

36 John Carroll, *Environmental Diplomacy: An Examination and a Prospective of Canadian-U.S. Transboundary Environmental Relations* (Ann Arbor: University of Michigan Press, 1983), 195–96.

37 Don Munton, "Acid Rain and Transboundary Air Quality in Canadian-American Relations," *American Review of Canadian Studies* 27 (1997): 327–58.

38 Daniel Macfarlane, "'A Completely Man-Made and Artificial Cataract': The Transnational Manipulation of Niagara Falls," *Environmental History* 18 (2013): 759–84 and Daniel Macfarlane, "Creating a Cataract: The Transnational Manipulation of Niagara Falls to the 1950s," in *Urban Explorations: Environmental Histories of the Toronto Region,* ed. Colin Coates, Stephen Bocking, Ken Cruikshank, and Anders Sandberg, 251–69 (Hamilton: L.R. Wilson Institute for Canadian History, 2013).

39 Greg Donaghy, *Tolerant Allies: Canada and the United States, 1963–1968* (Montreal and Kingston: McGill-Queen's University Press, 2003), emphasizes cooperation rather than conflict in the Canadian-American relationship during the Pearson era.

40 Murray Clamen and Daniel Macfarlane, "The International Joint Commission, Water Levels, and Transboundary Governance in the Great Lakes," *Review of Policy Research* 32 (2015): 42 and 56–57.

41 Under-Secretary of State for External Affairs (USSEA) to Secretary of State for External Affairs (SSEA), 18 July 1956, in Greg Donaghy, ed., *Documents on Canadian External Relations* (*DCER*), vol. 22, pt. 1, 1956–1957 (Ottawa: Department of Foreign Affairs and International Trade, 2001), document 377.

42 Ministry of Foreign Affairs, Indonesia, ed., *Asia-Africa Speak from Bandung* (Djakarta: Ministry of Foreign Affairs, Republic of Indonesia, 1955), 161–69.

43 Joseph Levitt, *Pearson and Canada's Role in Nuclear Disarmament and Arms Control Negotiations, 1945–1957* (Montreal and Kingston: McGill-Queen's University Press, 1993), 229–30. For a discussion of the anti-nuclear movement in Canada, see Brookfield, *Cold War Comforts*, 71–97.

44 SSEA to Canadian Delegation to UN General Assembly, 27 November 1956, *DCER*, vol. 22, pt. 1, doc. 383.

45 SSEA to Canadian Delegation to UN General Assembly, 30 November 1956, *DCER*, vol. 22, pt. 1, doc. 385.

46 SSEA to Canadian Delegation to UN General Assembly, 5 October 1956, *DCER*, vol. 22, pt. 1, doc. 378.

47 USSEA to SSEA, 18 July 1956, *DCER*, vol. 22, pt. 1, doc. 377.

48 See Milton Katz, *Ban the Bomb: A History of SANE, the Committee for a Sane Nuclear Policy, 1957–1985* (Westport, CT: Greenwood Press, 1986), 16.

49 UN General Assembly, "Report of the United Nations Scientific Committee on the Effects of Atomic Radiation," Supplement No. 17, A/3838, 1958, 41.

50 Michael J. Tucker, "Canada and the Test-Ban Negotiations, 1955–71," in *An Acceptance of Paradox: Essays on Canadian Diplomacy in Honour of John W. Holmes*, ed. Kim Richard Nossal, 115–40 (Toronto: Canadian Institute of International Affairs, 1982).

51 E.L.M. Burns, *A Seat at the Table: The Struggle for Disarmament* (Toronto: Clarke, Irwin, 1972), 154. On Canadian diplomatic efforts at the 1962 General

Assembly session, Under-Secretary of State for External Affairs Norman Robertson later wrote that the Canadian-brokered compromise had "the distinction of being one of the most confused expressions of the General Assembly's sentiments ever adopted." See Memorandum for the Minister, "Possible Canadian Initiatives in the Field of Disarmament at the 18th United Nations General Assembly," 16 September 1963, LAC, RG 25, vol. 11528, file 28-4-UNGA.

52 Lester Pearson, *Mike: The Memoirs of the Right Honourable Lester B. Pearson*, vol. 3 (Toronto: University of Toronto Press, 1975), 69–75.

53 UN General Assembly, "Report of the United Nations Scientific Committee on the Effects of Atomic Radiation," Supplement No. 16, A/5216, 1962, 35.

54 "Statement by General E.L.M. Burns, Canadian Delegate – First Committee, 11 October 1962," Press Release No. 4, 11 October 1962, LAC, RG 19, vol. 4284, file 8203-03-2-pt.1.

55 Burns, *Seat at the Table*, 171. For a detailed analysis of key policy documents comparing the disarmament policies of the Diefenbaker and Pearson governments, see Albert Legault and Michel Fortmann, *A Diplomacy of Hope: Canada and Disarmament, 1945–1988* (Montreal and Kingston: McGill-Queen's University Press, 1992), 204–5.

56 DEA Information Division, "Eighteenth Session: An Assembly of Opportunity," 19 September 1963, No. 63/19.

57 DEA Information Division, "Urgent Need for Suspension of Nuclear and Thermonuclear Tests," 18 October 1963, No. 63/20.

58 CANDEL-NY to DEA, "18th UNGA: Activities of CANDEL," 13 December 1963, LAC, RG 25, vol. 10793, file 24-12-9-1-pt.2.

59 United Nations General Assembly, Resolution 1896: Effects of Atomic Radiation, 11 November 1963.

60 UN General Assembly, Resolution 1910: Urgent Need for Suspension of Nuclear and Thermo-Nuclear Tests, 27 November 1963.

61 SSEA to USSEA, "Instructions for the Canadian Delegation to the 18th UNGA," 12 September 1963, LAC, RG 25, vol. 11528, file 28-4-UNGA.

62 Memorandum for the Minister, "Possible Canadian Initiatives in the Field of Disarmament at the 18th United Nations General Assembly," 16 September 1963, LAC, RG 25, vol. 11528, file 28-4-UNGA.

63 See, for instance, DEA Information Division, "Canada at the Geneva Disarmament Table," 26 March 1964, No. 64/6.

64 "Report for Inclusion in 'Review of the Work of the Twenty-First Session of the United Nations General Assembly – Item 35: Effects of Atomic Radiation: Report of the United Nations Scientific Committee on the Effects of Atomic Radiation,'" LAC, RG 25, vol. 10793, file 24-12-9-1-pt.2.

65 Legault and Fortmann, *Diplomacy of Hope*, 356–60.

66 Barbara Ward and René Dubos, *Only One Earth: The Care and Maintenance of a Small Planet* (New York: Norton, 1972), 219.

67 Barbara Johnson and Mark W. Zacher, "An Overview of Canadian Ocean Policy," in *Canadian Foreign Policy and the Law of the Sea*, ed. Johnson and Zacher (Vancouver: UBC Press, 1977), 357.

68 Ibid., 356–57; A.E. Gotlieb, "Canadian Diplomatic Initiatives: The Law of the Sea," in *"Freedom and Change": Essays in Honour of Lester B. Pearson*, ed. Michael G. Fry, 137–43 (Toronto: McClelland and Stewart, 1975); Barbara Johnson, "Canadian Foreign Policy and the Fisheries," in Johnson and Zacher, *Law of the Sea*, 61–65, and, for the definition of straight baselines, 66.

69 Quoted in Gotlieb, "Law of the Sea," 144.

70 Quoted in ibid.

71 Ibid., 144–47.

72 Ibid., 144 and 147–50; Johnson, "Fisheries," 68–70. These sources provide context and explanation for the 1970 amendment to the Territorial Sea and Fishing Zones Act.

73 But note, for example, Martin's statement to Parliament that the "era of inexhaustible water supplies is fast fading." See House of Commons, *Debates*, 11 May 1964.

74 MacDowell, *Environmental History of Canada*, 195; P.A. Larkin, *Freshwater Pollution, Canadian Style* (Montreal and Kingston: McGill-Queen's University Press, 1974), 49–53; and Jack D. Bails, "Mercury in Fish in the Great Lakes," in *Environmental Mercury Contamination*, ed. Rolf Hartung and Bertram D. Dinman, 31–37 (Ann Arbor: Ann Arbor Science Publishers, 1972).

75 O'Connor, *First Green Wave*.

76 Pearson addresses of 1969 and 1972, in Fry, *Freedom and Change*, 245–47.

Publications by Lester B. Pearson

Organizing the United Nations for Peace. Toronto: The Canadian Club, 1944.

With Herbert H. Hannam. *Food and Agriculture in World Affairs*. Ottawa: Canadian Federation of Agriculture, 1944.

"Canada and the Post-War World." *Canadian Affairs* (April 1944).

"UNRRA Faces Action." *Free World* (November 1944): 461–64.

"Canada Looks Down North." *Foreign Affairs* (July 1946): 639–47.

"Canada and the North Atlantic Alliance." *Foreign Affairs* (April 1949): 369–78.

"Canada and the North Atlantic Treaty." *Academy of Political Science Proceedings* (May 1949): 332–42.

"Canada's Policy for Peace." *Canadian Unionist* (July 1949): 157–58.

"Implications of a Free Society." *Canadian Unionist* (September 1949): 198–200, 203–5.

"Straight Talk from Mike Pearson." *Maclean's Magazine*, 15 October 1949, 8–9, 62–67.

"Planning Canada's Foreign Policy." *United Nations World* (July 1950): 52–53.

"Canadian Policy in the Present International Crisis." *External Affairs* (December 1950): 437–40.

"The Basis of Canadian External Policy." *External Affairs* (February 1951): 38–46.

"Why Canada Must Rearm." *Public Affairs* (Spring 1951): 1–3.

"Canada, the United Nations, and a Two-power World." *External Affairs* (May 1951): 154–60.

"North Atlantic Council Meeting." *External Affairs* (September 1951): 298–99.

“The Development of Canadian Foreign Policy.” *Foreign Affairs* (October 1951): 17–30; *External Affairs* (October 1951): 339–43; *External Affairs* (November 1951): 377–80.

“Partners in Democracy.” *State Government* (August 1952): 70–74.

“The International Situation.” In *Canada: Nation on the March*, 3–11.Toronto: Clarke, 1953.

“Co-ordination of Canadian Policy at the United Nations.” *External Affairs* (January 1953): 12–16.

“National Freedom and International Cooperation.” *External Affairs* (May 1953): 172–77.

“Canada’s Northern Horizon.” *Foreign Affairs* (July 1953): 157–91.

“Co-operation and Unity in the English-speaking World.” *External Affairs* (December 1953): 360–2.

“Tribute to Dr. George Patterson.” *External Affairs* (February 1954): 45.

“H. Hume Wrong.” *External Affairs* (March 1954): 74–78.

“Some Thoughts on Canadian External Relations.” *Canadian Historical Association Reports, 1954*, 69–76.

“Heartening Achievements in World Security Struggle but Complacency Unwarranted.” *Monetary Times Annual National Review* (1954): 25–26, 28.

“Western European Union: Implications for Canada and NATO.” *International Journal* (Winter 1954–55): 1–11.

Democracy in World Politics. Toronto: Saunders and Co.; Princeton: Princeton University Press, 1955.

“After Geneva: A Greater Task for NATO.” *Foreign Affairs* (October 1955): 14–23; *External Affairs* (October 1955): 25–60.

The Crisis in the Middle East, October-December 1956. Ottawa: Queen’s Printer, 1957.

The Crisis in the Middle East, January-March 1957. Ottawa: Queen’s Printer, 1957.

Where Do We Go from Here? A Lecture. Minneapolis: University of Minnesota Press, 1957.

“Force for the U.N.” *Foreign Affairs* (April 1957): 395–404; *External Affairs* (May 1957): 169–75.

“Pearson on the Norman Case.” *Maclean’s Magazine*, 6 July 1957, 14–15.

“Where Canada Stands in the World Crises.” *Maclean’s Magazine*, 6 July 1957, 13–14, 47–52.

The Free Press: A Reflection of Democracy. Williamsburg: Colonial Williamsburg, 1958.

Politique mondial et démocratie. Paris: La Colombe, 1958.

“A Measured Defense for the West.” *Orbis* (January 1958): 428–34.

Diplomacy in the Nuclear Age. Toronto: Saunders and Co.; Cambridge, MA: Harvard University Press, 1959.

“Ten Years of NATO.” *NATO Letters* (May 1959): 3–5; *International Journal* (Spring 1959): 79–84.

"The New Face of Diplomacy." In *Perspectives on Peace, 1910–1960*, 121–34. London: Stevens, 1960.

"After the Paris Debacle." *Foreign Affairs* (July 1960): 537–46.

"Crying for a Vision." *Atlantic Community Quarterly* (Fall 1960): 309–16.

"The Winds of Change." In *The Promise of World Tensions (Conference on World Tensions 1960)*, edited by Harlan Cleveland, 137–40. New York: Macmillan, 1961.

"The United Nations and Peace." In *A Critical Evaluation of the United Nations*, 9–24. Vancouver: UBC Press, 1961.

"My Hopes for Peace." *United Church Observer,* 15 October 1961.

"Foreword." In *Restless Nations: A Study of World Tensions and Development. Conference on Tensions in Development, 1961*. New York: Dodd, Mead, 1962.

"Introduction." In *The Liberal Party*, by J.W. Pickersgill. Toronto: McClelland and Stewart, 1962.

"Tested Principles and Policies: The Liberal Platform." *Saturday Night*, 26 May 1962, 16–17.

"Where Is North America Going?" In *Fourth Seminar on Canadian-American Relations at Assumption University of Windsor, November 8, 9, 10 1962*, 1–11. Windsor: Assumption University, 1962.

"Pearson Lists 10 Needs for a Healthy Canada." *World Affairs* (February 1963): 13.

The Four Faces of Peace and the International Outlook. Toronto: McClelland and Stewart, 1964.

"Government's Job: To Create an Environment for Progress." *Monetary Times* (January 1964): 4–5.

"A New Kind of Peace Force." *Maclean's*, 2 May 1964, 9–11.

"Keeping the Peace." *External Affairs* (June 1964): 240–53; *Survival* (July-August 1964): 150–58.

"Keeping the Peace." In *The Quest for Peace: The Dag Hammarskjöld Memorial Lectures*, edited by Andrew W. Cordier and Wilder Foote, 99–117. New York: Columbia University Press, 1965.

"Good Neighborhood." *Foreign Affairs* (January 1965): 251–61.

"The Face of the World in 1965." *External Affairs* (March 1965): 82–87.

"Canadian Stand on Rhodesia." *External Affairs* (December 1965): 534–35.

"Liberalism." In *Politics: Canada, Problems in Canadian Government*, 2nd ed., edited by Paul Fox, 348–49. Toronto: McGraw-Hill, 1966.

"The Control of Proliferation: The Broader View." In *The Adelphi Papers*, 21–26 (1966).

"Toward Effective International Law." *American Bar Association Journal* (November 1966): 1017–20.

"Forty Years On: Reflections on Our Foreign Policy." *International Journal* (Spring 1967): 357–63.

"Search for Peace." *Ecumenical Review* (April 1967): 196–97.

"Next Steps in Trade Liberalization," *Atlantic Community Quarterly* (Summer 1967): 254–56.

“Changing Canadian Federalism.” In *Canadian Federalism: Myth of Reality*, edited by J. Peter Meekison, 406–12. Toronto: Methuen, 1968.
“NATO and a Changing Europe.” *Atlantic Community Quarterly* (Spring 1968): 5–16.
“Late Norman A. Robertson.” *External Affairs* (September 1968): 346–48.
Partners in Development: Report of the Commission on International Development. New York: Praeger, 1969.
Peace in the Family of Man. New York: Oxford University Press, 1969.
“The New Approach – Through Cooperation.” *Commonwealth Journal* (February 1969): 23–35, 79–84.
“Beyond the Nation-State.” *Saturday Review*, 15 February 1969, 24–27, 54.
“NATO and a Changing Europe.” *Atlantic Community Quarterly* (Spring 1969): 90–104.
“NATO: Retrospect and Prospects.” *International Journal* (Spring 1969): 79–84.
“Freedom and Change.” *Queen’s Quarterly* (Spring 1969): 18–28.
“International Economic Co-operation in a Changing World.” *Australian Outlook* (August 1969): 111–19.
“The Commitment to Development Assistance.” *Banker* (September 1969): 870–73.
“International Economic Co-operation in a Changing World.” *Australian Outlook* (August 1969): 111–19.
“Crying for a Vision.” *Atlantic Community Quarterly* (Autumn 1969): 309–16.
Atlantic Community Quarterly (Spring 1970): 57–66.
Words and Occasions: An Anthology of Speeches and Articles. Toronto: University of Toronto Press, 1970.
The Crisis of Development. New York: Prager, 1970.
“The UN at 25.” *Saturday Review* (June 1970): 16–18, 42.
“Conflicting Perspectives on the Development Problem: An Introduction.” *Journal of International Affairs* (1970): 155–63.
The Commonwealth 1970: Smuts Memorial Lecture. Cambridge: Cambridge University Press, 1971.
“Federalism for the Future.” In *Canadian Federalism: Myth of Reality*, 2nd ed., edited by J. Peter Meekison, 156–66. Toronto: Methuen, 1971.
Mike: The Memoirs of the Right Honourable Lester B. Pearson. 3 vols. Toronto: University of Toronto Press, 1972–75.

Contributors

Stephen Azzi is associate professor in the Clayton H. Riddell Graduate Program in Political Management at Carleton University.

Robert Bothwell is the Gluskin Professor of Canadian History at the University of Toronto.

Isabel Campbell is a military and naval historian with the Directorate of History and Heritage, National Defence Headquarters.

Michael K. Carroll is associate professor of history at MacEwan University.

Adam Chapnick is deputy director of education at the Canadian Forces College and professor of defence studies at the Royal Military College of Canada.

John Dirks is an instructor of history at Trinity College, University of Toronto.

Greg Donaghy is head of the Historical Section at Global Affairs Canada.

John English is director of the Bill Graham Centre for Contemporary International History at the University of Toronto.

Norman Hillmer is professor of history and international affairs at Carleton University.

Brendan Kelly recently completed his PhD in history at the University of Toronto and is currently book review editor of *International Journal*.

Peter Kikkert is assistant professor of history at Sheridan College.

Maurice Jr. M. Labelle is assistant professor of history at the University of Saskatchewan.

P. Whitney Lackenbauer is professor of history at St. Jerome's University.

Adam Lajeunesse is assistant professor and the Irving Shipbuilding Chair in Arctic Maritime Security at the Mulroney Institute of Government, St. Francis Xavier University.

Daniel Macfarlane is assistant professor at the Institute of the Environment and Sustainability at Western Michigan University.

Michael W. Manulak is a fellow at the Balsille School of International Affairs.

Asa McKercher is assistant professor of history at the Royal Military College of Canada.

Galen Roger Perras is associate professor of history at the University of Ottawa.

Timothy Andrews Sayle is assistant professor of history at the University of Toronto.

Lara Silver lectures in the Department of History, University of British Columbia.

Ryan Touhey is associate professor of history at St. Jerome's University.

Jennifer Tunnicliffe is L.R. Wilson Assistant Professor of History at McMaster University.

Index

Note: Abbreviations in the subentries follow the list on page xiv. Subentries for "Arab-Israeli conflict (1947–48)" and "Arab-Israeli crisis (1967)" are listed in chronological rather than alphabetical order. For ease of reference, the United Nations is indexed as "UN."